How Ireland Voted 2011

How Ireland Voted 2011

The Full Story of Ireland's Earthquake Election

Edited by

Michael Gallagher

Professor of Comparative Politics, Department of Political Science, Trinity College, University of Dublin, Ireland

and

Michael Marsh

Professor of Comparative Political Behaviour, Department of Political Science, Trinity College, University of Dublin, Ireland

palgrave
macmillan

First published 2011 by
PALGRAVE MACMILLAN

Palgrave Macmillan in the UK is an imprint of Macmillan Publishers Limited,
registered in England, company number 785998, of Houndmills, Basingstoke,
Hampshire RG21 6XS.

Palgrave Macmillan in the US is a division of St Martin's Press LLC,
175 Fifth Avenue, New York, NY 10010.

Palgrave Macmillan is the global academic imprint of the above companies
and has companies and representatives throughout the world.

Palgrave® and Macmillan® are registered trademarks in the United States,
the United Kingdom, Europe and other countries

ISBN: 978-0-230-34881-3   hardback
ISBN: 978-0-230-34882-0   paperback

This book is printed on paper suitable for recycling and made from fully
managed and sustained forest sources. Logging, pulping and manufacturing
processes are expected to conform to the environmental regulations of the
country of origin.

A catalogue record for this book is available from the British Library.

A catalog record for this book is available from the Library of Congress.

10 9   8   7   6   5   4   3   2   1
20 19 18 17 16 15 14 13 12 11

Printed and bound in Great Britain by
CPI Antony Rowe, Chippenham and Eastbourne

Contents

Appendices
Michael Courtney

List of Tables and Figures

Tables

Figures

Notes on Contributors

Fiona Buckley is a lecturer in the Department of Government, University College Cork (UCC), where she specialises in gender politics and the politics of the Republic of Ireland. She is currently studying part-time for her PhD in Queen's University Belfast. Her thesis examines the role of women in ministerial office.

John Coakley is a professor in the School of Politics and International Relations at University College Dublin. He has published extensively on Irish politics, comparative politics and nationalism. His publications include *Politics in the Republic of Ireland* (5th edn, Routledge, 2010; edited with Michael Gallagher) and *Making and Breaking Nations: Nationalism, Ethnic Conflict and the State* (Sage, 2012).

Michael Courtney is a Government of Ireland IRCHSS doctoral candidate in the Department of Political Science at Trinity College Dublin. His research examines how the social characteristics of TDs structure attitudes within Irish political parties at the national level. He contributed a chapter on Irish immigration policy to the recent book *Next Generation Ireland* edited by Ed Burke and Ronan Lyons.

Kevin Cunningham is a research student in the Department of Political Science at Trinity College, Dublin. Taking the case of immigration, his thesis aims to evaluate the effect of changes in governmental policy on the politicisation of issues. His research interests also include election forecasting and extremism.

David Farrell is Professor of Politics and Head of the School of Politics and International Relations at UCD. He is co-editor of *Party Politics* and of the Oxford University Press series on 'Comparative Politics'. His latest book (with Russell Dalton and Ian McAllister) is *Political Parties and Democratic Linkage* (OUP).

Michael Gallagher is head of the Department of Political Science at Trinity College Dublin. He is co-editor of *The Politics of Electoral Systems* (Oxford, 2008) and *Politics in the Republic of Ireland*, 5th edn (Routledge,

2010), and co-author of *Representative Government in Modern Europe*, 5th edn (McGraw-Hill, 2011).

Pat Leahy is the political editor of the *Sunday Business Post*. He holds a degree in law from UCD and is a former Reuters fellow at Oxford University. He is a regular contributor to television and radio programmes and published his first book, *Showtime: The Inside Story of Fianna Fáil in Power*, in 2009.

James McBride is Director of the Irish Social Science Data Archive, which is based at University College Dublin. His research and teaching interests include Irish voting behaviour and public opinion.

Claire McGing is a doctoral student in the Department of Geography, NUI Maynooth. Her PhD examines gendered experiences of electoral politics in Ireland. This research is funded by the NUI Maynooth John and Pat Hume Scholarship and the Irish Research Council for the Humanities and Social Sciences (IRCHSS). Her supervisor is Adrian Kavanagh.

Peter Mair died in August 2011. Until that time, he was Professor of Comparative Politics and Dean of Graduate Studies at the European University Institute in Florence and was co-editor of the journal *West European Politics*. He co-authored *Representative Government in Modern Europe*, 5th ed (McGraw Hill, 2011) and co-edited *Accountability and European Governance* (London: Routledge, 2011).

Michael Marsh is Professor of Comparative Political Behaviour and Dean of the Faculty of Arts, Humanities and Social Sciences at Trinity College Dublin. He is a co-author of *The Irish Voter* (Manchester, 2008) and principal investigator of the 2002, 2007 and 2011 Irish election studies.

Gary Murphy is Associate Professor of Government in the School of Law and Government at Dublin City University. He has written extensively on Irish politics. Recent publications include *In Search of the Promised Land: Politics in Postwar Ireland* (Mercier Press, 2009); *Continuity, Change and Crisis in Contemporary Ireland* (Routledge, 2010) co-edited with Brian Girvin; and *Regulating Lobbying: A global comparison* (Manchester University Press, 2010) with Raj Chari and John Hogan. He is visiting Fulbright Professor of Politics at the University of North Carolina, Chapel Hill, for the academic year 2011–12.

Eoin O'Malley is a lecturer at the School of Law and Government, Dublin City University. His main areas of research include executive power and Irish politics which have been published in many international peer-reviewed journals. He is co-editor of the journal *Irish Political Studies* and of a new book *Governing Ireland* (IPA, 2011) as well as being author of *Contemporary Ireland* (Palgrave Macmillan, 2011).

Theresa Reidy is a lecturer in the Department of Government at University College Cork. Her teaching and research interests are in the areas of Irish politics, public finance and political science education.

Richard Sinnott is Professor of Political Science at University College Dublin. He is the author of *Irish Voters Decide* (Manchester, 1995), co-author of *People and Parliament in the European Union* (Oxford, 1998) and *The Irish Voter* (Manchester, 2008), and author of a wide range of articles on Irish and European public opinion and political behaviour.

Maria Laura Sudulich is a post-doctoral fellow at the Department of Political Science at the University of Amsterdam. She holds a PhD in Political Science from Trinity College Dublin. Her work focuses on electoral campaigns, new media and their impact on political parties.

Jane Suiter is a lecturer in Government at University College Cork. Her research interests revolve around the interaction of elections, voters and economics.

Matthew Wall is a post-doctoral researcher at the Free University, Amsterdam. He completed his PhD thesis on African elections in the 1989–2008 period at Trinity College Dublin. He has published several research articles on Irish politics, online politics, and campaigns.

Preface

On 7 May 2010 residents in the west of Ireland experienced their first earthquake 'since records began'. It registered 2.6 on the Richter scale, and one resident was quoted as saying 'We didn't know what it was. We thought it might have been a meteorite or something.'

Nearly ten months later, the whole of Ireland experienced a political earthquake, and it too was by far the largest since records began. No one mistook this for a meteorite. The effects were felt well beyond the island of Ireland. Whereas most elections in Ireland might live down, as far as their impact on the wider world is concerned, to the apocryphal headline 'Small earthquake in Ireland, not many people hurt', the 2011 election caught the attention of the media and some members of the broader public across Europe and further afield. Those with any claims to particular knowledge of Irish elections encountered an unprecedented level of media interest, with broadcast and print journalists from all corners of Europe waiting patiently outside the offices of academic or other commentators for the previous interview to finish.

This interest had two sources. First, ever since Ireland had reached an agreement – known, not entirely popularly, as 'the bailout' – with the International Monetary Fund, the European Central Bank and the European Union in November 2010, concerns had been growing that if Ireland was unable to meet the terms of this arrangement, this could not only be disastrous for Ireland's economy but might also lead to the demise of the single European currency, the euro. Thus, many more people than usual felt they had a stake in the outcome of an Irish election. Second, all the evidence was that the election was going to produce dramatic political change – that, after nearly eighty years of something very close to stability, with the same two parties, in the same order, occupying first and second positions at every single election from 1932 onwards, a whole new political order might now be born. At least, the opinion polls said that – yet, some hoped, and others feared, that change of the magnitude these adumbrated could not possibly occur, and that once voters got into the polling booths old habits would reassert themselves. In the event, change was on a truly unprecedented scale, and the 'earthquake election' tag, which as far as we know was first employed to describe Denmark's 1973 election, was fully justified.

This volume in the *How Ireland Voted* series, the seventh, aims to do justice to the transformation of the political landscape that occurred on 25 February 2011. The first three chapters analyse pre-election developments. Chapter 1 traces the background to the election by outlining the dramatic events that had transformed the political and economic landscapes since 2007, most notably the change of leadership of the government in May 2008 and the banking crisis that arose, or finally became apparent, in September of that year and was to dominate the work of government for the rest of the life of the 30th Dáil. Chapter 2 analyses the parties' manifestos, which are sometimes launched with as much publicity as the parties can muster and then consigned unread to the archives but which, when examined closely, can convey a lot about what the parties stand for. Chapter 3 examines the parties' selection of their candidates, asking whether the exceptional circumstances of the election brought forward a new type of candidate or whether the candidates selected were, by and large, of much the same backgrounds as those picked at earlier elections.

The next three chapters consider various aspects of the campaign. Chapter 4 reconstructs the course of the campaign and, based on interviews with key personnel, it presents and assesses the parties' perspectives on what went right and what went wrong for them. Chapter 5 considers the role played by the internet in what became known online as GE11 or on Twitter as #ge11, asking whether the internet can be considered to have taken centre stage as a key arena of political conflict or whether it remained marginal to the outcome. In Chapter 6 six Dáil candidates give their personal accounts of what it was like to face the voters on doorsteps across the country and, in a first for this series, a Seanad candidate conveys the unique experience of the 'Discover Ireland' route to parliament.

Chapters 7 and 8 analyse different aspects of the results themselves. Chapter 7 spells out the scale of the earthquake, noting the extent to which the results differed dramatically not just from those of 2007 but from those of every election since the 1920s, while at the same time observing that the election result displayed strong elements of continuity with what had gone before. Chapter 8 analyses survey data to investigate the reasons for the earthquake, asking who switched away from the government parties (and, just as interesting, who did not) and why. This chapter, too, identifies a pattern of continuity amidst the change. Chapter 9 considers aspects of preference voting – the facility offered to voters under Ireland's PR-STV electoral system to rank order candidates – in 2011 in the context of what we know about previous elections. Chapter 10 focuses on the presence, or absence, of women in the campaign, in the context of Ireland's status as a country where women are more under-represented than in most European countries. In Chapter 11, the election of the Seanad, Ireland's upper house of parliament, is analysed. A chapter on this subject has featured in every *How Ireland Voted* book since 1989, but it may never do so again given the declared intention of the Fine Gael–Labour government to introduce a referendum to abolish the Seanad before the next election. Chapter 12 discusses the putting together of the new government, a task which, in contrast to 2007, contained few surprises but which nonetheless produced a number of contentious decisions. Finally, Chapter 13 puts the scale of the political upheaval seen in Ireland in 2011 into the context both of previous Irish electoral history and of post-war European politics, showing how truly exceptional the election was. Appendices to the book contain the full election results, information on all 166 TDs and on government ministers, and other relevant background information.

At the front of the book we have included a chronology of the election campaign, and this is followed by a selection of photographs and campaign literature that capture the spirit of election 2011. We thank the *Irish Times* for permission to reproduce these photos, the photographers who took the pictures, and Peter Murtagh for helping us to obtain them.

As always, we thank our contributors, who responded with the appropriate combination of cooperation, patience and alacrity to the demands of a book being produced on a very tight schedule. We are pleased that this volume, like its two predecessors, is being published by the major international publisher Palgrave Macmillan, and in particular we would like to thank Amber Stone-Galilee for her enthusiastic response to our initial proposal and Liz Blackmore for fast-tracking it through the production schedule.

As this book was about to go to print, we learned of the sudden death on 15 August 2011 of one of the contributors, Peter Mair, while on holiday in his native County Sligo. Both of the editors were proud to have worked with him in the past, and we were very pleased that he agreed to write the final chapter in this book, placing the results of Ireland's 2011 election in a broader comparative context, a task for which he was uniquely well qualified. He was co-editor of the first book in the series, *How Ireland Voted 1987*, and had contributed chapters to several others. We dedicate this book to his memory.

Michael Gallagher and Michael Marsh
Dublin, 2011

Dedicated to the memory of Peter Mair (1951–2011)
– scholar, colleague and friend

The IMF's Ajai Chopra, now almost a household name, in Dublin in November 2010. (RTE)

A protestor makes her point as ministers meet to consider 'bailout' terms. (Dara Mac Dónaill)

The Greens announce that they are leaving government. (Eric Luke)

Brian Cowen announces that he will not contest the forthcoming election. (Eric Luke)

Brian Lenihan, Minister for Finance, showing the strains of office. Mr Lenihan died four months after the election. (Eric Luke)

An alternative election poster by UpStart.ie. (Dara Mac Dónaill)

Not everyone welcomed canvassers: a front door in Dublin Central. (David Sleator)

Labour leader Éamon Gilmore, and Dublin South candidates Aidan Culhane and Alex White, highlight Labour's unique record on the bank guarantee. (Eric Luke)

FG's finance spokesman Michael Noonan explains a point. (Matt Kavanagh)

Éamon Gilmore reads the tea leaves. (Matt Kavanagh)

Brian Cowen votes in Mucklagh, Tullamore. (Brenda Fitzsimons)

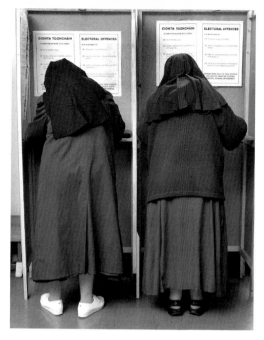

Nuns voting, with a photographer on hand to record this staple image of Irish election days. (Matt Kavanagh)

Former Taoiseach Garret FitzGerald at the main Dublin count centre, observing what was to be his last election. (Cyril Byrne)

Sorting and counting ballot papers. (Cyril Byrne)

Completed ballot papers. (Cyril Byrne)

FF Minister Pat Carey loses
his seat. (Cyril Byrne)

New FF leader Micheál Martin does his best to put a brave face
on his party's election performance. (Brenda Fitzsimons)

Taoiseach elect, Enda Kenny, taking a break from talks with Labour. (Bryan O'Brien)

Anti-coalition Labour members in resolute mood. (Matt Kavanagh)

FG heavyweights Phil Hogan and Michael Noonan ponder negotiations. (Alan Betson)

FG and Labour negotiators step it out. (Alan Betson)

Labour delegates study the Programme for Government. (Alan Betson)

Taoiseach and tánaiste elect. (Alan Betson)

FG press conference after the coalition deal is approved by parliamentary party. (Brenda Fitzsimons)

President Mary McAleese with the new government. (Brenda Fitzsimons)

Glossary and Abbreviations

Glossary

Áras an Uachtaráin, residence of the President of Ireland
ard-fheis (plural ard-fheiseanna), national conference (of a political party)
Ceann Comhairle, speaker or chairperson (of the Dáil)
Dáil Éireann, directly-elected lower house of parliament to which the Irish government is answerable
Fianna Fáil, the largest party in Ireland from 1932 until 2011
Fine Gael, second largest party in Ireland from 1932 to 2011, now the largest party
Leinster House, seat of houses of parliament
Oireachtas, parliament (has two houses: Dáil and Seanad)
Seanad Éireann, indirectly-elected upper house of parliament
Sinn Féin, republican party
Tánaiste, deputy prime minister
Taoiseach, prime minister
Teachta Dála, Dáil deputy

Abbreviations

CSO	Central Statistics Office
DL	Democratic Left
DUP	Democratic Unionist Party
ECB	European Central Bank
ESB	Electricity Supply Board
EU	European Union
FF	Fianna Fáil
FG	Fine Gael
GAA	Gaelic Athletic Association
Grn	Green Party
HSE	Health Service Executive
IMF	International Monetary Fund
Lab	Labour Party
MEP	Member of the European Parliament
MW	Mid-West

N	North
NC	North-Central
NE	North-East
NUI	National University of Ireland
NW	North-West
OMOV	one member one vote
PDs	Progressive Democrats
PR-STV	proportional representation by the single transferable vote
RTÉ	Raidió Teilifís Éireann, the national broadcasting station
S	South
SC	South-Central
SDLP	Social Democratic and Labour Party, second largest nationalist party in Northern Ireland
SE	South-East
SF	Sinn Féin
SIPTU	Services, Industrial, Professional and Technical Union
STV	single transferable vote
SW	South-West
TCD	Trinity College Dublin
TD	Teachta Dála (member of the Dáil)
ULA	United Left Alliance

Chronology of 2011 Election Campaign

18 Jan   Following the latest in a series of poor opinion poll findings, leading to renewed speculation about his continued leadership of FF, Brian Cowen places a motion of confidence in himself before a meeting of the party's TDs. He receives majority support (the figures are not disclosed) but the Minister for Foreign Affairs, Micheál Martin, who had opposed the motion, resigns from government.

20 Jan   With three ministers already having stated that they would not be standing at the forthcoming election, three others now announce that they too will be leaving the Dáil at the dissolution. Over a period of around 18 hours all six tender their resignations as ministers. It seems that Cowen's intention is to replace them with younger TDs, giving these a boost in the election, but FF's coalition partner the Green Party say this would be cynical and unacceptable and Cowen is compelled to abandon the plan, distributing the vacant portfolios among existing FF ministers.

22 Jan   After renewed pressure following this debacle, Cowen announces that he will stand down as FF leader but will remain as Taoiseach.

23 Jan   The Greens, who on 22 November last had announced that they would leave the government and trigger a general election once the passing of the budget measures was completed in early spring, now state that their patience is at an end and that they are pulling out of the government with immediate effect, though they will support the passage of the Finance Bill over the next week. The government now contains only seven ministers, the constitutional minimum.

26 Jan   FF TDs elect Micheál Martin as the new party leader. He immediately appoints his own front bench, which contains some people who are not even TDs.

1 Feb   Brian Cowen advises the President to dissolve the 30th Dáil. The election is set for Friday 25 February, and the campaign officially begins.

3 Feb   Launching Labour's economic plan, leader Éamon Gilmore says that the December 2010 ECB-backed loan provision was a 'bad deal' for Ireland and that Labour in power would insist that it be renegotiated. The Irish people would be able to decide whether budgetary policy is to be made by the democratically elected government or by the ECB; as the media sum up his statement, 'It's Frankfurt's way or Labour's way'. The head of the ECB, Jean-Claude Trichet, is, he says just 'a civil servant' who will have to change the ECB's policy if given political instructions to do so. Two days later Labour's former Minister for Finance Ruairí Quinn says that such comments are 'part and parcel of an election campaign' and acknowledges that there are many parts of the package that are not open to renegotiation.

Bookmakers make a Fine Gael–Labour coalition 1–14 to be the next government, i.e. pretty much a certainty.

4 Feb   With the campaign yet to take shape, there is considerable coverage of the difficulties in arranging a debate between the party leaders. While the leaders of most parties declare themselves ready to take part anywhere, any time, FG leader Enda Kenny seems reluctant to commit himself to a 3-way debate with the leaders of FF and Labour, citing a number of reasons.

5 Feb   *Irish Times* reports on a FG briefing documents for candidates and party workers that gives advice about lines of attack they can deploy against Labour.

6 Feb   Gerry Adams is interviewed on RTÉ radio, and when the questions turn to economics listeners can hear him rustling papers, apparently trying to find the right briefing note.

7 Feb   FF publishes manifesto; leader Micheál Martin emphasises that it contains 'no new spending commitments'.

Enda Kenny declares that FG will end the policy under which Irish is a compulsory subject in the Leaving Certificate exam, taken by final-year second-level school students at the age of 17. Other parties, and some voices within FG, criticise this.

All parties outline plans for political reform. The unusual prominence given to this suggests either that their focus groups have told them that this is a salient issue for the electorate, or that with their hands tied on economic issues they are giving prominence to those areas where they can actually do something.

8 Feb   TV3 stages first leaders' debate of the campaign. It was planned as a 3-way debate, but FG leader Enda Kenny has declared that it does not fit into his schedule and he is not present. Micheál Martin is generally reckoned to have come out the winner in the head-to-head confrontation with Éamon Gilmore.

10 Feb SF, Socialist Party and United Left Alliance launch their manifestos.

Michael Noonan says that Labour is evolving into 'a seriously high-tax party'.

11 Feb Labour launches its manifesto. Éamon Gilmore says yesterday's comments by Michael Noonan are 'old-fashioned, out of date and wrong'.

Green Party launches its manifesto.

13 Feb New Red C poll in *Sunday Business Post* is widely interpreted as showing that FG is on course for possible single-party government, with support of 'like-minded Independents'. The odds on a Fine Gael–Labour coalition are now 1–4, while a Fine Gael majority government shortens to 8–1.

John Giles, former Irish international football captain and manager and subsequently well known as a football analyst on TV, launches Labour's policy document on sport, while admitting that as he is not resident in Ireland he does not actually have a vote.

14 Feb Enda Kenny flies to Berlin for a meeting with German Chancellor Angela Merkel, arranged through their common membership of the European People's Party. Kenny says he emphasised the importance to Ireland of retaining the 12.5 per cent corporation tax rate, but FF dismisses the visit as a 'photo opportunity to make himself look prime ministerial'.

RTÉ televises the first ever five-way leaders' debate between Enda Kenny, Éamon Gilmore, Micheál Martin, Gerry Adams and John Gormley. The main focus is on Kenny given that he missed the earlier debate (8 February), and he is generally perceived to have acquitted himself well.

15 Feb FG launches manifesto – though this is, in essence, a gathering together of the policy documents it has already released. More strong criticism by FG and Labour of each other.

16 Feb TG4 stages the first three-way leaders' debate; the debate is conducted through Irish, but it is recorded and broadcast with English subtitles.

Labour runs newspaper ads modelled on supermarket ads, using the slogan 'every little hurts' and alleging that the FG programme contains a number of 'stealth taxes'.

17 Feb   FG finance spokesperson Michael Noonan says that on the economic front, regardless of who is in government after the election, 'it's going to be dreadful'. He says that under FG's plans, every household will be paying an extra €1,700 a year in taxes by the end of 2014, while under Labour's plans the figure would be €3,060.

21 Feb   Gerry Adams raises a rare laugh when he alludes to his consistent denial, in the face of some public scepticism, that he was ever a member of the IRA. Canvassing in County Cork, he says that earlier he had met some members of the Irish Farmers' Association, and 'I made it very, very clear that I am not and was not a member of the IFA – so let's put that to one side'.

22 Feb   RTÉ televises final leaders' debate of campaign, between leaders of three main parties. Commentators are struck by the absence of hostility between FG and Labour leaders. Meanwhile, Labour advertisements drop the anti-FG approach and instead speak of the advantages of 'balanced', i.e. coalition, government.

24 Feb   Although FG support in the polls has remained stable after its growth in the first two weeks of the campaign, the betting market's view of its prospects grows ever more favourable. A FG–Labour coalition remains favourite, but now at 1–2, while a FG majority government is only 5–2 compared with 18–1 at the outset of the campaign, and the third favourite is a FG minority government at 7–1.

Enda Kenny is seen as all but certain to be the next Taoiseach, on offer at an unbackable 1–100. At the start of the campaign he had been the least popular of the three main party leaders, but by election day he was the most popular.

25 Feb   Election day

27 Feb   Result known in broad terms; the consensus is that FG would find it impossible to form a minority government with support of Independents and that a FG–Labour coalition is the only viable option.

1 Mar   Talks between the negotiating teams of FG and Labour begin.

2 Mar   At just after 8 a.m., the 166th and final seat in the 31st Dáil is filled with the election of Seán Kyne in Galway West, where there have been two recounts.

5 Mar   Negotiations between FG and Labour continue, and in the early hours of Sunday 6 March agreement on a programme for government is reached.

6 Mar   The programme is ratified separately by FG and by Labour. In FG's case it is put to and ratified by the parliamentary party, with no opposition. In the case of Labour it is put to a delegate conference attended by 1,100 members and is overwhelmingly approved on a show of hands. However, two TDs, Tommy Broughan and Joanna Tuffy, oppose it.

9 Mar   31st Dáil meets for the first time. Seán Barrett (FG) is elected Ceann Comhairle (speaker), then Enda Kenny is elected Taoiseach by 117 votes to 27. When the government is announced, with 10 FG ministers and five from Labour, it is praised for being strong on experience, but criticised for being too old, too male, and too Dublin-centric. There is particular controversy over the fact that Joan Burton, Labour's deputy leader and finance spokesperson, is not given one of the two Finance portfolios but instead becomes Minister for Social Protection, which some attribute to gender bias.

10 Mar   Appointment of the 15 Ministers of State ('junior ministers'), who are not full members of the government.

20 Mar   John Gormley announces that he is standing down as leader of the Green Party.

21 Mar   Closing date for nominations of Seanad candidates.

27 Apr   The poll closes in Seanad election and counting of the votes begins.

29 Apr   Counting of votes in Seanad election ends; 43 senators from panels, and six returned by university graduates, have been elected to the 24th Seanad.

20 May   Taoiseach announces the names of his 11 nominees to the 60-member Seanad, thus finalising the composition of the Houses of the Oireachtas.

27 May   In a vote open to all party members, Éamon Ryan is elected new leader of Green Party.

10 Jun   Death through illness of Brian Lenihan, Minister for Finance 2008–11, and Fianna Fáil's only remaining TD in Dublin.

21 Jul   Eurozone leaders agree to reduce by around 2 percentage points the interest rate on Ireland's (and Greece's and Portugal's) loans under the 'bailout' agreement, thus enabling the government to claim success in its attempts to renegotiate the terms.

1
The Background to the Election

Gary Murphy

The end of the 30th Dáil and the calling of the election

Shortly after midnight on the night of Wednesday 19 January 2011, Taoiseach and leader of Fianna Fáil Brian Cowen rang the Minister of State for Children, Barry Andrews, at his home to offer him the post of Minister for Justice as part of a proposed cabinet reshuffle that he was to announce to the Dáil the following day. Andrews refused the offer, claiming that while he was flattered he had to decline on the basis that he was anxious to press ahead on the referendum for children's rights that he had long been piloting. The offer of a senior ministry to Andrews was the sequel to a carefully choreographed series of ministerial resignations, which saw Mary Harney, Dermot Ahern, Noel Dempsey and Tony Killeen give their letters of resignation to the Taoiseach earlier that night. These were then disclosed to the media. They were joined by Batt O'Keeffe just before midnight, although that resignation was not announced until the following day. With the resignation of the Minister for Foreign Affairs, Micheál Martin, the previous day, following the failure of a bid to oust Cowen as leader of Fianna Fáil, the Taoiseach had expected to announce six new ministers to the Dáil. This reshuffle was in fact a last-ditch desperate attempt by Cowen to refresh the Fianna Fáil faces in his government, with a general election looming once the Green Party had announced in November 2010 that it wanted the election held in early 2011. With Fianna Fáil standing at an all-time low in public opinion polls and heading for electoral meltdown, Cowen's plan to announce six new Fianna Fáil ministers, presumably to give the appearance of a revitalised party, was to backfire spectacularly once his coalition partners

1

the Greens interpreted it as a cynical return to stroke politics and refused to agree to it.

Thursday 20 January 2011 was one of the most amazing days in the history of Irish politics. Minister for the Environment and leader of the Greens John Gormley had become aware of the ministerial resignations and impending reshuffle only on the early morning news bulletins. At an emergency meeting of the Greens at 9.30 a.m. they decided they would not immediately pull out of government but would first tell Cowen that they would not support any new appointments. With the government dependent on their support Cowen was in a bind, but he initially refused to back down from his reshuffle plan. At this stage it was not even clear that he had six replacements lined up, but he told the Greens he was preparing to push ahead with a new cabinet. The Greens told him they could not be a part of it, prepared a statement, and readied themselves for an appearance on the famous plinth of Leinster House to announce they were withdrawing from government. Cowen blinked first and after a third meeting with Gormley that morning stated that he would be reallocating the vacated portfolios to his existing ministers, who would take these on in addition to their current ones.

He announced this to a stunned Dáil at 1.30 p.m. that day and named 11 March 2011 as election day, and the Greens declared that they were staying in government. Then the recriminations began. Both Cowen and Gormley went on RTÉ television's *Six One* news to give their versions of a meeting that representatives of Fianna Fáil and the Greens had had the previous day where the issue of the reshuffle was brought up by Cowen. An angry Taoiseach maintained that while the Greens had reservations, they understood that it was his prerogative to change the Fianna Fáil ministers and that by refusing to recognise this they had altered a long-standing tradition relating to a Taoiseach's right to change his cabinet. For their part Gormley stated that the Greens could not have been any clearer in telling Fianna Fáil that a reshuffle was the wrong signal to send out to the Irish people currently going through the worst recession in living memory and that they could not support it.[1]

Just two days after overcoming a leadership challenge from his then Minister for Foreign Affairs, Micheál Martin, Brian Cowen, with his botched reshuffle, had made one of the greatest errors in modern Irish political history. While the government was clearly in its last days, Cowen was desperate to lead his party into the general election in the hope of revisiting his barnstorming performance in the 2007 election where he was widely seen as the man who had turned around that particular campaign for Fianna Fáil. He thus risked all on appointing a new ministerial team that he could put before the electorate as the renewed face of Fianna Fáil. In fact, to all but the most partisan Fianna Fáil activist it seemed an act of utter folly and one that clearly would not find favour with the electorate. Once the Greens refused to agree to it Cowen had literally nowhere to go politically. Two days later he paid the ultimate price when he announced on Saturday 22 January 2011 that he was stepping down as leader of Fianna Fáil. The following day the Greens finally pulled out of government, leaving Cowen leading a cabinet with just seven members, the constitutional minimum, and unable to appoint any more because this would need the approval of the Dáil. The date of the general election was then moved from March back to February once the Greens, from the opposition benches, agreed to support the passing of the Finance bill, which was deemed necessary under the conditions of the international rescue package, discussed below, agreed with the European Union (EU) and International Monetary Fund (IMF). The annual Finance bill was hurriedly rushed through both houses of the Oireachtas, being passed by the Seanad on Saturday 29 January. This paved the way for the Dáil to be dissolved on 1 February and Brian Cowen called the election for 25 February.

It was all a very long way from the heady days in the immediate aftermath of the general election of 2007 when Bertie Ahern, fresh from a third consecutive election victory, formed a coalition with the Greens and the Progressive Democrats (PDs) promising a continuation of the economic policies that had delivered him and Fianna Fáil such political success. The intervening three and a half years, however, were to see a series of tumultuous events which, by the time the government fell, had witnessed Ahern resign from office as Taoiseach, the PDs go out of existence, the state bail out the banks by guaranteeing all their deposits and obligations in probably the most momentous political decision taken by any government since independence, the country enter a severe and prolonged recession, and the EU and IMF come to the rescue of the Irish economy in the form of a multi-billion euro contingency fund to ensure that the country remained solvent.

Perhaps most astonishingly of all, on the eve of the election Fianna Fáil, which had received 42 per cent of the vote at the 2007 election, stood at between 12 per cent and 16 per cent in the opinion polls. This cataclysmic fall in support for the party that had dominated Irish politics since its foundation was perhaps the most dramatic backdrop to the election of 2011. With the election of Micheál Martin as leader of Fianna Fáil on 26 January 2011, the party that had been led with phenomenal success by Bertie Ahern for over 14 years would head into the general election having had three leaders in less than three years and with an incumbent barely a week in the job. Moreover, before Brian Cowen's attempted reshuffle Micheál Martin's own leadership challenge against Cowen had been decisively rebuffed by the Fianna Fáil Dáil party and he had been forced to resign from the cabinet of which he had been a member since 1997. Within a week he would remarkably be leader of the party, but he would be facing into an election where the most likely result would be the decimation of Fianna Fáil. In that context the major question to be decided during the campaign was whether Fine Gael would gain enough momentum to secure the holy grail of an overall majority, or whether it would have to form a coalition government with the Labour Party. No other result seemed possible given the extraordinary events witnessed by the 30th Dáil.

Party competition

Entering into the 2011 general election campaign Fianna Fáil had been in power for close to 21 of the previous 24 years. A classically populist party since its foundation in 1926 and probably best described as a catch-all party,[2] it hovered consistently at above 40 per cent of the vote at election time, only dropping to 39 per cent on two occasions in 1992 and 1997 (see also Chapter 13). While it had traditionally governed alone, often in minority governments, the party had broken one of its supposed 'core values' in 1989 by going into coalition with the PDs, in effect a breakaway party from Fianna Fáil.[3] Fianna Fáil's commitment to coalition was copperfastened when it entered into another coalition, this time with Labour in 1993. Once Fianna Fáil accepted the politics of coalition, party competition became more volatile and unstable, which was signified in 1994 by the change in government during the 27th Dáil when the Fianna Fáil–Labour government collapsed and was replaced by a coalition of Fine Gael, Labour and Democratic Left.[4] The 1997 election saw the return of Fianna Fáil to government, this time in partnership with the PDs and supported by a number of independents. This government would prove to be first in over 30 years to be returned to office in 2002 when Fianna Fáil received over 41 per cent of the vote, only barely missed out on an overall majority and decided to coalesce with the PDs once again. A persistent feature of Irish politics up to the 2011 election had been the hegemonic position of Fianna Fáil. Its decision to abandon opposition to coalition government presented it with a variety of new strategic opportunities and the party unquestionably learned to take advantage of these, as symbolised by its bringing the Green Party into coalition after the 2007 general election. Such coalition building was of course founded on the presumption of Fianna Fáil polling in its normal range of around 40 per cent, thus giving it the possibility of choosing alternative coalition partners and possibly governing in perpetuity. It was to be denied this possibility by vengeful voters in February 2011.

The inclusion of the Green Party in the coalition government after the 2007 election was a personal decision made by Bertie Ahern to give him a stable majority after the virtual wipeout of the PDs at that election. Ever since their foundation in 1985 as a small economically right-wing and socially liberal party, the PDs had been confounding various media commentators who had constantly predicted their demise. The result of the 2007 election, however, left the PDs on the political equivalent of a life support machine. They returned with just two seats and would never recover. The Greens, who had their first TD elected in 1989, moved centre stage in 2007 when their six seats seemed to make a stable government more possible. While Bertie Ahern could have tried to form a coalition with the PDs and independents, bringing the Greens in would give him much more room for manoeuvre in terms of a Dáil majority. Although the Greens had also won six seats in 2002, the Dáil arithmetic after 2007 left them at least in a position to negotiate a programme for government. However, as the Greens did not hold the position of 'kingmaker' in being able to threaten to leave government and form an alternative coalition, their ability to insist on a number of core principles was significantly reduced.[5] After some tense discussions in relation to a programme for government they eventually signed up to enter coalition with Fianna Fáil and the PDs in June 2007. Their experience in government, however, was to be a bruising one.

For Fine Gael, the 2011 election seemed finally to be the golden opportunity to overtake Fianna Fáil as Ireland's largest party. Moreover, the implosion of the Fianna Fáil vote in the opinion polls meant that any traditional pattern of voting behaviour clearly would not apply to the 2011 election with the result that the possibility of an overall majority for the perennial runners-up of Irish politics was not out of the question. The early 1980s saw Fine Gael, best described as another catch-all party, get to within five seats of Fianna Fáil and gain over 39 per cent of the first preference vote, being the dominant party in two coalition governments with the Labour Party. This, however, proved to be something of a false dawn, as by accepting coalition in 1989 Fianna Fáil opened itself up to alliances that would once have been the sole preserve of Fine Gael. After the disaster of the 2002 election where Fine Gael returned with a historically low 31 seats, the party's long-term future seemed in grave doubt. Enda Kenny took over as leader following the resignation of Michael Noonan and faced a mammoth task to make Fine Gael a relevant force again in Irish politics. While Kenny did not manage to get Fine Gael into government in 2007, he did increase the party's share of the vote by 5 per cent to over 27 per cent and won back 20 seats to leave it with a respectable 51 and within striking distance of forming the next government. Nevertheless, for the more restless members of Kenny's parliamentary party the prospect of spending another five years in opposition did not fill them with any great enthusiasm and his leadership would face serious internal criticism over the course of the 30th Dáil. This was due in the main to a belief amongst many in Fine Gael that Kenny was not up to the job of bringing the party back into government. He was perceived as a poor media performer who was weak on various policy details and was unable to capitalise on Fianna Fáil's woes.

The 2007 election was a tremendous disappointment to the Labour Party. The merger between Labour and Democratic Left in January 1999 into a new Labour Party had no electoral effect at either the 2002 or 2007 general elections with Labour's votes remaining static at a disappointing 10 per cent and 20 seats. After the 2002 election the new Labour leadership under Pat Rabbitte had nailed its colours firmly to the mast of the Mullingar Accord with Fine Gael, whereby the two parties in effect presented themselves as part of an alternative coalition to the then Fianna Fáil–Progressive Democrat alliance. The voters were unimpressed, however, and Labour came out of the election having to rethink its electoral strategy yet again. It resolved under a new leader, Éamon Gilmore, to go back to the idea of presenting itself as an independent party, having come to the conclusion that any floating vote that was on offer would certainly not be swayed by Labour presenting itself as the willing junior partner to Fine Gael in government. In that context the 2011 election would be critical for Labour as it sought a way back into political relevance by being in government.

Added to this traditional mix was a cocktail of left-wing groups. These included Sinn Féin, which had had a disappointing election in 2007 and, with its ongoing central role in the Northern Ireland peace process, was keen to make inroads in the Republic, and a number of smaller groups that would eventually come together under the banner of the United Left Alliance. With voter disenchantment with the governing parties at an all-time high, there was certainly a constituency which was receptive to the sometimes radical economic solutions proposed by such groups. The 2007 election had been a poor one for independents of all hues. Given the clear choice between two opposing sets of alliances the voters deserted independents and returned only five of them, down from a near-record 13 in 2002. By the calling of the 2011 election, however, the prospects for independents seemed very strong indeed. The implosion of Fianna Fáil's standing in the polls meant that an extremely large number of votes that would once have been the preserve of Ireland's largest party could now conceivably go to any of the established parties or to the raft of independents that were keen to offer themselves to the electorate. In that context, as Brian Cowen attempted to reshuffle his cabinet in January 2011 he knew that he was only delaying what seemed destined to be the most historic general election in Irish politics since 1932 and one that would probably change political competition in Ireland forever.

Another coalition for Fianna Fáil

Fianna Fáil, the Greens, and the PDs, with 86 seats between them, negotiated a programme for government after the 2007 general election and seemed to have a pretty secure majority. Bertie Ahern's paranoia about stability was somewhat reinforced when during the negotiations to form a government, he agreed deals with the independents, Jackie Healy-Rae, Michael Lowry and Finian McGrath, which mainly concerned the provision of resources to local amenities in their constituencies. McGrath read parts of his deal into the Dáil record though Fianna Fáil insisted that these were in reality non-deals as the projects would go ahead in any event.[6] Despite some opposition to the very idea of going into government with Fianna Fáil, with one Green TD, Ciaran Cuffe, writing after the election that 'a deal with Fianna Fáil would be a deal with the devil', the Greens agreed at a special convention to enter government on 13 June 2007.[7] The then leader Trevor Sargent had made it clear that while he would not lead the Greens into a government with Fianna Fáil, he would be happy for a different leader to do so and he later had no qualms accepting a junior ministry in government. He thus stepped down as leader and was replaced in July by the newly appointed Minister for the Environment, John Gormley, who had led the programme for government negotiations with Fianna Fáil and who defeated a vocal critic of the coalition, Patricia McKenna, by a margin of two to one. The Greens did quite well when it came to the spoils of office; they gained two seats at cabinet, through Gormley and Éamon Ryan who became Minister for Communications, Energy and Natural Resources. They also received a junior ministry, the aforementioned Sargent, and two Seanad seats.[8] They did, however, have to compromise on a number of important policy initiatives including the use of Shannon airport by US troops mostly on their way to or from Iraq and the construction of a new motorway near the famous 'Hill of Tara', an area of immense cultural significance for many Green members.[9] On his election Gormley announced that it was now time for the Greens to communicate to the public what they had achieved in the programme for government and he quickly settled down to the business of government.

For their part, the other minority government party the PDs were barely in survival mode after their disastrous election. Their leader Michael McDowell had rather sensationally and petulantly announced his resignation from public life on the night of the election count, having been ironically beaten for the last seat by John Gormley. While former leader Mary Harney was reappointed to the cabinet, retaining the Health portfolio, she was also forced into resuming the leadership of the party albeit in a caretaker capacity. With their only other deputy Noel Grealish declaring no interest in leading the party, the PDs were forced to look beyond the ranks of their TDs for a fresh face to reinvigorate the party's fortunes. After some internal wrangling a competition was eventually held between the party's two senators, Ciaran Cannon and Fiona O'Malley, who both owed their positions to being included by Bertie Ahern among his 11 nominations to the Seanad. Cannon eventually prevailed in April 2008, but the fact that he was never elected to any national position did not augur well for the party's fortunes, nor did the fact that it had taken so long to fill the vacancy for leader.

The penchant for changing leaders after the election also infected the Labour Party, which came out of the 2007 election somewhat battered by the experience of actually losing a seat after having spent ten full years in opposition. Beaten by Pat Rabbitte for the Labour leadership in 2002, Éamon Gilmore eventually became Labour's tenth leader in September 2007 after Rabbitte announced his resignation the previous month. Gilmore was elected unopposed having set out an ambitious plan to have Labour lead the next government and offer itself as an alternative option to the voters beyond Fianna Fáil and Fine Gael. This would ultimately manifest itself in the 'Gilmore for Taoiseach' posters that sprang up during the 2011 general election campaign. Following his election as leader, Gilmore began attacking the government, and Fianna Fáil in particular, and repeatedly emphasised that Labour would not enter a coalition with Fianna Fáil after the next election. This was to counter the speculation which haunted Labour throughout the 2007 campaign that if the numbers stacked up it might well have entered government with Fianna Fáil. It was clear in that context that the fateful decision by

Dick Spring to bring Labour into government with Fianna Fáil in 1993 still scarred the party.

For its part Fianna Fáil, basking in the glow of a third, and perhaps somewhat surprising, election victory in a row given the media spotlight surrounding Bertie Ahern's finances, settled down to making the coalition work. Fianna Fáil, initially uneasy coalition bedfellows with the PDs and the Labour Party between 1989 and 1994, had, under Ahern, mastered the art of making such governments work. The Taoiseach, seemingly quite satisfied with the work he had achieved, declared that he would retire from public life by the time he was 60 in 2011, before the ending of the 30th Dáil. But the question of Bertie Ahern's finances which dominated much of the election campaign would not go away. Ever since the *Irish Times* revealed in September 2006 that Ahern as Minister for Finance between 1993 and 1994 had received payments of between €50,000 and €100,000 from a variety of business acquaintances and that the matter was being investigated by the Mahon tribunal, the issue had stalked both Ahern and Fianna Fáil but had done no real damage to either electorally.[10]

Yet the issue was to reappear dramatically in September 2007 when Bertie Ahern gave public evidence at the Mahon tribunal. The rationale behind these public hearings was to give Ahern the opportunity to explain apparent discrepancies between his accounts to the tribunal of various payments he received and the evidence from banking records that the tribunal's legal team had uncovered in the course of its investigations. The crux of the inconsistency was a bank lodgement by Ahern of IR£24,838.49 on 11 October 1994 that he claimed was made up of the proceeds of two 'dig-outs' from friends and acquaintances, one of which he received at a dinner following a football game in Manchester. The bank record for the day, however, showed that the lodgement was probably £25,000 sterling. If the tribunal judges accepted this as accurate then all sorts of awkward queries relating to how Ahern had come to obtain £25,000 in sterling would have to be explained.[11] Moreover, it would have the effect of bringing into doubt everything Ahern had told both the tribunal in private session and the media, including whether he had received any other payments.

After four days in the witness box and increasingly odd explanations as to the sources of his money, the carefully painted picture by Ahern's spin doctors of his having 'bent over backwards to cooperate with the tribunal' was ruined when it had emerged that he signed an affidavit in 2005 that omitted vital information that he had transferred IR£50,000 from his account to that of his then partner, Celia Larkin.[12] Most of Ahern's answers as to the sources of his money were opaque, were not backed up by any documentary evidence and consisted of explanations from the Taoiseach that were different from his previous enunciations on the matter of his finances.

Finally Ahern was reduced to telling the deeply sceptical tribunal judges that he could not remember a number of crucial events central to the controversy, most particularly the buying of £30,000 sterling in the early 1990s which he stated might have been done in instalments or by somebody else, whom he could not name, on his behalf.[13]

The sheer oddness of Ahern's evidence emboldened the opposition to act. Éamon Gilmore upped the ante considerably by calling on the Taoiseach to resign in the light of his evidence, while Fine Gael went even further by calling for a vote of no confidence in Ahern when the Dáil resumed after its summer break. Enda Kenny preceded this no confidence motion by declaring in a television interview that through his rambling and incoherent answers Ahern had adopted the motto of Louis the Sun King: '*L'État c'est moi*' ('I am the state').[14] This was a particularly damning criticism since Ahern had long claimed that he had been 30 years in politics and had no interest in personal enrichment. Indeed he had told the tribunal that he 'endeavoured to serve the country to my utmost. I have no interest in personal gain or benefit and never had'.[15] The accusation also of course brought to mind visions of the former Fianna Fáil leader Charles Haughey's own woes in relation to financial donations, his resignation statement from the Dáil stating that he had 'done the state some service', and his penchant for expensive Parisian shirts. Ahern's attempts to distance Fianna Fáil from this era were crumbling around him in the light of his evidence to the Mahon tribunal. The vitriolic nature of the debate in the Dáil was highlighted by Enda Kenny bluntly declaring that Ahern had not told the truth to the Irish people and by Éamon Gilmore claiming Ahern's story was 'cock and bull'. For its part Fianna Fáil, in the guise of Tánaiste (deputy prime minister) Brian Cowen, accused the opposition of hypocrisy, while John Gormley rather uneasily told the Dáil that the Greens were not the moral custodians of Fianna Fáil and would wait for the outcome of the tribunal.[16] With that the government won the vote by 81 to 76. An opinion poll just over five weeks later at the beginning of November, however, found that three-quarters of voters indicated that they did not believe that Ahern had provided full disclosure about his personal finances to the Mahon tribunal.[17]

The leadership change in Fianna Fáil

In November 2007 the Mahon tribunal began to dig further into two large deposits to Bertie Ahern's accounts in December 1993 and September 1994 of just under IR£50,000. These investigations were ultimately to lead to Ahern's resignation as Taoiseach and leader of Fianna Fáil in May 2008. Two months earlier the final political unravelling of Bertie Ahern's political career began to play out. Gráinne Carruth, his secretary for a period in the mid-1990s, gave evidence to the tribunal that she had in effect lodged sterling sums of money to Ahern's account at the Drumcondra branch of the Irish Permanent building society. Ahern had claimed that monies lodged for him by Carruth were from his salary cheques and Carruth maintained this line. However, when the tribunal showed unequivocally that documentary evidence pointed clearly to the fact Carruth had made a number of sterling lodgements she stated: 'I have to accept as a matter of probability in my dealings here yesterday that it was sterling.'[18] This evidence was the beginning of the end for Ahern. While there had long been doubt as to how Ahern had come into significantly large amounts of money, this was the first time that there was indisputable and inescapable conflict between his version of events and what the tribunal had clearly established to be the facts. Equally damaging was the perception that Ahern had left his former secretary dangling by herself in front of the unforgiving gaze of the tribunal.

Ahern's political support ebbed away as both the Greens and PDs urged him to clear up the contradiction between his evidence and that of Gráinne Carruth. Seemingly unable to do so and with increasing disquiet within Fianna Fáil, on 2 April 2008 Ahern announced his decision to resign as Taoiseach and leader of Fianna Fáil as from 6 May 2008. He had had an extraordinary career and stated that, like everything else he did in his political career, his decision was based solely on what was best for the country: 'I have served the country and the people I have had the honour to represent in Dáil Éireann honestly … I know in my heart of hearts that I have done no wrong and wronged no one.'[19] Ahern would spend the next month on a type of valedictory tour, the highlight of which was an address to the United States Congress on 30 April 2008 before he stepped out of the political limelight. His woes at the Mahon tribunal would last beyond his exit from the political stage as he found himself the subject of much public ridicule after an appearance at the tribunal in June 2008 where he told the astonished judges that he had won an amount of money on a horse.[20]

Brian Cowen had long been seen as the heir apparent to Ahern. Deputy leader since 2002, Minister for Finance since 2004 and Tánaiste since 2007, he was widely popular in the party and had been singled out by Ahern as his likely successor – much to the chagrin of other senior Fianna Fáil politicians, most notably Dermot Ahern. Two days after Bertie Ahern stepped down Cowen was nominated by Brian Lenihan and Mary Coughlan for the leadership and the following day Fianna Fáil confirmed he was the sole nominee for the position. He was elected on 9 April 2008 and would succeed Ahern as Taoiseach in early May. Cowen immediately repaid the faith shown in him by his nominators by naming Coughlan as Tánaiste and Minister for Enterprise, Trade and Employment and, even more crucially and surprisingly, naming Lenihan as Minster of Finance. He thus overlooked the claims of more senior members of Bertie Ahern's cabinet for two of the most important positions in government. By the time Cowen resigned the leadership of Fianna Fáil and was replaced as Taoiseach just over two and a half years later, he had presided over the implosion of both the Irish economy and Fianna Fáil's standing in the polls. Neither was an edifying sight.

The most immediate hurdle that Cowen had to face was the upcoming Lisbon treaty referendum scheduled for 12 June 2008. Just a week after becoming Taoiseach Cowen had confirmed that he had not in fact even read the treaty and seemed unable to come to terms with the vigorous opposition to the treaty. This came both from the right, in terms of the newly formed Libertas group and a number of extreme anti-abortion groups, and the more usual anti-EU treaty suspects from the left in the form of Sinn Féin and the People Before Profit Alliance. To make matters worse for the treaty's advocates, Ireland's EU Commissioner Charlie McCreevy also declared that he had not read it either, nor would he expect any sane sensible person to do so.[21] While this was probably an accurate summation of the treaty it was clearly politically naive and played into the hands of the No campaigners. This rather blasé attitude to the voters also spoke of a mindset where Yes campaigners believed that European referendums could somehow be passed by faith alone.[22] For their part the No campaigners were much more engaged with the issues and had been preparing for the campaign since the beginning of 2008. Moreover, the Taoiseach's robust partisan political nature came to the fore when after an opinion poll showing a majority of Fine Gael voters were intending to vote No he stated that all parties would have to 'crank up their campaign'. This was widely seen across the political spectrum as an attack on Fine Gael, although Cowen later claimed that his remarks had been taken out of context.[23] Nevertheless, they distracted attention from the real issues and from the Yes campaign's attempt to fend off the aggressive and sometimes misinformed views on what the treaty, if adopted, would mean for Ireland. These included the perpetual concerns in EU referendums of a further erosion of sovereignty, the spectre of conscription, the threat to Irish neutrality and a permissive abortion policy being introduced into Ireland via the back door. Ultimately the Yes campaign was the political equivalent of the proverbial damp squib and had to a significant extent been put on hold until Bertie Ahern stepped down as Taoiseach, which contributed in no small manner to its defeat. The failure to convince the electorate that issues surrounding abortion, conscription and corporate taxation were not part of the treaty played a significant part in the defeat of the referendum by 53 per cent to 47 per cent on a turnout of 53 per cent.[24] This was a significant blow to Cowen, barely a month in office, but European referendums had been lost before without any serious political impact for the governing parties. A much greater crisis was brewing, however, which would impact on Fianna Fáil like nothing else in its history.

Notwithstanding the change of leadership in Fianna Fáil and the defeat of the Lisbon treaty the coalition was showing itself to be quite stable after its first year in office. While there was much sniping both internally and externally at the Greens for propping up Fianna Fáil and reneging on some pre-election pledges, they were certainly proving effective coalition partners. For the PDs, however, the end was nigh. The election of Ciaran Cannon was greeted with indifference by the wider public and with little support, a stagnant organisation, and practically no funding beyond the state-granted leader's allowance, the four parliamentary party members, with the support of former leader Des O'Malley, arranged for a special delegate conference to take place on 8 November 2008 to argue for the winding up of the party. The result was 201 votes to 161 to bring the PDs to an end.[25] Over their 23 years in existence they had had a rather remarkable impact on Irish politics, particularly in the economic sphere, but they exited with a whimper as one of their core policies, namely 'light-touch regulation', was to contribute dramatically to the collapse of the Irish economy.

The state rescues the banks

On the night of Monday 29 September 2008 the chief executives of Ireland's two largest and most important banks, Brian Goggin of Bank of Ireland and Eugene Sheehy of Allied Irish Banks, came together at 6.30 p.m. to ring the Taoiseach requesting an immediate and urgent meeting with him and the Minister for Finance, Brian Lenihan. Although the request was granted by the government, the well-heeled bankers who turned up at the Department of Finance at 9.30 p.m. were made to wait for two hours to have their case heard. In the meantime, Cowen, Lenihan, the governor of the Central Bank, the secretaries general of the Departments of the Taoiseach and of Finance, the chief executive of the Financial Services Regulatory Authority, the Attorney General and a whole raft of advisors were grappling with a crisis of unprecedented proportions within the history of the Irish state; the very survival of the Irish banking system and with it the continued prosperity of the Irish state and its people. The bankers outlined their case, which was that they feared the immediate collapse of Anglo Irish Bank and perhaps one more financial institution, and that if that was allowed to happen, contagion in the banking system could well sweep away their institutions as well. Shares in Anglo Irish Bank had fallen by close to half that day alone and threatened to be much worse the following day, leading to what would be the inevitable failure of that bank and the very likelihood of a domino effect on all other Irish banks. Goggin and Sheehy were joined by their respective chairmen Richard Burrows and Dermot Gleeson at the meeting and told the politicians in no uncertain tones that the government had to act or the entire Irish banking system could well fail. One of their suggestions was that the government could nationalise Anglo Irish Bank. In colourful but angry terms, the Taoiseach told them that the government would not be taking that course, using the immortal line: 'We're not fucking nationalising Anglo.'[26] The rationale behind this was that to do so would put all other banks under probably fatal strain.

That September night was, for the Irish government, the culmination of a six-month period of acute national and international turbulence on the stock market which had spawned a fiscal crisis that threatened to undermine the very solvency of the state. The Irish stock market lost €3.5 billion of its value on 17 March 2008 after the US investment bank Bear Stearns collapsed due to its exposure to the subprime property market. Shares in Anglo Irish Bank fell 15 per cent on the same day, prompting Seán FitzPatrick, chairman of Anglo Irish Bank, to ring Cowen, then Minister for Finance, who was in Malaysia, over fears of a run on the bank's deposits. Cowen attempted to assuage market fears through issuing a statement saying that the situation was an international development rather than a national development.[27] Nevertheless, it was the beginning of a prolonged period leading up to the guarantee where it would become clear that Anglo Irish Bank's over-exposure in the property market would have a traumatic effect on both the Irish state and its economy. In the weeks leading up to the guarantee scheme the government began to put in place contingency measures for a worsening of the banking sector and prepared for the possible nationalisation of one or more of the state's financial institutions, and even a merging of Allied Irish Banks and Bank of Ireland. Just two days before the fateful night of 29 September, the Department of Finance had commissioned an emergency report from Merrill Lynch seeking an outline of the state's options in a rapidly worsening economic climate. The 16-page report was e-mailed to senior Finance official Kevin Cardiff that evening at 6.43 p.m. and outlined as one option, in just seven lines, a blanket guarantee of all deposits and obligations of the six Irish banks, but warned that the wider market 'will be aware that Ireland could not afford to cover the full amount if required'. Staggeringly, it estimated that this amount could be in excess of €500 billion.[28]

The cabal of politicians, civil servants and advisors who met on that September night had taken the view that doing nothing was not an option. Leaving the markets to decide would inevitably lead to the loss of Anglo Irish Bank within days, possibly also Irish Nationwide Building Society, and perhaps others as well. The experience of the fall of Lehman Brothers, the enormous Wall Street investment bank, just two weeks earlier in the United States showed the huge risk with leaving the market to decide. In that context the group led by Cowen had concluded that some form of state underwriting of the banking system was necessary. When told by Sheehy and Goggin that Ireland's two largest banks were at risk, Cowen was initially suspicious. Allied Irish Banks in particular had some past history in relation to being aided by the state. In 1986, during a serious recession, it sought government help to the tune of IR£100 million after its purchase of the Insurance Corporation of Ireland went disastrously wrong. The scale of that particular rescue was seen as overly generous to the bank, and here it was again seeking government assistance. But Cowen and his team were clearly in a bind and had to do something. Not wanting an Irish bank to fail or be taken into public ownership the decision was taken to guarantee the deposits, loans, obligations and liabilities of the six Irish banks, a total sum of €440 billion, more than twice the country's gross national product. An incorporeal cabinet meeting took place to approve the measure, with ministers contacted by phone between 3 a.m. and 5 a.m. In what was perhaps a sign of the coming confusion and dissension that would tear the government asunder over two years later, Minister for the Environment and Green Party leader John Gormley could not be contacted on the fateful night of the bank guarantee scheme and had to be roused from his bed by the

Gardaí with a message to ring the Taoiseach's office. Meanwhile, the chairman of Anglo Irish Bank, the bank at the very centre of the storm, Seán FitzPatrick, slept soundly in his bed.[29] The trouble with the Irish banks was that they were massively reliant on borrowed money from international banks and regularly had to borrow new money to cover loans that were due for repayment. Moreover, recourse to foreign funds began to quickly dry up from early 2007 when 'foreign investors started dumping Irish bank shares because of the banks' heavy exposure to a property sector that had all the hallmarks of a bubble'.[30] As the Irish property market began to crash spectacularly in the autumn of 2008, a concomitant collapse of the banks' liquidity ensued due to the enormous sums loaned by all the main banks, particularly Anglo Irish Bank, to property developers. With the fear that the Irish banks would be unable to borrow if one or two of them went under and the realisation that such an event could lead to the collapse of the entire Irish economy, the bank guarantee scheme was announced at 7 a.m. on the morning of Tuesday 30 September to an initial welcoming at home from both the media and the opposition political parties, with the exception of the Labour Party, but a much less friendly reception from abroad, highlighted by downright hostility from the British government and a statement from the European Commission that the guarantee would be investigated.

Things would quickly begin to go wrong, however, for Brian Lenihan and the government. They had taken a decision in early September 2008 to bring the budget forward from its normal date in early December to the middle of October. This seemed more to do with the optics of a government being seen to be getting things done than anything more substantive, and the budget when produced was nothing short of a public relations disaster. Ending his budget speech with a rhetorical flourish that it was a call to patriotic action, one of Lenihan's initiatives was to abolish the automatic entitlement to a medical card – in effect, to free medical care – for people over 70.[31] This entitlement, introduced on a seeming whim by a previous Fianna Fáil Minister for Finance, Charlie McCreevy, just before the 2002 election, was likely to cost the state significant sums in a country with an increasingly elderly population. That elderly constituency revolted like never before, and after a week of political chaos, where a significant number of government TDs had threatened to vote against the government, and which had seen Fianna Fáil backbencher Joe Behan resign from the party and the independent TD Finian McGrath declare he would no longer be supporting the government, Cowen overruled Lenihan and announced an about-turn on the medical card issue.[32] It was a spectacular display of political ineptitude on behalf of the government and of how weak Cowen's leadership had become less than six months after he had attained the highest office in the land.

In December 2008 the government presented to the public its blueprint for dealing with the increasingly grim economic crisis, the *Plan for Economic Renewal* which quickly sank without trace.[33] A month later on 15 January 2009 Lenihan announced that Anglo Irish Bank was to be immediately nationalised, thus negating at once one of the main reasons for introducing the bank guarantee scheme. Revelations that Seán FitzPatrick had arranged for loans of well over €100 million for himself from Anglo Irish Bank and then colluded with Irish Nationwide Building Society chief executive Michael Fingleton to conceal this from Anglo Irish Bank's own auditors and shareholders was the final nail in the coffin of Anglo's reputation.[34] Its demise and the later declaration by FitzPatrick that he was bankrupt was an eloquent metaphor for the state of the Irish economy.

As it became clear that the bank guarantee scheme was not a panacea for the economic crisis but rather a gigantic millstone around the necks of ordinary Irish people and of the Irish state itself, in January 2010 the government agreed to a framework of inquiry into the banking crisis and commissioned a number of reports for consideration by the Dáil. Findings by former IMF officials Klaus Regling and Max Watson in their report of May 2010 clearly concluded that the banking meltdown was a result of domestic decisions rather than the global economic crisis. In their executive summary they came straight to the point, stating: 'Ireland's banking crisis bears the clear imprint of global influences, yet it was in crucial ways "home-made".' A parallel report by the new Governor of the Central Bank, Professor Patrick Honohan, while principally focusing on failures of the regulatory agencies of the state, concluded that in its budgetary and macroeconomic policy between 2003 and 2008, the government had relied to an unsustainable extent on the construction sector and other transient sources for revenue. Ten months later in March 2011 a third report by former IMF economist Peter Nyberg found that the main reason for the crisis was 'the unhindered expansion of Ireland's property bubble', and went on to criticise the 'herd mentality' that saw all financial institutions copy the risky lending practices of Anglo Irish Bank.[35] Unfortunately for the citizens of the Irish state, the consequence of this behaviour was to saddle the country with a colossal debt. Politically, the result would be the electoral meltdown of Fianna Fáil.

Mid-term election day: June 2009

The first manifestation of this meltdown came on 5 June 2009 when the governing parties faced into European Parliament (EP) and local government elections, plus two by-elections, that two years into their tenure would serve as a barometer of their standing with the public. The results would be nothing short of catastrophic for both Fianna Fáil and the Greens. The rejection of the Lisbon treaty had brought onto the political scene the Libertas group, which, rejoicing in its role in defeating the treaty, announced that it was considering running candidates in the 2009 elections to the EP and reckoned it could win up to 70 seats across Europe.[36] In December 2008, under the leadership of Declan Ganley, it reconstituted itself as a pan-European political party declaring its intention to run candidates in all the states of the European Union and in March 2009 Ganley announced he would spearhead this assault by running in the Ireland North-West constituency. Once the campaign began, however, it was clear that Ganley and Libertas had vastly overreached themselves. While Ganley himself ran a high-profile campaign, his candidates both in Ireland and across Europe had minimal impact and suffered from a rather inchoate campaign structure and little voter recognition.

As with all EP elections in Ireland, the campaign very rarely dealt with any European issues and instead focused on personalities. Ireland was now divided into four constituencies, each with three seats; its total of 12 seats marked a reduction of one since 2004. Worried by Ganley's candidacy, Fianna Fáil chose the veteran Donegal TD, and former MEP, Pat 'The Cope' Gallagher, to contest the North-West constituency. While Fianna Fáil was confident of holding its seats in North-West, East and South, it faced an uphill battle in Dublin where its incumbent MEP Eoin Ryan faced significant competition from two well known anti-Lisbon campaigners, the sitting Sinn Féin MEP Mary Lou McDonald, and the veteran socialist Joe Higgins. For its part, Fine Gael was confident that it would hold a seat in each constituency but was hoping to retain its two seats in East in the face of a strong challenge from Labour's candidate Nessa Childers, while Labour itself was hopeful of picking up seats in East and South.

A typically dull campaign led, however, to a decent turnout of 59 per cent. The results were everything that Fianna Fáil feared with Ryan losing his seat and the party gaining just 24 per cent of the national vote. It marked the first time since the 1927 general election that Fianna Fáil had failed to win the most votes in a national election, as Fine Gael, with 29 per cent, overtook it. The Greens also fared poorly. On the opposition benches there was general jubilation in Labour as the party gained two seats, at the expense of Fine Gael in East and the independent Kathy Sinnott in South. Independent MEP Marian Harkin held off the challenge of Ganley in North-West,and Joe Higgins, two years after being rejected by the voters of Dublin West in the general election, took a seat in Dublin at the expense of Sinn Féin's McDonald.[37]

These results were mirrored in the local government elections held on the same day with Fine Gael again emerging as the largest party in terms of votes and seats. The election campaign was dominated by the state of the economy with one candidate declaring the election to be 'the most national election I have been involved in as a local councillor'.[38] Coming just after an emergency budget in April that increased taxation and cut public expenditure, these elections promised more grim news for the governing parties. Fianna Fáil's campaign was further hampered by internal divisions over candidate selection and strategy: selection conventions were replaced by a process of interviews, which was resented by significant sections of the party membership, particularly those who were not on the ballot. This selection strategy had no impact, however, as Fianna Fáil suffered a crushing reverse, losing 84 seats from what was seen as a terrible result in 2004, finishing with 218, and seeing its share of the vote fall nearly 8 per cent to 25 per cent. The results were even worse for the Green Party, which lost 15 of its 18 seats and received a negligible 2 per cent of the vote. Only one-third of voters who supported it in the 2007 general election stuck with it at this election, which augured very badly for its prospects come the next general election.[39]

For the opposition parties it was again a good day for Fine Gael which won an extra 43 seats bringing its total to 340, while claiming 32 per cent of the vote. For its part Labour increased its number of seats by 31, winning 132 seats. While Labour continued to poll remarkably poorly in the west of Ireland, winning only five of 208 seats in Connacht–Ulster, crucially for the future general election it did very well in Dublin, where it gained the largest number of seats in three of the four city and county councils. This was certainly a good harbinger for the party, which was exuding increasing confidence in terms of its future general election prospects, and its performance in Dublin would be central to that election. As is normal in local elections there was a significant number of independents elected, some 123 in total, and there was a big breakthrough in particular for the People Before Profit Alliance, which won five seats in Dublin. The one opposition party to be dissatisfied with its local election result was Sinn Féin; its share of the vote slightly decreased and it failed to make any seat gains.[40]

Overshadowing the European and local government elections, however, were the two by-elections held on the same day in Dublin Central and Dublin South. Fine Gael in something of a coup managed to persuade the RTÉ broadcaster George Lee to be its standard-bearer in Dublin South, where the vacancy arose from the death of the long-standing Fianna Fáil minister Séamus Brennan. Lee had previously entertained, but decided against, the idea of standing for the party in the 2002 general election in the Dun Laoghaire constituency. In 2009 he succumbed to the approach made by Fine Gael apparatchiks Frank Flannery and Tom Curran. His candidacy immediately gave Fine Gael an immense credibility boost, as a man generally trusted by the public as an economics expert in a time of unprecedented financial turmoil had made a significant political investment. Lee romped home, gaining over 27,000 first preference votes and winning over 53 per cent of the vote.[41] His time in Fine Gael was, however, to be both short-lived and underwhelming. In Dublin Central the vacancy was caused by the death of the long-serving independent TD, Tony Gregory. Fianna Fáil, in either an astonishing show of hubris or a nod to the Bertie Ahern political machine, decided to run the former Taoiseach's brother Maurice Ahern, who was then 70 years old, rather than the former Dáil candidate Mary Fitzpatrick who was known to be outside the Ahern tent. The voters of Dublin Central delivered a brutal rebuke to the Ahern machine when Maurice Ahern won just 12 per cent of the first preference vote and polled in a humiliating fifth place. To make matters worse, he also lost his council seat on the same day, while Fitzpatrick comfortably won a seat in the same ward. It was an eloquent verdict on the Ahern years with one noted political observer astutely commenting that 'showtime politics was buried in a Dublin Central grave'.[42]

The last days of the Fianna Fáil empire

Despite Fine Gael's political success in the middle of 2009, questions about Enda Kenny's leadership continued to manifest themselves. What originally began as political mutterings became more pronounced when George Lee, after only eight months as a TD, resigned his seat, claiming that he 'had virtually no influence or input into shaping Fine Gael's economic policies at this most critical time'.[43] Four months later, Richard Bruton, deputy party leader and spokesman on finance, who rather ironically was seen as having prevented Lee from having any major input into Fine Gael economic policy, launched a leadership heave against Enda Kenny when he refused to publicly back him during a number of media appearances. The backdrop to the heave was the publication of an Ipsos/MRBI opinion poll on 11 June 2010 which showed Fine Gael at 28 per cent – the first time since September 2008 that it had fallen below 30 per cent – which placed it in second place behind Labour.[44] Given that Fianna Fáil was at a historic low of 17 per cent in the same poll, it was too much for Bruton and his followers in Fine Gael and they attempted to oust Kenny as leader. However, their strategy was botched from the beginning and they seemed somewhat surprised that Kenny did not simply resign in the face of such open revolt in his parliamentary party. Spurred on principally by his trusted aide, Carlow–Kilkenny TD Phil Hogan, Kenny showed his political mettle by sacking Bruton from his front bench, much to the deputy leader's surprise. Although faced with the outright opposition of a significant number of leading members of his front bench, Kenny prevailed in the leadership battle, due to the support of a number of rural backbenchers, senators and MEPs, and won a confidence motion on 17 June 2010. It was to be the turning point on his long march to the office of the Taoiseach.

While there was no corresponding outright split in Fianna Fáil there was a steady erosion of both the party's parliamentary strength, and its reputation for good government in the second half of the 30th Dáil. In April 2009, the government announced its intention to deal with the problem of impaired assets in the banking system by setting up what it called the National Assets Management Agency (NAMA). The Minister for Finance, Brian Lenihan, confidently predicted that NAMA would stabilise the banking sector and was an essential component of the state's economic recovery. Eventually established in September 2009, NAMA's principal function was to acquire the distressed property-related loans of the Irish banks, estimated at that stage at some €80 billion, in return for government bonds, with the aim of allowing the banks to begin lending to viable businesses and increase credit generally within the Irish economy. However, NAMA soon became perceived in the public consciousness as the agency through which the government put the interests of the banks ahead of the interests of its people. The Irish economy continued to plummet. Gross domestic product (GDP) shrank in 2008 by almost 4 per cent and in 2009 by over 7 per cent (see Figure 1.1). There were concomitant increases in both emigration and unemployment (see Figure 1.2). The government was faced with rapidly and seemingly never-ending rises in interest rates for borrowing money on the international bond markets, public spending on education, health and social welfare was slashed, and a pay cut in public sector pay was introduced.

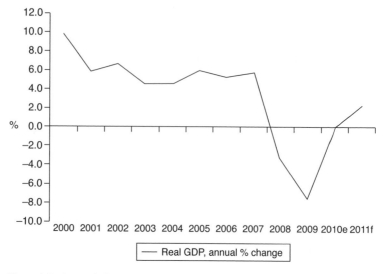

Figure 1.1   Annual change in GDP, 2000–11

Note: 2010e, estimated; 2011f, forecast.
Source: www.esri.ie/irish_economy/, accessed 1 June 2011.

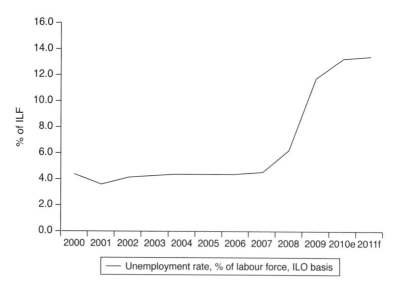

Figure 1.2   Rate of unemployment 2000–11

Note: 2010e, estimated; 2011f, forecast.
Source: www.esri.ie/irish_economy/, accessed 1 June 2011.

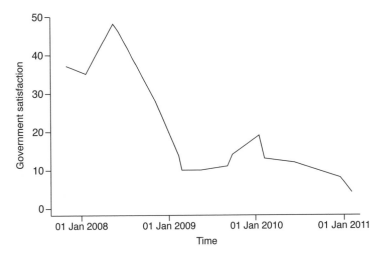

Figure 1.3   Satisfaction with government 2007–11

Source: IPSOS/MRBI polls.

As the economy imploded public satisfaction with the government began to go the same way (see Figure 1.3). The second half of 2009 would also see Fianna Fáil begin to unravel internally. In August 2009 both its TDs in Sligo–North Leitrim, Jimmy Devins and Éamon Scanlon, resigned the whip over cuts to cancer services in Sligo general hospital. Much more serious, however, was the resignation as Ceann Comhairle (speaker of the Dáil) in October 2009, of John O'Donoghue after a lengthy succession of newspaper reports over expenses he incurred during overseas trips.[45] There was some good news for the government in the same month when it managed to get the Lisbon treaty passed at the second time of asking with an overwhelming majority of 67 per cent in favour, a switch of over 20 per cent, with 41 of the country's 43 constituencies voting Yes. This was the highest Yes vote in a referendum on Europe since the Maastricht treaty in 1992, and the turnout of 58 per cent was the highest in a European referendum since the original vote on joining the EEC in 1972. The overriding rationale of the electorate seemed clearly to be that it was safer to be an integral part of the European Union in troubled economic times with the 'Vote yes for jobs' slogan of the Yes side being particularly resonant.

The acceptance of the Lisbon treaty did not, however, bring with it any recovery in the country's economic fortunes as unemployment and emigration continued to rise and the banks continued to need yet more injections of government capital. The impression of a government hopelessly adrift in a sea of incompetence was perhaps best summed up by the resignation of Willie O'Dea as Minister for Defence in February 2010. O'Dea had got himself into serious difficulty when it transpired that he had made a sworn statement in the summer of 2009 in connection with a High Court case taken by Limerick Sinn Féin local election candidate Maurice Quinlivan. While O'Dea initially accepted making comments about Quinlivan which were published in a local paper he denied making other unpublished comments that figured in the court case. It later transpired that O'Dea had in fact made the comments. Amidst allegations from Fine Gael in particular that O'Dea had committed perjury the government initially won a vote of confidence in the minister but he resigned the following day stating that his continuance in office would cause distraction from the vital work of the government, though it was widely believed in political circles that he could not remain in office.[46] Less than a week later the former Green Party leader Trevor Sargent stood down as Minister of State in the Department of Agriculture after accepting that he had 'made an error of judgement' in contacting the Gardaí about a case involving a constituent.[47] The following month, Minister for Arts, Sport and Tourism Martin Cullen resigned as a TD for Waterford on health grounds, which opened the way for a cabinet reshuffle in which Tony Killeen and Pat Carey were promoted to full minister and nobody was demoted. This was widely seen as a missed opportunity by the Taoiseach but it was clear that Cowen was intent on going into the next general election with an experienced cabinet team behind him. Just eight months later, by January 2011, that view had changed leading to the hopelessly inept further reshuffle attempt described at the start of the chapter.

The government's majority in the Dáil was, however, becoming more tenuous and was further weakened when in June 2010 Fianna Fáil Tipperary South TD, Mattie McGrath, lost the party whip for voting against a bill to ban stag hunting, a bill introduced by the government at the Greens' behest. This was followed by the decision of Donegal North-East TD Jim McDaid in November 2010 to resign his seat. That same month saw Fianna Fáil lose the seat in Donegal South-West that had been held by Pat 'The Cope' Gallagher before his election as an MEP. The seat had been vacant since Gallagher's election as an MEP in June 2009, and in July 2010 the High Court granted Sinn Féin's Pearse Doherty a judicial review into why a by-election had not been held in the intervening 12 months. The High Court later ruled that the delay offended the terms and spirit of the constitution and the government announced it would hold the by-election on 25 November 2010, which Doherty comfortably won, gaining 40 per cent of the first preference vote. By then the government was in freefall both economically and politically. As the interest rate for government borrowing became more punitive by the week, rumours abounded both nationally and globally that Ireland would have to seek a bailout of its own from the EU, the IMF, or both. On Sunday 14 November 2010 Minister for Justice Dermot Ahern told RTÉ's *The Week in Politics* programme that speculation that the government was going to seek aid from the EU and the IMF was 'a fiction'.[48] This line was reiterated by other senior ministers and by the Department of Finance in the following days, but on 19 November the government declared that it had officially opened talks with the EU and the IMF. On 28 November the government finally accepted access to an €85 billion rescue package for the Irish state. A week earlier, on 22 November, the Green Party announced that it would stay in government to pass the December budget but that it then wanted an election to take place in the second half of January 2011. The writing was on the wall.

With the EU/IMF deal effectively keeping the state alive economically and the Greens putting the government on election notice it was only a matter of time before Fianna Fáil had to face what was looking like an increasingly vengeful electorate, judging by opinion polls which at the end of 2010 showed Fianna Fáil mired at 17 per cent (see Figure 1.4). The first poll of 2011 had Fianna Fáil on 14 per cent, prompting Micheál Martin to act. Declaring to RTÉ that the 'presentation of the IMF coming into the country, that to me was a watershed moment',[49] Martin threw down the gauntlet to his Taoiseach and set out his stall to replace Brian Cowen as leader of Fianna Fáil. No other cabinet member joined this attempted leadership coup, with Minister for Finance Brian Lenihan denying that he had called on dissident Fianna Fáil TDs to seek a no confidence motion in Cowen. Thus Martin went alone and failed dismally, with Cowen winning a confidence motion by what was considered to be a comfortable (though undisclosed) margin on 18 January 2011. The Taoiseach then, in a desperate attempt to freshen up his own Fianna Fáil team, botched his reshuffle attempt over the following two days and was gone as leader of Fianna Fáil within the week. Martin comfortably won the ensuing leadership election ahead of his former cabinet colleagues, Brian Lenihan, Mary Hanafin and Éamon Ó Cuív. His reward would be to lead his party into an election campaign where the only certainties were that Enda Kenny, long considered a political lightweight by practically everyone in Fianna Fáil, was destined to be Taoiseach, and Fianna Fáil itself was equally destined to receive its lowest ever vote in a general election.

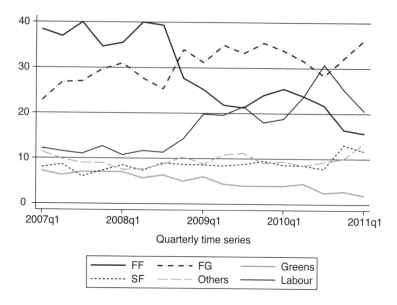

Figure 1.4   Party support 2007–11

Note: This is a quarterly series, compiled by averaging all RED C, IPSOS MRBI and Lansdowne polls published in each quarter.

Source: Compiled by Michael Marsh.

Notes

1. Events described here are drawn from accounts in the *Irish Times*, 21 and 22 January 2011, *Irish Independent*, 21 and 22 January 2011.
2. Liam Weeks, 'Parties and the party system', pp. 137–67 in John Coakley and Michael Gallagher (eds), *Politics in the Republic of Ireland*, 5th edn (Abingdon: Routledge and PSAI Press, 2010), at p. 143.
3. Michael Laver and Audrey Arkins, 'Coalition and Fianna Fáil', pp. 192–207 in Michael Gallagher and Richard Sinnott (eds), *How Ireland Voted 1989* (Galway: PSAI Press, 1990).
4. John Garry, 'The demise of the Fianna Fáil / Labour "Partnership" government and the rise of the "Rainbow" coalition', *Irish Political Studies* 10 (1995), pp. 192–9; Kevin Rafter, *Democratic Left: the life and death of an Irish political party* (Dublin: Irish Academic Press, 2011), pp. 155–9.
5. Nicole Bolleyer, 'The Irish Green Party: from protest to mainstream party?', *Irish Political Studies* 25:4 (2010), pp. 603–24, at p. 615.

6. Eoin O'Malley, 'Government formation in 2007', pp. 205–17 in Michael Gallagher and Michael Marsh (eds), *How Ireland Voted 2007: The full story of Ireland's general election* (Basingstoke: Palgrave Macmillan, 2007), at pp. 210–1.

7. O'Malley, 'Government formation in 2007', p. 209.

8. In a later government reshuffle the Greens would also gain an extra junior minister.

9. Bolleyer, 'The Irish Green Party', p. 615.

10. See Michael Marsh, 'Explanations for party choice', pp. 105–31 in Gallagher and Marsh (eds), *How Ireland Voted 2007*, at pp. 110–11, for how little impact this had on the 2007 election.

11. Michael Clifford and Shane Coleman, *Bertie Ahern and the Drumcondra Mafia* (Dublin: Hachette Books, 2009), pp. 321–2.

12. Clifford and Coleman, *Bertie Ahern*, p. 324.

13. *Irish Times*, 21 September 2007.

14. *Irish Independent*, 24 September 2007.

15. Clifford and Coleman, *Bertie Ahern*, p. 323.

16. *Irish Independent*, 27 September 2007; *Irish Times*, 27 September 2007.

17. *Irish Times*, 3 November 2007.

18. Clifford and Coleman, *Bertie Ahern*, p. 356.

19. Clifford and Coleman, *Bertie Ahern*, p. 360.

20. *Irish Times*, 5 June 2008.

21. Stephen Quinlan, 'The Lisbon Treaty referendum 2008', *Irish Political Studies*, 24:1 (2009), pp. 107–21, at p. 113.

22. Gary Murphy and Niamh Puirséil, 'Is it a new allowance: Irish entry to the EEC and popular opinion', pp. 76–96 in Brian Girvin and Gary Murphy (eds), *Continuity, Change and Crisis in Contemporary Ireland* (Abingdon: Routledge, 2010), p. 94.

23. Quinlan, 'Lisbon Treaty', p. 113.

24. Richard Sinnott, 'Attitudes and behaviour in the referendum on the Treaty of Lisbon', March 2009, Report prepared for the Department of Foreign Affairs, available at www.dfa.ie/uploads/documents/ucd%20geary%20institute%20 report.pdf, pp. 27, 39.

25. *Irish Times*, 10 November 2008.

26. Cowen is cited in Pat Leahy, *Showtime: The inside story of Fianna Fáil in power* (Dublin: Penguin, 2009), p. 332.

27. Tom Lyons and Brian Carey, *The FitzPatrick Tapes: The rise and fall of one man, one bank and one country* (Dublin: Penguin, 2011), pp. 129–30.

28. Lyons and Carey, *The FitzPatrick Tapes*, pp. 181–2.

29. This account of the night of the bank guarantee scheme draws from the following: Matt Cooper, *Who Really Runs Ireland: The story of the elite who led Ireland from bust to boom and back again* (Dublin: Penguin, 2009); Leahy, *Showtime*; Lyons and Carey, *The FitzPatrick Tapes*; Shane Ross, *The Bankers: How the banks ruined the Irish economy* (Dublin: Penguin, 2009).

30. Ross, *The Bankers*, p. 83.

31. www.budget.gov.ie/budgets/2009/FinancialStatement.aspx.

32. Leahy, *Showtime*, pp. 335–6.

33. Gary Murphy, *In Search of the Promised Land: The politics of post war Ireland* (Cork: Mercier Press, 2009), p. 13.

34. For the complicated story of FitzPatrick's loans from Anglo and from Irish Nationwide see Cooper, *Who Really Runs Ireland*, pp. 211–17.

35. Klaus Regling and Max Watson, *A Preliminary Report on Ireland's Banking Crisis*, May 2010; Patrick Honohan, *The Irish Banking Crisis: Regulatory and Financial Stability Policy 2003–2008*, May 2010; Peter Nyberg, *Misjudging Risk: Causes of the systemic banking crisis in Ireland*, March 2011. All three reports are available at www.bankinginquiry.gov.ie/.

36. *Irish Times*, 16 July 2008.

37. For a comprehensive account of the 2009 European Parliament election campaign see Stephen Quinlan, 'The 2009 European Parliament Election in Ireland', *Irish Political Studies*, 25:2 (2010), pp. 289–301.

38. Cited in Aodh Quinlivan and Liam Weeks, 'The 2009 local elections in the Republic of Ireland', *Irish Political Studies*, 25:2 (2010), pp. 315–24, at p. 317.

39. Quinlivan and Weeks, 'The 2009 local elections in the Republic of Ireland', p. 320.

40. For a comprehensive account of the 2009 local elections see Quinlivan and Weeks, 'The 2009 local elections in the Republic of Ireland'.

41. Kevin Rafter, *Fine Gael: Party at the crossroads* (Dublin: New Island, 2009), pp. 231–2.

42. Leahy, *Showtime*, p. 341. 'Showtime' was the termed coined by Fianna Fáil to describe the 2002 election campaign. See Gary Murphy, 'The background to the election', pp. 1–20 in Michael Gallagher, Michael Marsh and Paul Mitchell (eds), *How Ireland Voted 2002* (Basingstoke: Palgrave Macmillan, 2003).

43. *Irish Times*, 9 February 2010.

44. *Irish Times*, 11 June 2010.

45. For a detailed account of O'Donoghue's expenses travails see Ken Foxe, *Snouts in the Trough: Irish politicians and their expenses* (Dublin: Gill and Macmillan, 2010).

46. *Irish Times*, 19 February 2010.

47. *Irish Times*, 25 February 2010.

48. See www.rte.ie/news/2010/1114/okeefeb.html.

49. *Irish Times*, 19 January 2011.

2
The Parties' Manifestos

Jane Suiter and David M. Farrell

It has become the norm in parliamentary democracies for political parties to publish manifestos (or 'programmes') setting out their policy priorities for the period following the election. The common definition of a manifesto is that it represents the policy package a party puts to the voters at election time. There is something of a feedback loop here: research shows that voters use the parties' policy positions as a guide to their voting intentions,[1] while at the same time parties tack and change their policy positions in their efforts to woo voters. Manifestos are also a crucial component in the government formation process. Generally we find that the content of manifestos forms the basis for government coalition programmes and that parties are more likely to form a coalition if the policies expressed in their manifestos are similar (see also Chapter 12).

The significance of the parties' manifestos was brought into particularly sharp relief in the 2011 election campaign. The design, content and import of the manifestos were very much conditioned by the peculiar circumstances of this election. The fact that the election date was earlier than anticipated was bound to affect final preparations, even though all parties knew a reasonably early date was likely following the Green Party's announcement on 22 November 2010 that it would be pulling out of government. The terms of the European Union/International Monetary Fund (EU/IMF) bailout were bound to constrain the scope for new initiatives, particularly any involving large-scale investment of public funds, or indeed any talk of tax cuts. And, relatedly, the singular focus on the economy, almost to the exclusion of any of the other usual policy suspects such as health or crime,[2] was bound to produce a policy debate skewed in that direction. In the case of Fianna Fáil the sudden replacement of its leader was bound to cause a last-minute flurry of activity by the new leader to put his stamp on the party's policy ambitions. In addition, the likely result, given the polls, meant that Fianna Fáil could be sure it would not be in government, while Fine Gael and Labour each knew the most likely outcome was a coalition.

In short, in 2011 policy – and especially policy relating to the economic meltdown – was expected to matter, and we could expect this to be reflected in the manfestos of the parties. Second, we could expect the particular focus on the EU/IMF bailout to have an impact on party positioning on the left–right scale. Third, we could expect the length and content of the manifestos to be affected by the early election date, the likely coalition result and also the constraints on policy flexibility resulting from the bailout.

The parties' manifesto preparations[3]

It is no exaggeration to say that Fianna Fáil was in a very different place from where it had been in the 2007 general election. In that election, the emphasis was on the image of being full of new ideas – that there was 'more to come'. To that end, great effort was put into developing a very long and detailed document: among the longest of all the parties in that election (Table 2.1 below).

Things were very different this time. The mantra of the outgoing party leader, Brian Cowen, had been to place all emphasis on the four-year plan that had been agreed as part of the EU/IMF bailout. Had Cowen remained as leader it seems that the manifesto would simply have focused on this issue, the rationale being that there was little point raising new policy proposals that would only lay the party open to the inevitable 'why only now?' charge.

The election of Micheál Martin as party leader allowed a last-minute shift of emphasis, with a third of the document devoted to political reform. While it might have struck some as unusual to privilege this one dimension, the party leadership felt that it was timely, as reflected in the media debate (if less clearly in wider public opinion, as shown by the poll analysis reported by Marsh and Cunningham: see Chapter 8, p. 188). It was also understandable enough, given Martin's known views in favour of wide scale political reform.[4] In any event, the party needed to come up with something new, and what better area than one that has few cost implications. The rest of its manifesto was lacking much coverage of the usual policy areas with scant reference to either health or education policy. Indeed, one Fianna Fáil TD who retained his seat remarked that it was essentially the outline of the EU/IMF agreement.

Fine Gael was the last to publish its manifesto (on 15 February). There had been some media speculation that the date was designed deliberately to distract attention from the first of the major leaders' debates, as an insurance against the risk of a poor performance by the party leader. The more likely explanation has to do with the success of the party's 'five-point plan' strategy. By the end of the campaign Enda Kenny was being derided for his repeated references to it – most notably by the Fianna Fáil leader in a heated exchange during one of the TV debates – but there is little doubt that it did have some prominence: the party's focus groups indicated that it resonated with groups of voters. According to the party's key organiser, Mark Mortell, 'the five-point plan was designed to communicate to a wider electorate, largely uninterested in policy detail, that the party had a workable plan for government'.[5]

Figure 2.1   Fine Gael's five-point plan

'Fine Gael has a clear plan and a detailed programme in our 5 Point Recovery Plan

- **Jobs.** To get Ireland working we need jobs. Over the next four years Fine Gael will invest an extra €7bn in new energy, water, broadband and telecoms infrastructure to generate on average 20,000 jobs each year. We will cut employers' PRSI, abolish the airport departure tax and change the welfare system to encourage job creation.
- **Budget.** Fine Gael will prioritise cutting waste over raising taxes. This will protect jobs as public spending is cut. By cutting waste, income tax will not be increased. Fine Gael will take on vested interests – the bankers, the bondholders, the developers and the unions. We will aggressively cut the waste in our public service to keep all taxes as low as possible.
- **Public Sector.** Fine Gael will make the public sector better, smaller and cheaper. We will reduce the cost of the Public Sector by 10%, saving €5bn by eliminating waste and abolishing 145 Quangos. We estimate 30,000 administrative and bureaucratic positions can be eliminated by natural wastage, voluntary redundancy and relocation. We will replace the outdated and inefficient annual budget system with an open and transparent system to manage the nation's finances.
- **Health.** Our Health system doesn't work for the people who need it most. Fine Gael's Health Strategy will eliminate long waiting lists, end the unfair public-private two-tier system and replace it with a universal health insurance system based on the renowned Dutch model. A greater emphasis on diagnosis and treatment in the community will ensure shorter hospital stays. Hospital funding will be radically overhauled so that the money follows the patient.
- **New Politics.** Politicians should lead the way by taking cuts right at the top. Fine Gael will reduce the number of politicians by 35% – fewer TDs and abolition of the Seanad. Salaries for Ministers and office holders will be capped and a car pool system will replace State cars. Major reform will allow the Dáil to challenge Government decisions, better local government and a Citizens' Assembly to address major issues like Electoral Reform and Constitutional change.'

The 'five-point plan' strategy was playing out so successfully that it was decided to delay the manifesto launch until late in the campaign, when most of the major policies had been released via a series of mini-manifestos during the first few weeks. As a result, when the document finally emerged it contained few, if any, surprises. In the years leading up to the election, considerable effort had been placed on drawing up detailed policies on a range of areas, and a series of weighty documents had already been produced, a number of which received a fresh dusting off and relaunch as the campaign unfolded. The party had learned important lessons from the 2007 campaign, one of them being that the 'contract' concept it had used then came unstuck over lack of detail: it was determined that the 'five-point plan' strategy should not face the same problem.[6]

The consequence of having had so much policy development was that there was a lot of policy to promote. Hard decisions had to be taken on the manifesto content – which, nonetheless, ended up being almost twice the average length of the manifestos of the parties in this election. The task fell on a policy group chaired by Simon Coveney comprising a mix of frontbench spokespeople and a backroom team of party workers. This was a clearing-house for sifting through the detailed policies and prioritising the issues to include in the manifesto. As the election date drew near the plan of the campaign settled on setting out a comprehensive response to the government's four-year plan: it was out of this that the 'five-point plan' emerged.

The Labour Party's manifesto was drawn up by a committee chaired by Brendan Howlin and passed by the party's Central Council comprising representatives of all the constituency parties and the various sections (women, youth, etc.). Drafting started well in advance of the election, and from quite early on it was evident that the three main themes (that were to form the three chapters of the manifesto) were jobs, reform and 'fairness'.

With much the same sense of resignation as felt by the other mainstream parties, the manifesto was heavily conditioned by the dire economic circumstances. As one strategist commented: 'this was not the sort of election one went into politics for'. The emphasis was on presenting policies that would stand up to scrutiny, and while that meant that there was little scope to differentiate the party from the two larger parties, some effort was made nevertheless to mark out a different position, such as with regard to the speed of reducing the deficit and the weight given to taxation rises over service cuts, although even here the choices were more constrained than in any previous campaign.

According to the Labour strategist, the other unusual feature of this campaign was the way in which the parties found themselves more inclined to defend their manifestos than promote them. This, plus the lack of anything dramatically new to present, influenced the decision to launch the manifesto later in the campaign – on 11 February: the day after Sinn Féin's manifesto launch, the same day as the Green Party's and just four days before Fine Gael's. In 2007 Labour and Fine Gael launched their manifestos on 7 May – over two weeks before polling day on 24 May. This may well have been an unusual election in terms of the heavy focus on policy, but it was also unusual in that the policies being emphasised were determined more by the (dire) economic circumstances than by any bright new initiatives of the political parties.

The Greens sought to follow their practice in previous elections of being as membership-inclusive as possible in preparing their manifesto and key policies. In the years leading up to the election, grassroots-based policy groups, in large part overlapping the policy interests of the government ministers and ministers of state, beavered away in the background, preparing documents that were fed into the party's policy steering group whose members included senior politicians and the general secretary. The role of the steering group was to act as an interlocutor between the vaious policy groups and the party's national council.

Being in government did, however, affect the policy process in a number of respects. In the first instance, there was a concern to cut the party's policy cloth to suit its status as a government party: the policies had to be realistic – less emphasising new policies and more promoting the policy achievements of the preceding four years; they had to reflect the 'times that we're in'. Second, headquarters had to contend with the haphazard engagement of its key spokespeople, who, as busy government ministers and ministers of state and also as election candidates, had far less time to devote to drafting policy than they had in previous elections.

As the election date drew near the policy steering group invited the policy groups to update and finalise their policy priorities, and these were then knitted together to form the basis of the manifesto. While inevitably dealing with the party's environmental niche (though with a strong injunction throughout to avoid raising issues that might leave the party open to the charge of being 'nutty Greens'), given the circumstances, inevitably the principal focus was on the economic crisis, with the party seeking to portray a realistic and responsible image.

'Niche' positioning was also a feature of Sinn Féin's manifesto preparations, not least in its inevitable emphasis on the 32-county dimension. But, as for the other parties, the principal focus was on the economy, only in this case the mission was to separate Sinn Féin from the pack. Much play was made of the point that the party political consensus of sticking with the terms of the bailout was out of kilter with a lot of the independent economic commentary, which tended to stress the possibility that some of the debt emanating from the banks could be walked away from. The party also sought to distinguish itself from the pack with a different emphasis on how and how quickly to cut the deficit. All this was summed up by the slogan 'There is a better way'.

The manifesto was drawn up by a 26-county strategy group with feed-in from the party leader and the party's TDs: final sign-off was by the party's Ard Comhairle. There had been a long lead-in – preparations started directly after the 2009 local elections – but as the government started to show real signs of instability the pace picked up. It was always intended to focus on policy, and to that end the decision was taken to launch the manifesto with two weeks of campaigning still ahead (on 10 February). The economy was not the sole focus: political reform also featured prominently, as did key niche issues such as the cross-border links and the taxi industry.

The length of the manifestos in 2011

All major Irish parties have regularly issued manifestos as part of their general election campaigns and the length of these documents has increased considerably over time.[7] As discussed above, it is clear that the demands of government in the midst of crisis in 2011, combined with the party's knowledge that it would not be in government following the election, took its toll on the Fianna Fáil manifesto (see Table 2.1). Central areas such as health and education did not appear heavily in the document, and this is reflected in the collapse in the length of the manifesto from almost 45,000 words in the preceding election to less than 14,000 words in 2011. The Green Party also produced a shorter manifesto in 2011 than during the 2007 campaign, at just over 14,000 compared with over 19,000 at the previous election, although this was still a longer document than those produced in 1997 and 2002.

Table 2.1   Length of party manifestos 1997–2011

	Words 1997	*Words 2002*	*Words 2007*	*Words 2011*
Fine Gael	24,190	9,303	39,475	39,099
Labour	32,735	25,470	50,789	34,417
Fianna Fáil	37,986	32,489	44,915	13,655
Sinn Féin	3,830	19,605	34,470	15,095
Green	9,324	9,776	19,271	14,135

Labour also produced a shorter manifesto, although one longer than those of Fianna Fáil and the Green Party. Fine Gael, on the other hand, produced a similar length of document as in 2007 at just over 39,000 words, considerably longer than its efforts during previous campaigns.

The content of the parties' manifestos

The authors of this chapter were invited by RTÉ to come up with a user-friendly way of comparing the main political parties' election manifestos in a number of key policy areas. The policy areas included in the project were chosen using an extensive RTÉ audience survey into the issues that were having the greatest daily impact on the electorate.[8] After selecting ten specific areas, we examined the party manifestos of the five parties that had representation in the 30th Dáil – Fianna Fáil, Fine Gael, Labour, the Greens, and Sinn Féin. The ten areas were jobs stimulus, the abolition of the Health Service Executive (HSE), welfare cuts, whether to renegotiate the interest rate paid to the bailout fund, whether to renegotiate with some bank bondholders, greater emphasis on tax in the Budget, whether to reverse the minimum wage cut, measures to deal with negative equity, increase in third level fees and charges, and the abolition of the Seanad.[9]

We looked at the parties' positions in each given area and how each party's manifesto proposed to deal with these policy areas. However, in some cases the manifestos were narrow in focus. This was particularly the case for the Fianna Fáil manifesto where due to the pressures of government the party utilised the detail of the bailout fund on economic matters and included a section on political reforms. The party did not include a section on the traditional area of health. Where the party's manifesto did not deal with the policy in a particular area other party documents were used.

The comparison of the main manifesto commitments revealed a remarkable degree of consensus on the majority of the issues. For example, all five parties agreed on some sort of jobs stimulus, with Fine Gael largely targeting measures such as tax incentives and VAT restructuring. Labour, on the other hand, focussed on a €500 million Jobs Fund. The job stimulus plans of these two parties were subsequently to be included in the programme for government, and thus formed the basis of a government jobs initiative launched in May 2011.

What was most remarkable was the degree of overlap in the party manifestos between many of the main policies of Fine Gael and Labour. Both parties also agreed on renegotiating the rate paid to the bailout fund and renegotiating with some bank bondholders as well as reversing the minimum wage cut. The newly elected coalition was to act quickly on all of these in European summits and in post-election negotiations with the IMF on the minimum wage. Both parties also largely agreed with the necessity for a deal for those in negative equity. Fine Gael put forward a deferred interest scheme which would allow borrowers who can pay two-thirds of their mortgage interest to defer the remaining interest payments for up to five years. Labour also proposed the introduction of a two year moratorium on housing repossessions and also planned a Personal Debt Management Agency. While there was no formal 'backdoor' communication between the parties at manifesto design stage, both were very aware of the content of each others' policies, much of which had been published over the previous 12–18 months. Both were thus able to avoid a myriad of issues which could make government formation more difficult.

In fact, of the top ten areas coded by the project in only three were there significant differences in emphasis between Fine Gael and Labour. First, Fine Gael called for the abolition of the HSE and its being split into two separate bodies – a commissioning authority for the acquisition of care services that would be abolished once universal health insurance is introduced and a care services authority for the provision of care services of children, the elderly, and other vulnerable groups. Labour had a different emphasis: although not planning to abolish the HSE itself it did propose to split the functions along a similar line to Fine Gael.

Second, the parties differed on the reintroduction of fees for third-level education, one good reason for the decision to steer clear of this matter in the early stages of the new government. Labour was firmly opposed to the reintroduction of fees which it had abolished in a previous coalition. Fine Gael, on the other hand, was in favour of increasing student contributions so they would cover one-third of the cost of third level education. The plan was to do this with the introduction of a graduate tax with the eventual phasing out of registration fees. This issue was to prove the subject of some discussion between the two parties after the election when the Programme for Government was being drawn up (see pp. 272 and 280 below).

The third area in which the parties differed was perhaps the best known and the one which Fianna Fáil tried, largely in vain, to highlight during the campaign, namely the balance between tax and spending in the Budget. Fine Gael put the least emphasis of all the parties on taxation in its deficit reduction strategy. It proposed that tax increases would constitute only 27 per cent of the adjustment measures to reduce the budget deficit. Other revenue-raising measures such as the sale of state assets and spending cuts would make up the rest of the budgetary adjustment. Labour, on the other hand, planned to close the gap in the public finances on the basis of a 50:50 ratio of tax to spending cuts, and its manifesto argued: 'Labour believes the composition of the adjustment should be fairer and more balanced, including fairer taxation and on-going investments in education and other vital services.' There were also differences in the sell-off of state assets: Fine Gael set out a proposal to privatise the delivery of utilities through a sell-off of state assets with the proceeds being invested in a new state company, NewEra, while Labour explicitly ruled out any sell-off or 'short-termist privatisation of key state assets, such as Coillte or the energy networks'.

This discussion gives us a good overview of the main areas of difference and similarity between the manifestos and the parties' policy positions. But it is not systematic. Hence in the following section we will turn our attention to the examination of the content of the manifestos in a quantitative and standardised fashion.

Analysing the parties' manifestos

The comparative analysis of party manifestos has developed in leaps and bounds in recent years. For long, the hand coding methodology developed by the Comparative Manifestos Project (CMP) held sway.[10] The CMP project has been in operation since 1979, and these data have been widely utilised in the scholarly literature. A second approach to text analysis replaces the hand coding of texts with computerised coding schemes. A third technique, and one representing a radical departure from linguistic-based schemes, treats texts 'not as discourses to be read, understood and interpreted for meaning – either by a human coder or a computer programme applying a dictionary – but as collections of word data containing information about the position of the texts' authors on predefined policy dimensions'.[11] Developed by Kenneth Benoit and Michael Laver, this probabilistic Wordscores method of computerised text analysis was first used for an analysis of Irish party manifestos in the 1997 elections and the technique was extended to the analysis of Irish parliamentary speeches and the 2002 election manifestos.[12] We have chosen to utilise it here not only because there is good evidence that it is accurate in an Irish context, but also for the more pragmatic reason that the CMP coding is not available at the time of writing.

Utilising Wordscores allows us to track the movement of parties between elections on any given dimension such as economic or social policy (for more details, see the Appendix to this chapter). The Wordscores technique does have its critics, some of whom have argued that while the approach has great promise, 'the jury is still out on whether that will be fulfilled'.[13] However, the technique has been broadly validated by its growing use in cross-national research, such as when examining Danish party manifestos.[14]

Given the focus on the economy we will confine much of our analysis to that dimension. Figure 2.2 gives our manifesto-based estimates of the policy positions of the Irish parties in 2011. The scale contrasts higher taxation and government spending, on the left, with lower taxation and spending, on the right. As noted above, this was the substantial theme of the election campaign and one that was central to all of the party manifestos. However, as we saw, the policies of the three largest parties were greatly constrained and to a greater extent than ever before. All three of the larger parties and the Greens had pledged to broadly implement the EU/IMF deal agreed by the government the previous November and thus none could promise spending hikes or tax cuts. Sinn Féin, as we saw, was an exception, promising that it would tear up the deal, thus allowing itself significant room to diverge from the other parties on this crucial dimension.

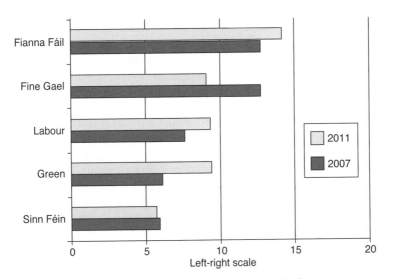

Note: 0 is the most left-wing position and 20 the most right-wing.

Figure 2.2   Estimated economic left-right positions of Irish parties 2007–11

As we might expect we can see a substantial impact of this context on the left-right scale. The wordscoring results suggest that the main substantive changes were a sharp shift from the right to a more central position by Fine Gael and a slight shift rightwards by Labour and the Green Party. As a result none of the three was significantly distinguishable from one another in the centre, relative to 2007 where Labour and the Greens were significantly to the left of Fine Gael. At the same time, Fianna Fáil shifted slightly to the right and Sinn Féin to the left, with each respectively occupying the extreme positions on each end of this dimension. Utilising the tax and spending dimension, derived from the 2007 CMP scores, a very similar pattern is found.

While Fine Gael emphasised spending cuts to a greater extent than tax rises the state of the public finances meant that it could not focus on tax cuts, the traditional focus of parties on the centre right (although one that all parties had tried to make their own in 2007). Thus Fine Gael rhetoric shifted from promising tax cuts in 2007 to job creation with a promise of 'a clear, credible jobs plan. We will create over 45,000 additional work experience, training, and internship opportunities, and increase total employment by at least 100,000 jobs.' The manifesto also promised that the Government would invest in the economy. 'Our NewEra plan will invest an extra €7 billion in energy, communications and water to give Ireland the world-class infrastructure it needs to compete. Since it will be funded in significant part through the sale of non-strategic state assets it will not increase the Government deficit.' In contrast, in its 2007 manifesto Fine Gael promised to 'cut taxes for all taxpayers, with a focus on relief for families and first-time homebuyers'. Labour's previous manifesto rhetoric also saw a decisive shift. In 2007 the party had five big spending commitments, from more hospital beds, to increased numbers of Gardaí, free pre-school education, money for carers and a 'Begin to Buy' scheme to allow people who are working to buy a stake in a home. In 2011 there was a €500 million Jobs Fund but no specific commitments, particularly on welfare where the predominance of mentions were on cutting down welfare fraud. Fine Gael, on the other hand, made specific references to keeping 'the Old Age Contributory and Non-contributory Pension at its current level'. It also pledged that 'working-age payments to carers, the blind and the disabled will also be maintained'. The result was a shift to the centre ground leaving Fine Gael occupying broadly the same space as the Labour Party.

The other party which saw a significant shift in its position between the 2007 and 2011 elections was Sinn Féin, which produced a distinctly left-wing agenda in its manifesto.

- The introduction of a 1 per cent Wealth Tax. This would be an income-linked Wealth Tax for high earners levied on their assets over €1 million in value, excluding working farmland.

- The introduction of a third tax rate of 48 per cent on individual income in excess of three times the average industrial wage (€100,000) per annum.
- Standardising all discretionary taxation expenditures (tax relief paid at either the standard or marginal rate depending on income) with a view to ultimately eradicating tax reliefs that do not return a value for society.
- Restoring the minimum wage at €8.65 an hour.
- Removing the income levy/Universal Social Charge from low earners in the 'no-tax' bracket and keeping minimum-wage earners out of the tax bracket.

This combination of traditional left-wing economic policies which allowed the party to distance itself from the EU/IMF deal ensured that it occupied its own distinctive space on the left.

Overall, the text analysis of the manifestos shows that the mainstream parties, notably Labour and Fine Gael, shifted positions to occupy the centre space on all dimensions, while Sinn Féin tracked left. Both Fianna Fáil and the Greens also shifted slightly right, the Greens to join the mainstream parties at the centre and Fianna Fáil to occupy the most right-wing position on the spectrum (see Figure 2.3).

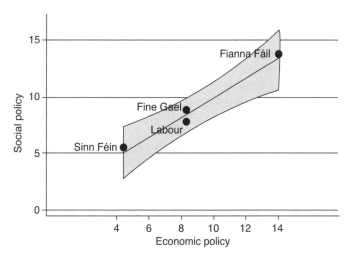

Figure 2.3   Positions on economic and social policy

Note: Based on Wordscores estimates. The shaded area represents a 95 per cent confidence interval around the left–right and social policy issue placements. The social policy dimension is measured from the expert results reported in Kenneth Benoit and Michael Laver, 'Estimating party policy positions: Comparing expert surveys and hand-coded content analysis', *Electoral Studies* 26 (2007) 90–107.

When we think more deeply about this it may not be as much of a puzzle as it appears at first glance. Parties that expect to be in coalition together can be expected to produce manifestos that are broadly similar in style. We also know that mainstream parties will tack towards the centre and the median voter, while niche parties will tend towards the mean position of their own supporters.[15] Broadly, it appears that both of these effects were in play during the process of writing the 2011 party manifestos.

It was clear long before the election that by far the most likely outcome was a coalition agreement between Fine Gael and Labour. Fianna Fáil's electoral position had deteriorated dramatically and it was also associated with the centre-right policies of its previous 14 years in government. A combination of circumstances including the early election meant that little attention was paid to the production of the party's manifesto, with large parts of the EU/IMF agreement simply being inserted. In addition, Fianna Fáil downgraded areas such as health and education, traditionally associated with spending. Its reliance on the text of the agreement with the EU/IMF and its consequent inability to promise increased spending, as it had in 2007, meant that it moved towards the centre-right of the spectrum.

Fine Gael, on the other hand, was keen to emphasise that a Fine Gael-led coalition with Labour would work. In the past the parties had negotiated a joint manifesto, but on this occasion both parties chose to go it alone, leaving them vulnerable to attack on their incompatibilities from both Fianna Fáil on the right and Sinn Féin on the left. The result appears to have been a change in the use of language on the part of Fine Gael, which saw the party shift decisively towards its putative smaller coalition partner. Perhaps reflecting its ambitions to overtake Fine Gael as the larger party, Labour also moved slightly towards the centre and towards Fine Gael, but by no means by such a large margin. The result was that among the larger parties Sinn Féin had the rhetoric of the left freely at its disposal and was able to occupy this space unchallenged, arguably the mean position of its voters. It is notable that in the previous three elections Sinn Féin has been positioning itself more as a party of the left and moving away from its previously conservative stance on social issues, one frequently seen with nationalist parties.

Overall, then, we can see that as expected there were shifts in the left–right placement of Irish parties during the 2011 election campaign. The larger parties and expected coalition partners Fine Gael and Labour moved closer together. This is likely to have been a consequence of the constraining EU/IMF deal combined with the pressures for would-be coalition parties to move together. Sinn Fein's distinctive position on the deal allowed it to break to the left and notably to also shift its position on the social dimension thus beginning to look more like a traditional left-wing niche party rather than a nationalist party, conservative on social issues and with a distinctive identity on Northern Ireland, as previously. The demise of the PDs created a space on the right that was filled by Fianna Fáil. However, given the shortness of that party's manifesto, due in part to the demands of office and the earlier-than-anticipated election date, it is too early to read much into this.

This was the most unusual of elections in a number of respects, and certainly with regard to the prominence given to the policies of the competing parties. Election 2011 saw great interest in policies by the media and voters alike. It also witnessed a policy agenda that was heavily conditioned by the economic situation, which set important constraints on virtually all the established parties, resulting in the parties that were to form a coalition government occupying similar territory on the centre ground, flanked by Fianna Fáil on the right and Sinn Féin on the left. A different election in a different context may well see the parties revert to type, but only time – and the next election – will tell.

Appendix: about Wordscores

The Wordscores technique simply counts the number of times any given word is used and utilises it to estimate the policy positions of texts. The technique requires that we input so-called 'virgin' texts and provide a measurement of their score on any dimension of interest. There is a choice of several data sources to provide this initial positioning of political parties' manifestos including expert surveys, public opinion surveys and of course comparative manifesto data. Repeated studies have shown that party expert surveys in which country experts are asked to place parties relative to one another on a variety of dimensions, are among the most valid.[16] The scores utilised in this analysis are the 2007 expert survey analysis included in Benoit and Laver,[17] which we have chosen for reasons of timeliness and face validity.[18]

The expert survey of Irish party positions on policy was conducted during the period of two weeks before and roughly one month after the 2007 Irish general election, which took place 24 May 2007. The survey closely followed the expert placement methodology used in previous surveys. Each policy dimension consisted of two endpoints anchored at 1 and 20, generally corresponding to the 'left' and 'right' positions respectively. Respondents were asked, for each policy dimension, to locate the main list of political parties on two scales, one indicating a party's position, and another indicating the importance that the party attached to this policy dimension. A total of 237 experts were identified, based on the mailing list of the Political Studies Association of Ireland. These experts were invited to participate in the survey by email. The sample was randomly divided into two groups: 128 experts were contacted two weeks before the election, and 127 experts were contacted one week after the election. By clicking on a URL in the email containing a unique respondent identifier, each expert was directed to an online survey. A total of 54 valid returns were received, a response rate of 22.7 per cent. The mean policy positions identified by the experts in 2007 were utilised as the virgin texts.

In order to ascertain whether the patterns we report in this chapter were the result of any peculiarity in coding in the 2007 expert surveys we also ran the technique utilising both scores on the basis of the CMP data (formerly known as the Manifesto Research Group) and those generated from previous Wordscores in 2002. The CMP data is made up of data from manifestos of the major political parties in 51 parliamentary democracies covering all democratic elections since 1945. The analysis is carried out by human coders using some 56 standard categories coding so-called 'quasi-sentences'. The real advantage of the dataset is that it allows researchers to compare party policy positions across both space and time. However, there has been some debate not only about the fact that the CMP does not provide any measurement of uncertainty but perhaps more importantly for the purposes of this chapter on the salience of party competition.

One problem is the measurement of the left–right measures, where the number of quasi-sentences in each category is summed and expressed as a percentage of the total set of quasi-sentences in the manifesto. This gives an indication of the degree of attention given to a particular policy theme in a manifesto. These frequencies can then be added together or used to outline dimensions of political competition, such as the left–right spectrum where individual measures are grouped into left and right and one subtracted from the other. The resulting data measures positions from –100 on the far left to +100 on the far right. The insight is that the more a party emphasises left-wing issues the more left-wing it is, and vice versa for right-wing.

There have been doubts raised over whether it is possible to equate salience or the emphasis in a manifesto with positioning as well as on coder reliability. For example, in 2007 on the key left–right position all Irish parties received a negative score indicating that from a comparative perspective all including the then PDs were centre-left. However, in this chapter we are interested in the relative movement of parties in Ireland along the left–right scale, rather than on cross-country comparisons, and thus the substantive position behind the starting point is less important. As a result we ran the wordscoring technique utilising figures from the CMP and uncovered a largely similar pattern to that outlined here. Fine Gael moved decidedly centre-left; Fianna Fáil shifted a little to the right, as did the Greens; and Labour remained largely static. We also tested whether utilising former Wordscores results rather than the expert survey as a base would result in a different analysis. We used the scores reported in Benoit and Laver with the 2007 manifestos as the virgin texts. We then utilised these scores as a reference category with the 2011 manifestos as the virgin texts and again came up with broadly similar results.

Notes

1. Russell Dalton, David Farrell and Ian McAllister, *Political Parties and Democratic Linkage* (Oxford: Oxford University Press, 2011).
2. On this see Marsh and Cunningham, this volume, Chapter 8, p. 187.
3. Much of this section is based on a series of face-to-face interviews with the key party personnel involved. As some preferred to remain anonymous we have chosen not to name any of our interviewees. We are very grateful to them for their time and frankness.
4. See, for instance, the record of his comments at the 2010 MacGill Summer School, reported in Joe Mulholland (ed.), *Reforming the Republic: The MacGill Report 2010* (Dublin: MacGill Summer School, 2010).
5. Noel Whelan, 'Election shaped by meltdown of FF brand', *Irish Times*, 2 April 2011.
6. Whelan, 'Election shaped by meltdown'.
7. On the history of manifestos in Irish elections, see Peter Mair, *The Changing Irish Party System* (London: Frances Pinter, 1987). For more recent analyses, see John Garry and Lucy Mansergh, 'Party manifestos', pp. 82–106 in Michael Marsh and Paul Mitchell (eds), *How Ireland Voted 1997* (Boulder, Colorado: Westview Press, 1999); Thomas Däubler, 'The preparation and use of election manifestos: learning from the Irish case', paper presented at the annual conference of Political Studies Association of Ireland, Dublin Institute of Technology, October 2010.
8. The RTÉ audience survey was carried out on 28 January to 1 February inclusive and a total of 1,207 people completed the survey. The margin of error was +/– 4 per cent. We are grateful to Stephen Quinlan and Mark Canavan for helping us to code the parties' manifestos.
9. For more information see www.rte.ie/news/election2011/party_comparison.html.
10. Michael Laver and Ian Budge (eds), *Party Policy and Government Coalitions* (Basingstoke: Macmillan, 1992).

11. Kenneth Benoit and Michael Laver, 'Estimating Irish party policy positions using computer wordscoring: the 2002 election – a research note', *Irish Political Studies* 18:1 (2003), pp. 97–107.

12. Michael Laver and Kenneth Benoit, 'Locating TDs in policy spaces: Wordscoring Dáil speeches', *Irish Political Studies* 17:1 (2002), pp. 59–73.

13. Ian Budge and Paul Pennings, 'Do they work? Validating computerised word frequency estimates against policy series', *Electoral Studies* 26:1 (2007), pp. 121–9.

14. R. Klemmensen, S.B. Hobolt and M.E. Hansen, 'Estimating policy positions using political texts: an evaluation of the Wordscores approach', *Electoral Studies* 26:4 (2007), pp. 746–55.

15. Lawrence Ezrow, *Linking Citizens and Parties: How electoral systems matter for political representation* (Oxford: Oxford University Press, 2010).

16. Kenneth Benoit and Michael Laver, *Party Policy in Modern Democracies* (London: Taylor & Francis, 2006).

17. Kenneth Benoit, Michael Laver and Slava Mikhaylov, 'Treating words as data with error: uncertainty in text statements of policy positions', *American Journal of Political Science* 53:2 (2009), pp. 495–513.

18. We also replicated the analysis utilising CMP data from 2007 which resulted in similar findings.

3
Candidate Selection

Theresa Reidy[1]

The 2011 election took place in a more politically charged atmosphere than previous contests. The collapse of the economy, the banking crisis and the application for an EU/IMF loan contributed to the heightened political tensions (see Chapter 1) and meant that the political landscape was markedly different from the 2007 election. The dramatic shift in Irish economic fortunes precipitated significant movements in support levels for all the political parties. Indeed, 'change' became something of a mantra in public discussions of politics before the election. This gave rise to widespread speculation about new political parties and movements. A record 566 candidates chose to contest the election, an increase of 96 on the 2007 election. Wicklow had the highest number of candidates with 24 names on the ballot paper, while the average across all constituencies was over 13.

Several small groups emerged but all failed to organise a national campaign with candidates in every constituency. Most ended up as loose political umbrella groups. These included New Vision, Fís Nua, the People's Convention and Democracy Now. The last of these, which in the event did not get off the ground, attracted a lot of media attention and involved several high-profile media personalities (Éamon Dunphy, Shane Ross, David McWilliams and Fintan O'Toole). The group had intended to establish itself as a 'non-ideological' political party and it hoped to attract candidates from across the ideological spectrum. It had a number of policy goals which included restructuring Irish bank debts (commonly referred to as 'burn the bondholders' during the campaign) and ending cronyism in Irish politics. A number of Independent TDs (including Finian McGrath and Catherine Murphy) had also been invited to become involved. Some preliminary planning had been completed but the group abandoned its plans to contest the election when the Dáil was dissolved ahead of schedule. Shane Ross decided to contest the election as an Independent and was elected in Dublin South, while McGrath and Murphy were re-elected as Independents.

Of the groups that did emerge, few registered as political parties. Fís Nua did but too late to have its party affiliation on the ballot paper. In contrast, the United Left Alliance (ULA) formed as a new political movement, incorporating three registered parties but did not itself register as a new political party. The ULA incorporates the Socialist Party, People Before Profit and the Workers and Unemployed Action Group. These groups campaigned as a single party and are treated as such here.

The first section of this chapter will document the rules governing the selection of candidates and the selection strategies of the five main political parties: Fianna Fáil, Fine Gael, Labour, the Green Party and Sinn Féin. This will be followed by an examination of the practice of candidate selection in 2011. It will pay particular attention to the main factors influencing candidate selection and the challenges which arise for parties in the course of the process. Finally, the chapter will profile the candidates who contested the 2011 general election, looking at the political backgrounds and experience of candidates.

Political recruitment is one of the key functions of political parties. Parties identify, select and prepare candidates for election. Candidate selection takes place within political parties and the practice of selection varies internationally. National structures governing candidate selection are rare and parties usually have discretion to set their own regulations. The US primary system is probably the best known selection procedure. Rules change and develop over time. The practice of candidate selection in Ireland is devolved and all parties operate a selection process using local conventions at constituency level. All but Fianna Fáil operate a one member one vote (OMOV) system, which empowers the party membership in candidate selection. Tension between the membership and the national executive of the party is a feature of the selection process and this is examined in the ensuing section. Ireland is unusual in a comparative context in that independent candidates, not affiliated with a political party, feature strongly in electoral contests.

Parties are involved in a delicate process when it comes to picking candidates for the coming election, with many factors that need to be borne in mind. Electability is the critical aspect but parties also consider a range of variables, which include age, experience, gender, geography and the strategies being operated by competitor parties. Added to this, each party must develop a strategy on the number of candidates it will field taking into account its current position and projections for the election. Deciding on the number of candidates was a particular concern among all the parties in 2011, arising from the sharp change in support levels in opinion polls. For parties with an upward trajectory in the polls, candidate numbers had to be increased to maximise seat gains. Parties with a downward trajectory face a more difficult scenario. In particular, Fianna Fáil had to tackle a major challenge in that it had many more candidates in the field than would normally be run by a party with support levels below 20 per cent. A major element of its strategy was to reduce the number of candidates that it was fielding. Over-selection and under-selection are always a concern at elections and can present a complicated challenge under proportional representation by the single transferable vote (PR-STV). This was especially the case in 2011.

Candidate selection: party rules and strategies

The formal rules governing candidate selection are contained in the constitutions or regulations of each of the political parties. Party headquarters manage the national selection processes and varying levels of influence and/or control are exerted by the central executives of the parties. Parties provide guidelines on the number of candidates to be selected and any other criteria that are to be employed. Selections are made at local level but party executives ratify all candidates and reserve the right to add candidates as needed. In exceptional cases, incumbent TDs have been deselected at previous elections. All parties use PR-STV for the counting of votes at selection conventions.

Each party's rules ascribe a role to the party executives in the management and organisation of the selection process. However, the rules say little about the overall strategy adopted by individual parties and this clearly is a central focus for parties. Decisions on the overall number of candidates to be run must be made in the context of the political circumstances of each election. This section will document the specific rules governing the process in each party and outline the party strategies that were developed and employed for the 2011 election.

Party strategy is heavily influenced by two factors: the existing position of the party (incumbent candidates and party network), and projections based on opinion polls and research. Each party engages in market research on an ongoing basis and this becomes central to decisions on candidate selection. In all cases, party strategists refer to opinion polls as a factor in the decision making at the 2011 election. In addition to polls, most parties conduct qualitative and quantitative research at national and constituency level over the course of the electoral cycle. The fluidity of the electoral landscape in 2011 and the uncertainty about the election date meant that many parties had tentative plans in place. These plans were amended and accelerated once the election date was announced.

Parties were advanced in their candidate selection plans when the election was called. Selection conventions are usually organised in the months before a general election and this election, though not legally required until 2012, had been anticipated for some time. Most conventions are organised on a constituency basis, although Labour split a small number of constituencies along geographic lines. The convention is usually chaired by a party notable from outside the constituency. All of the parties held conventions for the 2011 election. Four parties fielded a candidate in every constituency (Fianna Fáil, Fine Gael, Labour and the Green Party), and Sinn Féin stood in all but five constituencies.

Seeking out candidates to contest elections is a practice in all of the parties and the 2007 election was notable for the number of sportspersons who were persuaded to contest the election on behalf of several parties. 2011 saw a decline in the number of candidates approached to contest, arising from their pre-existing public profile. Strategists put this down to the negative experience of Fine Gael with George Lee.[2] Candidate profiles in a later section in this chapter reinforce this point, and previous electoral experience was a particular advantage in the main political parties.

One striking trend from Table 3.1 is the sharp rise in the number of independents contesting the 2011 election, close to double the number in 2007. There are varying explanations proffered to explain the strength of Independents in Irish elections[3] but the unpredictable electoral environment was identified by many as a factor.

Table 3.1   Number of candidates by party, 1997–2011

	1997	2002	2007	2011
Fianna Fáil	112	106	106	75
Fine Gael	90	85	91	104
Labour	44	46	50	68
Green Party	26	31	44	43
Sinn Féin	15	37	41	41
ULA	–	–	–	20
Others	195	138	108	215
Total	484	463	470	566

Fine Gael

Fine Gael fielded the highest number of candidates at the election. Its candidate selection strategy had been in development since the 2009 local elections and preparations were well advanced by the time the election was called. Phil Hogan TD and Frank Flannery are credited as being the architects of its strategy. Fine Gael headquarters commissioned both national and constituency level research in the years preceding the election. This work included opinion polls as well as small group research on policy, brand strength and SWOT (Strengths, Weaknesses, Opportunities, Threats) analyses.

Decisions on candidate numbers and selection criteria at conventions were very much informed by the constituency level research. The party increased its overall number of candidates based on its findings and, notably, in five constituencies it ran four candidates, a risky strategy under PR-STV. Local opinion polls were also crucial for decisions on vote management within individual constituencies. Where local polls identified that the party vote might be skewed between candidates, party head office devised vote management strategies to maximise gains for the party. Head office managed the process and, where necessary, decisions were enforced by the Director of Elections, Phil Hogan. Fine Gael invested considerable time and resources in research in advance of the election and the output was used to inform all areas of party strategy.

The formal rules for selecting candidates in Fine Gael are set down in the party constitution. A selection convention was held in each constituency at a date decided by the Executive Council. The candidate selection strategy operated by Fine Gael has top-down and bottom-up elements. Formally, the party leader proposes the selection convention directive and this is ratified and enacted by the Executive Council (previously known as the National Executive). The selection directives are informed by advice from four sources: the Executive Council, the National Election Committee, party head office and constituency strategy committees. Each constituency has a strategy committee which was established and assigned a series of tasks in advance of the election, including reviewing previous election results and tallies, speaking with potential local candidates and reporting back to head office. The National Election Committee and the Executive Council liaise on overall election strategy. The party leader is guided by the submissions from the four sources, although it is clear that the Executive Council and party head office are most influential in the decision making. It is rare for the Executive Council not to ratify the directive of the party leader (this occurred once in 2002) and there is considerable discussion and close cooperation between the Executive

Council, head office and the party leader in advance of directives being proposed. Fine Gael selection conventions began in November 2009 in Kildare South with the final convention in Louth on 25 January 2011. Each party member with at least two years' membership is entitled to vote in their constituency convention. The OMOV system has been in place since 1996.

The Labour Party

Similar to Fine Gael, the Labour Party was preparing for the election in the face of a strengthening position in the opinion polls and considerable disarray among the governing parties. Labour also commissioned its own opinion polls and again, these were used to inform party strategy. The strength of the party, in both its own and national media polls, led to a decision at the Executive Board to run additional candidates so as to maximise seat gains. It was agreed that all incumbent TDs would have a running mate. Jack Wall TD in Kildare South was the only exception to this rule; the decision to run just one candidate here was based on local opinion polls that suggested splitting the party vote might endanger the existing seat. In its decision making on candidate numbers, the party was influenced by evidence which suggested that it had under-selected in 1992 (in other words, it did not field enough candidates to maximise its seat gains)[4] and it was keen to avoid the same mistake in 2011. The party ran 18 more candidates than in 2007 and 26 more than in 1992.

Rules governing the selection of Labour Party candidates are set out in the party constitution. Responsibility for the process is allocated to the Organisation Committee.[5] Conventions are organised at local level and the Organisation Committee has discretion to decide on the number of candidates to be selected and may specify other criteria to be fulfilled. Election planning had been in train since the 2009 local elections. A three-person candidate team was established in each constituency to conduct interviews with potential candidates. The committee must comprise two party members and a present or former Oireachtas member; in addition, at least one must be male and one female. A separate board is constituted for each constituency by the Organisation Committee. The candidate team occupies a central and powerful role in the process, as only candidates nominated by the panel can go forward to the selection convention. The candidate selection team was also tasked with identifying and approaching new candidates and the party estimates that about 20–30 per cent of candidates emerged in this way. The party operates the OMOV system at selection conventions. The candidate team also makes recommendations on the addition of candidates after selection conventions have taken place (additions included Lorraine Higgins in Galway East and Mary Moran in Louth).

Fianna Fáil

The formal rules governing candidate selection in Fianna Fáil organise the process on a constituency basis. A call for nominations is issued to each cumann (branch). All declared candidates go before a convention. Fianna Fáil operates a delegate voting system with each branch entitled to three votes. Selection conventions are chaired by a party notable from outside the constituency and instructions on selection criteria are provided by party headquarters.

Fianna Fáil and the Green Party were projected to receive a significantly reduced share of the vote in pre-election opinion polls. For Fianna Fáil, this resulted in a strategy of reducing the number of candidates in the field, in an attempt to concentrate the vote on 'winnable' seats. The outcome of this strategy was that Fianna Fáil ran just 75 candidates in 2011. Despite the sharp drop in the number of candidates, many Fianna Fáil candidates believe that there were still too many candidates and this contributed to seat losses (Dun Laoghaire was identified as the main example of this over-nomination – see pp. 59–60 below). As Table 3.1 outlines, Fianna Fáil ran 31 fewer candidates in 2011 than in 2007. Indeed, Fianna Fáil could not have achieved an overall majority, a psychological blow for the long time dominant party of Irish politics.[6]

Fianna Fáil was in a position of considerable disarray facing into the 2011 election. In addition to the challenge of declining support in opinion polls, Fianna Fáil strategists also faced uncertainties around which incumbent candidates would seek to contest the election. A raft of retirements began in mid-2010 and accelerated around Christmas 2010, with many high-profile TDs and ministers indicating that they would not be contesting the election. This development eased one source of difficulty for the party, by reducing the number of candidates in the field, but it also meant that Fianna Fáil lost some of its highest vote-getters, such as ministers Dermot Ahern and Noel Dempsey and Taoiseach Brian Cowen. A change in party leader at the beginning of the campaign further complicated the selection strategy. Consequently, Fianna Fáil operated a fluid strategy on a very tight timeline.

Fianna Fáil has been identified as operating a centralised candidate selection process at previous elections,[7] but this was not the case in 2011. The party leader and head office are the central players in candidate selection within Fianna Fáil. The party was unprepared for the election with one candidate describing the party as 'spiralling into the abyss' in the months before the election. The overall party strategy was to reduce the number of candidates. This was achieved by controlling the selection criteria at conventions and directly encouraging candidates to withdraw at conventions (Jim O'Callaghan in Dublin South-East is identified as an example of the latter). However, head office did not pursue its strategy of reducing numbers in a very active manner until a new party leader, Micheál Martin, was elected at the start of the campaign. Head office exercises its power through the party leader. Difficulties around the leadership of Brian Cowen had been brewing for some months before the election; these problems took the focus from party organisation and constrained the ability of head office to act on candidate selection. Party retirements were considered difficult to manage and head office was not in a position to force candidates to declare their intentions. With the appointment of Micheál Martin, a more active strategy was pursued and the new leader approached a number of candidates in an attempt to persuade them not to stand for the election. The decision by Cork North-Central TD Noel O'Flynn not to contest the election is an example of this direct intervention. In addition, Limerick TD John Cregan decided to stand down at the start of the election, once his more junior running mate was appointed to Martin's front bench and he was not. In both cases the effect was to help reduce the number of candidates in the field.

The practice of candidate selection in Fianna Fáil was also complicated by residual anger from the strategy employed at the 2009 local elections. In 2009, candidate selection decisions were made centrally after an interview process. Party branches lost their role and this contributed to resentment among members and TDs. With the party in disarray nationally, and resentment from grassroots members over the 2009 candidate strategy, head office was forced into a more conciliatory and, ultimately, more passive role than it had played at previous elections.

The Green Party

Smaller political parties operate a more decentralised process with fewer guidelines from the central executives of the party. This is possible as parties are usually running just one candidate in each constituency and other factors such as geography and balancing a party ticket on age and gender grounds are therefore less of a concern.

Green Party candidate selection is managed by an Election Task Force (ETF) whose members include the cathaoirleach of the party, the general secretary, communications manager, members of the parliamentary party and party members. The role of the task force is to liaise with constituencies in the candidate selection process. In 2007 the party had run a candidate in every constituency (and two in Dublin North) and the ETF decided that this strategy should be repeated in 2011. It was considered especially important that, after its term in government, the party contest each constituency. Pragmatism was also an essential element and the party had a strong incentive to maximise its vote nationally: parties must reach a threshold of 2 per cent of the national vote to be eligible for state funding.

The party strategy was summarised by one of its candidates as 'ten serious candidates, ten full-blooded candidates (candidates that had an existing profile in the area, perhaps as councillors, but were unlikely to challenge for a seat) and the remaining candidates were intended to maintain the party presence in an area'. Indeed, a number of the candidates in the final category made very little effort at campaigning and many could be classified as 'paper' candidates. Some effort was put into picking candidates that might contest future elections and develop the party. However, the sudden calling of the election meant that less time was invested in this process than the party would have liked.

Within the Green Party constituency organisations have a lot of autonomy and can organise their own conventions. The date is notified to head office. The returning officer must be drawn from outside the constituency. The Green Party allows postal voting at its selection conventions. All candidates require ratification by the ETF, once they have completed a declaration of interest form. The ETF can deselect candidates but this did not occur in 2011.

Sinn Féin

Within Sinn Féin, decisions on candidate numbers and national strategy are decided by the Ard Comhairle. Sinn Féin has an election department which has an overall coordinating role, while each constituency has a local election strategy group, made up of local members. The election strategy group is responsible for managing the selection process; it issues the call for nominations and interviews candidates who have been nominated. The strategy committee makes a recommendation to the selection convention but does not have the power to veto any candidate. Members are given seven days' notice of the convention and the convention must be attended by a member of the Ard Comhairle, the body that has ultimate ratification power. The Ard Comhairle also has the power to deselect candidates but this was not applied in 2011. Sinn Féin ran 41 candidates. It ran two candidates in just three constituencies: Carlow–Kilkenny, Cavan–Monaghan and Mayo. The fact that Carlow–

Kilkenny is a two-county constituency creates an obvious logic of running one candidate from each county. The same applies in Cavan–Monaghan, which in addition is Sinn Féin's strongest constituency and one where it was aiming for two seats. A seat in Mayo was added to the 'target list' after the election of Pearse Doherty in the Donegal SW by-election in November 2010 and the ensuing high opinion poll ranking. Geography was an important factor in Mayo. Therese Ruane in Castlebar was challenging for the vote previously held by Beverley Flynn, while Rose Conway-Walsh was located in Belmullet. In addition to local opinion polls, Sinn Féin also engages in small group research at national and local level. This research is used to identify likely voters. At local level, focus groups were used within constituencies to identify issues of relevance to particular sets of voters and to develop strategies to target these voters.

United Left Alliance

Candidate selection for the ULA took place within the constituent political parties which subsequently amalgamated to form the ULA. The parties had an uneven network across the country and a limited party structure. Individual candidates have a great deal of influence within the movement.

Candidate selections in practice

Having considered the formal rules governing candidate selection and the macro-strategies devised by the parties, it is interesting to explore the practice of candidate selection. The process itself is the preserve of party members and elites. In practice, there is tension between these two groups for control. During the 1990s, parties developed their candidate selection rules, all but Fianna Fáil moving to the OMOV system. This conferred more power on the party members but in all cases parties have retained some centralised control, so that overall party strategy can be executed.

Selection conventions take place behind closed doors and are the starting point in an election campaign for many of the members. There is a somewhat militaristic rhetoric to be found among members in all parties with discussions on territory, battlegrounds and campaigns a common feature. Conventions are an opportunity for parties to prepare for the coming campaign. Local factions compete for supremacy and party headquarters is often the silent but potent background force laying down the rules of battle. Conventions can be marred by party infighting and occasionally by some very public disagreements. In 2011, there were very few public conflicts. It is hard to assess whether this was down to better management of the selection process or, more probably, the enormity of the political challenges and the collapse of the government, which precipitated an early election. Some examples illustrate the practice of candidate selection within parties and also highlight the challenges and dilemmas that parties face.

Fine Gael operated a centralised and tightly controlled selection process in 2011. All but six conventions had been held by the end of 2010 and the party provided instructions on the number of candidates in all cases. Eight selection conventions were given geographical selection criteria and gender was a selection criterion in just one constituency.[8] While each party member has a vote at the convention, the party centre retains a strong influence on the final outcome by setting the criteria for selection. The gender selection criterion in Dun Laoghaire is perhaps the best example of the party setting clear rules to favour or disadvantage specific candidates. The gender directive caused controversy at the convention with many seeing it as a deliberate strategy to ensure the selection of Mary Mitchell O'Connor. While Fine Gael did give some consideration to gender as a factor in candidate selection strategy, the Dun Laoghaire directive reflected a more ruthless objective of the party centre to ensure its preferred outcomes.

Galway West highlights further dynamics of candidate selection for Fine Gael. The failure of outgoing TD Pádraic McCormack to be selected by party members at the Galway West selection convention came as a surprise. McCormack had been the sitting TD for 21 years and was chairman of the parliamentary party at the time of the convention in December 2010. There was some speculation after the convention that he might be added to the party ticket; precedent within Fine Gael is that incumbent TDs are usually added to the ticket if they were not selected at convention. The constituency was complicated by geography with the two candidates selected at convention, Senator Fidelma Healy Eames and councillor Brian Walsh, located in the same part of the constituency as McCormack. The party was keen to ensure that a candidate would be located in Connemara. Following some consultation, McCormack, who was aged 68, announced that he would not accept being added to the party ticket and that he was retiring from party politics. Two additional candidates, Seán Kyne and Hildegarde Naughton, were added by the National Executive (the former gives an account of his campaign in Chapter 6, this volume). The candidates were added to provide geographical balance, and also to ensure that Éamon Ó Cuív of Fianna Fáil would have a Fine Gael candidate in his area.

Fine Gael made additions to its ticket in 15 constituencies, adding 18 candidates in all, geography and competitor party strategy being the guiding principles. Many of the candidates added had previously contested selection conventions, though there were some exceptions. Ciaran Cannon was added to the ticket in Galway East. Having joined the party after the dissolution of the Progressive Democrats (PDs), it was felt that he would not have a sufficient support base to come through the selection convention. Cáit Keane also joined from the PDs and unsuccessfully contested the selection convention in Dublin South; she was then added to the ticket in Dublin South-West.

The Labour Party increased its candidate nominations, running two-person tickets in several constituencies for the first time. This new approach occurred without significant problems, though Sligo–North Leitrim and Laois–Offaly presented some difficulties. In Sligo–Leitrim, two candidates went before the selection convention, Labour councillor Veronica Cawley and former journalist Susan O'Keeffe. Both candidates ended up on 71 votes, and the tie-breaker decision was that a name should be drawn from a hat. At this point, O'Keeffe emerged as the candidate but it subsequently transpired that the party had new rules in place when a tie occurred at a convention; the party executive board was to make the decision. The executive board (previously known as the general council) is a national body which is elected at the party conference. O'Keeffe also emerged as the candidate from this process. Cawley left the party over the decision and contested the election as an Independent. The dispute became difficult with several members of the party resigning just days before the election as a result of the selection controversy, and some contested the election as Independent candidates. A similar scenario developed in Laois–Offaly.

Dissatisfaction with the outcomes of selection conventions regularly gives rise to members leaving their party and contesting the election as Independents, often termed 'gene pool' Independents. Parties go to considerable effort to avoid these disputes as they can dilute party vote share and contribute to ill feeling, making it more difficult to manage the election. There are two main reasons for members choosing the Independent route. The first and more prevalent is that the candidate has not been selected by their party to contest the election, or the selection criteria rule them out of the contest. In 2011, this category would include candidates such as John Foley in Laois–Offaly and Tom Fleming in Kerry South, who both decided to contest the election having been dissatisfied by outcomes at Fianna Fáil selection conventions. The second and smaller group are candidates that have a policy disagreement with their party.

Sligo–North Leitrim illustrates the 'gene pool' issue for Labour but it is a phenomenon in all of the political parties. Fianna Fáil had been particularly plagued with this problem at previous elections. Independent Fianna Fáil has become a political label and a number of dynasties (Healy Rae and Blaney) were successful in successive elections under this brand. Despite these notable exceptions, in general, former party members tend not to perform very well at elections and only a small number are elected at each election (Tom Fleming in Kerry South is a 2011 example). There were fewer party disputes in 2011 but the early election is more likely to have been a factor than any increase in party discipline.

Fianna Fáil faced the most challenging political circumstances of all the parties and its candidate selection process was both more interventionist (managing retirements) and more decentralised (greater opportunities for the local organisation to make decisions) than on previous occasions. This was a departure from the trend established in recent elections which had seen Fianna Fáil selection processes become more centralised. In 2011, its traditional approach was complicated by declining support, retirements, a new party leader and uncertainty about the final election date.

TD retirements were higher in 2011 than at previous elections and Fianna Fáil was particularly affected (see list of retirements in Appendix 5, this volume). While retirements were essential for Fianna Fáil to reduce the number of candidates on the party ticket, it made the selection process more complex. The late decision by Taoiseach Brian Cowen to retire from politics created a vacancy in the Laois–Offaly constituency. More than 750 delegates attended the convention, which selected the Taoiseach's brother, councillor Barry Cowen, to stand in his place. Sitting TDs John Moloney and Seán Fleming were also returned. This resulted in a dispute with councillor John Foley, who had previously been Brian Cowen's running mate in Offaly. He went on to contest the election as an Independent.

A number of selection conventions, delayed by the evolving political situation, became ratification conventions. These conventions were used to formally agree incumbent TDs as the election candidates for the party. They took place in the early stages of the campaign and Cork South-Central is an example. Constituency organisations provided advice on candidate selections in several cases, which went against party strategy of running tight tickets. In Longford–Westmeath, a three-candidate strategy was recommended by the local organisation and agreed by party headquarters. In Clare, the local organisation interviewed potential candidates in a search for a second candidate. Dr John Hillery was recommended and agreed centrally. In Dun Laoghaire, a single-candidate strategy was recommended but the convention selected the two sitting TDs, Barry Andrews and Mary Hanafin, both ministers. Party disorganisation, incumbency and the involvement of dynasties have all been cited to explain this case. Dun Laoghaire is used most frequently to highlight the flaws in the election strategy of Fianna Fáil. The refusal of either of the sitting TDs to move constituency and the failure of the party to insist on such a move highlight the major problems within the party. Some analysts suggest that this may have cost Fianna Fáil a seat in Dun Laoghaire. Incumbency was also an issue in Kerry South, where John O'Donoghue was selected to contest the election. O'Donoghue had been embroiled in an expenses scandal that required him to resign as Ceann Comhairle (speaker) of the Dáil in 2009. This contributed to considerable personal unpopularity, which, when combined with the national swing against Fianna Fáil, made him unlikely to hold his seat. The convention rules stipulated one candidate. Councillor Tom Fleming and Senator Mark Daly withdrew their names at the convention. However, Fleming left the party shortly afterwards and contested the election as an Independent, as mentioned above. Despite a goal of reducing the number of candidates contesting the election, head office acquiesced to the addition of candidates in some constituencies and added candidates itself in a number of areas to provide geographical balance and support for existing candidates. Lisa Chambers in Mayo was the last candidate added to the Fianna Fáil ticket in the first week of the campaign.

Candidate selections are often presented as the murky side of intra-party politics and disputes about selections are common and often unpleasant. While there were some instances of disagreement within parties, on balance selections for the 2011 election were more orderly and less contentious than has been the case at previous elections. Conventions were very well attended in some of the parties, with several hundred in attendance at nearly all of the Fine Gael conventions and more than 1,500 members at its Cork South-West convention. Labour Party candidates noted high turnout at their conventions and it was not unusual for Sinn Féin to have close to 100 members at some of its conventions. In many cases Sinn Féin candidates were selected unopposed and the conventions became election rallies. Fianna Fáil had some variation in attendance with Laois–Offaly achieving one of the highest turnouts at 750 members.

Parties manage competing forces when selecting candidates. It is essential that electable candidates are picked but it is best if party harmony can be maintained. Parties must balance obligations to incumbent TDs with the need to ensure geographical balance, new candidates within parties, retirements, some gender balance in representation, all the while keeping their competitor in mind. In many ways, it is remarkable that there were so few contentious selection conventions. Party constitutions and rule books provide all of the details on the formal rules for candidate selection but the dynamics of intra-party organisation and management are best illustrated with examples from contests.

The candidates

Failures within the political system were the subject of sustained public discussion following the economic collapse. The debate spilled over into the election campaign and the electoral system, constituency workload of TDs and the incentives within the political system were all subject to examination. Repeated calls were made for more 'experts' to enter politics. Studies have documented the localist character of Irish politics and specifically how this dynamic translates in candidate selection practice.[9] The aspiration for a new breed of politician forms the backdrop to an examination of the profiles of the candidates who contested the 2011 general election.

The profile of candidates is of interest because little is known about the preferences of the party selectorate. Few studies have investigated which criteria party members prioritise in their decision making when they are selecting candidates. While party strategists all cite electability, a more complex set of factors are considered to be at play among party members. Localism is a key feature of Irish politics and it is likely that it is an important factor for party members when selecting candidates. Apart from a study on members of Fine Gael, there is little in the line of detailed information on party selectors.[10] It is possible to speculate on some features that may be important for party members by drawing inferences from the profile of the candidates that were chosen. This does not provide a complete answer because nothing is ever known of those that did not make it through the selection convention process. Inferences about selector preferences are thus based entirely on an examination of successful candidates.

The occupational background of the candidates is set out in Table 3.2, which employs the classification scheme used in the *How Ireland Voted* book series. Occupations are subdivided into seven categories. Commerce includes business people, the self-employed, financial consultants and auctioneers. Higher professional includes barristers and doctors while lower professional is mainly comprised of teachers and nurses. Non-manual includes secretaries, sales persons and public sector employees while manual employee covers occupations such as

Table 3.2   Occupational backgrounds of candidates, 2011

Occupation	Fianna Fáil	Fine Gael	Lab	GP	SF	ULA	Others	Total	%
Farmer	7	13	0	1	2	0	20	43	7.5
Commerce	17	33	7	10	7	1	54	129	22.8
Higher professional	23	17	11	10	3	0	26	90	15.9
Lower professional	12	25	30	8	7	2	25	109	19.3
Non-manual employee	8	7	5	1	3	1	14	39	6.9
Manual employee	0	1	5	1	4	4	14	29	5.1
Other	7	8	7	10	9	10	36	87	15.4
Unknown	1	0	3	2	6	2	26	40	7.1
Total	75	104	68	43	41	20	215	566	100.0

Note: Full-time politicians and public representatives are classified under their previous occupation.

tradespersons and manufacturing workers. The 'other' category is the most diverse and includes students, the unemployed, retired persons and occupations as varying as artists and house husbands.

The professions contributed 35 per cent of all candidates in 2011. Professionals as a group have long been the dominant occupational background among candidates at general elections. Nearly a quarter of candidates came from a commerce background and this marks a small decrease in the number from the 2007 election. This is noteworthy only in the sense that there had been much public criticism of the Fianna Fáil and Green Party government for not having sufficient numbers of business people in their ranks. Despite this, fewer business people contested the 2011 election. In general, the candidates who were business owners tended to run small businesses such as pubs, shops and auctioneering firms. Just under a quarter of Green Party candidates were from business backgrounds, while over a quarter of Independent candidates were business people.

Table 3.2 confirms some of the occupational stereotypes associated with individual political parties. There were no farmers among the Labour and ULA candidates, while Fine Gael selected 13 farmers to contest the election and 20 farmers stood as Independents. The decline in members of the farming community contesting the election is an established trend and there was no marked change in 2011.

Business backgrounds were more common among Fianna Fáil, Fine Gael and Independents than among the left-leaning parties of Labour, the Green Party and the ULA. Labour drew just under half of its candidates from the professions, reinforcing a perception that the Irish Labour Party is not a party of the working classes; teaching and law were the dominant backgrounds among its candidates. The occupational category 'other' shows an upward trend from 2007 and it is worth noting that a significant number of candidates listed their occupations as unemployed, which contributes to the upward trend in this category.

Manual employees, who are more likely to stand as candidates for left-leaning parties or as independents, had the lowest level of representation among candidates in 2011, a trend well established from previous elections. The professions and commerce dominated, suggesting a middle-class orientation among the majority of the candidates contesting the election. Among the lower professions, teaching was dominant while law dominated the higher professions along with small numbers of architects, lecturers and accountants. This finding is not unusual and similar patterns can be identified internationally. In a study of Labour Party members in the UK, it was highlighted that party selectors are conscious that they are choosing candidates for parliament and are keen to ensure they get quality representation. This was a key factor in why selectors often chose candidates with higher levels of education or from a higher social class than themselves.[11]

Finally, among Independent candidates, there was a marked increase in the professional and commerce categories. The number of Independent candidates in the election was almost double the 2007 number but the occupational profile diverges from 2007. It is not possible to explain the precise reason for the changes, but it could be interpreted against the backdrop of the public debate on the lack of 'experts' in politics in Ireland. A number of prominent banking specialists, management consultants and economists put their names forward for the election. Stephen Donnelly (Wicklow) and Shane Ross (Dublin South) were both elected, while Paul Sommerville (Dublin South-East) was unsuccessful. As candidates, they all received a lot of attention in the economic debates in advance of the election and their presence explains the rise in the higher professional category for Independents. There was also a sharp increase in the number of Independent candidates from a business background. Many of these were small business owners, quite a number from the construction sector. They received less attention in the course of the campaign and for the most part did not perform very well in the election.

In general, public debate around the election focused on the need for a new (and often unspecified) type of politician. One of the most interesting findings from Table 3.3 is that only a small number of candidates with no previous political experience contested the election for political parties.

This suggests that the election remained the preserve of political insiders or experienced contestants. Fianna Fáil had just five new candidates while Fine Gael had three. Of the parties, the Green Party fielded the highest number of new candidates with 37 per cent not having any previous political experience, a figure that suggests that the party's structures and candidate base have not stabilised, with a lot of change between elections. It ran 14 new candidates in 2007. This contrasts with Sinn Féin, which has a smaller turnover of candidates.

Table 3.3   Political experience of candidates, 2011

Party	TD	Senator	Cllr	Previous electoral experience[a]	MP or MEP	New[b]
Fianna Fáil	51	5	13	1	0	5
Fine Gael	43	10	47	1	0	3
Labour	16	6	37	6	1	2
Green Party	6	3	3	15	0	16
Sinn Féin	4	0	22	9	1	5
ULA	0	0	6	5	1	8
Others	6	1	41	50	0	117
Total	126	25	169	87	3	156

[a] Previous experience refers to candidates who were not public representatives when they were selected, but had previously run for election at either European, Dáil, Seanad, or local government level.
[b] New is defined as having no previous experience as a candidate in any public election.

Over 150 new candidates did contest the election in total with the vast majority of these, 117, coming from the ranks of the Independents. On balance, the information on the occupational background and political experience of candidates suggests that the political parties did not present a more diverse group of candidates to the electorate than on previous occasions. Diversity was provided by the Independents but middle-class backgrounds predominated, even with Independents.

Independent candidates include many former party members. A significant proportion of independent candidates can be identified as 'gene pool' independents. It is difficult to give precise figures as some candidates have moved parties on more than one occasion but at least 40 of the independent candidates had previously contested the election on behalf of other political parties. The 'gene pool' independents include at least ten former members of Fianna Fáil, five from Fine Gael, four from Sinn Féin, five former members of the Progressive Democrats and three former Green Party candidates. Unusually, the Labour Party had a high number of gene pool candidates at 12. Several of these arose from the disputes about candidate selection in Sligo–North Leitrim and Laois–Offaly that we mentioned earlier.

The final candidate feature to be considered is a family link in politics. The political dynasty is a feature of Irish politics, and this did not diminish in the 2011 election. Table 3.4 outlines details of candidates with a close relative (parent, aunt, uncle, brother or sister) who has previously held political office. Dynasties are not a feature among candidates in Sinn Féin or the ULA, and in the case of the Green Party, the one candidate with a family relative in politics had links with Fianna Fáil. Family links remain a prominent feature in Fianna Fáil, Fine Gael and Labour. This is especially true of Fianna Fáil on this occasion, with over 40 per cent of its candidates having a family member previously in politics. This represents an increase from 32 per cent in 2007, suggesting that family dynasties were more likely to contest the election.

Table 3.4 Gender and family links of candidates, 2011

Party	Total	Women	%	Family Link[a]	%
Fianna Fáil	75	11	14.7	31	41.3
Fine Gael	104	16	15.4	21	20.2
Labour	68	18	26.5	13	19.1
Green Party	43	8	18.6	1	2.3
Sinn Féin	41	8	19.5	0	0
ULA	20	5	25.0	0	0
Others	215	20	9.3	7	3.3
Total	566	86	15.2	74	13.1

[a] Family link is defined as where a family relation has held office at either local or national level.

Table 3.4 also includes details on the percentage of women contesting the general election. 2011 saw an increase in the number but a decline in the percentage of female candidates. Low female participation in elections is a long-standing feature of Irish elections and is discussed in detail in Chapter 10.

Information on the ages of candidates contesting elections is not easily available. The sharp increase in the number of retiring TDs afforded parties the opportunity to introduce younger personnel. It is difficult to assess if that did occur. Sixty-eight candidates under 35 contested the election, with the youngest candidates aged just 21 (Cian Prendiville in Limerick City and Darcy Lonergan in Cavan–Monaghan). Fine Gael ran 18 candidates under 35. The oldest candidate in the election was Ian McGarvey who stood as an Independent in Donegal North-East.[12] Early research on the age profile of members of the new Dáil suggests a marginal reduction in the age of members.[13]

Conclusion

'New' politics and demands for new political parties were particularly prevalent in the months before the 2011 election. Despite this, the evidence from the candidate selection process is that business as usual prevailed within the political parties. Parties adapted their strategies to the new political realities but there was no obvious change in direction to be found in the selections of any of the main parties.

Candidate selection is a critical step in any election. From the ranks of the candidates put before the electorate come the future parliamentarians and members of government. Consequently, parties spend a lot of time and effort managing the selection process. Inevitably, there are competing forces to be found within the process. The tension between party centre and the party membership was less evident in 2011 than at previous contests.

The nature of the 2011 contest had some impact on the particulars of the relationship. In the centre–periphery struggle in Fine Gael, central forces were prominent and the party centre reinforced its position in candidate selection. The process was carefully managed with considerable dialogue and interaction between the levels. This may have eliminated some of the tension but undoubtedly party headquarters achieved its preferred outcomes in nearly all conventions. The reverse is true within Fianna Fáil where the combination of political circumstances gave rise to a weakening of centralised control over the process. Some cooperation between local constituency structures and party headquarters was maintained during the process but the party suffered from widespread disillusion and disorganisation, and candidates interviewed for this chapter remarked on a sense of chaos. Weak leadership provided by Brian Cowen diminished the ability of head office to provide its managing role. The leadership change when it occurred was too late to have a decisive impact as many of the decisions had already been taken.

The Labour Party faced intra-party conflict arising from candidate selections and 12 Labour 'gene pool' Independents contested the election. Multi-candidate tickets became a more common feature of candidate strategy, and managing candidate rivalries, a long term problem for Fianna Fáil and Fine Gael, became a more prevalent part of Labour's experience.

In smaller parties, greater freedom is afforded at local level. Branches are often organised around public representatives and their own personal network so it is more difficult for the party centre to exert control. This confers power on the local branches to pursue their own preferred approach and that remained the case in 2011.

The most striking feature relating to candidates remains the dramatic increase in the number contesting the election and the completely decentralised and autonomous process which takes place when individual members of the public choose to contest the election as Independent candidates.

Notes

1. I am particularly grateful to the party strategists and candidates who participated in interviews for this chapter. All of the data listed in tables were sourced from candidate websites, political parties and candidate interviews.
2. George Lee was the economics editor with the national broadcaster RTÉ and won a landslide victory in the Dublin South by-election in June 2009. Controversially, he resigned his seat and quit politics just eight months later, amid recriminations within Fine Gael.
3. Liam Weeks, 'Minor parties in Irish political life: an introduction', *Irish Political Studies* 25:4 (2010), pp. 473–9.
4. In Michael Gallagher and Michael Laver (eds), *How Ireland Voted 1992* (Dublin: Folens and PSAI Press, 1993), p. 65, it is suggested that Labour may have missed out on up to seven seats as a result of under-nomination.
5. www.labour.ie/party/constitution.
6. The decision to run just 75 candidates, fewer than the number required for an overall majority, was the subject of considerable discussion in broadcast media, newspapers and online discussion fora such as www.politics.ie.
7. This centralised selection process in Fianna Fáil is discussed by Liam Weeks in 'Candidate selection: democratic centralism or managed democracy?', pp. 48–64 in Michael Gallagher and Michael Marsh (eds), *How Ireland Voted 2007* (Basingstoke: Palgrave Macmillan, 2008).
8. The use of a gender-based selection criterion in Dun Laoghaire is discussed in greater detail in Chapter 10 at pp. 228–9.
9. Michael Gallagher ,'Candidate selection in Ireland: the impact of the electoral system', *British Journal of Political Science* 10:4 (1980), pp. 489–503.
10. Michael Gallagher and Michael Marsh, *Days of Blue Loyalty: The politics of membership of Fine Gael* (PSAI Press 2002).
11. John Bochel and David Denver, 'Candidate selection in the Labour Party: what the selectors seek', *British Journal of Political Science* 13:1 (1983), pp. 45–69.
12. Candidate age details provided by the *Irish Times*, 25 February 2011, and the *Donegal Daily* at www.donegaldaily.com/2011/02/26/irelands-oldest-voter-casts-her-vote-in-rathmullan/, accessed 26 February 2011.
13. Mark Farrelly, 'Election 2011 – an age old story? An age profile of the 31st Dáil'. Blog posted on www.politicalreform.ie, 31 March 2011. See also Chapter 7, pp. 167–8 below.

4

Campaign Strategies and Political Marketing

Pat Leahy

If the country's still (apparently) booming economy, and the desire of voters to ensure those conditions continued, was the most important factor in deciding the 2007 general election, then the economy would also be central to the 2011 election. But in a very, very different way. The economic crash, the banking collapse and bailout and the consequent deep recession were more than just the background to the 2011 general election campaign; the economic, fiscal and financial issues dominated every debate. Together, these were the *only* issue of the campaign. How they dealt with the issue, and how they negotiated the torrents of emotion emanating from the public – anger, fear, impatience, even hope – would determine the parties' fates.

On St Bridget's Day, 1 February, Taoiseach Brian Cowen, quoting Raftery the Poet (*Anois teacht an earraigh / beidh an lá ag dul chun sineadh / 's tar eis na féile Bride / ardoigh me mo sheol*)[1] told a subdued Dáil what it already knew. The 30th Dáil was no more. The general election was coming at last, and it would be as different from the previous contest as it was possible to imagine. In fact, the starting gun had been effectively fired months earlier by the Green Party when it announced in the wake of Ireland's application to the European Union (EU) and the International Monetary Fund (IMF) for financial assistance that the party would force an election in the early part of 2011. In modern politics it's difficult to disentangle the political communication and campaign strategies that parties implement during the phase prior to the actual declared campaign from those which take off the day the Dáil is dissolved. In fact, the pre-campaign positioning is in many respects just as important, especially as spending limits and disclosure requirements during the campaign proper limit some of the initiatives that parties may wish to pursue.

All parties' preparations moved up a gear from the November announcement (with the possible exception of those of the Greens themselves). The slow-motion collapse of the coalition government and then of Fianna Fáil itself in January only heightened the sense that the battle had already been joined. By the time of Cowen's announcement that the day of polling had been set for 25 February, the parties had been in election mode for months. Yet, however intense the pre-election period has been, and however well-advertised the coming contest, there is always a discernable intensification of activity and mood when the Dáil is dissolved and the campaign proper starts. TDs scatter to their constituencies in the four corners of Ireland, to be dragged out of them only under extreme duress; many of the party headquarters' staff relocate to a specially designated election facility, designed for the daily press conferences and to bring all the campaign staff under one roof; the media tools up for blanket coverage. However hectic the pre-campaign, everyone feels the difference when the Dáil actually rises. When it's on, it's really on. Campaigns matter.

The state of the parties, January 2011

How did the different parties approach the campaign? What was their state of readiness and how had they planned their strategies?

Fine Gael

Fine Gael had been preparing for this moment for months, for years. 'You never really stand down the election committee – it continues even in peacetime', explained Mark Mortell,[2] a pivotal figure in the Fine Gael election effort. As the full extent of the banking disaster was gradually unfolding throughout 2010, and both the government's fiscal position and its standing with voters commensurately deteriorated, it became increasingly apparent to Fine Gael strategists that a 2011 general election was likely. Paradoxically, the failed heave against Enda Kenny actually served in the longer term to strengthen the party, 'stiffening Kenny's resolve'[3] and bringing in Michael Noonan to the finance brief, an appointment that was to prove immensely significant. Noonan's return was one of two significant personnel moves. Mortell, a leading executive with public relations agency Fleishman Hillard who was also an influential advisor to Kenny, joined on a full-time basis in September 2010. Despite his veteran status, Noonan brought energy as well as experience to the front bench. He had been among the very first to recognise, back in 2008, that the banks faced a crisis of solvency, not just liquidity, and though he was presented by the party as a serious man for serious times, he clearly relished being back at the centre of politics. Mortell was instrumental in giving the party's election preparations a strategic communications focus that largely enabled it to fight the election on its chosen grounds.

By the autumn, detailed planning was underway. Even before the Green Party's announcement of 22 November, Fine Gael was expecting to mount a campaign in the first half of the new year. Indeed, the party tried to use the budget and IMF bailout as a sort of dry run for the election campaign, rehearsing messaging and strategies, and developing its idea of a 'five-point plan' which would become the centrepiece of the election pitch. Its aim was to be 'ready to go'[4] from the start of the year.

In planning its campaign, Fine Gael came to one very important conclusion – that its principal opponent would not be Fianna Fáil, but rather the Labour Party. The party leadership and those planning the election campaign had doubts about the accuracy of the *Irish Times* polls that showed Labour leading Fine Gael, but there was no doubt that there was a surge in support for Labour which posed a significant threat, if not to Fine Gael's chances of leading the next government, then certainly to its hopes to dominate it. They figured voters had made up their mind on Fianna Fáil, but many of them had yet to decide between Fine Gael and Labour. 'Our research was telling us this clearly – people were choosing between us and Labour', said Mortell. 'That affected what we wanted to do, and how we were going to do it' (see Chapter 8 for evidence of this in campaign polls). They set about trying to persuade them to choose in favour of Fine Gael. In other words, they put Labour, not Fianna Fáil, in their gunsights.

This was to have profound consequences for the way that the party designed and approached its campaign. Fine Gael strategists were heavily influenced by the advice of its American political consultants, Greenberg Quinlan Rosner, in reading the mood of the electorate and crafting a message that would fly with voters. The five-point plan which would form the centrepiece of the party's political marketing (see Figure 2.1) arose not just from the Americans' input, but also from exchanges among the backroom staff, particularly between Ciaran Conlon, Andrew McDowell and Seán Faughnan in the autumn of 2010. Constant referral to the five-point plan by the candidates and the leadership was to become a point of parody, even for Fine Gael itself; Kenny himself jokingly referred to it in his homecoming speech in Mayo after he was elected Taoiseach.

But the party understood one of the tenets of a modern political campaign, as Leo Varadkar[5] observed on a television documentary broadcast soon after the election – when the politicians are almost physically sick of mentioning something, the public might just be starting to hear it.

Along with the five-point plan, the other central plank of the Fine Gael strategy – and the one principally directed at winning votes from Labour – was the Fine Gael pledge not to increase income taxes. The complementary promise was that the greater part of any future budgetary adjustments would be met by spending cuts, rather than new taxes. It was a tactic directly aimed at Labour, enabling Fine Gael to target Labour as a high tax party. When the campaign started, it was to prove highly effective.

But for all the careful preparation and meticulous, poll-tested planning, events also moved in Fine Gael's favour. Party strategists felt something decisive move in the political landscape with the arrival in Dublin of personnel from the IMF in November; many voters finally and irrevocably gave up on Fianna Fáil. 'Suddenly we felt the whole country tune in to hear what we were saying', said Ciaran Conlon,[6] a key Fine Gael figure and manager of the campaign. Tellingly, a similar thought had occurred to Seán Dorgan, the Fianna Fáil general secretary, who was in Donegal assisting with the by-election campaign. 'After the IMF', he observed, 'it was like a different country.'[7]

Though the tweaking of candidate lists, aided by the intensive use of local opinion polls, continued until the very last minute, Fine Gael reckoned it was as ready as it would ever be from the beginning of January; as the new year dawned, Enda Kenny was the unbackable favourite to become Taoiseach. It was a remarkable turnaround for a man who only months before had had to face a challenge from within his own parliamentary party. In truth, Kenny's apparent weakness as a potential Taoiseach had been all over everyone's polls and focus groups for years. But Fine Gael insiders were dismissive of the notion, held by some inside as well as outside his own party, that the electorate would never settle for Kenny as Taoiseach. They reckoned there was no mysterious alchemy to becoming Taoiseach. All they had to do was ensure that Fine Gael got enough votes. By the beginning of the year, he now seemed ready to confound those who said he would never succeed to the highest office.

Yet it could hardly be said that he had arisen in the midst of the crisis to stand ready as a national leader. Rather, he had stayed standing for long enough to see the prize come to him; perhaps the most underestimated man in Irish politics, certainly the most resilient. In the past year, he had demonstrated tenaciousness and an even temperament. However you chose to describe him, by the time the election was called at last, it was going to take an earthquake to stop him from winning it.

Labour

Labour still harboured hopes, albeit slim, of doing just that. The party's 'Gilmore for Taoiseach' slogan had been coined as part of a plan not just to promote the leader, but to emphasise the party's independence from Fine Gael in the next general election. Labour strategists believed that they had to show ambition to achieve a step-change in their position as the third party of Irish politics, and the Taoiseach slogan was a reflection of that. On the choice that always faces Labour leaders, Éamon Gilmore had taken the key strategic decision not to join an alliance with Fine Gael, but rather to fight the contest as an independent party on an independent platform. In fact, Labour had drifted apart from Fine Gael after their shared failure to wrest power from Fianna Fáil in 2007. Then, the two parties agreed a common platform and held joint events as part of the 'alliance for change'. Now, for all the likelihood of a coalition government between the two parties, they were as far away from each other on policy as they had been since the 1980s. For example, while Fine Gael had backed the bank guarantee of September 2008, Labour had opposed it. On other issues too, Labour's stance – or rhetoric, at least – had moved to the left, Fine Gael's to the right.

By the middle of 2010, as Labour's poll numbers surged, the party was faced with the dizzying prospect of its 'Gilmore for Taoiseach' slogan actually coming true. Gilmore himself had proved to be a brilliant Dáil performer and had succeeded in articulating the anger that many voters felt about the deteriorating economic situation and especially about the Fianna Fáil–Green government's perceived mixture of haplessness and helplessness. As the banking crisis deepened, Joan Burton's criticisms of the government produced more and more media 'hits' for the party. Arguably, it spent too much time and energy wondering how best to capitalise on its new-found support, and not enough consolidating it; too much time telling people that Éamon Gilmore should be Taoiseach and not enough time telling them why. Nonetheless, by the turn of the year, Labour was in a high state of preparedness for the contest to come. Its campaign slogan – 'Jobs, Reform, Fairness' – had tested well in focus groups and the organisation was itching to go.

The campaign was largely built around Gilmore's appeal as leader. 'It was a central part of our campaign strategy – to make it about leadership', said the party's national organiser David Leach.[8] 'Every focus group, every poll showed Gilmore beating Kenny hands down. So obviously we wanted to play to our strengths.' Conscious that the last great Labour surge, the 'Spring Tide' of 1992, had produced fewer Dáil seats than it might have, party handlers had set about recalibrating their candidate and constituency strategies, adding new candidates and attempting to divide constituencies on a scale the party had not seen before. Labour would run candidates everywhere, and sitting TDs were required to accept a running mate, something that few relished. (In fact, only in Kildare South, where there was no conceivable chance of a second seat to add to Jack Wall's, did a sitting TD not share the ballot paper with a running mate.)

There was one further way in which Labour was determined to learn from past campaigns and past mistakes. In both 2002 and 2007 Labour had been praised for a thoroughly planned, expertly executed, 'professional' campaign. The only problem was that neither produced any new seats. Some in the Labour leadership felt that perhaps these campaigns had been almost too well planned – and consequently less flexible or reactive to events. So on this occasion, they decided to hold back much of their advertising budget in reserve. Whatever might develop in the course of the campaign, they reasoned, they would be in a better position to react to it if they had plenty of money at their disposal. 'We wanted to set up the campaign not as a supertanker, but as a speedboat', said David Leach. It would turn out to be a wise decision.

Sinn Féin

In preparing for the general election, Sinn Féin drew heavily on a detailed examination of the 2007 campaign that the party had conducted after expected and hoped for seat gains had failed to materialise. Among the lessons the party leadership drew from that experience was that the message the party was trying to convey to voters needed to be a lot sharper and more defined than it had been. As a small party, it didn't get too many bites at the cherry, either with voters or with the media. It knew it needed to make whatever attention it got count.

'We needed to hone our message', according to the party's director of publicity Seán MacBradaigh.[9] 'We needed to make it more direct and clear and deliver it to our target audience.' Party operatives at all levels, from candidate to canvasser, became aware of the need for all its communications and marketing efforts to be 'on message'. The party also wanted that message to separate Sinn Féin from the other parties, something that resonated with the growing numbers of people who were turned off by all the parties. That's what gave birth to the party's efforts to brand all other 'establishment' parties as part of a 'consensus for cuts', a broad consensus on economic policy shared by Fianna Fáil, Fine Gael and Labour that Sinn Féin stayed resolutely outside. 'We wanted there to be absolutely no ambiguity about where we stood.'[10] The party was also more aggressive in the Dáil. It had decided if its TDs were going to make any impact in the chamber, then 'the gloves had to come off'.[11]

The pre-campaign period also saw two hugely significant developments for the party. Firstly, the legal effort to force the government to hold the Donegal South-West by-election bore fruit, as the government had feared it would. In the High Court, Mr Justice Nicholas Kearns fairly flayed the government for its ongoing refusal to hold the by-election, and the Taoiseach was forced to name a date for the poll. Sinn Féin wanted a contest in Donegal because it knew it had an extremely strong candidate in Pearse Doherty, who had the benefit of not just a significant local base, but a national profile in the Senate, further bolstered by his successful High Court challenge. He duly romped home in the by-election. The result gave an enormous boost to the party organisation everywhere. By the time Doherty was hoisted aloft to hail his 13,000 first preferences, the party's preparations had been turbo-charged with an even bigger boost. Secondly, on 14 November, Gerry Adams announced that he would resign his seat in Westminster and stand in the Louth constituency. Having a northern leadership had damaged the southern party, and the Adams question had been agonised over within the party for years, without ever really being settled. Now it was. The arrival of Adams shifted the party's centre of gravity, and voters began to notice.

The Green Party

The Green Party faced into the general election of 2011 exhausted and largely demoralised after two and half years of more or less continuous crisis in government. Every one of its six TDs knew that there was a strong chance they would lose their seats; every one of the party's staff knew that they would then lose their jobs. Media coverage of the Greens tended to concentrate as much on their impending wipe-out as anything the party was actually saying. One commentator likened them to the 'early Christians' who would be massacred, though their beliefs would endure.[12] As Green candidates contemplated the lions in the arena, the promise of the political hereafter wasn't much of a consolation.

Despite having called time on the government in the aftermath of the IMF's arrival, and thus set the election countdown clock in motion, the Greens appeared to have done little to prepare for the election. In fact, the party's preparations appeared to be dominated by the effort to secure the passage of key legislation regarded as 'trophies' by the Greens before the government finally ran out of time. A ban on corporate donations and the establishment of a directly-elected Mayor for Dublin were most prominent among them. In fact, the Greens had fallen into two of the classic traps for a small party in Irish politics. In government, they had concentrated all their resources – physical and intellectual – on governing, and none on preparing for the next election. And in government with Fianna Fáil, they found themselves being contaminated by the larger party's unpopularity.

The party leadership felt that a 'narrative' highly unfavourable to the party had already settled among both the public and the media. 'It didn't matter what we did. We were going to be faced with an immoveable object: the narrative of propping up Fianna Fáil and everything that went with that', recalled party leader John Gormley.[13] To counteract this, the party strategists tried to construct a national and media campaign based around its policies, which they believed were actually quite acceptable to many voters. They told voters that if they wanted a Green voice, they had to vote for it, and said plainly they were prepared to enter government with Fine Gael if that's what the result threw up. 'It didn't matter what we said', reflected Gormley. 'They had made up their minds.'

The general distaste with which the party viewed political fundraising meant that there was little money in the party coffers to mount a serious publicity campaign. In Irish elections, small parties always battle with existential uncertainty. But even by those precarious standards, by January 2011, the Greens were on the edge of the abyss.

Minor parties and Independents

One of the most noteworthy features of the political climate in the period running up to the election was the general dissatisfaction with the political system as a whole and, consequently, with all the established parties. A survey published by anti-corruption campaign group Transparency International in December found that Irish people's trust in their politicians was among the lowest in the world, on a par with countries like Nigeria and Romania.[14]

An unprecedented number of non-party, small party and newly-independent candidates were to enter the electoral fray in response to this public restlessness. They were, and are, an eclectic bunch. A group of left-wing and far-left groups came together to form the United Left Alliance, an umbrella group rather than a party, which included the Socialist Party of the Dublin MEP Joe Higgins, several councillors of the People Before Profit organisation and some Independent left-wing figures such as the former Tipperary South TD Séamus Healy. There were also existing Independents such as Finian McGrath, who likewise

Figure 4.1   Leaflet of Independent candidate Paul Sommerville

sought to capitalise on their 'outsider' status, despite in his case having previously been a government supporter. A number of 'non-traditional' Independents would also stand, principally on a platform of opposition to the government's banking policy and the EU/IMF deal. These included a number of candidates with a high media profile – including the Trinity Senator Shane Ross, and financial commentator Paul Sommerville (see Figure 4.1) – and some without any, including Stephen Donnelly, who would stand in Wicklow. There were the traditional 'constituency-based' Independents, such as Michael Lowry and Michael Healy-Rae, son of the retiring Jackie. These included candidates who had recently left Fianna Fáil, such as Mattie McGrath of Tipperary South. Perhaps most intriguingly – certainly for the media – was a group of high-profile figures including

Ireland faces immense economic challenges in the next few years and we need people with expertise and passion to help us navigate the path.

There are solutions and there is hope.

We need to start looking at things differently, believing we can change this broken country.

We need fearless independents who will above all, put the country first.

Paul Sommerville has:
- 22 years' experience in International Markets.
- Economic Expertise

Paul Sommerville is:
- Passionate
- Straight-talking
- Independent thinker

Vote No.1
Paul Sommerville

Solutions

- Attack cronyism at all levels
- Provide debt restructuring solutions for ordinary citizens
- Renegotiate the EU/IMF deal
- Separate bank debt from Sovereign debt
- Put small businesses at heart of recovery
- Radical political reform needed
- Abolish NAMA
- Reform semi-state bodies
- Abolish HSE as it stands
- Ensure tourism at the forefront of the economy
- Revisit Croke Park Agreement

Please see www.paulsommerville.com for full 15 point recovery plan

---

journalists Fintan O'Toole and Éamon Dunphy who toyed in private and then publicly with running as a group, but ultimately withdrew. Even without them, it was a huge and disparate field of Independent candidates that were preparing for the election as 2011 dawned. Despite their many differences, there was one thing that united them – they all claimed to represent a potential new departure in Irish politics.

Fianna Fáil

If the preparations of Labour and Fine Gael were marked by a careful but keen anticipation of the contest to come, Fianna Fáil's approach to the election was characterised by chaos and terror. By the start of 2011, with an election certain within at most a few months, Fianna Fáil was uncertain of who would lead it into the contest, what its message to voters would be and how it would fight the campaign.

There had been an increasing volume of dissent about Cowen's leadership since the 2009 local elections, when the party suffered its worst ever result in a national election, winning just 25 per cent of the vote (see p. 19 above). He had been severely – perhaps fatally – damaged when he gave a hoarse, stumbling radio interview to RTÉ's *Morning Ireland* after a late night spent socialising with Fianna Fáil TDs in Galway at the party's September 2010 think-in. The Taoiseach and his ministers were forced to deny that he was hungover. After the arrival of the IMF – preceded by a week of denials from the government that such a move was afoot – the dissent about Cowen's leadership grew into open questioning among many TDs, and clandestine questioning by many others, about whether the party could afford to go into the election campaign with Cowen as its leader. As Christmas 2010 gave way to the new year of 2011, it was still an open question. 'It seemed to me that the party was sleepwalking towards the precipice and outright disaster', wrote junior minister Conor Lenihan later.[15]

There were other questions, too. After the Greens announced their departure, the party had to confirm whatever retirements were coming, get its lists of candidates finalised and then get support to candidates on the ground. However, headquarters found it difficult to force decisions from potential retirees. Retirements, including some of the highest-profile names in the party, continued until right up to the campaign. In all, 20 Fianna Fáil TDs chose not to contest the general election. Fianna Fáil would lose every one of the seats so vacated.

Even though the general disarray meant they weren't in a position to know some of the most basic elements of the campaign, party strategists had been working on the basis that its message would be built around the four-year fiscal and financial plan agreed by the government with the EU and published in November. They considered that some version of 'the four-year plan is the only game in town' would be employed – but exactly how that would be delivered and marketed was not yet settled. For the great election-winning machine of Irish politics, it was an astonishing state of affairs.

Nowhere was Fianna Fáil's unaccustomed disadvantage more evident than in the financial resources the party had at its disposal for the campaign. Money talks in modern politics, and as the biggest and richest party, Fianna Fáil had usually enjoyed a traditional advantage in this regard. No more. The party had about €1 million to spend on the campaign.[16] Labour, usually able to spend only a fraction of the

Fianna Fáil war chest, had less than €900,000.[17] Neither came close to the resources available to Fine Gael. In January, director of elections Phil Hogan told reporters that the party had some €2.25 million available in advance of the campaign, though figures published later would show the party's spending on the national campaign amounted to some €1.6 million.

Despite (or perhaps because of) relatively stringent campaign finance laws, election spending can often be pretty opaque – much of it, for example, takes place before the formal notification period for spending. Expensively obtained intelligence and advice is essentially invisible. Nonetheless, to those covering the 2011 general election, the advantage enjoyed by Fine Gael in sheer financial might was obvious. Its campaign was bigger, broader and more expensive than any of its rivals. In this respect, it had already supplanted Fianna Fáil.

The heave (finally) arrives

The Dáil returned earlier than usual in January, and when it did, Fianna Fáil was in ferment. In a febrile atmosphere rumour and counter-rumour abounded; when a supposed challenge to Cowen failed to materialise at the Fianna Fáil parliamentary party's first meeting, Miriam Lord of the *Irish Times* summarised, 'More night of wrong vibes than night of long knives as Cowen lives to fight another day.'[18] Perhaps. But events were moving quickly now. Following revelations[19] that he had played golf with the disgraced former chairman of Anglo Irish Bank Seán FitzPatrick back in July of 2008, just weeks before the bank's near collapse prompted the government's bank guarantee, Cowen told the party he would 'consult' with it about his future. That Sunday (16 January) he called a press conference in a Dublin hotel to announce that he intended to continue as leader of Fianna Fáil and, furthermore, that he was putting down a motion of confidence in his own leadership for the following Tuesday. Less than three hours later, his foreign affairs minister Micheál Martin announced he would be voting against the motion. The heave was finally on.

Except it was a mild-mannered affair, remarkably unfratricidal and undestructive by the usual standards of these things. Cowen and his lieutenants canvassed hard, but the outcome was fixed when none of Martin's frontbench colleagues saw fit to join him in rebellion. Of the two other potential leaders, Brian Lenihan confounded the expectation of many backbenchers – several of whom insisted that he had encouraged them to mount a challenge – when he announced his support for Cowen, while Mary Hanafin simply refused to say what she would do. Thus isolated, Martin lost, and resigned from cabinet. The mood among most Fianna Fáil TDs was utter despair, and resignation to their fate. It seemed there was no hope for the party. They were right, but there was one further twist yet to come. Whatever their real view of his leadership, Cowen's colleagues were unwilling to guillotine his premiership. Now, he was about to do it himself.

The coalition collapses

Perhaps not surprisingly, this most ill-starred of leaders brought his final tragedy upon himself. Having defeated Micheál Martin's leadership challenge on Tuesday (18 January), Cowen, claiming 'vindication', sought on the following day to reshuffle his cabinet, bringing forward the resignations of four members that evening – Dermot Ahern, Noel Dempsey, Tony Killeen and Mary Harney – some of whom complied with the request to resign more cheerfully than others. Another minister, Batt O'Keeffe, would follow early the next morning. Disaster awaited. Even those Fianna Fáil TDs whom he had intended to appoint to cabinet could see that such a blatant political stroke would backfire. More dangerously, he had failed to secure the agreement of the Green Party, which refused to back any new appointments. As accusations and threats flew, the Greens simply threatened to leave government immediately and vote against the new appointments in the House. Faced with the prospect of being defeated on a vote in the Dáil, Cowen had no choice but to back down. After a morning charged with high political drama, he was left with a cabinet of just nine ministers, and his authority in tatters. After repeated adjournments, a humiliated Cowen, shoulders hunched and eyes downcast, returned to the Dáil chamber and announced that the general election would be held on 11 March.

The Fianna Fáil parliamentary party was more or less in open revolt now, and on Saturday the seventh leader of Fianna Fáil at last faced political reality. At a packed, hastily arranged press conference in the Merrion Hotel, he announced his resignation as party leader. Fianna Fáil, he said, would fight the election with 'good heart and determination'. It was about the opposite of the truth.

But the implosion of Fianna Fáil had also collapsed the government. On the following day, the Green Party filed in sombre fashion into the same room, and announced that they were leaving government. 'Our patience has reached an end', said party leader John Gormley. Though the party would, he said, vote in favour of the finance bill in the Dáil in the following days.

After frantic talks with Fine Gael and Labour, agreement was reached that the finance bill would be rushed through the Dáil that week, clearing the way for a dissolution. After a brief leadership contest, Micheál Martin was chosen to lead Fianna Fáil. Five days later, his face was on the lampposts, and the election campaign was on at last.

The campaign

Cowen's lyrical farewell to TDs was his swansong as a player in national politics. Though still Taoiseach, he had no part in the Fianna Fáil campaign and fulfilled his duties in only a caretaker manner. For someone in whom such hopes had once been invested, by his own people and by the country, his end was brutal, even by the unsentimental standards of politics. By the time Cowen rose to announce formally his intention to bring the 30th Dáil to an end, he cut a figure that was almost tragic. There was always a strange sort of nobility to his honesty, his bluntness, his cussed refusal to engage with the norms of modern politics. But his administration had ended in an utter shambles.

It's not showtime, folks

P.J. Mara, who returned once more to the campaign team (though in a less prominent role than previously), used to say that Fianna Fáil's best card was that voters believed it was the only party which could really manage the economy. Now, the new leader of Fianna Fáil sought to make a virtue of his party's inability to mount the auction elections of old. 'There are no new spending commitments in this document', said Martin at the Fianna Fáil manifesto launch in the Hugh Lane Gallery, an event at which Éamon Ó Cuív, the Community and Gaeltacht Affairs minister, very publicly fell asleep.

The party's slogan, 'Real Plan, Better Future', sought firmly to place the emphasis on the future, rather than dwell on the past. Martin was a whirlwind in the early days of the campaign, his presence – or more likely the absence of Cowen – bringing some hope to the beleaguered party. In previous elections, the Fianna Fáil campaign had been the biggest and the brashest, the slickest and the smartest. This time, it was plainly cobbled together at the last minute on a shoestring. The party eschewed a dedicated election headquarters, and operated instead from rooms adjacent to the party's rented headquarters in a modern office building on Mount Street. Two burly security guards patrolled the door, in case of unwarranted intrusion. Perhaps remarkably, no custard pies made it in.

The campaign was based entirely around the new leader, and the schedulers ran Martin ragged. Other ministers played only bit parts. Members of the new front bench, some of whom – such as political advisor Averil Power – held no elective office at all, played a more prominent role than some ministers. Even Brian Lenihan was a shadow of the rambunctious and garrulous political presence of the previous two years.

Martin began his leadership of the party with the unconditional apology that Cowen had always been incapable of making. The opinion polls would soon show that the public approved of the new leader, but still had it in for the party.

'It's Frankfurt's way or Labour's way'

Labour unveiled a new campaign headquarters on Dublin's Golden Lane. It was certainly a golden opportunity for Labour. It had never been so high in the polls; never before could a Labour leader credibly offer to lead a coalition government. On the first day of the campaign, Gilmore stood on a box in headquarters to rally the troops, surrounded by 'Gilmore for Taoiseach' banners. The following day he launched the campaign, high above the heads of the people of Dublin in the Gravity Bar. Two days later, Gilmore laid out his aggressive approach, promising a renegotiation of the terms of the EU/IMF bailout deal. 'It's Frankfurt's way or Labour's way!' he thundered. 'Whoa', thought many voters. 'My money's on Frankfurt.' Labour had made its first misstep of the campaign.

'Hello Taoiseach!'

Enda Kenny hit the ground running, taking off on a high-octane tour of border counties, the media trailing behind. In Cavan a crowd cheered him, with one man repeatedly calling to him – 'Hello Taoiseach! Hello Taoiseach!' He turned out to be a Fine Gael councillor. But the point was made and the pattern set. Enda smiled and waved and winked, and gave the thumbs-up. But he also had a deadly serious message. Fine Gael had a plan, a five-point plan. And it would not raise income taxes.

In those crucial early press conferences Kenny performed well, taking some questions himself and passing others on to his frontbench colleagues. Despite confident predictions by its opponents, Fine Gael strategists didn't hide Kenny; or if they did, they hid him in full view. He was front and centre at many of the press conferences, though he was always surrounded by colleagues. This did not just offer practical support to the leader, it reinforced the idea of Kenny as leader of a strong team. Kenny was still regarded as weak on detail by the press corps, but discerning that the chances of catching him out with a killer question were diminishing, journalists began to lose interest in pursuing him. On day four, when one reporter mischievously asked him to explain what cloud computing was, he batted the question out of the park with a sufficient explanation and a large dollop of self-deprecation. I may not know how it works, was the message, but I know it's important and I'll listen to people who know what they're talking about on it. Game, set and match. It marked an important moment.

Then after some wobbles, including a bizarre series of excuses – at one stage he suggested that his empty chair would be a symbol of all those who had to emigrate[20] – Kenny swished aside TV3's requests for his appearance at the first leaders' debate. The Fine Gael backroom team held their breath. The debate happened. Kenny looked a bit silly for not turning up, but suffered no obvious damage (see Chapter 8, p. 194). Fine Gael was on its way.

The contours of the competing policy platforms and the competing campaign strategies soon emerged. Fine Gael promised no income tax rises, and though there were several tax increases elsewhere in its programme, its plan for controlling the public finances centred on a programme of great swingeing cuts to every area of public spending – a budgetary adjustment it said would be in a ratio of 73 per cent cuts to 27 per cent tax increases. Labour, essentially, promised less austerity over a longer period, while its programme featured cuts and tax increases in roughly equal measures. Both parties promised great things from a renegotiation of the EU/IMF deal.

Fianna Fáil had proposals on all of these things. But the voters had long since decided that Fianna Fáil's role in this election was to bend over and have its backside kicked. Hard, and repeatedly. Gradually, Fianna Fáil became irrelevant to the argument about who should be in the next government, and what it should do, though Martin remained an influential figure, especially in the television debates.

The Greens tried valiantly to get themselves into the election debate, but found it impossible to break through the toxic association with Fianna Fáil. Sinn Féin batted hard against all the other parties, claiming with some justification to be the only party offering an alternative to an economic consensus broadly shared by the other parties. Critics pointed out that there was a reason it was shared by the other parties and accused Sinn Féin of having a solution based on the economics of magical thinking. But it resonated with many people in the Sinn Féin target groups. An army of Independent candidates from the right to the far-left, and on all points in between, jostled furiously for attention.

'Howya Angela!'

During the 2007 general election campaign Fianna Fáil strategists contrived two set-piece events in order to bolster Bertie Ahern's flagging appeal to voters. He entertained Ian Paisley at the site of the Battle of the Boyne, and he addressed British parliamentarians at Westminster. Fine Gael had watched its enemies, and learned. This time it was Kenny who was doing the statesmanlike encounters, one with European Commission President José Manuel Barroso and the other, bang in the middle of the campaign, with German chancellor Angela Merkel. The photos from Berlin seemed to show Merkel looking a bit uncertain about the whole thing. Enda, naturally, looked delighted. So he should have been. It was a brilliant PR coup. Kenny mentioned the visit repeatedly over the following few days.

Eppur si muove

It was, Kenny noted at the launch of the party's manifesto, the anniversary of the birth of Galileo, the great astronomer. 'Measure what can be measured,' the Italian said, 'and make measurable what cannot be measured.' By now, more than halfway through the campaign, the opinion polls which measure political support were clear about one thing: Fianna Fáil was stuck in the mid-teens, and Labour's votes were ebbing away. But Fine Gael was on a roll. And every succeeding poll brought the same news: *eppur si muove*. Still it moves. Onward and upward.

This, now, became the central question of the final phase: would Fine Gael win enough support to form a government without the support of the Labour Party? Leading Fine Gaelers pooh-poohed the notion, and a battery of heavyweights was sent out to proclaim their preference for a stable and solid coalition with Labour. Kenny himself was asked the question by a journalist as a press conference: was he now looking for an overall majority? 'I'm not, actually ...'[21] he began, before giving the five-point plan another turn.

But even as they publicly dismissed the notion of a single-party government, the Fine Gael campaign went into overdrive behind the scenes, carefully recalibrating their operation on the ground to give weaker candidates a boost. Leaflets appeared in key areas of key constituencies – 'To maximise Fine Gael's representation, in this area, vote number one for ...' (see, for example, Figure 7.2). It just might be on, they figured. Michael Noonan and Leo Varadkar were the heavyweight heart of the Fine Gael campaign, and they hammered Labour relentlessly on tax. Day after day, Fine Gael repeated its simple message: We have a five-point plan; we won't raise income tax; Labour is a high-tax party. They hammered it home with relentless efficiency. It wasn't subtle, but the polls seemed to say it was working like a dream. For its part, Labour knew that like all left-wing parties, it would be vulnerable on the tax questions. Strategists believed that it could minimise the damage by its pledge that individuals earning under €100,000 a year would be unaffected by any of Labour's tax changes. But Fine Gael's message was simpler and sharper, and it put Labour on the hook.

As Labour, wounded by Fine Gael's attacks, tried to get beyond the charges of being the high tax party of the public sector interests, Siptu president Jack O'Connor, a prominent trade union leader, waded into the debate to ensure that the spotlight was firmly kept on it. A single-party Fine Gael government, he warned, would be 'a recipe for disaster'. Fine Gael's Lucinda Creighton shot back: O'Connor is right to be worried. Fine Gael would put taxpayers ahead of the 'vested interests that Mr O'Connor represented', she responded. 'Is Jack O'Connor a Fine Gael sleeper?' wondered one Fianna Fáiler.[22] Labour was bleeding now. The party launched its manifesto at the new stadium on Lansdowne Road, two days before the Ireland–France rugby international. As Ronan O'Gara and Jonny Sexton banged over penalties and the Irish pack practised lineouts on the pitch below, Éamon Gilmore stuck out his elbows and hit Fine Gael a few digs. Fine Gael, Gilmore asserted, would 'attack families by cutting child benefit'. A Fine Gael government would 'attack pensioners' and 'attack front-line services'. The mood was aggressive and determined. Labour candidates posed for pictures in the stands overlooking the pitch. The candidates clustered around their leader for the group shot. 'Everybody wave!' called the photographer. But Gilmore wasn't waving. He was drowning.

On the Tuesday week before polling day, Gilmore and his campaign managers and key strategists reviewed their latest private polling. It showed Fine Gael on 40 per cent, Fianna Fáil on 18 per cent and Labour on 16 per cent. The election was slipping away from Labour, and Gilmore was slipping towards disaster. It was a moment of profound crisis for the Labour campaign. At emergency meetings the leadership and the key campaign figures David Leach, Mark Garrett and Colm O'Reardon surveyed their progress and their prospects, with the gloomy polls hanging over them like a sword of Damocles. They made a vital decision. Labour changed tack, and went negative. 'We hit them as hard as we could for two days', recalled David Leach.[23] Labour targeted Fine Gael with a series of statements, attacking its plans to cut child benefit particularly. The party produced a series of newspaper advertisements, modelled on a Tesco advertising campaign and with the slogan 'Fine Gael

– every little hurts'. The ads claimed that Fine Gael policies would result in significant cost increases for ordinary people, while introducing water charges and cutting child benefit. (Labour strategists received several angry phone calls from Tesco. They waited in hope that Tesco would seek an injunction against them, which would have hugely increased the ads' impact, though sadly for Labour, no writ arrived.)

Just as importantly, Labour ceased talking about Gilmore for Taoiseach and directed its efforts instead at warning of the dangers of a Fine Gael single-party government. Now the wisdom of holding back on its budgets became clear. Labour printed 350,000 leaflets, which were distributed to candidates all over the country. Posters were heralding its warnings about Fine Gael, and a flurry of further newspaper advertising hammered home the message. On the doorsteps, Labour candidates pushed the message about Fine Gael cuts hard.[24]

Labour and Fine Gael had known before the campaign that they would most likely end up in government together – but also that they would be rivals for every vote until polling day. While backroom staff from the two parties had always kept in pretty close contact, especially as the government disintegrated over the course of the previous year, those relations had consciously ceased before the campaign. There were no contacts between the teams running the two campaigns until the election was over, though individual politicians from both parties did speak occasionally. The barbs were real; the withering of Fianna Fáil had made Fine Gael and Labour each other's principal rivals. At the same time, the knowledge that they would almost certainly be doing business in government kept the rivalry largely under control.

As the penultimate week progressed Fine Gael climbed higher in the polls, but Labour's decision to attack Fine Gael prompted crucial voters to ask themselves if they were willing to give Fine Gael that sort of an unqualified mandate. Perhaps, as Fine Gael strategist Mark Mortell believes, there is now an 'inherent distrust' of single-party government in Irish politics; either way, the tide was about to turn. As the campaign entered its final week, the battle lines were clear: Fine Gael was powering ahead, and Labour was desperately begging voters to give the party a slice of the government. Fine Gael began the week with a rally of its Dublin candidates, presided over by Newstalk broadcaster George Hook, whose station was advertising 'news without the state-run spin'. The day's polls were showing that not only was Fine Gael within touching distance of an overall majority, but that Kenny, derided by so many for so long, was the most popular choice for Taoiseach.

Kenny seemed to be bulletproof, unstoppable now. He brushed off a *Sunday Business Post* story about his teacher's pension, amassed after just four years in the classroom, promising not to take it up. He was within sight of the finish line now. But there were a few late stumbles to come. First, he did a poor interview with TV3. Then he faltered noticeably in the second half of the final television debate on RTÉ. There is never much attraction for a front-runner in taking part in leaders' debates – why risk your lead? Why offer your opponent an opportunity? Fine Gael had avoided danger by ducking the first debate, and achieving messy draws in the Irish language and five-way debates that followed. But in the final debate, between just Kenny, Gilmore and Martin, the Fine Gael leader did not perform well. It was watched by an average audience of 800,000 people. Two days later he did another poor interview with Bryan Dobson on RTÉ, flailing around the place as Dobson pressed him for detail. Labour, seizing the moment, turned up the volume again, constantly warning of the dangers of an overall majority.

Kenny's late slips were the only really serious lapse in an otherwise brilliant Fine Gael campaign. Liberated by the certainty of office, and a world away from the dreaded television studios, Kenny finished with a barnstorming speech on a Donegal hillside. 'Tomorrow, then, the people are in charge', the Taoiseach-in-waiting declared on the eve of election. 'Governments may govern, but it is the people who rule.'

Conclusion

From the position in which the party started, Fianna Fáil actually fought an impressive campaign, which failed to make any ground against a tidal wave of public animosity towards its candidates. It is difficult to think of any respect in which the Fianna Fáil campaign could have been more effective, in the circumstances. Labour's campaign was a near disaster, but turned into triumph by a brave and deft change of direction as it stared defeat in the face. Fine Gael started with an overwhelming advantage and managed it ruthlessly and efficiently, to produce the greatest result in the party's history. But arguably a late falter deprived it of the ultimate prize of an overall majority. Sinn Féin reaped the benefits of a smart strategy and a clear message, but even party elders were taken aback by their success. The Green Party struggled for relevance and impact, and was ultimately submerged in the government's unpopularity.

Who won the campaign? Whose strategy was most effective? At one level, the answer is simple – you can tell the guys who won, because they're in government. But that's not always the full story. It's easy to fall into the trap of assuming that everything the winners did worked, and everything the losers did failed. In fact, the story of campaign 2011 is much more complex; neither politics, nor life, is quite so simple.

Notes

1. 'Now with the coming of the Spring / the day will be lengthening / and after St Bridget's Day / I shall raise my sail.'
2. Interview with author.
3. Mortell, interview with author.
4. Interview with Ciarán Conlon.
5. 'The Naked Election', RTÉ 1 television, 7 March.
6. Interview with author.
7. Interview with author.
8. Interview with author.
9. Interview with author.
10. MacBradaigh, interview with author.
11. MacBradaigh, interview with author.
12. Deaglán de Bréadún, 'Even whitewash won't halt Green machine', *Irish Times*, 12 February 2011.
13. Interview with author.
14. *Global Corruption Barometer*, published by Transparency International, 9 December 2010, reported in Pamela Duncan, 'Corruption survey: public's trust in politics declines', *Irish Times*, 9 December.
15. Conor Lenihan, 'Meltdown', *Business Plus*, April 2011.
16. Seán Dorgan, interview with author.
17. David Leach, interview with author.
18. *Irish Times*, 14 January 2011.
19. Tom Lyons and Brian Carey, *The FitzPatrick Tapes: The rise and fall of one man, one bank and one country* (Dublin: Penguin, 2011), serialised in the *Sunday Times*, 9 January 2011.
20. Kenny's explanation and Michael Noonan's attempt to remain impassive were caught on camera and became one of the more popular YouTube clips which whizzed around political circles every day. See also Figure 5.2, p. 94 below.
21. Author's own campaign notes.
22. Author's own campaign notes.
23. Interview with author.
24. Author's own campaign notes.

5
Internet Explorers:
The Online Campaign

Matthew Wall and Maria Laura Sudulich

The idea of an 'internet election' was initially put forward in 1997.[1] However, there is little evidence to date that online campaigning has supplanted more traditional campaign practices. This is particularly true of Irish campaigns, which are hardware-rich affairs characterised by substantial volumes of face-to-face human interactions. A study of the 2002 Irish campaign was entitled 'None of that post-modern stuff around here',[2] and many 'pre-modern' patterns and practices endure in contemporary Irish politics. All of the coverage of the 2011 campaign attested to the ongoing centrality of the 'canvass' – meaning that, to be electable, Irish politicians must engage heavily in individual-level, door-to-door persuasion using a mixture of argumentation and personal charisma. No serious campaign consultant would advise his or her candidate to focus solely on online campaigning in an Irish election and an investigation of the campaign activities that corresponded to electoral gains in the 2007 Irish campaign found that posters and leaflets were the most effective campaign tools.[3] In 2011, posters and leaflets remained must-have items for any serious candidate. Indeed, one of the election's more amusing stories concerned the large number of heavy-duty posters that came loose and flapped around the country like deranged birds in the campaign's first week.

Nevertheless, Irish parties, candidates, and citizenry have made rapid advances and undergone remarkable changes in their political use of internet technologies since the 2007 election, and in this chapter we will describe some of these advances and changes. We begin by looking back to what happened in the 2007 Irish online election campaign, which was a dramatically narrower and more straightforward topic to study than its 2011 counterpart. We made a study of Irish party and candidate websites in 2007 and found that the parties had rather staid and conservative websites, which failed to capture much of the obvious potential of the internet as a medium for bottom-up communication.[4] As Table 5.1 shows, only one-third of candidates launched personal campaign websites in 2007 and these were mostly of the 'online postcard' variety, which advertised candidates' telephone numbers, emails, and (for incumbents and ambitious challengers) constituency clinic hours.

Table 5.1 Percentage of candidates with personal campaign websites (by party) in 2007

Party	Yes %	No %	N
Fianna Fáil	53	47	105
Fine Gael	29	71	91
Labour	36	64	50
Sinn Féin	5	95	41
Greens	34	66	44
Progressive Democrats	23	77	30
Independents	31	69	69
Total	32	68	430

Source: Maria Laura Sudulich and Matthew Wall, 'Every little helps: cyber campaigning in the 2007 Irish general election', *Journal of Information Technology & Politics* 7:4 (2010), p. 5.

We found that the decision to launch a candidate campaign website in the 2007 Irish general election seemed to have been driven by a desire to keep up with constituency opponents rather than strategic electoral considerations. It was impossible to assess whether running a candidate site directly persuaded large numbers of voters to choose one candidate over another, but those who ran personal websites performed marginally better than those who did not (winning about 5 per cent of a quota more at the polls), even when a wide range of correlated factors such as spending, incumbency, and party affiliation were controlled for.[5] A survey of candidates found that more than half of the candidates running in 2007 evaluated the role of a campaign website as fairly or very important, though pre-modern campaign tools were rated as more important by candidates.[6]

For the 2011 Irish online campaign, we collected data on the social networking activities of the main parties and of over 500 candidates, as well as conducting a set of interviews with party campaign staff members who were responsible for the main parties'[7] online campaigns. The 2011 internet campaign saw a wide array of activities, which were often both qualitatively and quantitatively different from those that took place in 2007. All of the campaign staff interviewed for this study pointed to increases in staff and monetary resources that were devoted to the 2011 campaign, relative to 2007. For instance, Fine Gael had a team of over 30 volunteers working full time on a bank of computers in party headquarters (HQ) (see Figure 5.1) exclusively on their online campaign, supervised by party campaign staff and assisted by external consultants (ElectionMall). Several interviewees indicated that the online campaign went from being a peripheral aspect of the 2007 campaign to being a central aspect of the 2011 campaign.

In this chapter, we separate our discussion into use of the web by three types of campaign actors: the parties, the candidates, and the voters.

We wish to begin, however, by briefly introducing two key ideas that have emerged from the study of online politics. These ideas are useful for gaining international and historical perspective on the relationship between the internet and political campaigning. The first concept is the 'post-modern' campaign, a category developed by campaign scholars seeking to explain the role of new communications technologies. The second idea concerns the changing nature of the internet, where the term 'Web 2.0' is the most common description of the internet that we are currently experiencing.

Figure 5.1   The Fine Gael online campaign team in action

Post-modern campaigns

A number of scholars have examined the historical development of electoral campaigns. To simplify a rich and complex literature,[8] most scholars agree that campaign practices can be divided into three historical phases: pre-modern, modern, and post-modern – with each phase being associated with a specific set of techniques, a prototypical model of campaign control and planning, a set of media and organisational resources, and a tendency towards certain campaign themes. Crucially, each new phase has been preceded by an advance in communications technologies. While each new phase is marked by novel communicative possibilities enabled by technology, elements of the previous phases remain and coexist with these new tools and techniques.

Campaigns in the pre-modern phase (which lasted, roughly, from the mid-nineteenth century to the late 1950s) relied on newspapers, billboards, and party publications for media coverage. They were characterised by their prioritisation of candidate–voter interaction through public meetings, whistle-stop tours, and door-to-door canvasses. Thus, Irish campaigns in the twenty-first century still have many 'pre-modern' characteristics.

The 'modern' phase (early 1960s to late 1980s) arrived with the advent of radio and particularly television – technologies that enabled politicians to speak directly to millions of voters. Modern campaigns developed a more centrally-managed, HQ-driven organisational structure. The modern period coincided with a fall in party attachment among electorates in established democracies around the world,[9] and a substantial consequent increase in levels of electoral volatility.

From the early 1990s onwards, many scholars argue that campaigns in established democracies, and particularly in the United States, have entered an identifiable 'post-modern' phase. One of the post-modern phase's defining characteristics is 'increasing efforts by the parties to reach individual voters via the internet, direct mail, and telemarketing'.[10] This 'post-modern' stage was first brought about by the development of satellite and mobile phone technology, but it has been most strongly driven by the explosion of the internet in recent years.

It was Barack Obama's use of the internet for fundraising and campaign coordination in his successful bid for the American presidency in 2008 that fully illustrated how politically advantageous post-modern campaign techniques could be. Over a million Obama campaign workers coordinated their campaign activities using an innovative web infrastructure developed by the campaign. For instance, Obama volunteers were given instructions regarding which areas and/or phone numbers to canvass through the 'MyBarackObama' online platform.[11] Thus the Obama campaign team was able to employ post-modern technologies and techniques to streamline the organisation of traditional or 'pre-modern' campaign activities. Another feature typical of the post-modern campaign phase is the use of 'narrowcasting' – a technique that involves targeting specific messages for small audiences. Specialist mailing lists and blogs can be used by politicians seeking to influence a specific audience of voters. We will see that the Irish Labour Party attempted to narrowcast as part of its 2011 online campaign.

While campaign phases are abstract ideal types, they allow us to think about how campaigning has been altered over time by the introduction of novel communications technologies. If we view online campaign instruments as one element in a larger campaign mix, which contains aspects from all three 'phases', it is difficult to deny that post-modern tools bring significant communicative and organisational advantages to both candidates and parties at a relatively low financial cost. Several of the campaign workers whom we interviewed argued that having a strong online presence is particularly important for engaging with younger voters, who have grown up with online technologies. Another point that was frequently brought up was the capacity of the internet to facilitate two-way communication between political actors and the public. Labour and Fine Gael online campaign staff both discussed the high volume of work entailed in responding to questions and requests on party sites and social networking profiles, and the Greens hosted an extensive online 'Questions and Answers' session on their site – responding individually to over 2,000 queries.

However, the costs of post-modern campaigning are on the rise. Several of the major parties in the 2011 Irish campaign engaged in extensive online advertising, in addition to maintaining their websites and social networking profiles. The Fianna Fáil campaign staff pointed us towards its 'empty chair' ad (see Figure 5.2), which mocked Enda Kenny's non-participation in the leaders' debate hosted by Vincent Browne (see Chapter 4, p. 83), as a successful instance of online advertising – they stated that this ad brought over 12,000 click-throughs to the Fianna Fáil site. A Green Party campaign member indicated that a representative of Google advised that a budget of €30,000–40,000 would be required to be competitive in the online advertising battle. This level of expense evidently militates against any levelling out of resource inequities among parties/candidates. Instead, it appears that monetary resources are vital to secure high visibility for parties and politicians online. Post-modern campaign tools allow the candidates and the voters to exert a much greater influence on the overall shape of the campaign, meaning that parties face a loss of the centralised control of their message that characterised the 'modern' campaign era, as well as a host of new concerns to do with site security and content moderation. Another interesting downside of online campaigning brought up by party campaign staff is the level of vitriol that is present in online discussions of politics, particularly when a stream of personalised comments are directed against a specific individual. Post-modern campaign techniques thus provide candidates and parties with both new opportunities and novel problems. They also sit alongside campaigning practices from the 'pre-modern' and 'modern' eras in contemporary politics, and they are often used to streamline or augment these more traditional approaches.

Figure 5.2　Fianna Fáil's 'empty chair' online ad

Web 2.0

While the phrase 'Web 2.0'[12] has been controversial among internet experts, the intuition behind the term is straightforward. Traditionally, mass media have had a rather one-way relationship with their audiences. Mass media produces and disseminates content, which the audience consumes. In its early days, the internet followed a similar pattern, with a very small number of content creators and a large number of passive consumers. The Web 2.0 concept holds that this relationship has changed, meaning that the nature of the internet as a communications medium has evolved over its brief lifetime. The Web 2.0 internet comprises a range of technologies and phenomena that have erased the barriers to content production and distribution that were inherent in previous communications media. It is a space where sharing and creating interactive content is not only possible, but also free and technically straightforward for anybody with an internet connection. The previously passive audience is now empowered to generate, publish, edit, and categorise material.

Paul Anderson[13] provides a detailed account of the specific technical developments underlying this shift, including the growth of social networking sites (such as Facebook and MySpace); the availability of free blog-creating toolkits such as Wordpress and Blogspot; the increase of online spaces to share photographs (Flickr) and videos (YouTube); the advent of wikis (Wikipedia); and the development of systems of searching for (Google) and for categorising online information (del. ic.ious, stumbleupon). A more recent innovation is 'microblogging', which involves sharing information in parcels of 140 or fewer characters with a network of self-selecting 'followers'. The microblogging market was created and is currently monopolised by Twitter. All of these services are typically free to use and, vitally, they all allow users with virtually no technical expertise to publish whatever content they choose, which can then be viewed instantly around the world.

While the advent of the internet helped to usher in the 'post-modern' campaign phase, the changing shape of the internet itself in the Web 2.0 era means that novel campaign techniques that exploit the networking and user-generated content potentialities of the modern internet are now emerging. Naturally, Irish parties and candidates are trying to exploit these opportunities in the competition for votes, and we describe the online activities of the parties during the 2011 Irish campaign in the next section.

The parties

Organisationally, there were striking similarities across the online campaigns of the major parties. Generally speaking,[14] planning, development, and content generation was led by party staff and volunteers, with the help of outside professional consultants and the oversight of the party leadership – who defined strategic goals to be pursued and provided guidelines for site and social networking content. In this section we look at the parties' websites and their social networking profiles.

Party websites

The parties' campaign websites were rather similar – each sought to integrate social networking features, inviting users to 'share' items such as policy documents and candidate speeches via their own Facebook, Twitter, Flickr and YouTube accounts. All of the sites housed the parties' policy documents, and campaign videos and videos of messages from party leaders were also common. Another widespread feature was a facility for signing up for email updates on campaign events and new site content; the Fianna Fáil online campaign team emphasised the importance of the party email list for distributing party messages and encouraging volunteers to street canvass and/or telephone canvass on behalf of the party. All party sites also contained invitations to join up with the party campaign.

Indisputably the most dynamic party website belonged to Fine Gael, though its malleability bordered on the schizophrenic at times. The campaign site was relaunched initially without any policy content, featuring a video clip of Enda Kenny sitting in a café, and a facility for registering personal details and leaving comments. According to the video, the site was designed in this way in order to get an insight into and to aggregate public opinion, and the Fine Gael campaign team member whom we interviewed stated that this feedback was used in deciding on certain elements of the party's policy platform, though it is unclear precisely how this process worked in practice.

During the campaign, the site's front page went through several phases, ranging from informative and innovative to bizarre and rather naive.[15] While these innovations attracted some criticism and mockery (most memorably in the form of a parody of the Enda Kenny video, which was digitally transformed to give the appearance of slurred speech and a black eye, and then posted on YouTube) they also meant that Fine Gael was highly visible online. The Fine Gael online campaign team member whom we interviewed stated that the party campaign site received over 400,000 hits. This was probably assisted by the Fine Gael campaign's focus on its 'five-point plan', which was detailed on the party's site. Furthermore, Enda Kenny specifically advised voters to visit the party site to check out these details of his party's policy platform on the Fine Gael website during the final leaders' debate. However, it is worth noting that Fine Gael's web campaign also ran into novel problems, particularly when its site was hacked early in the campaign – leading to concerns about the security of data entered by site users. Also, our interviewee from Fine Gael reported that some Fine Gael candidates had their Facebook pages temporarily taken down, when several Facebook users reported that they were fake. This type of collective 'hacktivism' appears unlikely to have been spontaneous.

Labour was also innovative in its website design. The Labour campaign site featured a page where users could generate a constituency-specific video message from Éamon Gilmore and email it to friends/contacts. This facility is shown in Figure 5.3. The innovation of integrating Web 2.0 content creation with email is a very interesting mixture of the 'narrowcasting' and 'viral' online campaign memes – it effectively allows users to choose which region to target in their narrowcast, which they then create and seek to disseminate virally. Labour's site also featured a broadcast of the party conference at which the membership voted to approve the Programme for Government that it negotiated with Fine Gael, and the party has been particularly active on YouTube since the election.

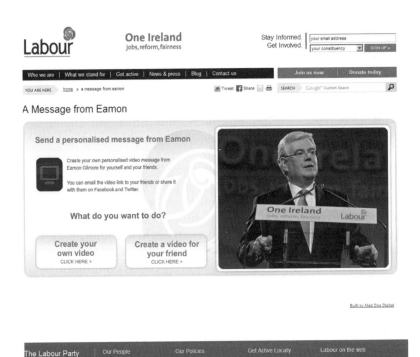

Figure 5.3   Labour's 'personalised message from Éamon'

The sites of Fianna Fáil, the Greens, and Sinn Féin were all highly pro-fessionalised and shared the common features described at the beginning of this section. However, while launching largely redesigned and faster websites compared to 2007, Fianna Fáil, the Green Party, and Sinn Féin did not display the same sort of thematic dynamism (which is typically referred to in website design circles as site 'freshness') as the Fine Gael and, to a lesser extent, Labour websites. The United Left Alliance site, while incorporating the common features of party campaign websites, was put together by a smaller team, with very limited resources, and consequently lacked some of the slickness of the other party sites in terms of appearance. Our interviewee from the Alliance informed us that the suddenness of the announcement of the election frustrated more ambitious medium-term plans for the campaign site.

Parties' use of social networking sites

The major parties also had profiles in the two most prominent social networking sites in the 2011 campaign: Twitter and Facebook. All of the party campaign staff members whom we interviewed emphasised the importance of party and candidate social networking presences during the campaign. The larger parties provided updates on breaking stories on their social networking profiles, to 'reward' followers. For instance, Fianna Fáil announced the results of its pre-election leadership contest on its Twitter feed, and the Greens pre-released sections of their party manifesto on theirs. Furthermore, party press conferences and events of all major parties included an online communication strategy – with campaign staff posting pictures or, in some cases, videos, of campaign events on the party Facebook or Twitter profiles in near real-time.

In Table 5.2, we show how popular each party's profile was on Twitter and Facebook as well as describing the number of 'tweets' that each party's profile had produced by 5 April 2011 and the launch date of each party's Twitter account. We can see that in terms of the timing of Twitter uptake and numbers of followers, Labour was well ahead of the other parties. Labour engaged in a particularly lively Twitter campaign in 2011 – with its campaign team interviewee indicating that party responsiveness in social networks was an important (and time-consuming) campaign priority. Once Fine Gael launched its profile in January 2009, the other parties quickly followed suit.

In terms of popularity, the Facebook figures are probably more electorally relevant, as Facebook is the most-consumed social networking site in Ireland. Fianna Fáil's unpopularity on Facebook is particularly striking, given the party's historical electoral dominance of Irish politics,

Table 5.2   Party profiles on Twitter and Facebook

Party	Twitter followers	Number of tweets	Date profile creation	Facebook profile 'likes'/friend
Fine Gael	4,855	1,630	26 Jan 2009	5,372
Labour	6,977	3,380	11 Jun 2007	5,631
Fianna Fáil	5,618	1,433	27 Jan 2009	2,950
Sinn Féin	4,696	2,396	03 Mar 2009	4,522
Greens	5,529	1,770	28 Jan 2009	523

Note: Different Facebook profile designs allow users different opportunities to express support. 'Official' and 'group' pages allow users to 'like' the organisation, while 'profile' pages allow users to 'friend'. Sinn Féin was the only party with a 'profile' Facebook page, the other parties all used 'official' pages.

although it is not incongruent with eventual results at the polls. Sinn Féin's strong performance and the Greens' weak performance at the polls were also somewhat foreshadowed by their Facebook profile popularity figures. These figures give a numeric indicator of the limitations of public interest in parties' social media campaigns. Even if we assume that each party's network is comprised of separate individuals, which is unlikely given that several politics junkies and media professionals engaged with multiple party profiles, the overall number of people 'liking' or 'friending' the mainstream parties on Facebook sums to less than 20,000 – a tiny proportion of the estimated number of individuals with Facebook profiles in Ireland. These figures indicate that, at the party level at least, the online campaign does not appear likely to have engaged large numbers of voters. On the other hand, the raw numbers of followers of a party social networking page may under-represent that page's potential reach, as each follower can resend party content to all of their followers.

The candidates

We focus on candidates' use of social media here. We do so firstly because this appeared to be very widespread across the field of candidates in 2011, and secondly because information on this type of web use in terms of output and numbers of consumers is easily available to researchers. In Table 5.3, we describe the proportions of candidates who had Facebook and Twitter pages, from a sample of 524 candidates, broken down by party affiliation. We can see that Facebook was significantly more popular among candidates than Twitter, and that Fine Gael had the highest proportions of candidates on both social networking sites. Sinn Féin

Table 5.3   Proportions of candidates from each party using Facebook and Twitter in the campaign

Candidates grouped by party	Facebook profile %	Twitter account %	N
Fine Gael	87	74	104
Labour	84	66	68
Fianna Fáil	61	40	75
Sinn Féin	85	41	41
Greens	62	48	42
United Left Alliance	84	52	19
Independents	67	44	175
Total	74	53	524

Note: information is unavailable for the remaining candidates.

candidates had the biggest disparity between Facebook and Twitter usage, with over twice as many on Facebook as on Twitter.

Candidate online campaigning has more than doubled in prevalence since 2007, when only 32 per cent of candidates had individual campaign sites (see Table 5.1). This increase partly reflects the efforts of the major parties to encourage their candidates to develop social networking presences. The larger party campaign teams whom we interviewed reported that candidates had received some form of instruction in the use of social networking sites. For instance, Fianna Fáil brought their candidates to a new media seminar in May 2009. The parties' online campaign teams also provided candidates with technical support in developing their social networking profiles (for example, by uploading videos or documents and posting links to these). Our interviewees indicated that party staff often had access to candidates' individual profiles, which they typically used to post party campaign material, but all party online campaign teams encouraged candidates to post their own content as much as possible. Social media usage among members of the United Left Alliance and Independents was impressive, considering that these candidates were not pushed towards social media by a party.

Internet campaign tools provide particularly useful possibilities to candidates who lack the resources that come with major party support. It is therefore unsurprising that social media use was a feature of several successful Independent campaigns. For example, Luke 'Ming' Flanagan TD has over 3,000 Twitter followers and over 1,700 Facebook 'likes' for his profile; John Halligan has over 2,600 Facebook followers, and Michael Lowry has highly popular Twitter and Facebook accounts – with over 5,000 friends on his Facebook profile. Shane Ross and Mick Wallace both launched Twitter sites in early 2011, just as the campaign was beginning in earnest, and both profiles now have substantial followings. However, some Independents such as Maureen O'Sullivan succeeded without large numbers of friends or followers, and others such as Tipperary North candidate Kate Bopp and Dublin South-East's Dylan Haskins were unable to convert popular social networking profiles into seats – although Haskins did particularly well for a non-affiliated first-time candidate, winning over 1,300 first preferences in a highly competitive constituency.

In terms of content, candidate social networking output often made for dull reading – anticipated campaign 'gaffes' online by candidates did not materialise, and one of the more common topics was the weather faced by canvassers. Several candidates posted links to party policy documents and pertinent media stories during the campaign. A large portion of the candidate Twitter content was personal in nature – in the sense that it dealt with what the candidate was doing that day (for example, going to a GAA (Gaelic Athletic Association) or rugby match), reading, watching, or thinking about.

As evidenced by the exceptional success of Independents in Irish politics, and as enshrined in the rules of the proportional representation by the single transferable vote (PR-STV) voting system, it is the *candidate* and not the party who must win votes in Irish elections. Not only that, but candidates from the larger (or more electorally ambitious) parties have to compete with opponents from within their own party. Thus candidates have strong incentives to distinguish themselves as individuals in their constituencies. As Facebook and Twitter both allow candidates to develop their own distinctive campaign styles and messages, the popularity of these tools in the 2011 campaign is not surprising. It appears that online social network use among Irish politicians is now very much a mainstream phenomenon. Overall, the figures displayed here indicate a considerably greater volume of online candidate activity in 2011 than we saw in 2007. With parties encouraging and assisting candidates to develop their online profiles, this trend is likely to continue in the near future. Post-election, one consequence of the popularity of social media among candidates is that large numbers of elected representatives are now active on both Facebook and Twitter – providing those who follow them with updates on the day-to-day business of the Houses of the Oireachtas.

The voters

Reliable cross-national figures on internet penetration levels are difficult to come by, but the internetworldstats.com site estimates that the 2010 internet penetration level in Ireland was just under 66 per cent of the population, meaning that Ireland lags behind world-leading European countries such as Iceland, Sweden, Norway, and Denmark. However, social networking sites are highly popular among Irish internet users: a study carried out at the end of the 2011 campaign (reported on RTÉ's website on 22 February) by Ipsos-MRBI found that approximately 50 per cent of the Irish population (above the age of 15) have a Facebook profile, leading to the estimate that there are 1.75 million Irish Facebook profiles online. Approximately 7 per cent of the Irish population was estimated to have a Twitter account. The highest reported volumes of social network site users are in the 15–24 age group, with nine out of ten in this group having a Facebook profile.

While data on politicised internet use by Irish voters in 2011 are still being collected, the Irish National Election Studies from 2002 and 2007 provide some useful insights. In 2002, the number who stated that they had found information about parties and candidates online was 5 per cent; in 2007, this proportion had more than doubled to 11 per cent. Studies of citizen political internet use in the UK tell a similar story, though direct comparison is difficult because the questions asked by researchers in the two countries are not identical. In their study of web use in the 2001 UK election, Lusoli and Ward[16] found that 5 per cent of survey respondents had visited the site of a political organisation, while a study[17] of the 2010 UK election found that this proportion had tripled: over 15 per cent had read or accessed official party sites. So, the evidence thus far points to online campaign consumption as a minority but growing phenomenon, in both Ireland and the UK.

The Web 2.0 character of the modern internet discussed at the beginning of this chapter means that it is now very straightforward to develop your own website. It is therefore not entirely surprising that literally hundreds of citizen-developed and managed sites covered the 2011 Irish election campaign daily (or in some cases, nearly minute-by-minute). While we cannot speak with certainty, we are confident that this election has received wider coverage (in terms of the numbers of people producing coverage and the volumes of news and analysis disseminated for public consumption) than any previous event in the history of Ireland. One downside of this fragmentation of content creation is that universal coverage of online politics becomes nearly impossible for academics. As social scientists, we are rather in the position of a flustered stenographer during a stormy court exchange – we cannot record the entirety of what's happening, but we try to pick up the most relevant content. That caveat aside, we both agreed that following the election online added a marvellous depth to the campaign – if sometimes making it a little more difficult to see the wood for the trees.

There has been an explosion of specialised sites dealing with specific aspects of Irish politics. Such sites provide valuable and often beautifully collated information about election results (electionsireland.org) or about the activities of members of the Houses of the Oireachtas (kildarestreet. com). Other examples of informational/political fanatic hub sites focus on more ephemeral aspects of politics. One very interesting example was electionleaflets.mygov.ie, which has scanned and collated over 250 separate election leaflets from the 2011 campaign, while Adrian Kavanagh's 'Irish general election facts and figures' blog provided detailed breakdowns of the candidates and constituency-specific analyses.

There were also a large number of weblogs, which focused on specific aspects of the campaign. The mamanpoulet.com feed had particularly interesting coverage of the online campaign, as well as linking to several other similar blogs. One interesting development in the blogosphere has been the emergence of academic blogs providing real time academic analyses of economic (economy.ie) and political (politicalreform.ie, reformcard.com) developments, while the votomatic.com site provided voting advice to users on the basis of a comparison of their opinions with the policies advocated by the main parties.

There were several election prediction hubs: politicalreform.ie had several posts seeking to derive seat predictions from polling data, the fullhouse.whitebox.ie site encouraged users to enter a prediction competition. Several bookmaking sites also provided continuously updated predictive information in the form of odds being offered for party seat bands, for the make-up of the next government, and whether individual candidates would win or lose their seat.

Several sites focused on citizen education and/or non-partisan political protest. An interesting development in this category involved candidate information collation – sites which captured contact details (or, in some cases, social networking details) of all of the candidates competing in the elections. While the mycandidate.ie site provided this service during the 2007 campaign, several sites did so in 2011 – these included: irishpoliticians.com, icitizen.ie, candidate.ie, and telluswhy.ie.

It should be noted that 'old' media organisations such as television and radio broadcasters produced well-developed and resourced election coverage sites. The rte.ie site, the tv3.ie site, the sites of the major national newspapers and the sites of national radio broadcasters were rich in detail and featured regularly updated content from multiple correspondents across the country as the campaign unfolded. There were also several 'new' media sites, which provided internet-only election coverage. These sites include: politics.ie, campaigntrail.ie, Storyful.com, thejournal.ie, sluggerotoole.com and irishelection.com. Some of these sites provided opportunities for a degree of interaction in the generation of political stories that was unthinkable in 'old' media formats.

Perhaps the most decentralised 'new' media source was Twitter.com, where, as we note above, about 7 per cent of the Irish population has a profile. Users of Twitter can mark the topic of their tweets using a hashtag with a specific label, and users can then view all tweets employing that hashtag in a single stream. For instance, tweets to do with the election campaign were typically labelled #ge11. We recovered over 109,000 individual tweets with this hashtag during the campaign. Interestingly, 'old' and 'new' media are now interacting in interesting ways – with political television programmes such as *Tonight With Vincent Browne*, *The Frontline*, and *Prime Time* all having their own hashtags which can generate thousands of tweets per episode. These tweets are typically integrated into the broadcast, with the presenters pausing to read out selected tweets. Another notable piece of Twitter coverage occurred as the votes were being counted, with each constituency being designated a hashtag, which journalists and citizens present at count centres used to construct a real-time narrative of the tally.

Conclusion

Overall, the 2011 campaign has seen a dramatic increase in the political use of the internet by all three types of actors considered in this chapter: parties, candidates, and voters. These changes are particularly striking when compared to the 2007 campaign, where political use of the internet was much more circumscribed. Web 2.0 platforms have transformed the online landscape and make the internet a significantly more attractive campaign arena.

Fine Gael appears to have led the way in the use of online technologies in the campaign, both through its innovative website and the proclivity of its candidates to use social networking tools. While it is not possible to directly estimate how these activities related to the party's performance at the polls, Fine Gael currently seems to be the Irish party best positioned to capitalise on emerging cyber-campaigning opportunities.

We found that social media use was widespread among candidates from all parties; the proportion of candidates with individual web presences in 2011 has more than doubled since 2007. We noted that Facebook was particularly prominent among candidates, with 74 per cent of the candidates whom we studied having a Facebook presence. This is unsurprising given the high numbers of Irish users of Facebook. Twitter was less widespread among candidates, but it offered the most diverse source of citizen coverage of the campaign, and has been integrated into several mainstream media. Finally, we observed that there was a rich array of citizen-generated coverage of the 2011 campaign available online.

It is difficult to predict how the internet/politics nexus will evolve between now and the next election campaign. At the moment, however, trends are pointing towards an ongoing growth in the use of the internet by parties, by individual politicians, and by politically-interested citizens. It appears that the internet is now an integral part of day-to-day political communications strategies, and that online strategy has become a major component of political campaigns in the Republic of Ireland. Whether the advent of online politics will bring changes to the substance, rather than simply to the style, of political communications and campaigning in Ireland remains to be seen.

Notes

1. Steven Ward and Rachel Gibson, 'The first Internet election? UK political parties and campaigning in cyberspace', pp. 93–112 in Ivor Crewe, Brian Gosschalk and John Bartles (eds), *Political Communications: The General Election Campaign of 1997* (London: Frank Cass, 1998).
2. Michael Marsh, 'None of that post-modern stuff around here: grassroots campaigning in the 2002 Irish general election', *Journal of Elections, Public Opinion and Parties* 14:1 (2004), pp. 245–67.
3. Maria Laura Sudulich and Matthew Wall, 'How do candidates spend their money? Objects of campaign spending and the effectiveness of diversification', *Electoral Studies* 30:1 (2011), pp. 91–101.
4. Maria Laura Sudulich and Matthew Wall, 'Keeping up with the Murphys? Candidate cyber-campaigning in the 2007 Irish general election', *Parliamentary Affairs* 62:3 (2009), pp. 456–75; Maria Laura Sudulich and Matthew Wall, 'Every little helps: cyber campaigning in the 2007 Irish general election', *Journal of Information Technology & Politics* 7:4 (2010), pp. 340–55.
5. Sudulich and Wall, 'Every little helps', pp. 340–55.
6. Sudulich and Wall, 'How do candidates spend their money?', pp. 91–101.
7. We conducted interviews with representatives from the online campaign teams of: Fine Gael, Labour, Fianna Fáil, the United Left Alliance, and the Greens. We were unable to interview a member of the Sinn Féin online campaign team. We would like to thank all interviewees for their cooperation and insights.
8. For a review see David Farrell and Paul Webb, 'Political parties as campaign organizations', pp. 102–28 in Russell J. Dalton and Martin P. Wattenberg (eds), *Parties without Partisans: Political change in advanced industrial democracies* (Oxford: Oxford University Press, 2000); Pippa Norris, *Developments in Party Communications* (Washington, DC: National Democratic Institute for

International Affairs, 2005); Paul Webb, David Farrell and Ian Holliday (eds), *Political Parties in Advanced Industrial Democracies* (Oxford: Oxford University Press, 2002).

9. Dalton and Wattenberg, *Parties without Partisans*; Rachel Gibson and Andrea Rommele, 'Measuring the professionalization of political campaigning', *Party Politics* 15:3 (2009), pp. 265–93.

10. Rachel Gibson and Andrea Rommele, 'Changing campaign communications: a party-centered theory of professionalized campaigning', *International Journal of Press/Politics* 6:4 (2001), pp. 31–43.

11. Cristian Vaccari, 'Technology is a commodity: the internet in the 2008 United States presidential election', *Journal of Information Technology & Politics* 7:4 (2010), pp. 318–39.

12. The expression 'Web 2.0' was first coined at a conference on changes in internet technology organised by O'Reilly Media and Media Live International in October 2004.

13. Paul Anderson, *What is Web 2.0? Ideas, technologies and implications for education, Feb. 2007* (Bristol: JISC), www.jisc.ac.uk/media/documents/techwatch/tsw0701b.pdf, accessed 19 June 2007.

14. The United Left Alliance departed from this model, with a decentralised approach to the online campaign that reflects the group's umbrella structure. Each Alliance candidate campaign team took leadership of the candidate's online campaign, and collaboration between candidates in online campaign activities took place on an informal, ad hoc basis. The United Left Alliance website was maintained by a small volunteer group (including a candidate) and content for that site was agreed by the Alliance's Steering Committee.

15. One of its more memorable incarnations featured an exhortation to send a Fine Gael (FG) Valentine (complete with FG-themed romantic poem) to friends on Valentine's Day. The Valentine's gimmick was just one of example of the several 'viral' online strategies used by Fine Gael during the campaign – the party posted a series of videos on its site (and on its YouTube account) where a young woman (described only as 'FG Girl') provided simple instructions on how to 'become part of the digital revolution' by following FG and its candidates on Facebook and by 'donating your status' (which involved posting FG campaign content on your Facebook wall for your friends to read). The site also briefly featured a Fine Gael game, which involved navigating Enda Kenny across a rolling 2D landscape in a 'platformer' game. However, the site also hosted substantial policy documentation around the five-point plan presented by Fine Gael in the campaign.

16. Wainer Lusoli and Steven Ward, 'Logging on or switching off? The public and the internet at the 2005 general election', pp. 13–22 in Stephen Coleman (ed), *Spinning the Web: Online campaigning during the 2005 general election* (London: Hansard Society, 2005).

17. Rachel Gibson, Marta Cantijoch and Steven Ward, 'Online citizen-campaigning in the UK general election of 2010: how did citizens use new technologies to get involved?' Paper presented at 'Internet, Politics, Policy 2010: An Impact Assessment', conference organised by the Oxford Internet Institute, Oxford, September 2010.

6
On the Campaign Trail

Seán Kyne (Fine Gael, Galway West)

Seán Kyne was first elected to Galway County Council in 2004 and was re-elected in 2009. He stood unsuccessfully for the Dáil and Seanad in 2007. He is an agri-environmental consultant and holds degrees in agricultural science from UCD. In 2011 he was one of four Fine Gael candidates in what was perceived to be a high risk and controversial strategy for the five-seat Galway West constituency. Despite being seventh of 17 candidates on first preferences, he won a seat, finishing just 17 votes ahead of the runner-up. His was the narrowest winning margin in the country, and, as a result of several recounts, he was also the last of the 166 TDs to be elected.

In December 2010, at the Fine Gael Galway West selection convention, I made a speech to those who had, in the particularly inclement winter weather, assembled in the Salthill Hotel. Following my contribution I withdrew, to the surprise of some, my name from consideration. I did this primarily because I believed that both I and the outgoing Deputy, Padraic McCormack, would be seeking support from the Connemara region and as a result I felt there would be little chance of success in such an eventuality. In a surprise result, Deputy McCormack subsequently lost out to Senator Fidelma Healy Eames and Councillor Brian Walsh, who were duly selected.

It was not until 8 January that Councillor Hildegarde Naughton and I were selected by party HQ in what was to prove a high-risk strategy of running four candidates with the aim of winning two seats. Galway West had not returned two TDs for Fine Gael since November 1982. I was selected as the Connemara candidate and was perceived by many to be a 'sweeper'.[1] I was determined to put in a good performance and my number one priority, backed by HQ and the local constituency executive, was to have Connemara to myself for canvassing. This was accepted by the other candidates with the proviso that I was not to canvass Galway City and the Oranmore electoral areas. The strategy was more or less obeyed. It meant that I had circa 30,000 voters in the Connemara area and could deliver my message of being 'a voice in government for Connemara'. It was widely anticipated that Fine Gael was on course to be in government and I was the Connemara candidate so the message was well received.

On the night after I was selected I held a meeting with three others in Moycullen, my home town, to start a campaign. We agreed to call a meeting for that Thursday night bringing together members from my home parish and the two neighbouring ones. We got a big crowd of over 60 and I addressed them together with other locals. Over the course of the next number of weeks I held meetings in Maam and Indreabhan with local party activists and supporters. Many doubted but a few influential people believed. It was arranged that former Galway football manager and TD for Mayo John O'Mahony would launch my campaign. This went off well. Former councillor and three-in-a-row All-Ireland winning footballer Pat Donnellan came aboard as an active part of my campaign team and attended all the local meetings in Connemara and indeed canvassed extensively. This was a huge credibility boost.

I had contested the 2007 election as a sweeper, receiving circa 2,000 votes. This was at a time when Fine Gael was recovering but where polls in Galway West showed us losing our only seat to the Greens. It was a time when Fianna Fáil was still very strong and was putting in a huge effort to win three seats in the constituency. In 2011 I reckoned that, with the sitting Deputy retired, I could and should more than double my vote. I believed that to stand any chance of being elected I needed to be ahead of one of my running mates and I also needed to be ahead of local Independent councillor Thomas Welby. This was my strategy therefore: market myself as the government candidate for Connemara, double my vote, be ahead of Welby and one of my running mates. If these elements clicked I believed I had some chance of success.

However, to many in the party I had no chance. I was nothing more than a sweeper. This view was furthered by much of the local media over the campaign. In constituency analysis I was viewed as 'the fourth candidate', 'the sweeper', 'the Connemara sweeper', and so on. However, my campaign was going well. There was no time to arrange a literature drop in Connemara due to its vastness so I had to settle for a good canvass, door to door. I knew I needed to expand my base into Connemara so I made a conscious decision not to personally canvass my home town and instead to allow others to do this while I would spread into Connemara. I received a good reaction at the doors in Connemara where meeting the candidate is very important. All rural areas were canvassed with locals, together with either myself or a family member, brother, sister, father, mother. If the candidate is not there himself/herself then I feel family members are important.

As the Connemara candidate, one issue on my mind as a huge negative for me and one that would be viewed in a negative manner was my competency in Irish. Galway West has the largest Gaeltacht in the country and Connemara is home to Raidió na Gaeltachta and TG4.[2] Up until 2011 I had never been interviewed in Irish, either live or recorded, and I had a huge psychological barrier to break regarding the native language. I had a basic knowledge from school and over a number of years, particularly after my local election success in 2009 (I was re-elected on that occasion), I began taking conversational Irish classes with a retired teacher. Over the years my command of Irish improved but my own views of my ability were still poor. I grasped the nettle in January 2011 and gave my first recorded interview in Irish, of 12 minutes which was edited down to five in studio. I got a great reaction. I began doing other interviews and I attended meetings in the Gaeltacht – something I hadn't the courage to do in the past. I did my first live interview in Irish, somewhat traumatic but I got great recognition over it, culminating in Minister Éamon Ó Cuív praising my Irish and stating that I was a much more credible candidate since beginning to speak the language.

Fine Gael's Irish-language policy, of removing compulsory Irish for the Leaving Certificate, was a huge issue in the campaign and one that caused huge anxiety in the party. I came out against the policy and at a public meeting with the 'mná na tí's' gave a speech in Irish where I said I was unhappy with policy on Irish and that consultation with me or the members of the Fine Gael party in the Connemara Gaeltacht had not taken place.[3] This was subsequently broadcast on *Prime Time* with subtitles. I received press coverage on the front of *Foinse*, on 'Morning Ireland', in the *Irish Times* and on Raidió na Gaeltachta. My stance on the issue gave me huge publicity and increased my profile considerably. Despite negative publicity surrounding the party's stance, my team and I put in a huge canvass in the Gaeltacht and we reaped an increased Fine Gael vote in the area as a result.

Two friends of mine took it upon themselves to organise a website for me as well as a Facebook and Google advertising campaign. They also took charge of press releases. The response was positive with an easy web-message section on the website for people to contact me during the campaign. It worked well.

I have a policy of never canvassing or speaking outside churches. In fact, I detest any type of canvassing except door to door. My team and I put in a huge personal and family canvass across Connemara and it paid off. A sense of belief started to envelop the campaign and some began to feel I had a real chance.

A couple of weeks before election day, the *Sunday Independent* ran an opinion poll showing me on 15 per cent of the vote and leading the field of four Fine Gael runners. This gave credibility to my campaign but I didn't believe for a minute that it could be true. Connemara had been over-polled. Some of my campaign team thought this was wonderful and that people wanted to back a winner. I told them to wait until the *Galway Advertiser* poll – scheduled to appear the following Thursday – and predicted that in that poll I would be on 2 per cent (I really believed I would be on 4 per cent but felt saying 2 sounded better). When the poll was published I was indeed on less than 2 per cent. I was annoyed because I knew it was not true and had the potential to do untold damage to my campaign as people would believe that I had no hope. All I could do was to keep the head down and keep canvassing, which I did. I was delighted when the polls finally closed as no more could be done and all that was left was to count the votes.

I was happy with the campaign although it was somewhat rushed due to the early election date. I had put in a huge personal effort into the campaign. It was the most intense seven weeks of my life: constant decisions, intense canvassing, press releases, media interviews, emails and phone calls, meetings, launches as well as the general pressure and unexpected controversies which are part and parcel of elections. And all before the marathon count.

I arrived into Leisureland, Salthill (the count venue), at around 8.45 a.m. on the Saturday of the count to do tallies. Nobody present could have anticipated that what lay ahead was the longest ever count in Galway West and one that would not end until the following Wednesday at 8.10 a.m. when I was elected and filled the last seat in the 31st Dáil.

On the official count I was ahead of Senator Fidelma Healy Eames by 56 votes, a sizeable amount, when she called a full recount on Sunday afternoon. This was agreed to by the Returning Officer but the result ended up nearly the very same at 54 votes. As each vote had to be checked and recounted, it was not until after midnight, in the small hours of Tuesday, that the count resumed where it had left off on the Sunday afternoon. Fidelma was eliminated and her votes distributed. I received a good transfer from her, as predicted from tallies during the night. However, we underestimated the transfer she would give Independent Catherine Connolly. Catherine was ahead of me by 63 votes. All that was left was for Brian Walsh's surplus votes to be distributed, of which I received 75 per cent and was elected by 17 votes.

As was widely expected and fully understandable, a full recount was called by Catherine and granted by the Returning Officer. Beginning on Tuesday afternoon, it ran through the night until eventually the result was declared and I was elected by the same margin – 17 votes – on Wednesday morning.

That slim margin proves that every single vote counts in an election. It was a marathon count which left all concerned tired, drained and at times emotional. But even after the campaign and the intense election count it was worth the effort, and I look forward now to the challenge of representing the people of Galway West to the best of my abilities in Dáil Éireann.

Ciara Conway (Labour, Waterford)

Ciara Conway was standing for the first time in a Dáil election. A service design and development facilitator with Barnardo's, she had been elected to Dungarvan Town Council in 2009. The incumbent Labour TD in Waterford, Brian O'Shea, announced in mid-January 2011 that he would be retiring at the election, so the candidate selection convention at which she and her running mate were selected took place only a few weeks before election day. Before her election, Waterford had not had a female TD since the death of Bridget Mary Redmond in 1952. This is her account, as told to her Parliamentary Assistant Jennifer Allen.

The call came on a Thursday afternoon. I was in Dublin, attending a meeting at Barnardo's, where I worked. Recognising the number I stepped out to take the call.

'You're getting the nod.'

'That's great ... thanks for letting me know...'

Oh. My. God.

Or as my daughter would say, O.M.G.

For a minute, everything stood still. There was a massive tornado headed this way, and I was standing there staring at it, waiting for it to hit.

I took a few seconds, and a couple of deep breaths, then rang my parents.

'It's on!'

After that initial phone call the euphoria and anxiety kicked in, and the tornado hit. A list of things that had to be done stretched out in front of me. This was 23 January. Within a few days, Brian Cowen would go into the Dáil and call an election. The adrenalin that was to get me through to 25 February and beyond had already begun pumping. I had to arrange leave from work, book a photographer, get posters and flyers designed and printed, get a loan, convene a team meeting, find a pair of shoes, warn the childminder, get a haircut … so much to do, so little time.

The campaign for Election 2011 had begun.

Within a few hours, HQ for the Conway Election team had been assembled in my parents' front room. This was to be the nerve centre for the action. Jan Rotte, a town councillor from Lismore in West Waterford, was to be the director of elections. We had a core group of around 15 or 20 people, many of them family, that we divided into groups and areas. My running mate was Séamus Ryan, a city councillor in the Waterford City South ward, so the Labour Party had the Waterford constituency nicely covered in terms of geographical spread. The South Ward had a number of high-profile people including John Halligan (Ind) and David Cullinane (SF), who would go on to become a TD and a senator respectively. It was decided that I would stay out of the South ward, while Séamus avoided Dungarvan, leaving the rest up for grabs. I had a natural base towards the west of the county and he the east, so we usually managed to avoid any doubling up of canvasses. Having a large family helped: on my mother's side there were plenty of Noonans, and the Conways were well known around Dungarvan, and in addition Cappoquin host to Conway's Hotel. Around Dungarvan, I was known through having been on the Town Council. We felt there was a large vote to be got in the Tramore area. During the last election Martin Cullen had secured a large number of votes from that area – but my feeling was that it was a vote for a minister rather than Fianna Fail.[4] I grew up in Tramore, and my father was well known as he'd spent 34 years teaching there. He and a small team made it their business to knock on as many doors as possible, and the recognition factor was no harm when Joe Conway turned up on the doorstep looking for a vote for his daughter. When it comes to strategies, our main strategy was to knock on as many doors as humanly possible and meet everyone we could.

Brian O'Shea had reconsidered his initial decision to run for another term just a few weeks beforehand, so there was a seat to be filled and an anti-government vote to be capitalised on. And there was no time to lose.

The next day I found myself standing in a photographic studio getting my picture taken for the election posters. I had brought an outfit, but I didn't like the colour or how I looked. Feck. I rang Noelle. 'Mam, will you go over to my house and find the other suit jacket? The black one? And there should be a white blouse hanging up that I just ironed? Can you bring them over please? Thanks Mam.'

She arrived within half an hour, while I continued to make and receive phone calls and answer the flurry of texts. I ditched the first outfit, bottoms and all, and ended up having the photo taken trouserless.

'Imagine if the other candidates could see you now – sure all we need is Gok Wan!'

Thus began the campaign in earnest. Next time there's an election, I hope to god it'll be in the summer. We had hailstones. We had snow. We had rain, fog, ice, frost and bitter, bitter cold. The first night we went out canvassing it was minus three degrees in Dungarvan. But there was no time to lose and I was determined to meet as many people as I could. Even as a teenager, and long before I could vote, I remember being impressed by the candidates who actually knocked on the door themselves, so I was determined to meet as many people as was physically possible.

It might have been freezing outside, but there was definitely a warmth in the reactions we were getting on the doorsteps; in many cases this was a fiery anger. Anger at the mess we were in, anger at having no job, and anger towards politicians. But while there was definitely an anger out there, more often than not people told me their stories of hardship with a quiet dignity. 'I'm not looking for much, just enough to do', was a common one. I can recall a man in West Waterford who told me 'All you can offer me now is hope. You're young, you're educated, and all that's left is hope.' Time and time again I met women who started off with an anger that ended up in teary eyes as they told me about the son gone to live in Australia, or the daughter who was getting ready to emigrate to Canada.

Often there were positive reactions simply because of the fact that, of the 15 candidates running in the four-seat Waterford constituency, I was the youngest at 30 years of age, and the only woman – and a single mammy at that. My daughter Aeva-May did her fair share of canvassing among her classmates and their families. I'm quite sure that there are some TDs who don't have half the knowledge or political acumen that she had at eight years of age. She was very understanding about the whole thing, though God knows it wasn't easy for her, or me either. It was tough – I'd say goodbye to her early in the morning as she was dropped off to school, and it could be 10 p.m. after a full day of knocking on doors before I'd see her again, when we were both exhausted. Ah, the guilt that goes with being a parent! To be fair to my own parents, there's no way I could possibly have managed without their help and support. They were, and still are, brilliant. In fact, the support I got from my whole family brought home to me just how lucky I am to belong to such a great clan of people. There was the childcare, and the fact that their house in Abbeyside was completely taken over as the election HQ. My mother Noelle and Mary-Ann, my sister, were constantly making soup and sandwiches and packing picnics to feed the troops as they braved the cold highways and byways of a wintry wet Waterford. My dad, Joe Conway, was out doing the whole east of the county, around Tramore and Waterford City, while other teams traipsed the roads around Tallow and Ring and West Waterford.

There are, of course, certain challenges that female election candidates have to contend with that would never bother the gentlemen. Mascara, for one. Is there really a waterproof mascara that will stay put as the rain is pelting in February half-way up the Comeraghs? I've yet to find it. Footwear is another one. You have to try and look the part when you're walking from house to house, but I've found to my detriment that heels, however low, were a bad idea. The blisters were bad. Then there's the whole issue of tights laddering, and not offering enough protection from the elements. In the end I decided the best way to tackle the frost was to opt for hiking boots under trousers. Waterford city councillor Pat Hayes spotted them one night and remarked 'Jaysus Ciara, if you'd only worn the boots at the beginning, we'd all be home in front of the fire at this stage!'

We had our fair share of injuries in Team Conway. There were a few falls, but they struggled on, fair play to them. My uncle Eddie Cashin hurt his leg at work one morning, and mid-way through that evening's canvass in Ballinroad, he looked down to see a swelling on his shin the size of a balloon. But he battled on through the throbbing. Out in An Rinn, another member of the team returned limping.

'What happened to you?'

He'd pulled a muscle in his leg going up and down the steep hills in Ring. In Tramore, we noticed that Aoife Harhen, a volunteer and best friend of my sister Doireann, was limping. It transpired that she'd broken her toe on the canvass a week beforehand, but didn't complain once, or even let on she was hurt.

Running for election, I was surprised at the changes some of my family were prepared to make. My uncle Dick Lanigan is famed as one of the most dyed-in-the-wool Fianna Fáil supporters you could hope to meet. But lo and behold, he travelled down from Glasnevin, and spent a few days in the country no less – knocking on doors in Clashmore and Ardmore in west Waterford. Miracles can happen.

The campaign flew, and all of a sudden it was the eve of polling day. In a last push, my brother Ruairí enlisted the help of some of the under-14 Abbeyside Ballinacourty GAA Club to drop some more leaflets around the Dungarvan and Abbeyside area. (They volunteered, so I've been assured that it doesn't count as child labour … .)

Polling day itself, 25 February, was something of a reprieve. My 18-year-old brother Joe was voting for the first time, as was my cousin Philip. We had a cake with candles to mark the occasion; every celebration needs a good cake. I went to the polling station accompanied by my sister and Aeva-May, and got some lovely words of encouragement from people I met there. At that stage, there was nothing I could do, all the work was done.

On the day of the count, I was full of great intentions of going to the cinema. This is something I've heard Ruairí Quinn say he's fond of doing as the count begins. We got some very early word from our people at the Butler Centre in Waterford City that the first few boxes had been opened and the tallies weren't great. Uh-oh.

Resolving to cut myself off from all media, I headed over to the town in Dungarvan, where people were full of encouragement. We had some lunch, did a bit of shopping. When I got back home, the phone was hopping.

'Where the hell were you?! The news is good! The tallies are good!'

I broke my self-imposed media ban, and switched on Waterford Local Radio (WLRFM), and remained with an ear on the radio and eye on the TV. It felt unreal, like waiting for an exam result.

I managed to stay away from the election count centre until 6 o'clock or so. My stomach was full of knots, but the fact that people were in good spirits and full of banter was a help – as was the tally sheet, which indicated that things were going in our favour.

The night drew on. John Deasy of Fine Gael took the first seat, about an hour before midnight. His running mate Senator Paudie Coffey claimed the second seat an hour or two later.

One by one, the Labour well-wishers and supporters had gone home as the night wore on, leaving a hardy bunch of political junkies and family. Things might have been quietening down in the Butler Centre in

Waterford City, but it was all go on Twitter and Facebook. As RTÉ ended its coverage for the night, it was left to the hardy news team in WLRFM and to the twitterati to let people know how things were going. Supporters in Waterford City and County who had gone home were in bed with their laptops, following the tweets and commenting on Facebook. All around the world, my family and friends were keeping up to date online – the likes of my cousin Clíona in Spain, my friend Jennifer in Ecuador and a plethora of aunts, uncles and cousins in Perth, Australia. Many people found themselves chatting to each other and getting to know each other, and figuring out their connection to me, via t'interweb.

At around the 3.45 a.m. the Returning Officer Niall Rooney took to the stage to make it official – I'd been elected!! The first female TD for Waterford since 1952 – Woop!

The relief!

The joy!

The exhaustion!

Back in Fungarvan, I tried to go to bed for an hour or two, but I didn't really get any sleep that night. Instead I found my mind whirring, so I ended up replying to the mountain of texts, Facebook messages and tweets.

After what must've been a ten-minute snooze, I awoke to a very important phone call – my first big task as newly elected TD.

Before the election, myself and Aeva-May, my daughter, had made a pact: if I got my seat, she would be allowed get a mobile phone.

She was staying in her godfather Thomas's house, and at 7 a.m. she was ringing me: 'Mam, did you win?! You did!? Can we go into town now to get my phone?! You promised mam.'

So I did a piece with Seán O'Rourke for RTÉ radio, along with Arthur Spring, and afterwards myself and Aeva-May went off shopping, to buy a shiny new pink and cream mobile phone.

Conor Lenihan (Fianna Fáil, Dublin South-West)

Conor Lenihan was first elected to the Dáil in 1997 and was re-elected in 2002 and 2007. Before entering politics he was a radio journalist. In 2004 he was appointed to a Minister of State position, and he remained a Minister of State until the change of government in March 2011, in his last position having

responsibility for science, technology, innovation and natural resources. He
was preceded into the Dáil by four relatives: his grandfather Patrick Lenihan,
his father and brother (both Brian Lenihan) and his aunt Mary O'Rourke. His
2011 campaign in Dublin South-West, where both incumbent Fianna Fáil TDs
lost their seats, was the subject of a documentary broadcast on RTÉ Radio 1,
entitled 'Dogfight'.[5]

The Dublin South-West constituency is probably one of the most
competitive constituencies in the country. Although situated south of
the river Liffey it has the feel of a Northside or more accurately a north
inner-city constituency. Indeed much of the early settlement of the
Tallaght area, which is at the core of the constituency in electoral terms,
was constituted from inner-city Dubliners who were moved out to the
area, in some cases en bloc, from run-down corporation flat complexes
that were considered well beyond the inhabitable. In other words, for
most of these residents, the move to Tallaght was a welcome break
away from flat dwelling to having a home of their own. When the first
residents moved in the houses were, in some cases, built literally without
connecting roads, services or infrastructure. The blight of bad planning
decisions forged the future identity of the area with well-known political
figures such as the late Seán Walsh, Mervyn Taylor, Chris Flood, the late
Larry McMahon and Pat Rabbitte being the early voices on behalf of
what was a growing, young population, situated in conditions that were
far from enviable in what had previously been an outlying rural village,
dominated in employment and social terms by the Dominican Priory.
Research based on the CSO surveys indicates an area or constituency that
is low in terms of the presence of the managerial or professional classes.
Relative to the country as a whole the area has a lower than average
proportion of people who hold third level degrees. The concentrated
voting population is either living in local authority housing estates or
has previously done so, either directly themselves or while growing up.
It is one of the youngest constituencies in the country and turnout has
traditionally been low. It has voted No in EU referendums on a number
of occasions.

The 1997 general election was something of a turning point for Fianna
Fáil in the area. After a barren ten years with just one seat the party
secured the prized second seat, and continued to hold this right up until
election 2011. Prior to my own arrival as a TD in 1997 Chris Flood held
the party banner alone. The local party organisation had been badly
damaged by the split when Mary Harney left to form the PDs, and for
ten years Fianna Fáil struggled to make an impact. 1997 marked a turning

point because, for the first time in a long time, the constituency joined the mainstream politics of the country with both Fianna Fáil and Fine Gael making ground at the expense of the left. Somewhat atypically the constituency had elected three left-wing seats (one Democratic Left and two Labour) in 1992, with Mervyn Taylor heading the poll off the back of huge constituency effort and the fabled 'Spring Tide' of the same year. In keeping with the economic downturn the constituency in election 2011 again swung to the left with two seats for Labour and one for Sinn Féin. Brian Hayes retained his seat for Fine Gael. Because the skills base within the constituency is more likely to be in the semi-skilled to unskilled range it becomes much more volatile and vulnerable when recession kicks in.

Election 2011 was a quite different election to any other I have fought in the constituency. In 1997 I fought a classic 'challenger' type campaign. I had been nominated over a year in advance by party headquarters, with Bertie Ahern determined that new candidates should get training, mentoring support and an opportunity to get out and about well before the campaigning started. I covered a lot of doors before the election, got stuck in on local issues and began to get coverage in the local media. Because I was new and not a public representative, having never served on the council, I could be more independent and critical. The result was a populist campaign, fought on the ground, with significant national media coverage, and a level of support that saw me scraping in to the then five-seat constituency which incorporated Tallaght and South Clondalkin. 2002 was a more nervous affair because I was now under pressure to deliver two seats for party headquarters, not made any the easier by Chris Flood's premature departure from the ticket through ill health. A vote management operation was imposed by headquarters which resulted in Charlie O'Connor and I being within 100 votes of each other and retaining our two seats. 2007 was the easiest election of all with it proving impossible for the opposition to disturb our two seats. In effect a high-spending and tax-cutting government was impossible to beat when combined with Bertie Ahern's obvious appeal in terms of popularity. The public clearly opted to ignore the difficulties that Bertie was experiencing with regard to his personal finances at the Tribunal at Dublin Castle. In fact in my own constituency there was strong support for him in his tribulations. Despite the popular lore, the Fianna Fáil campaign was not rescued midway through the campaign and it was fairly obvious from early on that the opposition were not at the races.

Election 2011 was fought, fairly exclusively, on the national issues. Unlike other or previous campaigns I have fought in Dublin South-West there were no local issues, distinct to the area, that became an issue during the campaign. The difficulties at Tallaght Hospital that featured heavily in both 2007 and 2002 got a mention but not in a way that was shifting votes one way or the other. The fact that both Fine Gael and Labour were promising to review the decision to give the Mater Hospital the privilege of being the site for the new, national, children's hospital, while not critical, probably did help both of those parties on the ground when it came to getting their message out. The two Fianna Fáil representatives in the contest were, in effect, forced onto the defensive over a decision that was not of their own making and was of benefit, in electoral terms, only to TDs standing on the northside of the city. The Tallaght Hospital Action Group have created a lot of noise over the years and none of it has ever been of any benefit to the Fianna Fáil TDs in the constituency. Clearly with such a large presence of young parents in the constituency the campaign on the hospital issue did cause damage. It probably hardened up left-wing votes in the constituency that otherwise might have opted for Fianna Fáil or Fine Gael.

On the doorsteps there was predictable hostility towards the government parties with Fianna Fáil getting the bulk of the blame for the downturn. The outright hostility to both Fianna Fáil and the Greens had been well flagged in advance in public opinion polls. From a Fianna Fáil perspective the combination of the bank guarantee, the IMF/ECB intervention in our economy, and the dramatic scenes of Dáil chaos as Brian Cowen tried to force through his cabinet appointments had well and truly put paid to any chance of there being just modest losses on the party's part. Most incumbent Fianna Fáil deputies were well conditioned to the concept that a wipe-out was on its way. The only hope of avoiding one was if the government had managed to remain in power up until 2012, which became an impossibility before Christmas 2010 as result of Green Party nervousness and the smaller party's inability to withstand further criticism from both the media and their own grassroots.

In my own case I had signalled in a radio interview some 18 months before the election that I believed, on the basis of our then national opinion poll rating, that there was a distinct possibility that Fianna Fáil could lose both of its seats in the constituency. When I informed party headquarters of this possibility the response was somewhat incredulous. They and many other commentators believed that I was exaggerating. It is fair to say that before the entry of the IMF, pretty much everyone within the party was clinging to the notion that the opinion polls were inaccurate and did not take into consideration the strength of the Fianna Fáil core vote. This was the rock of complacency on which the party perished. In effect the party struggled to absorb and properly analyse the impending wipe-out, which in my view, was very evident well before the IMF made its well-publicised entry into the country. There was a pressing need for a change of leadership before the election and indeed prior to Christmas 2010. However, few of the party's deputies had the stomach for such a fight and were all the more reluctant to do so given that there was no clear alternative candidate to Brian Cowen at cabinet level who was prepared to step out in order to take the leadership on. In the event Micheál Martin, by force of circumstances, did do so at a very late stage and clearly benefited from the fact that he had taken the initiative on the Cowen issue by beating Brian Lenihan into third place.

On the doorsteps, in the first week, it was obvious that voters were positive towards me on a personal basis, in particular because of the very high-profile stand that I took on the leadership issue. However the personal regard and well wishes were somewhat eerie in that they never came accompanied by an assertion of actual voting support. In effect, in the early days of the campaign voters were being polite but by implication marking out the ground. There was no sympathy for the government and no getting away from the assertion, by so many, that it had been Fianna Fáil's fault that the downturn had occurred. There was no way of sweetening the bitter pill of cutbacks, political pensions, payoffs to bankers, and the imposition of punitive income levies. For most voters Fianna Fáil had been in power too long and had fallen asleep at the wheel. There was a somewhat simplistic belief that an alternative would, by definition, be better and in some way would deliver slightly different medicine to the hardship message that Fianna Fáil had felt obliged to deliver. It may take a long time for Fianna Fáil to recover from this defeat, not least because the public themselves are only coming to terms, perhaps now, about how dire the situation facing the country actually is.

Tip O'Neill is famously quoted as stating that 'all politics is local'. In Ireland's case this is even more so the case: parochial and local issues play a significant part in the life of a TD or public representative. Our system of proportional representation means, in effect, when you belong to a large party, as Fianna Fáil was before election 2011, then the most serious threat to your security and continuance in Leinster House is coming less from the opposition and much more from your own running mate. In Dublin South-West my initial running mate was Chris Flood, at one point a junior minister, and he was subsequently replaced by his protégé Charlie O'Connor, a candidate with a long track record of service at local authority level. In effect Charlie O'Connor's vote was quite complementary to my own and this was borne out in a TG4 survey back before the election of 2002. His vote was much more pronouncedly local to his own area where he lived (Springfield in Tallaght) and geographically preponderant in the central to western districts of the constituency. My vote, according to the same poll, was more centre to east of the constituency reflecting the fact that my family home was located in Templeogue and I had a higher share of ABC1 voters. The most intense competition between the two candidates was in 2002, O'Connor's first time on a ticket with me, and my first re-election campaign. Tensions ran high but rapidly dissipated after we secured the two Fianna Fáil seats in 2002 and again in 2007.

There was very little tension in the campaign of 2011 and in fact very little contact at all between both of our campaigns. The sheer ferocity of the challenge facing Fianna Fáil meant we both effectively did our own thing. Charlie and I met on only one or two occasions during the campaign and generally at public meetings. Both of us had allowed an RTÉ documentary maker to follow us around for the duration of the campaign. The documentary, entitled 'Dogfight', depicted both of our efforts to get elected. Because of the editing needs of the documentary it tended to magnify both the hostility we met on the doorsteps and the element of tension between the two Fianna Fáil candidates. I was fairly candid about the competitive nature of things between Charlie O'Connor and myself. There was little room for negative campaigning by either of us given that we both knew that if we were to win one seat in the constituency the transfers of the other candidate would be vital if we were to scrape through with one. The actual tension between us is less than it is with our supporters and over the years both of us have acted, on occasion, to calm down the ardour of our activist antagonists. My activist base has its roots in the old Seán Walsh machine, while Charlie has an activist base in the Chris Flood machine which for many years had perceived themselves to have been downtrodden by the more dominant Seán Walsh faction. In my experience the kind of tension, evident in other constituencies within Fianna Fáil, has not been as bad in Dublin South-West as elsewhere. The three-in-a-row victories stretching from 1997 meant success rendered it unnecessary. I also believe that the general decline in the level of political activism, from its height in the 1980s, meant there was less room for the 'daggers drawn' contests so beloved of the Fianna Fáil party under Charles J. Haughey. Bertie Ahern's big achievement, internally within the party, was the introduction of a semblance of peace within the party and much less of the faction fighting that had become so much the norm in the aftermath of the Arms Trial of 1970.

Unlike many others, who are dismal about Fianna Fáil's future prospects, I believe the party has a future. However it will have to reinvest in its activist base, in particular the younger element, and open up the nomination process to full competition by allowing each and every member a vote in the convention contests. John Bruton initiated this reform within Fine Gael and it is the one reform to which one can attribute some of Enda Kenny's subsequent success. The party will also have to give a much sharper edge to its views on the economy and shake off the lethargy and complacency induced by years of devotion to the partnership process. It will also need to redefine the party's view on social issues in much the same way that David Cameron fashioned the 'big society' view in advance of his success in the UK. Any similar exercise in Ireland, by Fianna Fáil, would have to stress the importance and primacy of the private sector as engine of recovery and driver of economic growth.

Mary Lou McDonald (Sinn Féin, Dublin Central)

Mary Lou McDonald is vice-president of Sinn Féin and was fighting her third Dáil election campaign, having been unsuccessful in 2002 and 2007. In 2004 she was elected as an MEP for the Dublin constituency, and had a high profile in 2008 as the leader of Sinn Féin's campaign against the Lisbon Treaty, though she lost her European Parliament seat in 2009. Before becoming a full-time public representative she was a consultant for the Irish Productivity Centre. In 2011 she and Sandra McLellan (Cork East) became Sinn Féin's first female TDs since 1927.

The 2011 general election campaign was markedly different from that of 2007, when I first contested the constituency of Dublin Central. The economic collapse and the bursting of the Celtic Tiger bubble radically reshaped the political mood across the state and in the constituency. The fall from grace of former Taoiseach Bertie Ahern and Fianna Fáil redefined the state-wide and local political contest.

Although the 2007 election campaign had been a difficult one for Sinn Féin and for me personally, I had it in mind to take another run in the constituency and that opportunity presented itself in 2011. I had remained active on the ground in the constituency, particularly from 2009 onwards after the electorate relieved me of my duties as an MEP.

Almost two years of quiet, hard graft re-organising the Sinn Féin constituency organisation and establishing an election team culminated in the selection convention in November 2010. The local organisation supported my nomination and I was selected as the Sinn Féin candidate. Gerry Adams spoke at the convention and got the ball rolling for the campaign with a message of 'every vote will count. Remember Fermanagh–South Tyrone' – a reference to Michelle Gildernew's knife-edge victory in the Westminster elections.

The instability of the government, its narrow majority and the arrival of the EU/IMF made the political atmosphere volatile and the election campaign a very long one. From Christmas onwards activists were on 'red alert'. The Sinn Féin constituency office in Cabra was busier than ever and we opened a second election office in Ballybough. I was struck by the numbers of people, women in particular, who came forward to offer their help in the campaign. We consciously organised activities to suit people's availability, particularly women with young children. The maxim of Bobby Sands that everyone has their part to play became the credo of the campaign team. It worked, we built up what is described in political parlance as a formidable 'machine'.

From the outset local activists believed that we could take a seat in Dublin Central. They based their view on the 'political vibes' on the ground and the fact that a big political space had opened up with Bertie Ahern's exit from politics. I was, initially at least, more apprehensive. Once bitten twice shy, I was very aware that a seat in this very competitive constituency was a big ask. Fianna Fáil was down but not out, the Labour Party and Fine Gael surged ahead in Dublin according to opinion polls, and the Tony Gregory tradition was alive and well.

The election directorate began meeting weekly from November onwards and a detailed programme of work was drawn up. Dublin Central is a mixed but predominantly working-class constituency. Voter turnout is a challenge in every election. It was understood from the start that translating support into votes would be a decisive factor for us. We had to convince voters from the housing estates and flat complexes across the area that it was worthwhile to come out on the day.

Door-to-door canvassing was the major element of the campaign. There is no substitute for direct, one to one conversation on the doors. People wanted to talk – a lot. Not surprisingly local issues featured strongly but it was the focus on the 'big picture' – the economy, the cutbacks and the future of the country – that marked this election out as different. Discussions with disillusioned voters and non-voters were at times frustrating or demoralising but always interesting. One of the big management issues for the campaign was ensuring that the canvass moved along at a reasonable pace.

It is my long-held view that the lifespan of any political leaflet is short – from letterbox to bin. My election team held a very different view and we distributed thousands of pieces of literature over the course of the campaign. We blitzed housing estates, flat complexes, shopping centres, churches with copies of state-wide manifestos, local manifestos, profiles of the candidate, reasons to vote for Sinn Féin, reasons to vote at all.

A number of local community groups organised election hustings and for the most part they were well attended. The overwhelming public anger with the collapse of the economy, the frustration with the bailout for the bankers/cutbacks for the people approach of the Fianna Fáil–Green government, echoed loud and clear at each meeting. Fianna Fáil would be punished, that was clear. Who the beneficiaries would be in Dublin Central was not as clear cut.

Unlike 2007 I was not viewed as a sure bet. It was only as the election drew close and a Sinn Féin 'bounce' materialised in the opinion polls, that my name featured in any media commentary as a possible gain for the party. That was a good thing. There is nothing worse than being 'safe' in any election. I knew that the Sinn Féin position of opposition to the consensus for cutbacks had stuck a chord on the ground. The Sinn Féin articulation of dealing with the private bank debt (inelegantly expressed as 'burning the bondholders') was well received. As many people were looking for an alternative, Sinn Féin support strengthened – not dramatically but sufficiently to put candidates across the state into contention for seats.

One week out from polling day I told activist meetings that I thought we would win a seat. One last push, keep the concentration and energy levels, we're nearly there. The activists were buoyed up and they gave it everything. I spent the day of the election doing all the predictable things, visiting the polling stations and knocking some doors. Every vote would count. I have become allergic to the song 'Hello Mary Lou', it has been with me from birth and looks like haunting me to the grave. My sensitivities cut no ice with the election team. The song filled the Cabra air and echoed throughout the North Inner City. A group of women jived to it on Sheriff Street, proof positive according to one activist that the song was a vote-getter. I sincerely doubt it.

It was lunchtime before I got a phone call from the count. I kept away from the RDS until tea time. Candidates can be a distraction and even a pain in the neck when number crunchers and anoraks are doing the maths and reading the political tea leaves. My director of elections called the final result with remarkable accuracy. The lunchtime phone call was to tell me that we were going to win. That was still his view at tea time.

I had come in third on first preference votes but had to wait until the final count to get elected.

I was declared elected as a TD for Dublin Central surrounded by many of the people who had worked very hard, over a very long period of time, to make it happen. Nicky Kehoe, a friend and former Sinn Féin councillor, stepped forward and held my hand high. We made it – at last!!

Richard Boyd Barrett (United Left Alliance, Dun Laoghaire)

Richard Boyd Barrett came close to election in 2007 as a candidate for the People Before Profit Alliance. In 2009 he was elected to Dun Laoghaire–Rathdown County Council with over 4,000 first preferences, and in 2011 he became one of five United Left Alliance TDs elected to the Dáil. Before becoming a full-time public representative he worked as a teacher.

At the outset of our campaign, we understood that we had a very good chance of winning a seat for the People Before Profit Alliance (PBPA) in Dun Laoghaire. We had come very close in the previous general election of 2007 – narrowly missing out on the last seat on transfers – having initially received the fifth highest first preference vote in a five-seat constituency.

The subsequent local elections in 2009 confirmed our chances of winning a Dáil seat in Dun Laoghaire, when I topped the poll with almost double the quota in the Dun Laoghaire ward and my fellow PBPA candidate Hugh Lewis took a seat in the neighbouring Ballybrack ward, which was also part of the Dun Laoghaire constituency for the purposes of the general election.

We knew also that dramatic developments in the economic and political situation in the country, in terms of the onset of the banking and the economic crisis, were certain to translate into a massive decline in support for Fianna Fáil. Given the widely held understanding that this crisis had resulted from Fianna Fáil policies that had favoured the profits of developers, bankers and the super-wealthy, we were also confident that our brand of left-wing politics had been strongly vindicated and that this was likely to result in increased electoral support. Our strong record in local campaigning against privatisation, bin charges and for local amenities and housing, along with my own profile and association with some wider national campaigns against the bank bail-out were also likely to assist our campaign.

However, while we had all these factors going in our favour, we also knew that winning was far from a forgone conclusion.

The redrawing of the boundaries of the Dun Laoghaire constituency had seen it reduced from a five- to a four-seater. Added to that, we had extremely stiff competition in terms of rival candidates: two Fianna Fáil ministers, Mary Hanafin and Barry Andrews; a Green Party junior minister, Ciaran Cuffe; the leader of a resurgent Labour Party, Éamon Gilmore; and the racing certainty of at least one Fine Gael seat with Seán Barrett. The addition of a high-profile second Labour candidate, Ivana Bacik, further added to the tightness of the field.

So, while we knew we had a real chance of winning, we also understood that a small party taking a seat in this field would be a very considerable challenge.

My selection as candidate was a straightforward matter, as I had run previously and come so close in the general election, and had then gone on to win the council seat by such a wide margin. The formal nomination took place a few months before the election and was approved unanimously by a general meeting of the Dun Laoghaire PBPA branch.

Our campaign strategy was, in the first instance, *political* rather than logistical. For us the practicalities of the campaign had to flow from a political assessment of the crisis and issues facing the country, and how they were impacting on popular consciousness. We were convinced that the severity of the economic crisis and the desperate thirst for solutions had opened up popular consciousness to bigger political and economic questions in an unprecedented way. This was, we believed, in contrast to previous elections, where local issues often predominated.

We decided, therefore, that our election material – leaflets, newsletters and arguments on the door – had to lead with the big political picture, addressing the reasons for the economic crisis and a concrete programme of alternative polices that addressed it. In this regard, we also felt a critique of the failings of the government was not enough, although it was important; we also needed to spell out in easily understandable form an alternative set of concrete policies.

Secondly, we also believed that to fully define ourselves and distinguish ourselves, we needed to emphasise the fact that we were a political force based on deeds, not just words and promises. We were acutely aware that people were fed up with politicians that said what you wanted to hear but then behaved very differently in practice and implemented very different policies from those they promised. Indeed, this sense was one of the main motives behind the entry into political activity of most of the PBPA activists and behind the establishment of the PBPA itself.

For this reason, we put a strong emphasis on our record as grassroots campaigners on issues during *non-election periods* and as people who mobilised from the bottom through protests, mass meetings and *'People Power'* rather than simply statements and submissions as was common with mainstream political parties.

This emphasis was not simply a political device but reflected our actual practice over many years – whether we won or lost elections – and constituents in Dun Laoghaire were well aware of this. Indeed, a very common refrain among a significant layer of people in Dun Laoghaire, went along the lines: *'We don't agree with everything you stand for but we know you are honest, committed, hard-working and you are always there – we only see the others at election time.'*

Having said that, we put the lead political emphasis on the big questions facing the country – the banking crisis, jobs, public services, health and education, etc. We also very consciously rejected a view which separated or opposed the national issues from the local. We believed that the local issues and problems of particular services or amenities or housing were directly connected to the bigger questions of neo-liberal economic doctrine, privatisation and deregulation, and we sought to establish the connection between the national and the local in our election material.

For example, our campaign to stop the closure of Dun Laoghaire baths was not simply a parochial campaign but was linked to our record of opposing purely profit-driven developers' agenda, Public–Private Partnerships (PPPs) and the neo-liberal economic agenda generally, that had so demonstrably crashed the wider economy.

Similarly, our campaigns for more social housing, or against particular private residential developments or the privatisation of certain services, always highlighted the connection to our wider critique of a 'for profit' economic model which had now fallen flat on its face.

So our election material and arguments during the election emphasised how our local campaigning fitted in with that wider critique of a political and economic model that had failed and needed to be replaced, and that we could be trusted because we had shown in practice over many years – even when we were swimming against the tide – that we were genuinely committed to a different type of politics and society.

An important aspect of this approach was that we continued with our campaigning activities on particular issues during the election period even when it disrupted more straightforward election canvassing. We continued to organise protests and meetings on particular issues even though this put us under a lot of pressure in terms of the more conventional promotion of the candidate and vote-hunting, which all the rest of the candidates were engaged in. So for example, in the midst of the campaign we held protests and public meetings about recent cuts in bus services. However, this approach ultimately paid off electorally, as it convinced people that we were serious about the issues and not just self-promotion.

In terms of the more conventional election campaigning activity, we were very systematic in terms of mapping out the constituency for leafleting runs, door to door canvassing and postering. Roughly speaking, we divided and prioritised the constituency into three types of area:

1. Our strong areas, where we had a long history of campaigning and were well known to the people.
2. Other areas where we were not so well known but where we felt the profile of the constituents, in terms of being young, working class or likely to be sympathetic to campaigns we had been involved in, was likely to favour us.
3. Areas that were traditionally Fianna Fáil or Fine Gael and less likely to be favourable towards us.

We planned to canvass the first and second groups as a priority and to do them at least twice but only to mass leaflet the third type of area and, if time allowed, canvass those areas once.

We held regular large meetings for activists and supporters where everybody had a chance to input into the election campaign plan. These large meetings began several months before the actual election and became a critical organising centre for a campaign that built up steadily in its intensity as the election campaign proper (i.e., from the official date when the election was called) approached.

In addition to activists and supporters meetings, we also put a lot of focus on a couple of large publicly advertised meetings, which were addressed by both myself and other candidates from the recently formed United Left Alliance (ULA), which we had helped establish along with Joe Higgins's Socialist Party and Séamus Healy's South Tipperary Workers and Unemployed Action Group (WUAG). These public rallies were very successful, seeing attendances of over 200 people – including many new faces, who subsequently joined the canvassing and campaign team.

The establishment of the ULA was an important development in terms of the campaign as it allowed us to answer the question many people considering voting for us were asking – namely whether a small alliance could have any impact on the bigger national stage and the big economic questions facing the country as a whole. The sense that we were part of a wider national alliance that was seriously challenging for a number of seats across the country convinced many people, who wanted to vote for us but who weren't sure there was much point, that a vote for us would not be wasted.

Much of our press work was also organised centrally through the ULA, focusing on the bigger national issues, particularly the key economic issues such as the banking crisis, the IMF/EU deal and the austerity measures that flowed from those things. Again, this approach helped us get considerable national media coverage and convinced those considering voting for us that we were mounting a political challenge at the national and not just the local level.

Another very important aspect of our campaign was the approach we took to fundraising. For us fundraising was not just an end in itself but organising big fundraising events – gigs, social nights, etc. – was a way of pulling wider layers of people, who might not normally come to political events, into the campaign. We organised three major fundraisers over the course of the three-week campaign – with almost 300 people attending the biggest of those, when we held a concert at which local musicians who supported us performed.

Another key aspect of our campaign that was significant in terms of our ultimate victory was a focus on street canvassing at key hubs (shopping centres, village centres, post offices etc). While other parties did this occasionally, we did this on an almost constant basis throughout the day, often at several locations simultaneously. Our view was that daytime door-to-door canvassing was far less effective than being on the street, as you tended to get a lot fewer people in during the daytime. Having a very strong visual and street presence at multiple locations also strongly conveyed the sense to people that we were 'everywhere'. It gave a real sense of momentum and strength to our campaign.

New technology also played some role. We had a growing text and email list which we used throughout the campaign to notify members and supporters of the canvassing rota, assembly points and activists' meetings. This list grew substantially during the course of the campaign with people signing up to it at the various meetings, protests, rallies and fundraisers. Facebook similarly played an important role for advertising our various events and getting out statements and comments on issues that arose. We also put up a number of YouTube videos with the candidate speaking about key areas of policy, which received a reasonably high hit rate.

However, if there was one key factor that helped secure our ultimate victory it was people power. For a smaller party, we had one of the biggest election teams, if not the biggest team of all the parties and candidates in the field. These activists were not just foot soldiers but people who had come into our organisation or campaign through previous involvement in 'on the ground' campaigns on various issues that we had spearheaded. We had bus campaigners, Save Our Seafront campaigners, anti-war activists, students who had campaigned against student fees and many others who had campaigned on a variety of other issues local, national and international. Our campaign team tended to be younger than our rivals (though not exclusively young – we had pensioners too!), and almost of all our campaigners were people who had a fairly high level of politics and were capable of taking on questions and arguments, in what was the most politicised election in recent years. In contrast to previous (pre-recession) elections, factors such as the amount of money available to a party I think played less of a role. In this election politics and the big economic questions were pre-eminent. In this regard, a campaign team such as ours, which was highly politicised – through regular attendance at meetings where politics were discussed at a high level – and who had practical experience of campaigning on concrete issues was critical. This highly politicised character to the election favoured us significantly and made it by far the most enjoyable election campaign I had ever been involved in.

Paul Gogarty (Green, Dublin Mid-West)

Paul Gogarty was first elected to South Dublin County Council in 1999 and to the Dáil in 2002. Between 2007 and 2011 he was chair of the Oireachtas Committee on Education and Science. He was one of the most prolific tweeters in the 30th Dáil, and early on the morning of 26 February he became the first TD to concede the loss of his seat by means of a tweet.

During the 2002 general election campaign a number of my canvassers were outside a church in Lucan when they were approached by members of another small party to see how the campaign was going. 'How do you think ye'll do?', they asked. 'I think he's going to get elected', was the reply. According to eye-witnesses, the opposing team gave our canvassers a look of incredulity that wondered how we could be so naive as to think that a Green Party candidate in a three-seat constituency had even a whiff of a chance.

But we knew we had more than just a whiff of a chance. If anything, the votes were already in the bag before the election, based on strong work on the ground in the areas where I had a council seat. Canvassing during the election was an outright effort to stem the inevitable haemorrhaging of votes to rival parties with far better funding and much bigger teams of canvassers.

If we were quietly confident in 2002, the mood in 2011 amongst the team was cautiously pessimistic. There was always the hope against hope that personal work rate and track record would count for something when the voters filled in their ballot papers. While some members of my team urged positivity, I preferred to take a realistic approach and refused to play up my chances. We were gearing up for a hiding and there was no point in pretending otherwise. This was not to say we didn't fight our corner.

Everything had been organised to run as smoothly as possible. Candidate selection had taken place 15 months previously, giving plenty of time to prepare for a possible snap election. From a local organisational point of view, we did as much engaging and promotional work as was practically possible in the 12 months prior to the election being called. We always envisaged that we would be outgunned yet again during a three-week campaign and were hoping that keeping a high profile, visibility on the ground and sheer relentless slogging would keep me in with a fighting chance until the election was called. It had worked in 2002 and in 2007, why not again?

But this was an election campaign like no other. In the end my firm conclusion is that you could have put Mother Teresa up as a Green Party candidate and she would not have been elected in Dublin Mid-West. And I was certainly no Mother Teresa.

As soon as the election was called, we sprang into action. Posters were up within a couple of days. Volunteers were organised via web texts. This time around my campaign was handicapped by the lack of availability of a Director of Elections. There was no one living in the constituency who was available on a near-permanent basis to overview the campaign. However, I did have a very dedicated campaign manager, a former Lucan resident, who commuted from north county Dublin on a near-daily basis. I also had four or five other members of the team who were able to divide up the organisational work.

The canvassing team itself was smaller too. People had either died, moved away or were tied up with parenting duties. More recent recruits were thin on the ground. We had a small but dedicated bunch, occasionally reinforced by volunteers who travelled up from places as far afield as Donegal and Limerick.

The expectation was that, similar to 2007, we would only have enough person power to cover my strong areas of Lucan and Palmerstown. In 2007 we were unable to muster enough people to cover any of Clondalkin, something regrettable but which we were used to. The Clondalkin vote in 2002 and 2007 hovered around the four per cent mark, but in Lucan it was over 20 per cent, meaning that if only certain doors could be knocked on, they had to be in my strong area.

The campaign differed somewhat from 2007 in that we were more likely to have people out canvassing during the day rather than at night-time. This reflected the economic situation, where people were either unemployed, part time or flexible, or self-employed. In fact there were several nights where canvassing was abandoned due to lack of personnel, but there were always enough during the day, the exact opposite of what had happened four years previously.

The absence of canvassers was not down to people being afraid to canvass or having left the party, although we did have some of these. It was more related to commitments people had and the times they had them. The Green Party is not noted for having a high conversion rate of members to canvassers even during the best of times and so I knew, as ever, that I would be relying on a core group of members, family and friends to do 90 per cent of the heavy lifting.

A side effect of having to canvass throughout the day was the inability to cover shopping centres to any degree. Schools in the Lucan/Palmerstown area were covered, with specific leaflets on education issues, where I had a good track record, but shopping centres were left out. In hindsight, this would not have made any difference, except that it would have saved us from negative encounters. We also did a number of churches, a practice which I would rather avoid for honourable reasons were it not for the fact that most of your rivals are doing the same. Again I have never seen much benefit in hanging around outside a church. The best reaction I ever got was standing outside a church the week *after* I got elected.

I did attend a number of debates at constituency and national level which, while worthwhile in themselves, would not have gained me any votes and just resulted in my meeting fewer people.

There was no involvement from head office in my campaign. A number of head office staff came out at weekends to assist, but I generally avoided national press conferences as I felt I would be hard pressed to cover the doors and that going into the city centre for a press conference at which I would not be the main speaker would be a waste of time.

On the doors, people were generally polite but their dissatisfaction was clear. There was recognition for work I had done on various issues, but few guarantees of a number one. 'You've done a lot of work, but I'm not voting Green this time', or 'If you were running as an independent I'd give you my number one, but not as a Green Party candidate.'

In a minority of cases, incidents involving me as reported in the media (e.g., the Emmet Stagg Dáil incident) were thrown in my face with palpable venom. In 2011 I had a much higher national profile than in previous elections. Under normal circumstances this might be perceived as an advantage. But in the cauldron of negativity, it just helped to place you as a target.

Any positive contribution I did make, such as in the field of reversing education cutbacks, tended to be ignored or not to be known, despite consistent mentioning on leaflets, on the web and on the doors.

Online social media such as Facebook and Twitter had absolutely no impact on the campaign itself. Twitter served as a means for negative commentary to reach me directly and also acted as a welcome but unwise personal diversion from what was a fraught campaign.

Having kept track of how many people I personally met during the campaign, I estimate that I engaged with no more than 200 people face to face. That is a shockingly low amount, but is largely down to the large amount of time spent discussing and explaining issues on the doors. A subjective guesstimate suggests that approximately 40 per cent of those I spent time explaining and discussing things with ended up changing their minds and voting Gogarty No. 1. However it required at least 20 minutes in virtually all cases to achieve the desired result.

Looking back it is clear that the loss of my seat was inevitable and had been for at least two years. Green Party poll numbers had held up in government with Fianna Fáil for the first year of office. However, after the banking crisis and the harsh decisions that the government felt it had to make, numbers began to fall. We had expected a backlash, particularly after each budget. We did not estimate the extent of the backlash and anger, feeling that our belief that we were doing the right thing for the right reasons would suffice, along with our local reputations. How wrong we were.

The loss of my seat was overwhelmingly down to national factors, although I admit that mistakes I personally made over the previous two years would not have helped. In normal circumstances, hard work and face to face contact would reap its own rewards. This time it meant nothing as the narrative was that we had propped up a corrupt Fianna

Fáil government and had not stood up for the people. The truth did not matter in this case, just the perception.

What election 2011 means for future elections, I do not know. Clearly the factors that led people to vote Fianna Fáil for so many years have diminished. This was a national election on national issues and I believe that some candidates won votes that had very little to do with their own personal attributes. Will politics be back to normal next time? Will people vote for people they know work hard and with whom they have been in contact, or will they weigh up the national positions?

It is hard to say. But the new government will face some of the challenges the outgoing one faced, and so will its candidates in the next election. The next campaign is likely to again be focused on national issues rather than local ones. The Green Party faces a challenge in convincing the electorate that the national and international issues it is concerned about bear a real and immediate relevance to their lives. It may take most of us more than one election to make a comeback.

Averil Power (Fianna Fáil, Seanad election candidate)

Averil Power contested the general election for the first time in 2011. She came fourth on the first count in the three-seat Dublin North-East constituency, only 238 votes (0.6 per cent) behind the third-placed candidate, but ultimately failed to win a seat. She had been appointed frontbench spokesperson on political reform by the new leader Micheál Martin at the end of January 2011 even though she did not then hold an elected position. Since 2004 she had worked as policy advisor to Minister Mary Hanafin in a number of government departments. In the Seanad election she stood on the Industrial and Commercial panel and beat 33 other candidates to win the second of nine seats.

'If you think the general election was tough, you ain't seen nothing yet!' – words of wisdom from a hardened campaigner to this Seanad novice before I started out.

'No way!', I thought. My campaign team and I had canvassed 14 hours a day in the February 2011 general election in not only the worst political environment in Fianna Fáil's 85-year history, but also miserably cold and wet weather. A campaign to win a Seanad seat would have to be a walk in the park compared to that.

With my list of voters and their addresses in hand, I set off on a national tour of the homes of hundreds of county councillors.[6] I had a month to meet as many of them as possible and convince them that I was worthy of their No. 1 vote.

Two weeks later, I knew exactly what my friend meant about how gruelling the campaign could be. I'd already clocked up nearly 4,000 miles on a car that normally does less than 100 in a week. I had visited 11 counties, staying in a different place every night. I had drunk endless cups of tea and eaten a year's supply of sandwiches, cakes and buns. And not only had I met about 130 councillors, I'd also met many of their neighbours after getting lost and calling to the wrong house at the end of the wrong boreen!

I was starting to see why the vocational panel election has been termed the 'Discover Ireland' route to the Seanad.

I was only halfway through the campaign and already I was emotionally and physically exhausted.

To make matters worse, I had no real idea of how I was getting on. I'd been warned at the outset that commitments like 'I'll look after you', 'Sure you'll be up there anyway' or 'I'll definitely give you a vote' (e.g., not a 1, a 2 or even a 5!) could probably be written off as losses. 'The only fella you can really believe is the one who's willing to tell other people that he's giving you the No. 1', I had been told. In that case, I reckoned I only had about ten votes so far.

The internal competition between the Fianna Fáil candidates was intense. With approximately 260 Fianna Fáil councillors, TDs and Senators eligible to vote, the party was expected to win between 10 and 12 Seanad seats. The real question was which candidates would be successful. And with 32 Fianna Fáil candidates running, most were destined to end up disappointed on polling day.

Set against the backdrop of a disastrous performance in the general election, emotions and tensions were running high. Three-quarters of our outgoing TDs had just lost their seats. We had won only one out of 47 seats in Dublin. Twenty-five constituencies now had no Fianna Fáil TD, and our parliamentary party didn't include a single woman.

Within a few days of the general election, Fianna Fáil leader Micheál Martin had announced that he would be taking a hands-on approach to the Seanad election with the hope of getting women and younger people elected to the Upper House. He then commenced a round of meetings with Fianna Fáil councillors to convince them to support a 'preferred list' of Seanad candidates.

Of the 32 Fianna Fáil candidates on the ballot paper, ten – including myself – were on the leader's list. Two weeks into the campaign it was fair to say that the list was receiving a mixed reaction amongst the councillors.

Some voters were strongly in favour of Micheál's plan and were determined to back his strategy to rebuild the party. Others were vehemently opposed to it, either because they rejected the idea of a list outright or because their preferred candidate wasn't on it.

While fortunate to have been included on the list, I was very conscious that there were plenty of other people who deserved a place on it as much as I did. And I knew that I was going to have to very work hard to prove to the councillors that I deserved their support.

I had also been warned at the outset that, list or no list, I was up against it.

I had been elected to a range of positions in the party over the previous ten years, including Chairperson of the Trinity College Cumann, member of the National Youth Committee and secretary of the Dublin North-East constituency organisation. I had worked as a policy advisor in three government departments and helped to run national campaigns. I had also been knocking on doors in Dublin North-East five times a week for the previous three years in a bid to win a Dáil seat.

But I hadn't been a well-known figure nationally prior to the general election. And so, the word was that people who didn't know anything about my background were apparently being encouraged to believe that I was being promoted by the leader without having done the hard graft.

One rival was also reported to be trying to make an issue out of my husband's job as a political journalist, referring to me on the hustings as 'Mrs Sheahan'. I have to admit that I found this line of attack particularly cheap. Anyone who knows either of us is aware that we have always kept our personal and professional lives 100 per cent separate. And in this day and age, the notion of judging a woman not by her own work record or commitment, but rather by what her husband does for a living, is pretty outmoded.

As I made my way around the country, I tried to make as strong a case as I could for myself. I had contested a tough general election, when others had chosen not to run, and polled a close fourth on the first count in a three-seat constituency. I am involved in a wide range of community activities and genuinely want to serve the people of Dublin North-East to the best of my ability. I also have a real interest in national issues, particularly education, and am keen to make a strong legislative contribution in the upper house.

I hoped that our Seanad electorate could see that I had both the track record and the future potential to merit their support. As the weeks progressed, word started to come back that I was gaining ground. As one TD reported back to me, after I had met the councillors in his constituency, 'Once they saw that you didn't have horns growing out of your head, they actually really liked you!' To be fair to our councillors, I found them generally to be a very discerning bunch who make up their own minds rather than falling for false images put out by others.

The campaign itself was a real eye-opener. While visiting voters in their own homes in some of the most remote parts of the country, you get a real feel for them and the communities they represent. Over ten cups of tea a day, I also learned more in one month about our party organisation across the country than I had in the previous decade.

Having survived tough local elections in 2004 and 2009 (the number of Fianna Fáil councillors had halved during that period), the quality of our remaining councillors is impressive. I found it reassuring to see that while Fianna Fáil now has many constituencies with no TD, we still have over 200 councillors working hard in communities all over the country.

What surprised me, perhaps naively, was that although I had grown up in an urban council estate and come from a non-political family, I had a lot more in common with rural councillors than I thought. As I chatted with people in all corners of the country about Ireland's future and the type of policies that I felt our party should advance, I felt a real sense of common purpose and shared commitment.

Apart from Fianna Fáil councillors, I also called to as many Independents as possible and got more promises of No. 1 votes than I had expected. Of course, as with every election under proportional representation, transfers can make all the difference. So I also canvassed my local Fine Gael county councillor for her 18th preference (after she had voted for all 17 of her party's candidates on my panel).

Wherever I went, people were very obliging. Councillors welcomed me into their homes at all hours or made time to meet me during a busy day on the farm or in the office. Some families, whom I'd never met before, even offered me a bed for the night and a boiled egg in the morning. Between 9 am each morning and 11 pm at night, I met councillors in their homes, in car parks, at GAA clubs, on the sidelines at rugby training and in local cafés. The most memorable rendezvous was when I climbed into the passenger seat of one councillor's truck and he said 'Don't mind the gun.' When I saw the shotgun at my feet, I desperately hoped that none of my answers to his questions would make him angry!

While the travel was tough, one of the hardest parts of the whole campaign was the week between the close of polling and the count for my panel. The die was cast and there was nothing I could do, but my fate was unknown. I tried to distract myself as much as I could. I read books, walked the legs off my dogs Frankie and Charlie, and went kayaking in Dublin Bay. The latter proved to be the most successful distraction as the waves were high and for the three hours that I was focusing on not drowning I really didn't think about the election at all!

Finally, D-day arrived and I headed into Leinster House for the count. As I made the journey from Bayside to Kildare Street, I didn't know what to expect. I felt that the campaign had gone well in the end and was encouraged by the fact that many councillors had been ringing and texting me to wish me luck. But at the same time, I had to be prepared for the worst. In the end, I beat 33 other candidates to take the second seat overall on the panel and the first seat for Fianna Fáil. Having felt the bitter taste of disappointment in other campaigns, hearing the words 'Having reached the quota, Averil Power is deemed to be elected' was an incredible moment not just for me, but for my team who have worked so hard for me over the past few years.

Overall, Fianna Fáil performed much better than expected across the board, having attracted a significant number of Independent votes. We won 14 of the 43 panel seats, compared with 18 for Fine Gael, eight for Labour and three for Sinn Féin, ensuring that we are by far the largest opposition grouping in the Seanad. Half of the candidates on Micheál Martin's list were elected and we ended up with a good mix of people, with more experienced Senators there to show novices like myself the ropes.

Notes

1. A sweeper is a candidate who is added to a party ticket mainly in the hope that they will bring in additional votes that, upon their elimination, will be transferred to one of the party's stronger candidates, but who is not expected to be a serious challenger for a seat themselves.
2. The Irish-language radio and television stations respectively.
3. The mná na tí is the woman of the house; specifically, in this context, of the houses in which students from across Ireland stay while visiting the Connemara Gaeltacht in order to improve their Irish.
4. In 2007 Martin Cullen was Minister for Transport and headed the poll in the Waterford constituency with over 11,000 first preferences. He resigned his seat in March 2010 for health reasons and did not stand in 2011.
5. This can be found on the internet at www.rte.ie/radio1/doconone/radio-documentary-conor-lenihan-charlie-oconnor-irish-general-election-2011.html, accessed 21 June 2011.
6. For an overview of the Seanad election system, see pp. 247–50 below.

7

Ireland's Earthquake Election: Analysis of the Results

Michael Gallagher

The corresponding chapter in the 2007 book in this series described the election as 'the earthquake that never happened'. Change in 2011, in contrast, was truly seismic. Fianna Fáil suffered a negative tsunami of votes that has few parallels among governing parties anywhere, while Fine Gael, Labour and Sinn Féin all achieved record performances. The left as a whole achieved its highest ever level of support. There are strong elements of continuity amidst the upheaval, as we shall see, but by any standards this was an extraordinary election. In the next chapter Michael Marsh and Kevin Cunningham assess the evidence as to why the voters behaved as they did, and in Chapter 13 Peter Mair places the result in a comparative context and considers the implications for the party system. In this chapter we will discuss the results themselves in detail, identifying patterns in party gains and losses, asking why the conversion of votes into seats produced the highest level of disproportionality ever, and discussing the background of the members of the 31st Dáil.

Votes and candidates

More candidates stood than at any previous election – a lot more, in fact. Leaving aside the position of the Ceann Comhairle (Speaker of the Dáil), who is deemed automatically re-elected, an increasingly contentious provision of the constitution, 566 candidates contested the other 165 seats, the previous peak being 484 in 1997. Ballot access is not especially difficult; a candidate must either be nominated by a registered political party, be nominated by 30 registered voters, or lodge a deposit of €500. The rise in the number of candidates was due entirely to an increase in the number of Independents, of whom there had been just over 100 in 2007. While Fianna Fáil responded, probably inadequately, to its anticipated drop in support by reducing its number of candidates from 106 to 75, Fine Gael and Labour increased their numbers by 13 and 18 respectively, while Sinn Féin and the Greens were virtually unchanged.

As Table 7.1 shows, fewer than one in every three was elected, and a plurality of the 566 candidates did not even reach a quarter of the quota, thus failing to qualify for reimbursement of their campaign expenses. Over a third of all candidates won fewer than 1,000 first preferences; 69 per cent of those outside the four main groups suffered this fate. Only one candidate with more than 8,000 first preferences was not elected, and only one candidate with fewer than 4,000 first preferences was elected. In a comparative perspective, the low number of votes required for election is striking, and this plays a significant part in the close links that can exist between TDs and voters. In relation to the Droop quota, the tipping point for success tends to lie between 0.5 and 0.6 of the quota. Candidates whose first preference total lay within this band had a 42 per cent likelihood of election. Only 17 per cent of those whose first preferences amounted to between 0.4 and 0.5 of the quota (and just 2 of the 328 with less than this) were elected, while 86 per cent of those with between 0.6 and 0.7 of the quota (and 102 of the 103 with more than this) were elected.

The Fianna Fáil logo is usually the one that brings most benefit when next to the name of a candidate on the ballot paper, but on this occasion it was Fine Gael whose candidates fared best, with an average of nearly 8,000 first preference votes each. The average Fianna Fáil candidate won fewer votes than candidates of Sinn Féin, never mind Fine Gael and Labour. Only a quarter of Fianna Fáil candidates were elected, compared with almost three-quarters in 2011, which not only testifies to the party's slump in support but also reinforces suggestions that in 2011 it ran far too many candidates.

This is also reflected in the poor performance of ministers, who usually have the highest success rate of all. In 2011 only six cabinet ministers even stood for re-election, eight having resigned before the Dáil was dissolved and a ninth, the Taoiseach, having decided not to stand again. Just three of these six, and only two junior ministers, were re-elected. Remarkably, county councillors had a better election rate than ministers. There were limits to the public's appetite for new faces, though: as usual, the great majority of those with no elective status fared poorly, 72 per cent of them receiving fewer than 1,000 first preferences. Finally, it is worth noting that even though the proportion of female candidates dropped, as discussed in Chapters 3 and 10, for the first time women won on average more votes, and had a slightly higher success rate, than men. When we control for party and for elective status, gender explains little about the vote a candidate received, but at the very least these figures support the argument that parties have nothing to lose by selecting more female candidates in future.

Table 7.1   Fate of candidates at 2011 election

	Number	Average vote	Average Droop quotas	% elected	% not elected but qualifying for reimbursement of expenses	% not qualifying for reimbursement of expenses
All candidates	566	3,923	0.37	29	29	42
Fine Gael	104	7,708	0.71	73	27	0
Labour	68	6,350	0.62	54	46	0
Fianna Fáil	75	5,165	0.48	25	71	4
Sinn Féin	41	5,382	0.51	34	56	10
Green Party	43	954	0.09	0	9	91
United Left Alliance	20	2,971	0.31	25	20	55
Others	215	1,295	0.12	7	9	84
Cabinet minister	6	6,246	0.62	50	50	0
Junior minister	12	5,088	0.47	17	83	0
Non-ministerial TD	108	7,812	0.74	70	27	3
Senator	25	6,910	0.63	56	36	8
MEP	2	8,822	0.87	100	0	0
County councillor	154	4,906	0.52	36	51	13
None of the above	259	1,282	0.12	5	13	82
Male	480	3,896	0.36	29	28	44
Female	86	4,070	0.39	30	36	34

Notes: Candidates qualify for some reimbursement of campaign expenses provided their vote total at some stage of the count reaches a quarter of the Droop quota (for explanation of the Droop quota, see Appendix 4). Voting figures refer to first preference votes. 'County councillor' refers to those candidates who at the time of the election were members of a county or city council.

About 40 per cent of the candidates had also stood in 2007, and on average these now won 314 votes more than on that occasion. There is huge variation across the party system: candidates standing again for Fianna Fáil now received, on average, 3,267 votes fewer than in 2007, and Green candidates were down by nearly 1,700 on their previous tally, while candidates for Fine Gael, Labour and Sinn Féin each added on average over 2,000 votes to their 2007 figure. Again, while gender differences are small, they are to the benefit of women: female candidates standing again won on average 718 votes more than in 2007, while for male candidates the figure is only 247 votes.

Quantifying the earthquake election

This was truly an election like no other in Ireland, and like hardly any other anywhere else, as is discussed in more detail in Chapter 13. It is difficult to resist a *Guinness Book of Records* approach to discussing the results, so we may as well set out at the start the list of 'highests' and 'lowests' established on 25 February 2011.[1]

- Volatility was much higher than at any previous election (30 per cent).
- Fianna Fáil won its lowest ever share of the votes (17 per cent).
- Fianna Fáil won its lowest ever number of seats (20).
- Fianna Fáil lost more votes (24 per cent) and more seats (58) than any party has done before between elections.
- Fine Gael won its highest ever number of seats (76).
- For the first time since the 1920s, Fine Gael is the strongest party.
- Fine Gael gained more seats (25) than any party has done before between elections.
- Fianna Fáil and Fine Gael, traditionally the two main parties, between them won their lowest ever share of the votes (54 per cent).
- Labour won its highest share of the votes (19 per cent) since 1922.
- Labour won its highest ever number of seats (37).
- Labour achieved second-party status for the first time ever.
- The number of Independents elected (14) was the highest since 1951.
- The number of TDs retiring (36) was the highest ever.
- The number of TDs defeated (45) was the highest ever.
- The number of TDs elected who were not members of the previous Dáil (84, or 51 per cent) was the highest ever.

In most cases, as we shall see, these records were not so much broken as smashed, with 2011 representing a quantum leap from anything that had gone before. Figure 7.1 illustrates the extent to which the 2011 result was truly transgressive, marking a profound change not just from that of 2007 but from the previous 79 years of Irish political history. From the perspective of the post-2011 party system, the puzzle is not why there was such a large change in 2011 but why there was so much stability between 1932 and 2011, but that is not a subject for this chapter.

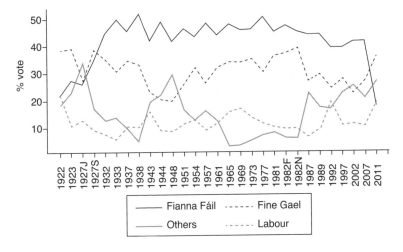

Figure 7.1   Party support 1922–2011

Starting with volatility, this is most often measured by the Pedersen index, which is calculated simply by adding the vote gains of those parties that made gains, plus the vote losses of those parties that made losses, and dividing the total by 2. That produces a minimum estimate of switching, which may in practice have been higher as vote flows may sometimes cancel each other out – and, of course, the electorate, and the corpus of voters, both change between elections. For the election as a whole this index produces a figure of almost 30 per cent, one of the most volatile elections in postwar Europe, as discussed in depth in Chapter 13. The average volatility per constituency was 31 per cent; in fact, only two constituencies produced volatility levels lower than the *maximum* figure seen in 2007 (20 per cent). As usual, volatility was highest in Dublin (average of 36 per cent per constituency), reaching a peak in Dublin Mid-West. Here, at least 46 per cent of voters switched, nearly all of them from the former government parties (Fianna Fáil was down 21 per cent, the Progressive Democrats 12 per cent and the Greens 7 per cent) to the former opposition parties (Labour was up 20 per cent, Fine Gael up 19 per cent, Sinn Féin up 3 per cent and the United Left Alliance up 4 per cent). Still, this was a nationwide phenomenon, and even in

Connacht–Ulster, where once again volatility was lowest, the average figure per constituency was 27 per cent.

Turnout was one of the few dimensions on which the election did not produce exceptional figures. Turnout rose by almost 3 percentage points so, after dropping at virtually every election from 1969 to 2002, it has now risen by around 7 percentage points over the last two elections and is above the 1987 level. The rise in turnout was greatest in Dublin (up over 5 percentage points), though overall Dublin's turnout level remains below that for the country as a whole. Between 2007 and 2011, the number of registered electors rose by around 98,000 while the number of valid votes rose by around 155,000. The latter statistic gives us confidence that turnout really did rise, which is not surprising given the strong emotions about the state of country, such as anger and outrage, expressed by many voters in election surveys (see next chapter).

Fianna Fáil

'This is not a wipe-out', declared outgoing junior minister Dr Martin Mansergh bravely as the results started coming in. If so, then, as Damon Runyon would put it, it will do until a wipe-out comes along. Disaster, cataclysm, catastrophe, or tragedy may sound too apocalyptic for an election result that did not, after all, result in anyone's death, while rebuff, reverse or setback or are hardly adequate to express the scale of what happened. Perhaps collapse, debacle, humiliation, or meltdown come closest to fitting the bill.

The facts can be simply stated. Fianna Fáil, having received 39 per cent of the votes or more at every election since 1932, plunged to just 17 per cent, losing virtually three-quarters of the seats it had won in 2007 (see Table 7.2). Having been the largest party at every election since 1932, it dropped to a distant third, with not much more than a quarter of the seats of Fine Gael. For an octogenarian or nonagenarian pro-Treatyite, who became politically aware at the 1932 election, 2011 was the election they had dreamed of all their life but never really expected to live to see. At every election since June 1927 – when in one constituency it did not have an official candidate – Fianna Fáil had won at least one seat in every constituency. In 2011, though, it was left unrepresented in 25 of the 43 constituencies and in eight of the 26 counties. A person so minded could walk from Gweedore in Donegal South-West to the south coast in Waterford and be in Fianna Fáil-free territory the whole way, apart from a 12-kilometre stretch in east Galway. Those who believed the opinion polls in the months before the election were not surprised by the outcome, but many had continued to believe, even as the ballot boxes were being opened, that things could not possibly be as bad for the party as these polls suggested.

Table 7.2   Result of 2011 election, with changes since 2007

	% vote	Change since 2007	Seats	Change since 2007	% seats
Fine Gael	36.1	+8.8	76	+25	46.1
Labour	19.4	+9.3	37	+17	22.4
Fianna Fáil	17.4	−24.1	19	−58	11.5
Sinn Féin	9.9	+3.0	14	+10	8.5
United Left Alliance	2.7	+1.6	5	+5	3.0
Green Party	1.8	−2.8	0	−6	0.0
Workers' Party	0.1	0	0	0	0.0
Christian Solidarity Party	0.1	0	0	0	0.0
Progressive Democrats	0	−2.7	−	−2	−
Independents and others	12.3	+7.1	14	+9	8.5
Total	100.0	0	165	0	100.0

Notes: For detailed results, see Appendix 1. Table refers to contested seats; Fianna Fáil also won the one uncontested seat (automatic re-election of Ceann Comhairle), giving it 20 seats out of 166 in the 31st Dáil. The Progressive Democrats had disbanded by the time of the 2011 election.

Virtually the entire top level of the party disappeared overnight from the scene. Of the 12 Fianna Fáil cabinet ministers in office at the start of January 2011, only four were still in parliament when the Dáil reassembled after the election. Four (Dermot Ahern, Noel Dempsey, Tony Killeen, Batt O'Keeffe) resigned from office by 20 January and did not stand at the election; a fifth (Micheál Martin) resigned from office to challenge for the party leadership; and the Taoiseach, Brian Cowen, remained in office but did not stand at the election. Of the remaining six, three (Pat Carey, Mary Coughlan, Mary Hanafin) lost their seats at the election, leaving only three (Brian Lenihan, Éamon Ó Cuív, Brendan Smith) who were re-elected, along with Martin, now party leader. This thinning out of the party's top echelon was to be deepened by the untimely death of Brian Lenihan less than four months after the election. The election also saw the retirement of former government ministers Bertie Ahern, Rory O'Hanlon and Michael Woods, along with seven current or former ministers of state (junior ministers). Another two former cabinet ministers (Martin Cullen and James McDaid) had resigned their Dáil seats in 2010. Finally, the election itself saw the defeat of 35 Fianna Fáil TDs, including four former cabinet ministers (Frank Fahey, John O'Donoghue, Mary O'Rourke, Dick Roche) and 13 former junior ministers (see Appendix 5 for full list of retiring and defeated TDs). Moreover, only two of the defeated ministers even ran in the Seanad elections, and neither of them was elected. At a stroke, Fianna Fáil was denuded of the great bulk of its senior and experienced figures – though, given the unpopularity that the Fianna Fáil 'brand' had acquired, being able to put unfamiliar faces forward in the aftermath of the election was perhaps no bad thing. Unfortunately, not one of the 20 members of its shrunken Dáil group was female, and some of its TDs were generally regarded as being among life's natural backbenchers rather than its frontbenchers.

There was no 'decisive battleground': Fianna Fáil lost votes everywhere. Having been the strongest party in 40 of the 43 constituencies in 2007, Fianna Fáil is now not the strongest in any; treating Independents as a group, Fianna Fáil is the second strongest in 12 constituencies, in 11 it is the third strongest, and in the other 20 it is lower than that. It was particularly weak in Dublin, where it won only 12 per cent of the votes and only one of the 47 seats – and, as we have mentioned, the winner of this seat, Brian Lenihan, one of the most respected politicians in the country despite the unpopularity of the policies he implemented while Minister for Finance between 2008 and 2011, was to die in June 2011. In no constituency did Fianna Fáil reach 30 per cent of the votes, and in two, both on the south side of Dublin, it fell below 10 per cent. These two constituencies sum up the way the party collapsed everywhere: Dublin South, where it received 9.4 per cent, is perhaps the most well-heeled in the country, and the adjacent Dublin South-Central (9.5 per cent) is one of the least prosperous. It lost votes in all social groups, as we will see in Chapter 8, and in every part of the country: from southern glens to western shores, from northern hills to Leinster's doors, the people arose and abandoned Fianna Fáil. Its 'best' performance compared to 2007 came in Mayo, where its support slipped by only 8 per cent (mainly because it had polled exceptionally poorly here in 2007). Everywhere else it dropped by at least 16 percentage points; there were seven constituencies in which its vote fell by over 30 points, the nadir being a 37-point drop in Dublin North-West. Fianna Fáil did not gain a seat anywhere, and in only three constituencies (Cork South-Central, Dublin West and Mayo) did it avoid losing a seat. In 19 constituencies it lost two seats and in the other 21 it lost one. As we will discuss later in the chapter, Fianna Fáil was for once significantly under-represented in terms of its seats:votes ratio, and its candidate nomination strategy was also the subject of much critical discussion.

If the point needs illustrating further, we can focus in particular on the constituencies of the party's former leaders to show how much has changed. In Laois–Offaly, represented by Brian Cowen from 1984 until he stood down in 2011, the party had on average won over 50 per cent of the votes at each of the previous ten elections, but it dropped 30 points to 27 per cent; though this constituency was still something of a success, in that it won two seats, one of just two constituencies in the country, the other being the leader's Cork South-Central, where it managed this. In Bertie Ahern's Dublin Central, it also dropped 30 points, ending up with no seats in a constituency where it had won two in 2007. In Longford–Westmeath, where it had routinely exceeded 50 per cent while Albert Reynolds led its team, it dropped to 19 per cent. In the Dublin North-Central constituency of his predecessor Charles Haughey it fell 31 per cent and was left without a seat. In Cork City, the bailiwick of Jack Lynch (leader 1966–79), the losses were a relatively minor 18 points and it lost only one seat, no doubt because its new leader Micheál Martin is a local TD. Seán Lemass preceded Lynch as leader; under him Dublin South-Central had been a Fianna Fáil stronghold, with the party able to take three seats out of five in 1965, but in 2011 it could not muster even 10 per cent of the votes and was left seatless. And in de Valera's Clare, where Fianna Fáil won almost 70 per cent of the votes in 1977, it was now down to 22 per cent. In short, Fianna Fáil's outflow of support swept the entire country, paying no heed to county or provincial boundaries.

Fine Gael

What is bad for Fianna Fáil is usually good for Fine Gael, and in 2011 Fine Gael capitalised fully on the collapse in support for its main rival. For the first time ever – or the first time since 1927 if we regard Fine Gael as essentially a continuation of Cumann na nGaedheal under another name – it is the largest party in the Dáil. Indeed, its 76 seats make it the dominant party in the 31st Dáil; it has more than twice as many seats as any other party, a feat that Fianna Fáil itself achieved only four times. It won four seats in one constituency (Mayo, the base of leader Enda Kenny), something no party has ever before achieved in a five-seat constituency. This is all the more impressive bearing in mind that Fine Gael won only 31 seats just two elections ago, in 2002, and there was speculation then that the party might not survive much longer. Comparing its 2011 performance with that of 2002, the party has gained two seats in nine constituencies and one seat in a further 23, with no gain in just seven (in the remaining three of the 2002 constituencies, boundary changes make direct comparisons difficult). In 2002 there were

13 constituencies in which the party failed to win a seat; in 2011 there was just one (Dublin North-West). The party did not lose a seat in any constituency, and though three of its outgoing TDs lost their seats, each was defeated by a running mate. In five constituencies it had more than one new TD elected (three new TDs in Cavan–Monaghan), a sure sign that the Fine Gael label was in itself very attractive to voters.

Fine Gael increased its support in all but four constituencies, with its greatest advances in Dublin, where in the space of two elections it has advanced in votes from 14 per cent to 30 per cent and in seats from just three to 17. Although its vote gains were impressive, they alone do not account for its seat gains; indeed, although it has never before won as many as 76 seats, its vote share remains more than three percentage points below the peak it attained under Garret FitzGerald in November 1982 (see Figure 7.1). In 2011 it was able to turn 36 per cent of the first preference votes into 46 per cent of the seats. Compared with its recent low point of 2002, its 2011 figures represented 161 per cent of the 2002 vote share but 245 per cent of the 2002 seat share. Its record haul of seats derived not just from its vote gains but also from two additional factors, disproportionalities in the electoral system and vote management, that we will discuss in greater detail later in the chapter.

Labour

Like Fine Gael, Labour had a good election. It won more seats than ever before, four more than the 33 it won in the 'Spring Tide' of 1992, and its share of the votes was its highest since 1922. As usual these days Dublin was the party's strongest area; though Fine Gael won slightly more votes than Labour in the capital, Labour took one more seat. Labour won two seats in six constituencies in the capital – including in two three-seat constituencies, a feat it has never achieved before. While a student of social democratic parties elsewhere in Europe would see nothing remarkable in this pattern, it represents the breaking of new ground for the Irish Labour Party.

The party more or less doubled its vote since 2007, with its largest nine gains all occurring in Dublin constituencies. There were particular successes in Clare (it won a seat for only the second time since 1951), Cork South-West (the first seat since 1977), and in Galway East (the first seat ever), while seats were retained in Galway West and Waterford despite the retirement of long-standing incumbents, which in the past has often meant the loss of a seat. Its gains were lowest in Connacht–Ulster, but its low 2007 base meant that the party virtually trebled its vote share here and won two seats for the first time since 1927. In a number of constituencies in the north-west Labour took in candidates from outside the party fold, but this policy did not work especially well. In Donegal North-East Jimmy Harte, formerly of Fine Gael and then Independent, did at least treble his vote, though he still came nowhere near election, but former Independent TD Jerry Cowley in Mayo, former Progressive Democrat TD Mae Sexton in Longford–Westmeath, and former Independent candidate John Kelly in Roscommon–South Leitrim fared no better than they had under their previous labels.

Labour did not lose any seats, none of its TDs was defeated, and only in one constituency (Kerry South) did its vote share decline. By any previous standards this was an exceptional performance, but it did not produce quite the degree of euphoria engendered by the 1992 election result. This was partly because of the hopes and expectations raised by the polls from mid-2010 that had shown Labour to be the strongest party (see Figure 1.4, p. 26), leading to the mass production of 'Gilmore for Taoiseach' paraphernalia that had a slightly forlorn air by the end of the campaign (see Chapter 4). With Fianna Fáil support collapsing Labour seemed well placed to pick up much of that party's working-class votes in particular, but while it did well it faced stronger competition on its left than ever before. Once the seat distribution was known it seemed almost certain that Labour would be the junior component in a Fine Gael-led coalition government, some way short of the 'partnership' status it had been able to claim in 1992, and this also dampened the mood. While this was an exceptionally good election for Labour, it remains below 20 per cent of the votes and has not shaken off its status as one of the weakest socialist/ social democratic parties in Western Europe.

Sinn Féin

In 2007 Sinn Féin had been expected to win 10–12 seats, and its eventual total of just four was a major disappointment. Its 2011 performance affirmed that it is well implanted in the political system south of the border, as it added more than 80,000 to its vote total and came back with 14 seats – the most ever, or the most since 1923, depending on how much continuity can be identified between today's party and the anti-Treatyites of the early 1920s, a contested subject. The most high-profile success was that of party president Gerry Adams in Louth (see p. 74 above). Some observers expected him to sweep home at the head of the poll, while others wondered whether the southern electorate, even in a border constituency, might be less than welcoming towards a candidate with such strong Belfast roots. In the event the former were proved correct, as Adams received the third highest vote total in the country.

Sinn Féin's strongest area remains the border: it won a seat in each of the five border constituencies, including two in Donegal, where it is the strongest party. It also won four seats in Dublin, but its performance in the capital was surprisingly muted: it is weaker here, with only 8 per cent of the votes, than in the rest of country, won only two-thirds of the votes that Fianna Fáil received, and gained just 1 per cent compared with its 2007 vote share. In five of the 12 Dublin constituencies its vote share actually dropped. Elsewhere in the country it achieved localised peaks of support and won seats in the south (two in Cork and one in Kerry) and in the midlands (Laois–Offaly and Meath West). With so little to choose in policy terms between the three main parties, and Sinn Féin standing as the main proponent of what seemed to be the popular policy of 'burning the bondholders' and rejecting the European Union/ International Monetary Fund (EU/IMF) bailout, it might be argued that Sinn Féin should have done even better, and that for some southern voters its republican dimension and a perception of domination by northerners remains unattractive. There may be something to this, and some Sinn Féin candidates still do not attract lower preferences from other parties' supporters, though others, such as Brian Stanley in Laois– Offaly, had no problem in this regard. Its Dáil group, with TDs such as Pearse Doherty, Mary Lou McDonald and Peadar Tóibín coming to the fore, has a much more youthful and somewhat more gender-balanced appearance than before. Overall, a leap from four to 14 seats must be seen as unambiguously a success, though Sinn Féin shows no signs of altering its status as a party of permanent opposition.

Others

The four main parties won 83 per cent of the votes and 147 of the 166 seats. In 2007 the largest of the rest had been the Greens, whose vote grew to nearly 5 per cent of the votes, and with six Dáil seats they earned two places in cabinet. In 2011, not even Martin Mansergh could dispute the deployment of 'wipe-out' to describe their fate. They lost votes in every constituency and lost every one of their seats. They ran one candidate in each of the 43 constituencies, but 35 of these candidates won fewer than 2 per cent of the votes. Although party leader John Gormley declared during the campaign that the party 'expected' to be fighting for the last seat in around nine constituencies, in the event not one Green candidate even achieved runner-up status. The Greens' performance had serious financial consequences. The party fell just 3,368 votes (around 78 votes per constituency) short of the level of 2 per cent of the votes nationally that would have enabled it to qualify for party funding, with drastic implications for its ability to employ full-time staff.[2] Moreover, only four of its 43 candidates – former cabinet ministers John Gormley and Éamon Ryan, former leader Trevor Sargent, and senator Mark Dearey – even reached the level of support necessary to qualify for reimbursement of expenses.

The Greens were overtaken by the United Left Alliance, consisting of the Socialist Party, the People Before Profit Alliance, and two other candidates. The ULA exceeded 10 per cent of the votes in five constituencies and it won a seat in each. MEP Joe Higgins regained his seat in Dublin West, as did Independent Séamus Healy in Tipperary South. Clare Daly in Dublin North was elected at the fifth attempt, and Richard Boyd Barrett took a seat in Dun Laoghaire, where he had come close in 2007, despite the constituency being reduced from five to four seats (see his account in Chapter 6). Finally, the most left-wing constituency in the country, Dublin South-Central, elected not only two Labour TDs plus a Sinn Féin TD but also Joan Collins of the ULA, who had earned national prominence in the dying days of the 30th Dáil by berating Bertie Ahern as he was standing outside Leinster House giving a television interview.

The Progressive Democrats had won nearly 3 per cent of the votes in 2007, more than either the Greens or the ULA managed in 2011, but in 2009 the party wound itself up. Table 7.2 therefore shows the party as having lost both of its seats – although some observers suggested that 2011 had nonetheless been a good election for the PDs, who retained a ghostly presence. At least five of the 166 members of the 31st Dáil were former PDs,[3] so even if the PD label has gone, something of what the party stood for remains.

Ireland has long been famous for electing more Independents than the rest of Western Europe together,[4] and it excelled itself in 2011, Independents reaching a 60-year peak. Fourteen were elected, and their combined vote, over 12 per cent, was the highest since June 1927. Most of these candidates had little support, over 70 per cent of them receiving fewer than 1,000 first preferences. Of the 14 successful Independents, five were incumbents, though only two of these (Finian McGrath and Maureen O'Sullivan) had been first elected as Independents; Noel Grealish had been elected for the PDs in 2007, Michael Lowry (the object of very negative findings by the Moriarty Tribunal in its report published in the weeks after the election) was first elected for Fine Gael, and Mattie McGrath had been a Fianna Fáil TD until he jumped ship in January 2011. Several of the others also had a party past: Tom Fleming had twice come close to election as a Fianna Fáil candidate; John Halligan had stood twice to little effect for the Workers' Party; Catherine Murphy had stood for the

Workers' Party and Democratic Left at past Dáil elections and had won a 2005 by-election before losing her seat in 2007; and Thomas Pringle had been elected to Donegal County Council as a Sinn Féin candidate.

The other five were relative newcomers; literally so in the case of Michael Healy-Rae, who succeeded his father in Kerry South. Luke 'Ming' Flanagan had been dismissed as a crank when he stood in 1997 and 2002, receiving fewer than 1,000 first preferences on a platform in which legalising cannabis loomed large, but he had subsequently enjoyed electoral success at local government level and now received nearly 9,000 first preferences. Shane Ross had extensive political experience, having been an Independent senator for 30 years. He had made one unsuccessful foray into Dáil politics, faring badly as a Fine Gael candidate in Wicklow in 1992, but now, aided by a high profile as a Sunday newspaper columnist, he soared to the top of the poll in solidly middle-class Dublin South, becoming the second highest vote-winner in the country with over 17,000 first preferences. In Wexford Mick Wallace was well known as the founder and, between 2007 and 2010, coach of Wexford Youths, a team in the second tier of Ireland's football (soccer) league, which earned him an endorsement from Irish international striker Kevin Doyle.[5] He was a high-profile builder, distinctive for his long white hair and earring, and did not declare his candidacy until three weeks before polling day.[6] His slogan 'For a New Politics' seemed to capture the somewhat inchoate and unfocused desire for change. Finally, the least expected success was that of Stephen Donnelly, a 35-year-old management consultant with no political background, who in the betting market was at 14–1 to win a seat in Wicklow early in the campaign. Stressing his economics expertise and making good use of media appearances, he built a successful campaign virtually from zero. The profusion of Independents cannot be ascribed to the rigidity of the party whip system in the Dáil: only one of these 14 TDs, Mattie McGrath, became Independent as a result of defying the party whip.

Votes and seats

The 2011 election was the most disproportional Irish election ever, with a score of 8.69 on the widely-used least squares index, compared with the previous peak of 6.62 in 2002. This is well above the typical level of a proportional representation (PR) system (usually around 5 or less), albeit still well below that of non-PR systems such as that of the UK where the figure is usually between 15 and 20.[7] As Table 7.3 shows, both of the incoming government parties won sizeable bonuses, while Fianna

Fáil was significantly under-represented. Fine Gael's bonus of 16 seats is the largest any party has ever won, and likewise Fianna Fáil's 'negative bonus' of ten seats was the worst any party has suffered. Sympathy for Fianna Fáil might be tempered, though, by the consideration that this is the first time it has ever been under-represented, and that at the previous ten elections its cumulative over-representation came to 64 seats. Labour's bonus of five seats was also a record for that party.

Table 7.3 Party shares of votes and of seats, 2011 election

	% votes	Hare quotas	Seats	Difference
Fine Gael	36.1	59.6	76	+16.4
Labour	19.4	32.1	37	+4.9
Fianna Fáil	17.4	28.8	19	–9.8
Sinn Féin	9.9	16.4	14	–2.4
United Left Alliance	2.7	4.4	5	+0.6
Green Party	1.8	3.0	0	–3.0
Others	12.7	20.7	14	–6.7
Total	100.0	165.0	165	0

Note: The Hare quota equals the total number of valid votes (2,220,359) divided by the number of contested seats (165), which equals 13,457. The 166th seat was that of the Ceann Comhairle, returned automatically as a Fianna Fáil TD.

Why was the outcome of the 2011 election so disproportional? There are two main explanations. One lies in an unusual feature of the Irish electoral system, and the other concerns vote management, or the distribution of a party's vote among its candidates.

The unusual aspect of Ireland's electoral system is not, as some Irish voters believe, the fact that candidates of one party compete against each other for votes – that is a feature of the electoral system in about half of the EU's 27 member states – but, rather, the use of very small district magnitudes, that is, the number of MPs elected from each constituency. In Ireland's 2011 election, the 165 elected TDs were returned from 43 constituencies, an average of only 3.8 per constituency. Most countries using any kind of PR electoral system employ larger district magnitude than this: for example, in Luxembourg average district magnitude is 15, in Belgium it is 14, in Finland it is 13, in Poland and Portugal it is 11, in Switzerland 8, and at Northern Ireland's Assembly elections 6. District magnitude is the key factor in determining how proportional an electoral system is: the smaller the district magnitude, the less proportional the election results are likely to be.[8] Elections are least proportional when district magnitude is 1, which is why non-PR elections, such as those in the UK and France, are the most disproportional in Europe.

District magnitude in Ireland has always been small – around 4, or less, at every election since 1937 – but until recently one factor in particular kept disproportionality down to the levels typical of PR systems. This was that Fianna Fáil, as the largest party, which under any electoral system is usually the beneficiary of disproportionality, generated some antipathy from supporters of all other parties, and these consequently tended to use their transfers against it. Once Fianna Fáil acquired a coalition ally, in the shape of the PDs, and became less transfer-unfriendly generally, its seat bonus rocketed: this bonus was just four seats in 1989 and three in 1992, but rose to 12 in 1997, 13 in 2002 and eight in 2007. The 1997 election set a new record for disproportionality, which was then broken by the 2002 election and, as we have said, this in turn was exceeded by the 2011 figure. In 2011 the largest party, now Fine Gael, did reasonably well in transfers from other parties' supporters (see below), and hence reaped this largest-party bonus.

The reason why district magnitude has so great an effect is simply that in a small constituency it is often impossible to produce proportional results. For example, if a party wins 15 per cent of the votes in a three-seat constituency it will either be greatly over-represented if it wins one seat (33 per cent of the seats) or greatly under-represented if it does not win a seat (0 per cent). In a ten-seat constituency, it will be over- or under-represented by only 5 per cent. Across the country as a whole, the various constituency disproportionalities often even themselves out, which is why Labour is usually pretty accurately represented overall, on average receiving about two seats more than its 'fair' share. If they do not even themselves out, though, a small-district electoral system has the potential to generate significant levels of disproportionality. This is made more likely when the number of constituencies itself is not large. If greater proportionality is wanted, the solution is obvious: use larger constituencies and ideally, into the bargain, use a permanent configuration of constituencies instead of redrawing boundaries after each census.[9]

There is a degree of chance in whether a given election does or does not produce reasonably proportional results, in that the over- and under-representations of individual parties might or might not even themselves out across the country. However, this does not mean that it is simply random whether we see major deviations from proportionality. This depends also on the distribution of votes among parties, and the evenness of a party's support across the country – as well as the spread of votes among a party's candidates within each constituency (vote management), which we discuss later. In 2011 Fine Gael benefited greatly from being by some way the largest party; not only was it the strongest party in 33 of the 43 constituencies, but in 18 of these constituencies it had around twice as many votes as any other party, and thus benefited from the large-party bias inherent in small constituencies. In three-seat constituencies such as Meath East, Roscommon–South Leitrim and Sligo–North Leitrim it was able to win 67 per cent of the seats with 40 per cent of the votes or less, and in five-seaters, such as Carlow–Kilkenny, Cavan–Monaghan, Dublin South and Wicklow, it won 60 per cent of the seats with fewer than 40 per cent of the votes. Fine Gael was over-represented at all levels of district magnitude, and it was most over-represented in five-seat constituencies, winning 55 per cent of the seats here for 38 per cent of the first preference votes. In all it was over-represented in 36 constituencies and under-represented in just seven, and the 'swings and roundabouts' effect, whereby a party is over-represented in some constituencies and misses out in about the same number of others, did not materialise. Given that it won 46 per cent of the seats with 36 per cent of the votes, there is every likelihood that, had it won the 40 per cent of the votes that at least one poll gave it during the campaign, it might well have achieved an overall majority.[10]

In contrast, Fianna Fáil was over-represented in just 14 constituencies and under-represented in the other 29 – an exact reversal of the 2007 numbers. In 2011, the five-seat constituencies came to Fianna Fáil's rescue, as the party won nearly half of its seats there. In the three-seat and four-seat constituencies the party was greatly under-represented, with a return of 9 per cent of the seats for 17 per cent of the votes, but it achieved parity of representation in the five-seat constituencies. Fianna Fáil's seats:votes ratio is affected also by the relative evenness of its strength across the country, which usually works in its favour but on this occasion worked against it. As Table 7.4 shows, Fianna Fáil had by far the lowest coefficient of variation in 2007, and the second lowest after Fine Gael in 2011, indicating relatively little variation in its vote across the country. When a party is strong, this is good; for example, if a party wins around 45 per cent of the votes in every constituency, it will win 50 per cent of the seats in each four-seat constituency and will almost certainly win a majority of the seats in a number of three-seat and five-seat constituencies. When it is weak, evenness of support is not helpful; if a party won precisely 9 per cent of the votes in every constituency, for example, it might not win any seats anywhere. Between 2007 and 2011 Fianna Fáil went from being a strong party to a weak one, and thus its fairly even cross-country support, reflecting the even cross-class support that it continues to enjoy (see Chapter 8), now worked against it. This was particularly apparent in Dublin, where Fianna Fáil won just one seat, whereas Sinn Féin, with only two-thirds of its vote, won four seats. Fianna Fáil's coefficient of variation in Dublin was only 0.19, with its strength everywhere in the range from 9 per cent to 17 per cent, whereas Sinn Féin's coefficient was 0.84, reflecting a range from 0 per cent to 22 per cent.

Table 7.4 Uniformity of party support across the country

	Mean	Standard deviation	Coefficient of variation
2011			
Fianna Fáil	15.7	5.0	0.32
Fine Gael	35.1	8.8	0.25
Labour	21.6	9.2	0.43
Sinn Féin	8.9	7.5	0.84
Independents	12.0	9.4	0.78
2007			
Fianna Fáil	41.7	6.7	0.16
Fine Gael	26.4	9.1	0.34
Labour	10.5	6.1	0.58
Sinn Féin	7.2	5.6	0.78
Independents	5.4	6.8	1.27

Note: The coefficient of variation is simply the standard deviation divided by the mean. The lower the coefficient of variation, the less variation there is in a party's strength across the country.

Vote management and intra-party competition

The other factor that can affect a party's conversion of votes into seats is the distribution of its votes in a constituency among its candidates there. For example, if a party were to receive 40 per cent of the votes in a five-seat constituency, then it might win either two seats or three seats depending on how these votes were divided among its leading three candidates. If two received around 16–17 per cent each, with the third getting only 7 per cent, it would almost certainly have to settle for two seats, but if each of its leading three candidates won 13–14 per cent then it would have a much better chance of taking three seats. Increasingly, party head offices do not simply let their candidates try to maximise their own votes and hope for the best; instead, the party puts some kind of vote management scheme into operation, with the aim of bringing about an even spread between the leading candidates. This typically takes the form of dividing the constituency geographically, 'awarding' specific slices of it to particular candidates rather in the manner of a nineteenth-century plenipotentiary deciding which of the rival colonial powers should be given which territory. The importance of vote management should not be exaggerated – in most constituencies, the share of votes that each party wins is the decisive factor, and it would make no difference how these votes are divided among its candidates – but it matters often enough that one of the larger parties might win, or miss out on, half a dozen seats depending on whether or not it manages its votes optimally.

Managing votes is easier said than done. For one thing, parties operate in a world of imperfect information; it may be apparent only retrospectively what should have been done, and where. Moreover, there are limits to the power of party head offices or anyone else to effect a vote management scheme, even if they know exactly what they want to do. From the perspective of the party's strongest candidate(s) in a constituency, a vote management scheme in effect requires them to steer some of their support to a weaker running mate, which carries the risk that the running mate might be elected at their expense, something that occasionally happens. If a strong candidate refuses to cooperate with such a scheme, there is not much that can be done, though one incentive to fall into line is that a TD who has put his or her own seat on the line for the good of the party will hope for preferment after the election whereas recalcitrant TDs may find themselves left out in the cold.

Vote management impinges on intra-party competition, which is liable to be at least as intense as competition between parties. This is usually a hidden aspect of campaigns, as parties attempt to present a united face to the world and candidates promote themselves without explicitly denigrating their running mates, although occasionally tensions become so great that, as past books in this series testify, candidates cannot refrain from telling the media about their grievances. For example, in Mayo Fine Gael held three seats and was pushing strongly for a fourth. Two of its TDs, leader Enda Kenny and Michael Ring, were regarded as safe, but the other incumbent, John O'Mahony, feared that if the non-incumbent on the ticket, Michelle Mulherin, was elected, this might be at his expense. After some negotiations between the various camps an agreement on division of the constituency was reached, giving Mulherin more of the constituency than she had had in 2007, and then there were moves to go further by trying to direct Enda Kenny's surplus votes to Mulherin by asking his supporters to give their second preference to Mulherin, which did not please O'Mahony. As described in one of the local newspapers:

While O'Mahony's people are unhappy with the vote transfer plan, those close to Deputy Ring and Councillor Mulherin are reported to have concerns that the territory allocated to them is too restricted compared to Deputy O'Mahony. It is understood Deputy Kenny conceded ground in central Mayo to Councillor Mulherin while she also secured additional areas in north Mayo that had previously been held by Deputy Ring.[11]

In the event, Fine Gael won so many votes in Mayo that it would have been virtually certain to take four seats even without any vote management.

Fine Gael took this aspect very seriously and voters in a number of constituencies were asked to rank the party's candidates in a specified order. In several Dublin constituencies, voters in particular areas received letters, signed by Enda Kenny or by the party's national director of elections Phil Hogan, asking voters to give their number 1 vote to the candidate perceived as weaker and the number 2 to the stronger (see the example from Dun Laoghaire in Figure 7.2).[12] Across the country as a whole, Fine Gael's vote management was outstanding. This was why, as mentioned earlier, with 36–41 per cent of the vote it was able to win three seats in a number of five-seat constituencies or to take two seats in several three-seat constituencies. In only two constituencies (Galway East and Longford–Westmeath) can we say that the party would probably have taken an additional seat with better vote management, and there are three (Cork South-Central, Donegal North-East and Tipperary South) where there is an outside possibility that an additional seat could have been won. In some other constituencies (Dublin North, Kildare North, Louth and Meath West) it was poor, but Fine Gael had sufficient votes to win a second seat anyway. These cases, though, are the exceptions to a general pattern of very impressive vote management by Fine Gael tacticians.

In contrast, Labour's vote management was frequently sub-optimal and sometimes costly. The most glaring example was in Cork East, where its leading candidate, Seán Sherlock, won almost 12,000 first preferences and its second candidate, John Mulvihill, just 5,701. As a result Mulvihill was eliminated on the seventh count when he was just 489 votes behind Sandra McLellan of Sinn Féin, and the transfer of his votes resulted in McLellan's election. Had around 700 of Sherlock's first preferences been diverted instead to Mulvihill, Labour would have won two seats here. Likewise, in Dun Laoghaire, had around 250 of party leader Éamon Gilmore's eleven and a half thousand first preferences been switched to

AN IMPORTANT MESSAGE TO FINE GAEL VOTERS
FROM JIM GILDEA
Constituency Director of Elections

Dear Voter,

May I first take the opportunity to thank you for the courtesy and support you have shown to our candidates and their canvassing teams over the last number of weeks.

Your support is much appreciated. In order to help us secure two seats for Fine Gael in the Dun Laoghaire constituency I am appealing to all Fine Gael voters in the Booterstown, Blackrock and Seapoint areas to vote **NUMBER 1 Mary MITCHELL O'CONNOR and to vote NUMBER 2 Seán BARRETT.**

Yours Sincerely,

Jim Gildea
Constituency Director of Elections

FINE GAEL ☆	**BARRETT, Seán** (Fine Gael) Ballinclea Road, Killiney		**2**
FINE GAEL ☆	**MITCHELL O'CONNOR, Mary** (Fine Gael) Johnstown Road, Cabinteely		**1**

It is vital that we manage our vote in Dun Laoghaire, and elect two Fine Gael TDs. I am happy to endorse this local strategy, requesting Fine Gael voters in Booterstown, Blackrock and Seapoint to vote **Mary MITCHELL O'CONNOR 1 and Seán BARRETT 2.**

Enda Kenny TD
Fine Gael Party Leader

THIS IS AN OFFICIALLY AUTHORISED VOTER REQUEST ISSUED BY THE FINE GAEL DIRECTOR OF ELECTIONS IN DUN LAOGHAIRE
For Confirmation,please telephone Fine Gael Headquarters at 619 8444

FINE GAEL ★

Published by Phil Hogan TD, Fine Gael Headquarters, 51 Upper Mount Street, Dublin 2; Printed by Fine Gael, 51 Upper Mount Street, Dublin 2a

Figure 7.2 Fine Gael vote management scheme in Dun Laoghaire

his running mate Ivana Bacik, Labour would have taken a second seat. There is at least some chance that better vote management in four other constituencies (Cork North-Central, Dublin Central, Dublin West and Longford–Westmeath) could have led to an extra seat. In some of the constituencies where Labour did take two seats this was despite poor vote management – or, more likely, a complete absence of any attempt at vote management. In Dublin South-West, for example, the leading candidate received over three times as many first preferences as his running mate. In Dublin Mid-West and Dublin South-East, though, Labour's vote management was good (or perhaps the votes simply fell optimally) and this played a role in bringing it a second seat.

We can examine this more systematically by considering the important ratio which, when a party is aiming at n seats, is between its first-placed candidate and its nth-placed. Ideally, the votes of the leading candidate will be as low a multiple as possible of the nth-placed. For example, Fine Gael was aiming at three seats in Dublin South; its strongest candidate here received 9,635 first preferences and its third-placed candidate received 7,716, giving a ratio of 1.25 to 1. In some cases this vote-balancing was almost perfect, with a multiple of 1.01 in Meath East and 1.07 in Limerick County. In contrast, Labour's multiple in Cork East was 2.08 and in Dublin West it rose to 3.58. Across the 35 constituencies where vote management was or could have been important for Fine Gael, the multiple was 1.52, while for the 15 constituencies where this applied to Labour, its multiple was 2.22.[13] The difference is due partly to Labour's lack of experience in this area – in the past, only rarely has the party been in with a serious chance of winning more than one seat in any constituency – and, in addition, Labour lacks the resources to conduct constituency-level opinion polls to find out how its candidates are faring. It may also be that many Labour incumbents are accustomed to operating in their constituencies without too much interference from head office and would resist attempts to get them to channel support to a running mate. This also applies to Sinn Féin, which had a chance of winning two seats in just one constituency, Cavan–Monaghan, but poor vote management (a multiple of 1.82) ensured that it was left with just one seat.

Fianna Fáil's problem in 2011 was winning votes rather than managing them, and its intra-party battles had an element of *sauve qui peut* about them. For example, open warfare over turf erupted in Louth, where senator James Carroll and county councillor Declan Breathnach were in contention for at most one seat.[14] Breathnach complained that the 'suits' in party head office had given Carroll too much of the constituency, including part of his own 'traditional stomping ground'. He stated: 'I am absolutely livid. There are posters up in Castlebellingham, Kilsaran and Duffy's Cross, areas that are my natural hinterland.' Carroll responded loftily that Breathnach's 'backbiting, sniping and negative remarks' were 'part of the politics of the past'. In the event, each candidate won about

0.4 of a quota and neither was elected. In all, there were 13 constituencies where Fianna Fáil ran two candidates but did not win a seat. The most high-profile case was Dun Laoghaire, where two ministers, Barry Andrews and Mary Hanafin, refused all pleas that one of them move to the adjacent Dublin South, where there was no Fianna Fáil incumbent (see p. 60 above). Neither was elected. There were four other constituencies where Fianna Fáil ran two incumbents but did not win a seat, and questions were asked afterwards as to whether head office or the leader should have been more active in insisting on a single-candidate strategy in these cases. For example, in Cork South-West the party's two TDs won 24 per cent of the votes between them, and the Labour candidate won just 14 per cent, but Labour won a seat and Fianna Fáil did not. The nine cases where it ran a non-incumbent alongside an incumbent, with neither being elected, also raised questions about its strategy.[15]

As noted already, the 75 candidates put forward by the party was an excessive number given its level of support. While it does not follow that a sole candidate would have won all the votes that two together won – obviously, some of those cast for the weaker candidate were personal votes – the argument is that a sole candidate can campaign and seek votes in all parts of the constituency, whereas when there is more than one candidate, each is often confined to a particular part of it and the stronger one does not become sufficiently well known to attract lower preferences across the whole constituency. The result can be what is known in Japan as *tomodaore*, meaning 'going down together', that is, splitting the vote in such a way that neither candidate is elected.[16]

When a party's internal transfer rate is close to 100 per cent, or even at the 80+ per cent level achieved by Fianna Fáil prior to the 1980s, then the number of candidates may not matter much, as pretty much all of the votes transferred from eliminated candidates will pass to other candidates of the party. This is why the parties in Malta, where internal transfer solidarity is close to 100 per cent, typically run many more candidates than there are seats at stake. But when a party's internal solidarity level drops to Fianna Fáil's 2011 figure of 58 per cent (see next section), it can matter a lot. In these circumstances, the usual vote management rules do not apply, because if the two candidates run virtually level with each other, and only 58 per cent transfer from the weaker to the stronger, the latter's votes will be only around 80 per cent of the two candidates' combined total. Thus, in the Cork South-West case already mentioned, although the two candidates together received nearly 10,800 first preferences, the internal transfer rate was only 57 per cent and even on the final count the stronger candidate had only 10,155 votes.

Vote transfers

Under proportional representation by the single transferable vote (PR-STV), voters can rank order as many of the candidates as they wish, and during the counting process a number of votes are transferred from one candidate to another, depending on the next preference marked (see Appendix 4 for a fuller explanation of the electoral system). This can occur either when a candidate is elected with a surplus over and above the quota, or when the lowest-placed candidate is eliminated. In either case, by examining the pattern of transfers we can draw inferences about the preferences of supporters of different parties, and about the extent to which voters are thinking along party lines at all when deciding how to fill in their ballot paper. We are interested both in intra-party transfers (when votes are transferred from a candidate of a given party, how many of these votes transfer to another candidate of the same party when such a candidate is available to receive transfers?) and inter-party transfers (when votes are transferred from the last remaining candidate of a given party, what proportions pass to candidates of other parties?).[17]

The strength of intra-party transfers can be seen as an indicator both of the level of party identification and of the primacy of party over candidate in the local campaign. Given the apparent decline in both of these, it is no surprise to find that internal party solidarity is not what it used to be. Prior to the 1980s Fianna Fáil's internal transfers flowed at a rate of over 80 per cent, exceeding 90 per cent in 1933. In 2002 Fianna Fáil's figure dropped to a record low of 62 per cent, dipping below Fine Gael's figure for the first time, and the 2011 figure was lower still (see Table 7.5). This casts doubt upon a popular interpretation of Fianna Fáil's vote in 2011, which was that, given the toxicity of the Fianna Fáil 'brand', those who still voted for it must be totally committed Fianna Fáil identifiers who would not abandon the party despite its multiple failings. In reality, evidently, the commitment to the party of its much diminished band of voters was questionable, implying that a good proportion voted for individual candidates regardless of, or even despite, rather than because of, their party label (this is discussed further in chapter 8). A voter in Carlow–Kilkenny who intended to vote for a Fianna Fáil incumbent, John McGuinness, explained to a local paper 'that she was voting for John and not Fianna Fáil',[18] and she was probably not alone in this. Four internal Fianna Fáil transfers were below 50 per cent, the weakest we can be precise about being just 45 per cent in Galway West,[19] and only one, in Mayo, reached 70 per cent. If Fianna Fáil's internal transfer rate everywhere had been 80 per cent, as in earlier decades, it would have won up to six additional seats: in Cork East, Cork South-West, Donegal South-West, Louth, Sligo–North Leitrim, and perhaps also in Carlow–Kilkenny. In contrast, neither Labour nor Fine Gael missed out on any seats due to insufficiently strong internal transfers.

Table 7.5 Transfer patterns at 2011 election (%)

From	Available	N cases	FF	FG	Lab	SF
Internal solidarity						
FF	FF	28	58.2			
FG	FG	29		67.8		
Lab	Lab	16			56.2	
Inter-party transfers						
FG	Lab	4			45.2	
FG	FF, Lab	4	20.7		45.2	
FG	FF, SF	4	24.3			10.0
Lab	FG	16		38.4		
Lab	FF, FG	16	10.4	38.4		
Lab	FG, SF	6		40.2		22.1
Lab	FF, SF	8	12.0			21.3
FF	FG, Lab	7		22.8	21.1	
FF	FG, SF	3		23.8		14.8
FF	Lab, SF	8			24.3	14.1
SF	Lab	15			32.2	
SF	FF, FG	18	11.4	24.4		
SF	FG, Lab	15		17.0	32.2	
SF	FF, Lab	14	11.7		33.4	
Grn	FF	15	14.8			
Grn	FF, FG	13	14.6	36.4		
Grn	FF, Lab	12	13.3		37.4	
Grn	FG, Lab	11		28.6	37.5	
ULA	Lab, SF	6			29.6	38.3

Notes: The 'Available' column shows those parties that, in every case, had a candidate available to receive transfers. 'Inter-party' transfers refer only to terminal transfers, in other words to cases where the party whose votes were being distributed had no candidates of its own left in the count. The cases analysed exclude surpluses that were based on the distribution of a package of votes from a candidate of another party.

Turning to inter-party transfers, the most striking feature is the absence of a strong relationship between any two parties. Between the two parties that went on to form the next government, enthusiasm was at most warm. Considering all Fine Gael terminal transfers when a Labour candidate was available, 45 per cent of the votes went to Labour, and the corresponding figure in the other direction was 38 per cent. At the 1973 election, the high point of coalition solidarity, these figures were 71 per cent and 72 per cent respectively.[20] As for the parties in the outgoing government, Green voters clearly had a positive antipathy towards Fianna Fáil, as indeed supporters of pretty much every party did. Even Sinn Féin supporters, who in 2007 had given more of their next preferences to Fianna Fáil than to Fine Gael, now preferred the latter by a ratio of more than two to one. Sinn Féin itself lost a little of its transfer-unfriendly gloss, being generally preferred to Fianna Fáil, and ULA voters were more inclined to give their next preference to Sinn Féin than to Labour, but in most pairwise comparisons Sinn Féin came off second best. Labour was the most transfer-attractive party, being the most common next choice for voters of Fine Gael, Sinn Féin and the Greens, and this assisted it in its achievement of the record seat bonus mentioned earlier.

This is borne out by the list of seats that were won and lost due to inter-party transfers (see Table 7.6). Of the 12 seats that were so affected, Fianna Fáil was the loser in ten cases and Sinn Féin in the other two. At least Sinn Féin was able to balance this by being the gaining party in two cases, both when it was in contention with Fianna Fáil. Fine Gael, Labour and Independents each gained three seats due to transfers from other parties, and while these gains made no difference to the composition of the next government, given its huge majority, the additional ten seats would have left Fianna Fáil in a much healthier position with 30 seats than it was with just 20.

Table 7.6   Constituencies where inter-party transfers affected the outcome

Constituency	Seat won by	At the expense of	Due to transfers from
Cork E	Sandra McLellan SF	Kevin O'Keeffe FF	Lab, Inds
Cork SW	Michael McCarthy Lab	Denis O'Donovan FF	SF, FG, Inds
Donegal SW	Thomas Pringle Ind	Brian Ó Domhnaill FF	SF, Lab, Ind
Dublin MW	Derek Keating FG	Eoin Ó Broin SF	FF
Dublin N	Alan Farrell FG	Darragh O'Brien FF	Grn
Dublin NE	Seán Kenny Lab	Larry O'Toole SF	FF, Ind, Grn
Dublin SE	Kevin Humphreys Lab	Chris Andrews FF	Ind, SF, Grn
Dun Laoghaire	Richard Boyd Barrett ULA	Mary Hanafin FF	Lab
Louth	Peter Fitzpatrick FG	James Carroll FF	Lab
Sligo–N Leitrim	Michael Colreavy SF	Éamon Scanlon FF	Lab
Waterford	John Halligan Ind	Brendan Kenneally FF	SF, Lab, WP
Wicklow	Stephen Donnelly Ind	John Brady SF	Ind, FF

Note: The counter-factual scenario is one where the votes transferred from the party or parties in the final column went equally to the two candidates in the previous columns, in which case the candidate in the third column would have taken the seat.

The members of the 31st Dáil

Turnover and experience

As we mentioned earlier, turnover reached unprecedented levels. Of the 166 people who had taken their seats at the start of the 30th Dáil in 2007, only 80, along with two TDs elected at by-elections in 2009 and 2010, became members of the 31st Dáil in 2011. Over a fifth of those 166 (36 in all) retired, and unsurprisingly these were a little older than other TDs, averaging 62 years of age in February 2011 compared with 53 for the rest (see Appendix 5 for full list). Obviously, the main reason so few were re-elected was the attrition rate among Fianna Fáil TDs; only 24 per cent of its 2007 TDs were re-elected (one as an independent), compared with 75 per cent or more of TDs of Fine Gael, Labour or Sinn Féin. Across parties, TDs re-elected in 2011 had won slightly more votes in 2007 than defeated TDs had (8,249 compared with 7,752), and this was particularly marked among Fianna Fáil TDs, where those TDs re-elected in 2011 had won on average 10,683 first preferences in 2007 compared with 8,248 for Fianna Fáil TDs defeated in 2011. Even in such an exceptional election, past performance did hold some predictive power.

Of the 166 members who took their seats at the first meeting of the 31st Dáil on 9 March 2011, only 82 had also belonged to the 30th Dáil. This is the first time since 1923 that a majority of those elected did not belong to the previous Dáil. Such a figure is exceptionally low by the standards of most established democracies, apart from Canada and Spain, though in post-communist countries it is the norm that around half of all deputies are replaced at each election.[21] Of the 84 non-incumbents elected, eight were former TDs returning after an absence (Eric Byrne, Seán Crowe, Frances Fitzgerald, Séamus Healy, Joe Higgins, Seán Kenny, Catherine Murphy, Liam Twomey), the other 76 being new TDs. Political generations come and go rapidly. Only three members of the 31st Dáil were TDs contemporaneously with previous Taoisigh Jack Lynch and Liam Cosgrave, and a further 20 rubbed shoulders with Charles Haughey and Garret FitzGerald, the dominant figures of the 1980s. Naturally enough, new TDs are most prominent within the parties that gained most: within the Fine Gael Dáil group nearly half of the TDs (34 out of 76) are first-termers, as are a bare majority (19 out of 37) Labour TDs. Collectively, the TDs of both Fine Gael and Labour exhibit a mixture of newness and experience, but the Fianna Fáil Dáil group, as well as being small overall, is short on fresh faces; only eight of its 20 TDs first entered the Dáil after 1997.

Some of these fresh faces will no doubt one day be party leaders, while others will be one-term deputies. Whatever the future holds, the 76 new TDs bring a wealth of divergent experiences to Dáil Éireann. One has worked in Afghanistan, another in Vanuatu. One was a non-attending member of the House of Commons for 19 years and led his party into the power-sharing agreement in Northern Ireland. One spent five years at Maynooth studying for the priesthood, another served a ten-year jail sentence for possession of explosives. Nearly half (33) were standing for the first time in 2011, but at the other end of the scale two had first stood in the early 1980s. One took part in protests against the Vietnam war in London in the late 1960s; another, born in the mid-1980s, founded an autism charity at the age of 16. One has suffered from cerebral palsy, and another had a stroke in 2008. Six were aged over 60 and another six were in their twenties. One new TD was the producer for ten years of RTÉ television's most watched programme, *The Late Late Show*; another is the manager of the county Gaelic football team. One was a speechwriter at the nuclear test-ban treaty commission in Vienna; another won 548 first preferences when standing for the Dáil in 1997 under the name 'A, Ming' on a platform of legalising cannabis. Two are Ireland's first openly gay TDs. While it might be going too far to say that 'all human life is there', it is certainly the case that the Dáil does not consist of 166 'identikit TDs'.

Routes to the Dáil

The two classic routes to Leinster House are, first, through local government and second, through family links. The first is as strong as ever. The great majority (133, or 80 per cent) belonged to a county or city council before entering the Dáil. A further nine reversed the sequence, leaving just 24 (14 per cent) who have never belonged to a local authority. Only ten of the 76 new TDs fall into this last category. The overwhelming majority of new TDs (71 out of 84) were members of a county or city council at the time of the election. Thus, while there were many new faces in the 31st Dáil, the owners of those faces have a similar profile to those of the people they replaced, contrary to some hopes that a fundamentally new political class would emerge out of the crisis (see also Chapter 3, pp. 63–4). Until recently, it was common for TDs to retain their local authority position along with their Dáil seat, the equivalent of the French *cumul des mandats*. Since 2004 this has been prohibited, a measure intended to bring about a degree of separation between national and local politics, but the fact that council membership is part of the political socialisation process for almost all national politicians may have its consequences nonetheless, in terms of how TDs see their representational role vis-à-vis their constituents.[22]

On the other hand, the number of TDs closely related to a former TD, which is usually around 20–25 per cent, showed a marked decline in the 31st Dáil. Only 26 have such a relationship, which could be judged significant in their election in 22 cases (13 per cent), less than half of the figure in the previous Dáil. Not surprisingly, these 22 were much younger when first elected to the Dáil (on average, 34 years old) than other TDs (average age 42), and all bar one were elected on the first occasion they stood. Fifteen of the 22 were sons of previous deputies, with four nephews and three brothers; as discussed further in Chapter 10 (see p. 231), this factor did not work to the advantage of any female TD in 2011.

About a quarter of the TDs were standing for the first time in 2011, while at the other end of the scale five were standing for the 11th or 12th time, having been contesting elections since the 1970s. Most (55 per cent) were elected the first time they stood, while a couple (Eric Byrne and Seán Kenny) tasted defeat five times before succeeding at the sixth attempt. Just over half of all TDs have won every election they have contested, while one (Eric Byrne) has been defeated a remarkable nine times in his lengthy political career.

Backgrounds of deputies

Like all of its predecessors, the 31st Dáil was heavily male-dominated, although at least the proportion of female TDs, at 15 per cent, is the highest ever (see Chapter 10 for full discussion). Occupationally, there is little change from previous Dála of the past 30 years (see Appendix 2 for full details).[23] Professionals make up around 45 per cent of Dáil membership (60 per cent among Labour TDs), and those with a 'commercial' background (mainly running a small local business such as a shop, a pub, a wholesaler and so on) make up around a fifth of all TDs (over a quarter in the case of Fine Gael). The collapse of Fianna Fáil in particular has accelerated the decline in the number of farmers in the Dáil; this is now down to just 12 (7 per cent), all of them representing either Fianna Fáil or Fine Gael. A little over a half of TDs have a third-level degree, a slight increase on 2007, the proportion being highest within Labour (69 per cent) and lowest among Sinn Féin TDs (29 per cent).

Despite the large number of newcomers, the 31st Dáil is not especially youthful. Overall, the median TD was born in 1960, first stood for the Dáil in 2002, and was first elected in 2007. Around 32 per cent of TDs were in their fifties on election day, and a further 19 per cent were in their sixties, with only 4 per cent in their twenties and 23 per cent in their thirties. TDs' average age was 49 on election day, more or less the same as in other recent Dála. Among the four main parties, Labour TDs remain the oldest at an average of 51, though this is four years less than in the 30th Dáil; as well as a number of new young TDs, the Labour Dáil group now includes first-time TD Michael Conaghan (66) and former TD Seán Kenny (the oldest member of the Dáil at 68). Compared with the population as a whole, those under 30 and those over 70 are the most likely to feel under-represented, something that may have both symbolic and practical consequences.[24]

Conclusion

The 2011 election was expected to be Ireland's earthquake election and it did not disappoint. Records fell left, right and centre, with the dominant party of the previous 80 years collapsing to a quarter of its previous strength while the perennial second and third parties won record numbers of seats and formed a government with the largest ever overall majority. Yet, within this appearance of dramatic change, there were strong elements of continuity. Most strikingly, as elaborated in Chapter 13, no new party won any seats; the election saw a rearrangement of the existing party system rather than its destruction. At the 2002 election Fianna Fáil, Fine Gael and Labour won 133 seats between them; in 2011, they again won 133 seats. The distribution of seats among these three mainstays of the party system was very different – Fine Gael won more or less the same number as Fianna Fáil had in 2002, Labour about the same as Fine Gael had in 2002, and Fianna Fáil just one more than Labour had in 2002 – but their collective strength is almost unaltered.

Attempts to predict the future development of the Irish party system do not have a good track record. When Bertie Ahern won his third successive election in 2007, no-one predicted that his party would plummet from 78 to 20 seats within four years. Now that Fianna Fáil has suffered this debacle, one prognostication would foresee 'normalcy' gradually reasserting itself. If Labour, with 20 seats in 2007, could leap to 37 seats at the following election, and if Fine Gael, with 31 seats in 2002, could come close to an overall majority two elections later, then perhaps Fianna Fáil too has every chance of bouncing back. Fianna Fáil might be inherently a large party that is temporarily in shrunken form but will soon revert to its usual shape. The more pessimistic assessment is that Fianna Fáil in 2011 engendered a degree of outright hostility that scarcely any party has ever generated before, and so it will take many years and a degree of reinvention before it will be trusted again with a role in government.

Moreover, critics have long alleged that the glue that has always bound the disparate members of Fianna Fáil together and is central to its appeal is not any common ideology but, rather, its near-permanent occupation of the corridors of power. Since 1932, Fianna Fáil has never spent more than one consecutive term out of office, so those who simply want to be on the winning side have naturally gravitated to it. After the 2011 election, though, it did not look as if Fianna Fáil could expect a rapid return to office. If the Fine Gael–Labour government succeeds in dealing with the country's economic problems, then there is no reason to expect a significant swing to Fianna Fáil; if it does not, it is hard to see why voters would turn to the party generally held responsible for those problems. In these circumstances, conditions might be conducive to the rise of a new party. Were the government to break apart, of course, Fianna Fáil might have hopes of once again being coalitionable. For the moment, though, voter attitudes to the party are very negative, as we shall see in more detail in Chapter 8.

Notes

1. Two of these records were a matter of decimal points. Labour won 19.4 per cent of the votes, compared with 19.3 per cent in 1992; Fianna Fáil and Fine Gael won 53.55 per cent of the votes between them, compared with 53.57 per cent in June 1927.
2. Nicole Bolleyer, 'The Irish Green party: from protest to mainstream party?', *Irish Political Studies* 24:1 (2009), pp. 603–23, at p. 620.
3. Ciarán Cannon was the last leader of the PDs, Noel Grealish was elected twice to the Dáil as a PD, Mary Mitchell O'Connor was elected to her local county council as a PD, and Derek Keating and Peter Mathews were past members of the party. In 2011, Grealish was re-elected as an Independent TD and the other four were elected for Fine Gael.
4. Liam Weeks, 'We don't like (to) party: a typology of independents in Irish political life, 1922–2007', *Irish Political Studies* 24:1 (2009), 1–27.
5. Former Ireland international captain and manager John Giles, better known to many younger voters as a match analyst on television, endorsed Labour's Aodhán Ó Riordáin in Dublin North-Central, and he too was elected. However, the endorsement of another former Ireland international, Paul McGrath, did not achieve the election of independent Victor Boyhan in Dun Laoghaire. Neither Doyle nor Giles, being UK residents, actually had a vote.
6. Photographs of all TDs, along with their electoral histories, can be found on http://electionsireland.org, maintained by Christopher Took and Seán Donnelly.
7. Michael Gallagher, Michael Laver and Peter Mair, *Representative Government in Modern Europe*, 5th edn (Maidenhead: McGraw-Hill, 2011), p. 391.

8. Rein Taagepera and Matthew Soberg Shugart, *Seats and Votes: The effects and determinants of electoral systems* (New Haven and London: Yale University Press, 1989), pp. 112–25.

9. For the rationale and elaboration of such a scheme, see John Coakley, 'Revising Dáil constituency boundaries: Ireland in comparative perspective', *Administration* 55:3 (2007), pp. 1–30, and 'Does Ireland need a constituency commission?', *Administration* 55:4 (2008), pp. 77–114.

10. With an additional 4 per cent of the votes Fine Gael would have been very likely to win an extra seat in Cork North-Central, Donegal North-East, Galway East, Kerry South, and Longford–Westmeath, and it would have had a reasonable chance of doing so in Cork South-Central, Dublin North-West, Dublin South-Central and Tipperary South.

11. Tom Kelly, 'Proposed vote transfer policy leads to tensions within Fine Gael ranks', *Connaught Telegraph*, 8 February 2011.

12. Letters lacking the explicit endorsement of a senior national figure may be suspected – with some reason, based on past experience – of constituting an attempted 'stroke' by one of the candidates.

13. As a comparator, the classic case of non-management or mismanagement of votes for many years was the Dublin Central constituency, where Bertie Ahern controlled the Fianna Fáil organisation and insisted on receiving as many first preferences as possible. Over the six elections of the 1987–2007 period, the average ratio between his first preference vote total and that of the *n*th-placed Fianna Fáil candidate was 5.50.

14. See the account in Olivia Ryan and Christine Doherty, 'FF candidates in Louth turf war', *Drogheda Independent*, 16 February 2011.

15. Carlow–Kilkenny, Cork East, Donegal South-West, Dublin Central, Galway West, Meath East, Meath West, Sligo–North Leitrim, and Wicklow.

16. This was a feature of the single non-transferable vote system, which Japan employed at elections prior to 1996. Examples, and comparisons with vote management in Ireland, are given in Michael Gallagher, 'The Japanese House of Councillors election 1998 in comparative perspective', *Electoral Studies* 20:4 (2001), pp. 603–25, at pp. 605–8.

17. As in Chapter 9, we exclude from the analysis all cases of simultaneous eliminations of candidates of more than one party, and distribution of surpluses when these votes are taken from a packet of votes received from a candidate of a different party. Unlike Chapter 9, the analysis includes first-count surpluses. See discussion on pp. 206–7 below.

18. Seán Keane, 'Checking the windows for a draught', *Kilkenny People*, 11 February 2011. For general discussion of the impact of party and of candidate on voters' decisions, see Michael Marsh, Richard Sinnott, John Garry and Fiachra Kennedy, *The Irish Voter: The nature of electoral competition in the Republic of Ireland* (Manchester: Manchester University Press, 2008), pp. 146–60.

19. In Roscommon–South Leitrim a Fianna Fáil candidate was eliminated simultaneously with a Green and an Independent; the proportion of the Fianna Fáil candidate's votes transferring to his running mate was somewhere between 33 per cent and 43 per cent.

20. Michael Gallagher (ed.), *Irish Elections 1948–77: Results and analysis* (London: Routledge and PSAI Press, 2009), p. 315. Of course, the range of options in 1973 was much less extensive.

21. Richard E. Matland and Donley T. Studlar, 'Determinants of legislative turnover: a cross-national analysis', *British Journal of Political Science* 34:1 (2004), pp. 87–108, at p. 93; Michael Gallagher, Michael Laver and Peter Mair, *Representative Government in Modern Europe*, 5th edn (Maidenhead: McGraw-Hill, 2011), p. 67.

22. Michael Gallagher and Lee Komito, 'The constituency role of Dáil deputies', pp. 230–62 in John Coakley and Michael Gallagher (eds), *Politics in the Republic of Ireland*, 5th edn (Abingdon: Routledge and PSAI Press, 2010).

23. Categorising TDs occupationally is not straightforward. As Noel Whelan notes, many TDs, in their campaign material or online biographies, downplay any pre-political occupation, presenting themselves as 'full-time public representatives'; some Sinn Féin deputies in particular, he says, 'appear to have had no occupation before politics or are shy about sharing it'. Noel Whelan, 'The continuity behind the Dáil transformation', *Irish Times*, 5 March 2011.

24. See discussion in Mary-Clare O'Sullivan, 'The social and political characteristics of the twenty-eighth Dáil', pp. 181–94 in Michael Marsh and Paul Mitchell (eds), *How Ireland Voted 1997* (Boulder, CO: Westview Press and PSAI Press, 1999), p. 184.

8

A Positive Choice, or Anyone but Fianna Fáil?

Michael Marsh and Kevin Cunningham

This chapter explores the motives, expectations and mood of voters in 2011, and draws on the results from an unprecedented number of campaign polls as well as the Lansdowne/RTÉ exit poll, carried out with voters as they left the polling station, to answer a number of questions about voting behaviour in this election. The first question must be about the collapse of Fianna Fáil. The scale of the losses suffered by that party is almost without precedent in a mature democracy, but the root cause is a simple one to identify, and it is argued here that the outcome was in essence a classic example of voters exacting punishment for what was widely seen as a succession of bad economic decisions. Fianna Fáil (and the Greens) destroyed the economy, and the voters went some way to destroying those parties in revenge. Such an explanation, however, does nothing to tell us why voters who left Fianna Fáil, and others, chose the alternatives they did: why Fine Gael rather than Labour, or why an Independent, or Sinn Féin, rather than either of the more established opposition parties? This leads into the second question: how did voters decide on the alternative to Fianna Fáil, and how far were voters in 2011 motivated in ways different from those of previous elections?

There was certainly some expectation that, such was the extent of the economic crisis, and so intense had been the debate around it over the previous two years and more, that voters would focus more than they usually did on party; national issues and the policy alternatives facing the next government would take priority over the importance and quality of a local candidate. A stronger emphasis on policy voting could provoke all sorts of change, but the most obvious question here is how far any change in focus contributed to the growing strength of centre-left and left parties and candidates, and a clearer left–right cleavage in the party system. To the extent that there was a national focus, whether greater or less than in recent years, the main talking point in the last week was on the composition of government. The Fine Gael–Labour government that was seen as the most certain of certainties over the last few months of 2010, if not earlier, now appeared only as a probability, as the option of an overall Fine Gael majority looked possible, if unlikely. In the end, of course, a Fine Gael–Labour government was formed, with a huge majority, but the third major question addressed here is was this government what people wanted, and was it seen, even by people who appeared to vote for that outcome, as a government that could lead the country out of its current malaise?

The collapse of the Fianna Fáil vote

Fianna Fáil's victories in 2002 and 2007 owed much to the perception that it had done a good job in relation to the economy, delivering an unprecedented level of prosperity with low taxes, growing incomes and high levels of employment. There were clouds on the economic horizon in 2007, as there had been in 2002, but the public had confidence in Fianna Fáil to weather the possible storms. In fact, Fine Gael in particular seemed unwilling to raise any fears as its own focus groups had told it Fianna Fáil would win any contest on the economy. In the terms used in political science, Fianna Fáil 'owned' the economy as an issue.[1]

Between 2008 and 2010 the confidence of the public was lost in as dramatic a fashion as anyone could envisage. There were two critical periods. First there was the month starting with the bank guarantee of 30 September 2008, and then two years later, there was a growing realisation that things were much worse even than they had seemed. The government announced it would withdraw from the international bond market as the only price at which it could borrow money was prohibitively high. It also admitted that the adjustment that would be required in the December 2010 budget was close to twice what the voters had previously been led to expect. Figure 8.1 shows the consequence of these series of events on Fianna Fáil support. It shows as points all of the polls taken by RED C over the inter-election period, and plots fitted lines between them, segregated by 30 September 2008 and 30 September 2010. Many voters who identify themselves with a party interpret economic news through partisan lenses. Such 'bias', for want of a better description, is limited and may be overcome by stark realities when these present themselves. The bank guarantee of September 2008 and the withdrawal from the bond market of September 2010 represented such stark realities for Fianna Fáil supporters.[2] There are parallels elsewhere. The most obvious is the collapse of the British Conservative Party's credibility on economic matters following its sudden withdrawal from the European exchange rate mechanism on 'Black Wednesday' in September 1992. It would be almost 20 years before that party again led its Labour Party rival in public perception of its capacity to run the economy.[3] How long it will take Fianna Fáil to regain its credibility must be unknown at present, but there can be no guarantee that it ever will do so. It is possible that, as with the effect of Black Wednesday on the Tories, uncertainty had been growing for some time over Fianna Fáil's ability to maximise economic prosperity. What is clear is that the initial episode had far-reaching consequences for the party.

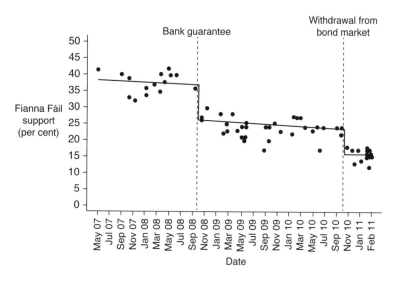

Figure 8.1   Fianna Fáil in the polls May 2007–February 2011

The pattern is clear. There is almost no trend in Fianna Fáil voting intention 2007–11 beyond an initial sharp fall to a lower level following the bank guarantee, and a subsequent fall two years later. Fianna Fáil's demise may thus be termed as a story of two bailouts. First, when the banks were bailed out; and second when it became clear that the entire country was to be bailed out. In the intervening period, Fianna Fáil did not suffer the loss of support that might have been expected given that what was originally termed 'the world's cheapest bailout' by Brian Lenihan[4] soon became what the International Monetary Fund (IMF) described as 'matching episodes of the most severe economic distress in post-World War II history.'[5] Nor were there any changes in subsequent months; there was no steady accumulation of discontent culminating in a final decision to vote for someone else. Good months, such as the green shoots of recovery early in 2010, were followed by bad months, as support fluctuated as if randomly around a new level established quickly after each crisis. Basically, after September 2008 Fianna Fáil support never again exceeded 30 per cent, and after September 2010 it never exceeded 20 per cent.[6] A number of events in the few months before the election might be thought to have played a role in the scale of the defeat, but it is hard to see any consistent traces in the polls of any event after September 2010. The arrival of the European Central Bank (ECB)/IMF in November only confirmed what had been clear to international investors for some time: the government's policy was not working. The tough budget seemed to have no great impact, nor did the acceptance of the ECB/IMF terms, and the shambolic collapse of the government and resignation of Cowen as Fianna Fáil leader seemed to be no more than temporary blips. In electoral terms, the question was not whether Fianna Fáil would suffer a heavy defeat, but simply how heavy that defeat would be and who would benefit most from government losses. The goose was cooked, but who would feed off the carcass?

Settling on the alternatives: uncertainty and change

In the absence of a strong anchoring point the electorate was very volatile in the last months and weeks leading up to the election. The polls, as described in Chapter 1, suggested that no other party had quite captured the public mood and provided a single alternative to Fianna Fáil. Fine Gael's support was up significantly without looking like it would dominate, while Labour's growth in the middle of the year was not sustained. Sinn Féin showed growth after the by-election win in November while Independents consolidated what looked like a strong showing. Evidence from a number of sources points to great uncertainty.

While political parties compete for votes in elections, in reality that competition may be limited. Many voters are effectively 'out of competition', having made a standing decision to support a particular party that allows no effective consideration of any other party. For example, a voter may be extremely committed to Fianna Fáil and would never dream of giving their first preference vote to any other party. In this case all Fianna Fáil has to worry about is making sure that that voter actually turns out to vote on election day. Other voters may be genuinely trying to make up their minds about which of a number of parties to vote for. If a voter is considering the merits of only *two* parties in particular – say, Fine Gael and Labour – then that voter is 'open to competition' between those two parties (and 'out of competition' for all the other parties). There may also be voters who are seriously considering voting for one or other of three or more parties and are thus open to competition between a range of parties. The existence of voters who are open to competition allows parties to compete with one another for votes (and not simply compete over which party can mobilise the largest proportion of 'its' voters).

The traditional picture of the Irish electorate was one in which a large number of voters were removed from competition between parties. Instead, voters followed loyalties established during and after the civil war. The more common view nowadays is of an *available* electorate, one prone to violent swings towards or away from particular parties; an electorate cut from its traditional moorings and free to float on whatever political tide is flowing. In short, many commentators believe that we now have an electorate that is open to competition between a range of parties; that we have, in fact, a large number of 'floating voters'.

Questions that are asked in surveys about party preference typically focus on the outcome of the choice voters make – did you (or will you) vote for party A, B or C? Typically, surveys ask respondents who they would vote for if an election were to be held tomorrow (or who they voted for in the last election). This ignores the other options that voters may consider. What surveys do not ask is whether the party indicated by the respondent is the respondent's very *clear-cut* choice or whether the party is selected by the voter after an effort to decide between *a number of* parties. RED C asked questions in a number of polls that were designed to find out how certain voters were in their ideas about who they would support and who they would not. The questions used here ask respondents to indicate, for each party, how probable it is that a given party would ever get their vote.[7]

A RED C poll carried out for Paddy Power on 1 February, three weeks before the election, put these questions to respondents and the results give us an insight into the state of the electorate at that time. Taken in comparison with results from the Irish Election Study of 2002–07 they underline the extent to which a sea change had taken place in Irish party politics. Moreover, this change took place well before the election as the results resemble quite closely those from a similar study carried out in June 2009.[8] A distinction is made here between what we might call 'core voters' – those who give a high score of 8 or more (out of 10) to just one party – and 'potential voters', those who gave a high score – 8 or more – to more than one party, as well as 'antagonistic' voters, those who give a party the minimum score of 1.

Table 8.1 describes the results. The first point to note is the very low figures for the core support in each party. The total across all parties sums only to 43 per cent, indicating that the majority of the electorate was still available. Not surprisingly, the major change from 2007 was the drop in Fianna Fáil core support, down from 21 per cent to just 9 per cent, but Fine Gael had risen from 8 per cent to 14 per cent. In the second row is the percentage of respondents giving the party a score of 1, indicating they would be very unlikely to support the party. Forty-seven per cent, up from just 18 per cent in 2007, gave this score to Fianna Fáil, making it almost as unpopular as Sinn Féin (52 per cent, almost unchanged from 2007), with significant consequences for its ability to collect transfers. The results also broadly indicated a lessening of confidence across the party system. In 2007, 54 per cent gave a 10 to at least one party, but in this poll only 41 per cent did so.

Table 8.1 Core and potential support 2011 (%)

	FF	FG	Lab	SF	Grn	Ind
Core support (8+, one party)	9	14	8	5	1	6
Antagonism (score of 1 for that party)	47	19	18	52	49	19
Potential support (8+, one or more parties)	19	35	29	15	7	23
Potential support shared with:						
FF	100	12	10	16	22	17
FG	23	100	49	16	34	30
Labour	15	41	100	24	38	33
SF	13	7	12	100	23	19
Greens	8	6	9	10	100	12
Independent	21	19	26	29	40	100

Source: Analysis of Paddy Power/RED C poll, 1 February 2011.

The potential support row sums to more than 100 per cent, 128 in fact, because some respondents indicate potential support for more than one party. Labour support was very high, well up on the 22 per cent in 2007, and not far behind that for Fine Gael. Independents also scored very highly, and the Greens and Sinn Féin were well above what they actually achieved. In the rows below the potential support row we can see how each party's support is shared. If we look at the Labour column, it shows us that Labour shared 49 per cent of its support with Fine Gael; the Fine Gael column shows that this was largely reciprocated, with 41 per cent of Fine Gael's support shared with Labour. Independent-inclined voters also leaned towards Fine Gael (30 per cent) or Labour (33 per cent) in large numbers. This sort of pattern of overlap between these two parties could also be seen in 2007 and earlier, although support was also shared significantly with Fianna Fáil then.[9]

The RTÉ/Millward Brown exit poll showed similar levels of uncertainly, asking voters when they made up their mind how to vote. This is a very different approach to a similar question – that of uncertainty – but this asks people to report on their own state of uncertainty while the previous analysis infers uncertainty from a number of evaluations of different parties. Only 36 per cent claimed to have decided before the election was called, with the remainder evenly divided between the day before, the week before and two to three weeks before election day. In contrast almost half of all voters claimed to have decided before the campaign proper began in 1997, 2002 and 2007. Forty-one per cent decided in the last week, including on the last day, a percentage well up on previous years.

Table 8.2   Time of decision (%)

	1997	2002	2007	2011
Day before election	12	10	13	20
Week of the election	15	14	17	21
2–3 weeks before the election	25	30	22	23
Before the election was called	48	45	48	36
Total	100	100	100	100

Source: Lansdowne/RTÉ exit polls 1997–2011.

Fine Gael and Fianna Fáil support was committed earlier than was support for other parties. Forty-eight per cent of Fianna Fáil voters and 42 per cent of Fine Gael voters decided early, compared with just 27 per cent of Labour voters. Uncertainty is also evident, as might be expected, in those voting Independent. This might suggest that Labour campaigned effectively, but it could be simply that Labour voters did generally make up their mind later than others. Fine Gael did best whenever people decided. Labour's poll ratings throughout suggest it lost support relative to its poll figures at the start of the election, although its private polls suggest it did improve in the final week when its focus changed to preventing a single-party Fine Gael government (see pp. 85–6 above).

Not only did people leave it late to decide, but there was a huge degree of change in voting behaviour from 2007. Both Chapter 7 and Chapter 13 demonstrate how unusual this election was in terms of aggregate change. Such measures of volatility can underestimate the degree of gross change: how many voters voted differently at the two elections. We have taken the composite of all polls taken during the campaign to examine preference change from 2007. We did this to give us a much larger sample than that which is normally available, even in the exit poll. Obviously the polls differ in their timing but all were quite close to the final result and the advantages, in terms of sample size, outweigh any disadvantages. Unfortunately polls are not good in assessing who actually votes. The exit polls do not talk to non-voters and campaign polls can only find out who is more or less likely to vote, so we cannot look so closely at the source of non-voters in 2011; for this there are some indications in the campaign polls and these will be discussed below.

A different way to look at this uncertainty is in terms of traditional loyalties. Political scientists have employed the term 'party identification' to describe the attachment that voters have had to parties, an attachment that can lead voters to screen out information critical of their party or excuse or rationalise what others would see as information damaging to that party. This helps to explain why such people would support the same party in election after election. Such attachment is low in Ireland these days and seems to have dropped a little further in 2011, judging by the exit poll. In 2002, 28 per cent of those voting felt 'close' to a party.[10] In 2011 it was just 25 per cent, the drop being accounted for largely by the decline in Fianna Fáil identifiers from 16 per cent to just 10 per cent of those voting. There was a marginal increase in Fine Gael and Labour numbers, but 2 per cent fewer identify with Fine Gael than Fianna Fail. Moreover, such attachment is still (as it was in 2002) more closely linked to a Fianna Fáil vote than to support for any other party. Fianna Fáil depended on its traditional supporters to a much greater extent than did other parties; 40 per cent of the party's vote came from those who felt close to the party, at least twice as high a figure as that for any other party. However, even those who did admit to being close to the party were much less likely to vote in accordance with their attachment than were identifiers with other parties. Only 61 per cent of Fianna Fáil sympathisers voted for the party, whereas the comparable figure for other parties was in the range of 80–90 per cent, as it was formerly with Fianna Fáil. The implication of these results is that Fianna Fáil has retained a reservoir of sympathy, despite its current travails. This improves its chances of making a significant recovery, although even if all those who declared support had voted Fianna Fáil it would still have come in a very poor second in 2011.

Table 8.3   Party choice of individual voters 2007–11 (%)

Vote in 2007	Vote in 2011					
	Fine Gael	Labour	Fianna Fáil	Sinn Fein	Green	Ind./Other
Fine Gael	77.0	10.4	2.4	3.1	0.8	6.2
Labour	12.6	66.3	2.9	5.0	1.1	12.0
Fianna Fáil	28.0	15.8	34.9	6.1	1.1	14.0
Sinn Féin	5.1	7.3	2.6	77.1	1.3	6.6
Green Party	22.5	24.7	2.5	4.9	29.1	16.3
Prog. Democrats	44.4	11.1	13.9	2.8	2.8	25.0
Indep. / Other	18.2	10.7	4.7	6.0	0.5	59.8
Did not vote	28.5	25.9	9.7	15.8	3.7	16.3

Sources: RED C, Millward Brown and OI campaign polls, and Lansdowne exit poll: see the Appendix to this chapter.

The same pattern is seen when we take a measure of attachment based on behaviour rather than explicit sympathy, by looking at past voting. Table 8.3 shows the vote or vote intention of respondents in 2011 tabulated against their vote (or non-vote) in 2007. In all, of those who voted for a party in 2007 and 2011, 45 per cent, almost half, changed their primary allegiance. If we include those who did not vote in 2007, and ignore those who would not say, half of all voters altered their behaviour from the previous election, an increase of almost 30 percentage points from the 1997–2007 average. While this is a very significant increase it does not indicate a change promoted by dissatisfaction with all parties. Indeed, this increase can be attributed largely to the exodus from Fianna Fáil. Fianna Fáil retained just one in three of its voters from the last election. Fine Gael and Sinn Féin each retained more than three of every four of their 2007 voters, but Labour, despite its massive overall gains, held on to only two out of three, a figure not much greater than that for Independents/Others. This further underlines the relative softness of the Labour vote.

Fine Gael was the main beneficiary of the exodus from Fianna Fáil, attracting 28 per cent of 2007 Fianna Fáil supporters while Green Party support dissipated to an even greater extent than that of Fianna Fáil. The Greens retained just 29 per cent of their 2007 vote share, with Labour (25 per cent) and Fine Gael (23 per cent) attracting the bulk of that vote.

New voters, or at least those who did not vote in 2007, opted almost equally for Fine Gael and Labour, with Sinn Féin and Independents/Others sharing most of the rest about equally. Fewer than one in ten voted Fianna Fáil, but even this was a much higher share than could be attracted away from other parties.

Sometimes voters change by staying home. While some voters move in and out of the electorate for reasons that are primarily circumstantial,[11] some may prefer to stay away rather than support a party they have traditionally favoured. There is some evidence that this was a behaviour adopted by Fianna Fáil voters. Those who reported voting Fianna Fáil in 2007 were much more likely to say they would not vote in 2011 than were those who voted for Fine Gael, Labour or Sinn Féin; 17 per cent of Fianna Fáil voters said they would stay home, as against 9 per cent of each of the others' supporters. So not only did Fianna Fáil lose to other parties, it also lost significantly through differential turnout. Many 2007 supporters stayed home while very few 2007 non-voters opted this time for Fianna Fáil.

Who voted for whom?

Before we go on to explore the reasons for choice it is worthwhile to establish the major demographics of party support. This is first because movements between parties by social groups may give some indications as to the motivations behind such changes, and second because the bases of support in 2011 may give us some pointers to the future.

What is normally unusual about Irish politics is the relative absence of a relationship between distinct socio-demographic groups and political party choice. The pattern continued in 2011. Table 8.4 shows party choice by social class. Apart from the relative strength of Fine Gael among the now small group of farmers, the more distinctive profiles are those of the smaller parties. While Sinn Féin has particular support in the semi- and unskilled working class, even this tendency is weakening.

The fall in support for Fianna Fáil was relatively uniform: between 21 per cent and 28 per cent in each social class. Differences between Fine Gael's and Labour's abilities to increase their vote share at the expense of Fianna Fáil was somewhat structured by social class. Whereas Fine Gael increased its support marginally better among middle-class deserters (an 11 per cent increase compared with 9 per cent), Labour picked up more than Fine Gael among working-class movers. The most dramatic change was the rise of 14 per cent (from 9 per cent to 23 per cent) in Labour's share of the skilled working-class vote. While this may be the result of the 'tax versus cut' policy differences between the parties, the overall outcome hardly points to a typical left–right divide. As usual, and something that might be regarded as highly irregular in other countries, the Labour Party does not dominate any one social class; rather, it is Fine Gael that has the largest support in every class – including unskilled workers.

Table 8.4   First preferences by social class from 2011, and change since 2007 (%)

	AB Middle class	C1 Lower middle class	C2 Skilled working class	DE Semi- and unskilled working class	F Farmers
Fine Gael	41 (+11)	36 (+13)	30 (+8)	30 (+7)	53 (+9)
Labour	22 (+9)	23 (+12)	23 (+14)	21 (+11)	5 (–1)
Fianna Fáil	14 (–23)	14 (–27)	15 (–28)	16 (–28)	23 (–21)
Sinn Féin	6 (+3)	9 (+3)	14 (+6)	17 (+4)	7 (+3)
Green Party	3 (–5)	3 (–4)	2 (–3)	2 (0)	1 (+1)
All Others	14 (+4)	16 (+4)	16 (+2)	14 (+6)	11 (+8)
Total	100	100	100	100	100
N	4,128	4,873	3,834	4,398	966

Source: See Table 8.3; bracketed figures estimated from 2007 exit poll.

Gains made by Independents and Others combined are almost entirely concentrated in the semi- and unskilled working classes and among farmers. This may be a reflection of the influx of support for far-left independents and those from the Fianna Fáil 'gene pool'. Nevertheless, the support bases of Independents and Others show a very flat profile.

We also looked at those who had shifted their allegiance from Fianna Fáil since 2007 using the set of polls used in Table 8.3. There is a possibility here that the destination of such voters might be more closely linked to class, as habit and traditional loyalty may weigh less heavily for these voters. In fact, this group looks much like the larger group of voters of which it forms a part. Those in the AB group were more likely to move to Fine Gael than those in the DE group, 33 per cent compared to 24 per cent, but that is the sort of difference we see in Table 8.4. Similarly, Sinn Féin won 9 per cent in the DE group but only 4 per cent in the AB category. Independents picked up between 13 per cent and 15 per cent in each group. There is this very little sign here of any significant realignment in terms of class.

Unfortunately the available data do not allow us to look within occupational groupings to distinguish those in the public as opposed to the private sector, a distinction that became politicised as the size of the public deficit expanded. In the past we have not seen much

Table 8.5 Vote distribution by age in 2011 and change since 2007 (%)

	18–24		25–34		Age 35–49		50–64		65+		Gender Male		Female	
Fine Gael	31	(+7)	30	(+7)	35	(+10)	36	(+7)	39	(+8)	36	(+9)	35	(+10)
Labour	24	(+12)	26	(+17)	24	(+14)	22	(+13)	18	(+8)	20	(+10)	23	(+13)
Fianna Fáil	12	(−23)	12	(−27)	12	(−28)	16	(−29)	25	(−24)	15	(−27)	15	(−27)
Sinn Féin	14	(+3)	13	(+3)	11	(+3)	10	(+4)	5	(+4)	12	(+4)	9	(+3)
Greens	3	(−5)	3	(−5)	2	(−3)	1	(−1)	1	(−1)	2	(−2)	3	(−2)
Inds/Others	16	(+6)	16	(+5)	15	(+4)	16	(+6)	12	(+5)	15	(+6)	15	(+3)
Total	100		100		100		100		100		100		100	

Source: See Table 8.3; bracketed figures estimated from 2007 exit poll.

difference in the party political allegiances of these two groups, although the former group is more heavily unionised.[12] The 2011 Irish Election Study does allow for such analysis and may show that these differences are now clearer.

Disaggregating vote share by age group in Table 8.5 reveals how Fine Gael increased its share by between 7 and 10 per cent in each age group, with the biggest gain in the 35–49 group where there was most volatility. Fine Gael stands as before, slightly favoured by older age groups. In contrast, Labour's gains range from 8 per cent to 17 per cent and are concentrated mostly around the 25–34 age group, reinforcing to some extent its support bias towards younger voters.

Fianna Fáil's losses range from 29 per cent to 23 per cent and are greatest in the age group 50–64, where it lost almost two-thirds of its 2007 vote share. The age profile of the Fianna Fáil voter is now heavily skewed towards the 65 and over age group where it holds the support of 25 per cent, as compared with 12 per cent in each of the 18–24 and 25–35 age groups. In 2007 the break was between those under and over 50. Perhaps this oldest age group was sheltered more from cuts, but it is also in that group that we would expect traditional loyalties to be at their strongest.

Previous volumes in this series have emphasised how a party's age distribution is a reflection of the relative age of the parties, as supporters grow into a habit of supporting a party over many years. If this is correct, it is bad news for Fianna Fáil. Unless the party is able to dominate the opposition there are signs that Fianna Fáil will fall behind Sinn Féin. Gains made by Sinn Féin range between 3 per cent and 4 per cent across the four under-64 age categories. The party even made gains in the 65-plus category.

In terms of gender, differences are much as they were in 2007. Sinn Féin remains much stronger among men. The previous disposition among women towards Independent candidates has now gone.

The bases of choice

There was some expectation that this election would be different from its recent predecessors in being focused more on what might be done than on who was to do it, with more emphasis on policy and less on personalities, and more concern with the national and less with the local. The evidence on this suggests that such change was somewhat muted. Table 8.6 shows responses to a question in the Lansdowne/RTÉ exit poll asking people to choose between several factors in terms of what was most important in their decision. This is a well established question, dating back to the 1980s. The main criterion for the great majority of voters was either the parties' policies or a candidate who would attend to local needs. This is in marked contrast to previous exit poll findings in some respects. At past elections, including 2007, the choice of Taoiseach has typically been more important and policies less important than was the case in 2011. The percentage picking 'candidate' is almost unchanged from 2007, suggesting that the national–local balance was not substantially changed. However, it should be acknowledged that this policy figure was lower, and the candidate figure higher, than comparable ones from an identical question in three Millward Brown/Independent Newspapers polls during the election. Across the three polls and about 3,000 respondents, average figures were Policies (46 per cent), Minister (15 per cent), Taoiseach (9 per cent) and Candidate (28 per cent). These vary little whether or not those with no vote intention are included or excluded. Perhaps the higher level of candidate-centred voting in the exit poll can be explained by the fact that those responding had just voted and were more conscious of the candidates who were standing.[13] Unfortunately, we cannot establish this by comparing findings on this item from campaign polls and the following exit poll.

Table 8.6 The most important criterion in deciding how to vote (%)

	2007	2011
The Taoiseach	12	7
The set of ministers that will form the government	23	13
The policies as set out by the parties	25	43
A candidate to look after the needs of the constituency	40	38
Total	100	100

Source: Lansdowne/RTÉ exit polls 2007, 2011.

It is remarkable that Fianna Fáil voters, who in 2007 were more inclined to stress what we might group together as national, non-candidate factors, were in 2011 the most inclined (with voters for Independents and Others) to stress the importance of the local candidate. This suggests that Fianna Fáil's incumbents, badly as they fared, still mitigated the anti-Fianna Fáil swing. Whatever their motivation, voters were more likely to choose Fine Gael than any other party. Fine Gael's lead was greatest where voters cited policy as the reason, with 47 per cent of this group choosing Fine Gael, compared to only 28 per cent of those wanting a local candidate. Despite its apparent ideological focus, it is notable that

Sinn Féin's best performance (as in 2007) was among those who want a good local candidate, 12 per cent of whom support that party compared with 9 per cent of policy- and minister-driven voters and 8 per cent of those who want to pick a Taoiseach. While these differences are small, they are contrary to what might have been expected. We will look at the importance of the party leaders in a little more detail below, but it is worth noting here that despite the emphasis on its leader in campaign material, Labour did worst among those who were picking a Taoiseach, and best among those wanting a good set of ministers. The latter group were 8 per cent more likely than the former to support Labour. Again, this difference is not large (though it is statistically significant) but it is notable for being the opposite of what we might have expected given the emphasis of Labour's campaign.

Policy and the vote

An emphasis on policy in this election is understandable, given the circumstances in which the election was being fought, but people may mean a variety of things by 'policies'. Fine Gael had its famous 'five-point' plan, for instance, to which Enda Kenny referred constantly, and other parties also had policy packages laid out in their manifestos (see Chapter 2). We can distinguish two very different ways in which these might lead a voter to choose one party over another. The first is that they prefer the general approach of one party to the other, in terms of the choices it will make. This may be because of ideology, or of practicality, or self-interest, or some other reason. For this to be the case the parties must offer different policies. In economic policy, for instance, a voter may prefer the speed with which one party addresses the budgetary deficit, or the mixture of taxation and cost-cutting strategies a government led by this party would follow. There were differences between the parties in 2011, not least in economic policy, and people could have chosen in this way. A second meaning does not require that parties have different policies but that voters judge each party in terms of its credibility. Everyone may agree that the crisis needs to be addressed, and all parties say they will do it, but who do voters trust most to accomplish the task? In 2002 and 2007 the voters thought Fianna Fáil would do the best job running the economy, perhaps unsurprisingly given the apparently strong record of economic growth enjoyed at the time. A variant on this is that different groups of voters may care about different policy areas, and what matters is credibility on the area that is most important. Voters preferred to trust

Fine Gael on health in 2007, but ultimately health proved less important than the economy.

Questions asked in polls are not always designed in such a way that we can extract either meaning from them, but there were questions asked in the exit poll and campaign polls that could throw some light on which of these meanings was most widespread. We can start by examining what issues the voters said were most important. The exit poll asked respondents what was the primary issue or problem that lay behind their decision on how to vote.[14]

Respondents were clear that it was the economy/banking crisis or anger directed against the political system/government and politicians, each at 36 per cent (see Table 8.7). The difference here may be cosmetic. It seems likely that the anger against politicians had its roots in the economic crisis. There is little difference between the parties in terms of the importance of the economy in particular, but Fianna Fáil voters were much less likely than those of other parties to emphasise anger or disappointment with politicians and the political system. Other issues that featured more highly in recent elections, such as health and crime, were now a marginal influence.[15] Using a slightly different methodology, an IPSOS MRBI/*Irish Times* poll invited respondents to say which issue would be the most important one for the new government to tackle, and

Table 8.7 The most important issue or problem in 2011

Issue		%
Economic crisis		35.6
The economy/managing the economy	17.7	
The banking crisis	12.9	
The EU/IMF bailout	5.0	
Economic issues		13.5
Unemployment/redundancies/job losses	5.7	
Pay cuts	5.4	
Higher taxes	1.5	
Mortgage increases/negative equity	0.9	
Political system		36.3
Anger with government/political system	22.7	
Politicians/government have let us down	13.6	
Other issues		6.2
Tactical/traditional		4.4
Don't know		0.7
Other		3.3

Source: Lansdowne/RTÉ exit poll 2011.

provided a list of seven items, asking people to pick one. Most chose jobs (51 per cent), or public finances (23 per cent), with health (10 per cent) a poor third. Political reform (6 per cent) and political accountability (5 per cent) were each chosen by relatively few,[16] as were emigration (2 per cent) and education (2 per cent). This is not to say these were not salient, but simply that they were not the most important issues.[17]

The major issue was, in broad terms, the economy, but who did people think best equipped to deal with it? A Millward Brown/Independent Newspapers poll on 31 January asked respondents to say which party would be best at dealing with each of four issues, three of them economic: the deficit, the health service, unemployment and the banks. Results are given in Table 8.8. In general, each item got a very similar response with about 20 per cent saying no party and 10 per cent not knowing, while Fine Gael and Labour were the top two parties. Of course we might expect that people would nominate the party they intend voting for as the best one. In such cases we are not necessarily finding reasons for voting so much as rationalisations for doing so. We expect a strong link, but it is the varying strength of the association between ranking and vote across questions and parties that can offer insights into possible causes of behaviour. There are several notable features. The first is that on the banks a larger percentage thought the problem beyond all parties. The second is that on unemployment Labour led Fine Gael. A third is there was very little faith in Fianna Fáil to solve any of these problems; Sinn Féin was seen as more credible than Fianna Fáil. Unsurprisingly, Fianna Fáil voters were often disproportionately inclined to see these problems as insoluble. As we have seen above, health was a marginal issue and the

Table 8.8   Party with best policy in selected areas (%)

	Deficit	Health	Unemployment	Banking
		Best policies to deal with:		
Fine Gael	32	32	24	27
Labour	18	19	29	18
Fianna Fáil	9	6	7	8
Sinn Féin	9	8	9	10
Green	0	1	1	1
Independents/Others	3	3	3	2
None of them	18	18	17	23
Don't know	11	12	10	12
Total	100	100	100	100

Source: Millward Brown/Independent Newspapers, 2 February.

overall link between each of these competencies and vote intention was weaker in the case of health than for the other issues: the salience of the deficit was most strongly linked to vote choice.[18] Only 65 per cent of those who thought either Labour or Fine Gael was the best option to solve the deficit problem intended to vote for each party; those who thought no party could do it favoured Fianna Fáil, Labour and Independents most. On the banking crisis the figures are very similar, but there the pessimists spread evenly across the same four parties. On unemployment, Labour's lead was not converted into votes: only 55 per cent of those who thought Labour was best to tackle this problem intended to vote for the party. Given the importance of these issues in the campaign, the association between rating and votes might be considered modest.

A later Millward Brown/Independent Newspapers poll (17 February), asked voters to prioritise three things: renegotiating the ECB/IMF deal, renegotiating with bank bondholders, and reducing the cost of public services. This question moves us slightly away from mere capacity and closer to actual policy differences. As the first priority, 51 per cent picked the ECB/IMF deal; 28 per cent, the bondholders; and 20 per cent, cost-cutting. Voters with different priorities tended to support different parties. Table 8.9 shows that those selecting cost reduction as a priority had a greater tendency to support Fianna Fáil (in particular) and Fine Gael, and were less likely to support Labour and Sinn Féin and Others; those targeting bondholders were more likely to support Sinn Féin and Labour. Even so, most of these differences are not large. In all three groups Fine Gael is the largest party, and Labour is second in two of them. One sign of a left–right difference is that 66 per cent of those who prioritised reducing costs opted for Fianna Fáil or Fine Gael, as against only 47 per cent of those who wanted to deal first with the bondholders.

Table 8.9 Party choice by priority for new government

	Renegotiate ECB/IMF deal	Renegotiate with bank bondholders	Reduce cost of public services
Fine Gael	38	33	40
Labour	20	23	15
Fianna Fáil	14	14	26
Sinn Féin	10	15	10
Green	1	1	0
Independents/Others	16	14	8
Total	100	100	100

Source: Millward Brown/Independent Newspapers, 17 February.

Some other questions were asked that also get closer to the first meaning of policies, where people pick a party because they want what it promises to do more than they want what others promise. This is sometimes called 'position issue' voting; people pick a party because its position on an issue is closer to their own one than is the position of any other party. In 2011 there were arguably more position issues separating the established parties than we have seen for some time. This was particularly clear with respect to the deficit (see also Chapters 2 and 4). All parties emphasised reducing the deficit through a mixture of cost savings and tax increases, but Fine Gael went furthest in ruling out most tax increases, and Labour, and even more so Sinn Féin, called for more taxes. A Millward Brown/Independent Newspapers poll on 31 January asked: 'In order to improve the public finances, should the next Government focus most on … ?', with a number of specified options: Raising taxes (7 per cent), Reducing public spending (65 per cent), Both (18 per cent) or Do not know (9 per cent). Tabulated against vote intention, this shows relatively little sign that people chose their party for its position on this issue. The small group that wanted higher taxes were less likely to vote Fine Gael or Fianna Fáil (41 per cent) than were those who favoured public spending cuts (48 per cent) but that difference is quite small, and there is no significant difference between those who said reduce spending and those who said 'both'.

A similar question was asked in the exit poll, this time spelling out the current realities more clearly: 'In order to reduce the deficit, the next Government should concentrate most on reducing spending on health, social services etc. and not raising taxes or increasing taxes and maintaining spending on health, social services etc.' Results are shown in Table 8.10. One thing that remains quite consistent across this analysis of issue voting is that Fine Gael was more attractive to those who were keen to cut public spending and the cost of public services. In general we have seen a 'Fine Gael/Fianna Fáil versus the rest' division on this issue, but not so here. In fact, apart from the 11 per cent difference in the two columns on the Fine Gael vote, differences are not significant. It is hard to argue from these results that the voters sent a clear message as to what they wanted done. The link between options and vote is clearer if we look just at those who say policy was their main motivation (see Table 8.6). The difference between the two columns in voting Fine Gael is now 15 percentage points, and it is 9 points for Labour but it remains insignificant for other parties. Much the same is true, though less pronounced, if we look at all those whose criterion was national rather than candidate-centred.

Table 8.10 Party choice by taxation/spending balance (%)

	Government should concentrate on raising taxes	Government should concentrate on reducing public spending
Fine Gael	32	43
Labour	23	19
Fianna Fáil	17	14
Sinn Féin	10	9
Green	3	3
Independents/Others	16	13
Total	100	100

Source: Lansdowne/RTÉ exit poll 2011.

Emotion and choice

It may also be the case that when people talk about policy they mean something much less concrete. They may simply be rejecting the performance of the previous regime, and in some cases also the inability of the then opposition to halt the collapse of the economy. We showed in an early part of this chapter that critical moments had a big impact on the level of support for Fianna Fáil, but for individuals these moments may be more personal ones. The Millward Brown poll of 31 January asked people about their direct experience of the failing economy. How much had the economic changes promoted personal insecurity? Had they lost a job, or had a salary cut or frozen, or worked shorter hours? Almost 80 per cent reported that they or someone in their household had experienced one of these. Significantly, those reporting none of the above were much more likely to vote for Fianna Fáil (24 per cent as against 14 per cent), but also more likely to vote Fine Gael. Those who reported one or more (and the number made no difference) were disproportionately more likely to favour Labour, Sinn Féin and Independents.[19] Another Millward Brown poll (17 February) asked about the future rather than the past: were people worried about paying household bills (68 per cent), a reduced standard of living (78 per cent), losing their home (41 per cent), or losing their job (27 per cent)? Only 16 per cent had no such worries. There is a link between such worries and voting. Again, those with no such worries were more likely to support Fine Gael and Fianna Fáil. We also see that those who voted Fianna Fáil in 2007 and who had experienced job insecurity in their household were less likely to stay with that party: 36 per cent of those who experienced insecurity stayed as opposed to 52 per cent of those who did not. Similarly, 33 per cent of those who were worried stayed as opposed to 52 per cent of those who were not.

Research within political psychology has demonstrated that emotion also plays a part in voting behaviour. While traditionally it was argued that emotion and rational calculation are inimical, more recent research has argued that emotions such as anger could have an impact on the way in which voters process information.[20] In particular an emotion such as anger could prompt a voter to engage more seriously with news and information and question predispositions. It was reported at the time that attention to news and current affairs programmes increased notably after September 2008. Confidence or hope could increase enthusiasm for participation. We also saw that many voters claimed that they were motivated to choose their party because of their anger at the economic situation and political system. The exit poll obtained responses to a question asking about people's emotional response to the 'way things are going nowadays'. On a 4-point scale from 'not at all' (1) to 'very' (4) voters were most typically Angry (3.3), Outraged (3.1), Worried (3.0) and Afraid (2.8). Sinn Féin voters were most angry (3.6), and most outraged (3.5), followed by Labour voters. Fianna Fáil voters were least angry (2.9) or outraged (2.6), though even they were clearly unhappy. Sinn Féin voters were also most worried, and Fianna Fáil voters least so. Hope and confidence were in shorter supply, but were greatest among Fianna Fáil voters and least among those of Sinn Féin. There is a weak left–right divide here as we saw on some issue questions and on experience of hardship and concerns about the future, with anger lower among centre-right voters and confidence higher. Even so, Fine Gael and Labour differences are barely significant in most cases and the sharper differences are between what after the election were to be the main two opposition parties, Fianna Fáil and Sinn Féin. The strength of the association between these feelings and party support varies, with the strongest links being with anger and outrage and the weakest ones with worry and fear.[21] It is notable that among those who voted Fianna Fáil in 2007, those who changed party this time were more angry and outraged than those who stayed: 3.4 as against 2.9, and 3.3 as against 2.6.

Party leaders

It is common nowadays – if not always – for commentators to focus on the party leaders as a source of support for or resistance to parties. Concern that Enda Kenny was holding back Fine Gael promoted a heave against him in June 2010 (see pp. 20–1 above), and a perception that Labour's chances were boosted by the apparent popularity of Éamon Gilmore led Labour to put most of its eggs in that basket at the start of their campaign, promoting Gilmore for Taoiseach.[22] Fianna Fáil, perhaps belatedly, dumped its leader as the campaign started. Two types of question are asked about leaders. The more common, most notably in the IPSOS MRBI/*Irish Times* series, asks about performance of leader of their party (or as Taoiseach). This is typically misinterpreted as a question about the respective merit of leaders vis-à-vis one another, but just because you think someone is doing a good job as leader of a particular party (particularly if it is doing well) does not mean you like them, or think they would make a good leader of a government, or would vote for them. The other question asks about best choice for Taoiseach. This is plotted through the campaign in Figure 8.2. The questions included the leaders of Fine Gael, Labour and Fianna Fáil.

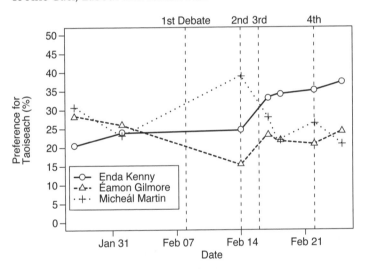

Figure 8.2   Best choice for Taoiseach over the campaign (other responses not shown)

Initially Kenny lagged behind Gilmore and Martin. The last of these seemed to make a very favourable impression initially, and indeed outstripped the others in two of the first three polls. However, the honeymoon was short-lived and by 17 February Kenny was in front and by the exit poll was well ahead. There is some volatility in this series with Martin ranging from 21 per cent to 39 per cent, Gilmore from 15 per cent to 29 per cent, and Kenny from 20 per cent to 37 per cent, but some of this is down to the OI Research/*Daily Star* poll on 14 February. Yet voting intentions for each of the parties remained pretty flat in this period with upward or downward trends of no more than 2–3 per cent at most (see the Appendix to this chapter). Moreover, trends did not match those for leaders. Kenny's approval seems to have grown throughout, while that of his party seems to have peaked mid-campaign. Hence there is little evidence here that leaders had a significant effect. Arguably Kenny's rise in the ratings was a consequence of Fine Gael's success rather than a contribution to it. Indeed, fluctuations in ratings of Micheál Martin and Éamon Gilmore may be merely owing to their performances in the first televised debate, a time when the focus on the three leaders was most intense. If we ignore the 14 February poll immediately after this debate, approval of both leaders appears to be much steadier with a slight decline throughout the campaign. The exit poll also reinforces the feeling that this was not an election about leaders, since only a handful of people mention the choice of Taoiseach as their primary basis of choice.[23]

Yet this was also an election in which the media placed great emphasis on leaders, with a series of debates including one in Irish (see the Chronology at the front of this volume). Kenny missed a TV3 debate (see p. 83 above), but did not seem to have suffered visibly from that decision. Figure 8.2 demonstrates that his rating remained static immediately after the first debate, marked by the first vertical line in the graph. According to the exit poll, those who watched no debates were as likely to support Fine Gael as those who watched at least one, and those who thought nobody won were also as likely to vote for Fine Gael as those who thought someone had won. Much the same is true for the other parties. Martin was thought to have performed best (23 per cent), ahead of Kenny (20 per cent) and Gilmore (11 per cent), with 28 per cent not watching and 12 per cent perceiving no winner. Only 35 per cent of those who thought Martin won voted Fianna Fáil; the comparable figure for Kenny and Fine Gael is 63 per cent, and for Gilmore and Labour 48 per cent. There is certainly a lot of room here for people to see 'their' leader doing well rather than to select a party on the basis of performance, and little sign that these events made much difference. However, we would need information on individual party preferences before and after these debates to be sure. What we might surmise is that the debates helped Kenny and may have boosted his personal rating because expectations for him were set so low, but it is hard to argue that this helped Fine Gael.

Preferences for government composition

In 1989, 1992 and 2007, when the Progressive Democrats, Labour and the Greens respectively entered into coalition government with Fianna Fáil, many argued, with some validity, that this was not what the people voted for. It is hard to make the same assertion of the coalition formed in 2011. First, the Fianna Fáil/Green government was resoundingly defeated, both parties were removed from office and, indeed, the Greens were removed from the Dáil altogether. The voters wanted a change. Second, as demonstrated in Table 8.11, the Fine Gael–Labour coalition was the option most popular with voters, with 43 per cent opting for this as against Fine Gael alone (18 per cent) and Fine Gael with Independents (12 per cent).

A critical factor in this was the effect of the collapse of Fianna Fáil on the preference for government. This dramatically altered the set of possibilities for government formation. Some coalition possibilities from previous elections were no longer realistic. This applies to all Fianna Fáil-led coalitions. Other coalition options, which would in the past have been too unlikely to consider, were now distinct possibilities. This is the case with Labour-led coalitions. The effect of this was that the only familiar alternative in 2011 was the Fine Gael–Labour coalition, which was able to build on support levels from 2002 and 2007, when it had achieved 19 per cent and 30 per cent support in the respective exit polls.

Table 8.11 shows how Fine Gael supporters were split in their support between a coalition with Labour (42 per cent support) and a single-party government (41 per cent support). There is generally no marked demographic base to this split, although farmers were slightly more likely to want the party to govern without Labour, as were voters in Connacht/Ulster rather than Munster or Leinster, and those aged over 65. Women preferred a coalition with Labour, but all of these differences are quite small. Interestingly and, counter to some expectations about greater policy salience in this election, there was no difference with respect to favouring tax increases as opposed to spending cuts. There was minuscule support in Fine Gael (2 per cent) for the viable coalition with Fianna Fáil. Considering the expected size of Fianna Fáil and its ideological proximity, this is one of the most emphatic manifestations of the antipathy of Fine Gael supporters towards Fianna Fáil.

Labour supporters were overwhelmingly in favour of the coalition with Fine Gael. They also exhibited little desire to rekindle the 1993–94 coalition with Fianna Fáil. Just 4 per cent supported a coalition with Fianna Fáil and left-wing independents. This is also surpassed by the 10 per cent support for a coalition with previously untouchable Sinn Féin.

Table 8.11 Support for coalition options for all respondents and for supporters of individual parties (%)

Coalition	All	FG	Lab	FF	SF	Green	Ind./ Other
Fine Gael/Labour[a]	43	42	76	27	14	43	28
Fine Gael	18	41	2	8	4	16	9
Fine Gael/Independents	12	14	1	7	5	9	32
Labour/Sinn Féin/Ind.	10	0	10	2	53	6	13
Fine Gael/Fianna Fáil	4	2	1	18	2	1	1
Labour/Fianna Fáil/Ind.	4	0	4	19	1	1	3
Labour/Fianna Fáil/Sinn Féin	1	0	1	4	5	0	1
Other	8	1	5	15	16	24	13
Total	100	100	100	100	100	100	100

[a] Includes 10 per cent support for Labour-led coalition.

Source: Lansdowne/RTÉ exit poll 2011.

Fianna Fáil supporters did not appear to show the same levels of antipathy to Fine Gael or Labour, demonstrating relatively strong levels of support for coalition with either (18 per cent and 19 per cent support each). Strikingly, the most popular option for Fianna Fáil supporters is the Fine Gael–Labour coalition. Perhaps this is recognition by a section of Fianna Fáil that time outside of government would be beneficial for their party.

Labour's message in the final week of the campaign that it would be undesirable if Fine Gael could form a single-party government may have found a favourable reception in the electorate (for a full discussion of the new strategy see pp. 85–6 above). This is not only because of the lack of support for such an outcome within Fine Gael; it is also because it is difficult to find additional support outside of Fine Gael, where supporters of other parties appear to be resoundingly in favour of the coalition over a possible single-party government.

Transfer patterns

We can get more information on what people might have wanted by looking at transfer patterns. While a voter can signal a coalition preference through transfers, it may also be the case that a preference order is simply indicative of support for particular candidates, or some combination of parties and candidates with no clear implications for government formation.[24] Of course these can be gleaned from the counts themselves and such an analysis is carried out in Chapters 7 and 9. However, polls, and particularly the exit poll, are also a valuable tool in this regard. This is because official transfers are a partial picture, and their validity as an estimate of the behaviour of all voters is unknown. Most votes do not transfer, and those that do may transfer many times with subsequent contamination. The exit polls can only indicate reported lower preferences but there is no reason to consider such reports any less valid than those of first preferences. In 2011 the exit poll asked a question designed particularly to establish the second party supported rather than, as previously, any other parties supported. The results are detailed in Table 8.12, which shows second preferences by first preferences. These results are very consistent with the overlap in support for parties near the start of the campaign, which was displayed in Table 8.1, and indeed also consistent with the evidence from the analysis of actual transfers (see Table 7.5). It again highlights the reciprocal support between Fine Gael and the Labour Party. Fine Gael voters who did vote for a second party were more inclined to transfer to Labour than anyone else, with 32 per cent opting for Labour as their next preference, and Labour voters were almost as enthusiastic in reciprocation. Fianna Fáil, in contrast, struggled in this respect, winning few transfers from other parties. Only 8 per cent of voters gave that party a second preference. Sinn Féin too remains relatively 'toxic', but Independents were very successful. In total 78 per cent voted for more than one party. This is more or less on a par with what was found for previous years.[25]

Table 8.12 First and second party preferences (%)

Second preference	Total	First preference					
		Fine Gael	Labour	Fianna Fáil	Sinn Féin	Green	Indep Other
Fine Gael	16	–	31	26	14	28	25
Labour	21	32	–	16	23	31	24
Fianna Fáil	8	11	6	–	9	9	10
Sinn Féin	6	5	10	7	–	3	8
Green Party	4	4	6	5	2	–	3
Indep / Other	22	21	32	18	37	25	10
No other party indicated	22	28	15	27	14	4	19
Total	100	100	100	100	100	100	100

Source: Lansdowne/RTÉ exit poll 2011.

Expectations about the government

An IO Research/*Daily Star* poll towards the end of the campaign indicated that more voters trusted in a Fine Gael–Labour coalition than the obvious alternatives. Fifty-seven per cent trusted a Fine Gael–Labour government to address the crisis, compared with 46 per cent for Fine Gael with Independents, 42 per cent for Fine Gael alone and a mere 22 per cent for a Labour–Fianna Fáil option. That is certainly not to say that voters were optimistic about the future. As we have already seen, they were neither optimistic nor confident. Most thought that the government should try to renegotiate the bailout: an early Millward Brown/Independent Newspapers poll (30 January) found 76 per cent of voters wanting renegotiation. However, only 39 per cent thought this effort was likely to succeed. Many voters also thought the policies of the two parties in government would be compatible (39 per cent), with government party supporters more confident (52 per cent and 49 per cent for Fine Gael and Labour respectively, with don't knows included), but that is not to say they expected much more than that the government would last.[26] When it came to the economy, in general 50 per cent thought they would be worse off next year[27] with only 9 per cent expecting things to improve; 74 per cent expected the recession to last more than three years.[28] This varied very little across the parties, but voters for Sinn Féin and Independents were somewhat more pessimistic about the next year.

Conclusion

This chapter posed a succession of questions about voters in 2011. The first was why voters forsook Fianna Fáil in such large numbers. The answer here is that it was the result of a dramatic loss of confidence in the government to manage the economy and widespread anger and outrage at the financial crisis for which the government was seen to be responsible, even if the blame was not directed only at Fianna Fáil and the Greens. Once lost, in September 2008, its good name was impossible to re-establish; a further sudden change two years later simply took the party to an even lower level. In what is a classic case of electoral accountability, the voters judged the record, found it wanting and accordingly decided they would not support Fianna Fáil, or the Greens. Of course the government tried to deflect blame, claiming for some time that the international financial situation was the cause of the crisis, but voters were not deflected and so punished those who were accountable. The second major question concerns the motivations of those who voted for parties other than Fianna Fáil in 2011. Clearly the movement away from Fianna Fáil was a national one and was based on what the government had (or had not) done. How far did such national motives underlie the choice of an alternative to Fianna Fáil? In particular, were there signs that the scale of the crisis had prompted voters to concern themselves more with the policy options facing the new government and less with the local record of a candidate? And, given an unprecedentedly large vote for what was seen as parties and candidates of the 'left', is there any sign that voters were consciously selecting left-wing policy options?

The evidence here is a little mixed, but in general it would seem that policy was said by voters to be more important to them that it had been in the recent past, and anecdotal evidence from the 'doorsteps' seems also to point to a greater engagement by voters in national issues (see the candidate contributions in Chapter 6). Even so, a substantial group of voters, not much smaller than in 2007, maintained that the candidate's ability to look after the constituency was still central to their decision. That these were more inclined than those citing 'policy' to vote Fianna Fáil does point to national concerns being more prominent in the vote for an alternative government. Evidence that voters were motivated by substantive policy concerns is harder to find. It is clear that the opposition won on perceived competence to deal with the crisis, and the choice between opposition options is predictable in these terms, but that is hardly new. There is less firm evidence that voters were making a choice about how the crisis should be dealt with. Perhaps the constraints of the bailout inhibited the sort of programmatic options that are common in modern democracies, and analysis of the manifestos suggests differences were muted, but there was an obvious increase tax/larger cuts difference between Labour and Fine Gael. There is some evidence that voters' preferences on this issue were linked to their vote, but the association is far from strong. More generally, there are some broader signs of differences in the impact of the crisis on voters for left and right parties, and some difference in the perceptions of the two groups about priorities, but these are not always strong and not present in the same way on all indicators. Within most sub-groups defined by experience or policy preference in the tables we have looked at here, Fine Gael was the preferred choice.

The decision of Labour to join Fine Gael in government, while it was what the voters wanted, ensured that the government versus opposition divide would not produce the right versus left competition that some commentators desired. The future is obviously very uncertain, and contingent on many events over the next few years, but the general argument here has been that the 2011 election was much more striking for the outcome – the collapse of Fianna Fáil – than for any sea change in the way people make their decisions on how to vote. Many who would formerly have described themselves as basically Fianna Fáil supporters did not so describe themselves this time and, even when they did, many did not follow their traditional behaviour on this occasion. Such was the assessment of that party's recent years in power that it must be unlikely that a faith so damaged can easily be renewed. The exit poll found three-fifths of voters did not see Fianna Fáil leading a government again in the next ten years. The more immediate question is perhaps whether Fine Gael, or even Labour, will do so, or whether a new party will emerge. Expectations as to what can be expected from the government may well be modest, but if Fianna Fáil can lose so much of its traditional support, much of that for Fine Gael and even more so for Labour must be even more conditional. We may have experienced an earthquake, but we should anticipate the possibility of severe aftershocks.

Appendix: the campaign polls

The polls during the campaign indicated some clear trends in support. Table 8.13 shows the averages for each week, the election result and the differences therein. As the campaign wore on, Fine Gael support increased and stabilised at its elevated level. Labour's support declined marginally throughout the campaign. Sinn Féin's surge in December 2010 and January 2011 looked short-lived. Support for Sinn Féin, Fianna Fail, Independents and the Green Party remained relatively constant throughout the campaign.

Overall, the polls provided a fairly accurate prediction of what happened. When the results were known it was evident that expectations of Fine Gael winning its best ever vote were misplaced and the collapse of Fianna Fáil's support would not be quite as great as suggested by the polls. Differences between the poll estimates and the outcome are slightly more marked if we take the last three polls than if we look at all 14 polls over the four weeks, although this applies mostly to the Fine Gael vote share. Common explanations for these 'errors' are that: (1) some voters might have deserted Fine Gael as the possibility of a single-party government became more real; and (2), some voters were too embarrassed to admit they would support Fianna Fáil.

Just as Michael McDowell had done in 2002, Labour's campaign in the last week certainly tried very hard to alert voters to the fact that one party could find itself with an overall majority. Campaign polls did reveal (see Table 8.11) that a substantial proportion of Fine Gael supporters favoured a coalition over a single-party government. As for the so-called 'shy Fianna Fáil' syndrome, a reference to a problem British pollsters had in finding Tory voters in the UK in the early 1990s, this is also a real possibility and there is evidence for this. The difference between the exit poll and the election in terms of Fianna Fáil support was far beyond what one might expect from randomness alone.

Table 8.13 Poll averages during the campaign (%)

	FG	Lab	FF	Green	SF	Ind/O
27 Jan–3 Feb (6 polls)	33.7	22.3	16.3	1.7	12.7	13.7
4–10 Feb (1 poll)	38.0	20.0	15.0	3.0	10.0	14.0
11–17 Feb (4 polls)	38.3	19.5	15.3	1.5	11.0	14.5
18–24 Feb (3 polls)	38.3	19.0	15.0	2.0	10.7	15.0
Election	36.1	19.4	17.4	1.8	9.9	15.4
Difference	+2.2	–0.4	–2.4	–0.2	+0.6	–0.4
Campaign average	36.3	20.6	15.6	1.8	11.6	14.2
Difference	+0.2	+1.2	–1.8	0.0	+1.7	–1.2

Sources: RED C/*Sunday Business Post*, 27 January; Lansdowne/Independent Newspapers, 28 January; RED C/Paddy Power, 31 January; Lansdowne/Independent Newspapers, 1 February; MRBI *Irish Times*, 1 February; Red C/Paddy Power, 1 February; RED C/*Sunday Business Post*, 10 February; IO Research, 14 February; Lansdowne/Independent Newspapers, 14 February; RED C/*Sunday Business Post*, 17 February; MRBI *Irish Times*, 18 February; Lansdowne/Independent Newspapers, 21 February; RED C/Paddy Power, 22 February; Lansdowne/RTÉ exit poll, 25 February.

An internal analysis of its last poll by RED C after the election did provide some support for both of these theories, but it also raised some other possibilities.[29] There were net shifts from Fine Gael to Labour and Independents in the last few days, and concerns about single-party government were linked to this. A second factor was the late awareness of local candidates, with Independents gaining here, but Fianna Fáil also being helped. This analysis also indicated evidence to support the 'shy Fianna Fáil' explanation, as indeed RED C analyses had done through the election. Those saying 'don't know' were much more likely to have voted Fianna Fáil in 2007 (55 per cent of those who refused to disclose their preference had supported Fianna Fáil in 2007), and were slightly more likely to vote for Fianna Fáil in 2011 than typical treatments of 'don't knows' would assume. Most significantly though, the RTÉ/Lansdowne exit poll also underestimated the Fianna Fáil vote, an error that cannot be explained by the fact that people said they were undecided rather than admit a Fianna Fáil preference.

Notes

1. This concept of 'ownership' was developed in John R. Petrocik, 'Issue ownership in presidential elections, with a 1980 case study', *American Journal of Political Science* 40 (1996), pp. 825–50.

2. It is arguable that the government's tough budget, introduced, several weeks earlier than normal, on 14 October 2008, compounded the loss of confidence in the government's capacity to manage the economy. This contained a reversal of the free health care provision for the over-70s introduced just before the 2002 election, and led to unprecedented protests by 'grey' voters with up to 25,000 marching on the Dáil (see p. 16 above). The government later backed down on this change, but the budget still marked the departure of the 'Celtic Tiger'. The second crisis point combined a number of events, all of which signalled that things were worse than had been generally suspected. The economics editor of the *Irish Times* described 30 September as 'an extraordinary day. The Government removed all doubt that an even harsher budget than planned will be introduced in the coming months … Government's borrowing agency unexpectedly cancelled scheduled fundraising efforts over the rest of 2010.' He also put the chances of an IMF intervention at 50:50 (Dan O'Brien, 'A historic day but no one knows what is yet to come', *Irish Times*, 1 October 2010). From that point until the next poll in October the main story in the press was the greater scale of the crisis, and talk about an all-party consensus on the means to reduce the deficit.

3. Paul Whiteley, 'The Conservative campaign', *Parliamentary Affairs* 50:4 (1997), pp. 542–54. Whiteley notes (p. 553): 'Periodically and rarely, however, a really major shock occurs which shifts the political equilibrium to a semi-permanent new level. The winter of discontent in the dying months of the 1974–1979 Labour government was one example of this, as was the Falklands war for Mrs Thatcher's government. Black Wednesday was also an example of this type of shock, in that it fundamentally changed the way that the electorate regarded the Conservative government.'

4. *Irish Times*, 10 October 2008.

5. Ireland: 2009 Article IV Consultation – Staff Report; and Public Information Notice on the Executive Board Discussion (IMF, 24 June 2009), www.imf.org/external/pubs/ft/scr/2009/cr09195.pdf.

6. An OI Research poll on 19 February 2011 for the *Daily Star* underlines the extent to which the electorate blamed Fianna Fáil for the economic situation. It asked in relation to a number of groups and individuals whether or not they should be tried for the notional crime of 'economic treason'. While below 'bankers' (86 per cent), Bertie Ahern, Fianna Fáil Taoiseach from 1997 to 2008, was cited by 65 per cent; Brian Cowen, Fianna Fáil Taoiseach 2008–11 by 47 per cent; and Brian Lenihan, outgoing Fianna Fáil Finance Minister by a mere 34 per cent.

7. 'We have a number of political parties in Ireland each of which would like to get your [first preference] vote. How probable is it that you will ever give your first preference vote to the following parties? Please use the number on this scale to indicate your views, where "1" means "not at all probable" and "10" means "very probable".' RED C also asked a variant of this question with a five-point labelled scale. The results are very similar in terms of highlighting

overlap between each party's support, and the unpopularity of Fianna Fáil, Sinn Féin and the Greens.

8. Authors' analysis of survey carried out as part of the European Election Study project: see www.piredeu.com.

9. Michael Marsh, 'Stability and change in structure of electoral competition 1989–2002', pp. 94–111 in Diane Payne, John Garry and Niamh Hardiman (eds), *Irish Social and Political Attitudes* (Liverpool: Liverpool University Press, 2006).

10. 2011 figure from exit poll; 2002 figure from Michael Marsh, Richard Sinnott, John Garry and Fiachra Kennedy, *The Irish Voter: The nature of electoral competition in the Republic of Ireland* (Manchester: Manchester University Press, 2008), p. 63.

11. Marsh et al., *The Irish Voter*, chapter 10.

12. For evidence from the 2007 Irish National Election Study see Michael Marsh, 'Voting behaviour', pp. 168–97 in John Coakley and Michael Gallagher (eds), *Politics in the Republic of Ireland*, 5th edn (Abingdon: Routledge and PSAI Press, 2009).

13. This question has often been asked in the past. Sinnott shows that in campaign polls in five elections between 1977 and 1987, policy was mentioned on average by 25 per cent, and the candidate by 40 per cent; calculations based on Table 7.1 in Richard Sinnott, *Irish Voters Decide* (Manchester: Manchester University Press, 1995), p. 169.

14. Lansdowne used 19 pre-coded response categories.

15. Health, crime and local issues were each mentioned by 2 per cent; choice of Taoiseach, emigration, education, single-party government and ensuring a strong opposition were each mentioned by 1 per cent. Crime was mentioned by less than 1 per cent. No mention of abortion is recorded.

16. Despite the emphasis in Fianna Fáil's manifesto on the subject, only 2 per cent of Fianna Fáil voters chose political reform.

17. There were few questions about political reform in various polls and these indicate little in the way of differences between supporters of different parties. Abolition of the Seanad got the support of 57 per cent in the 14 February Millward Brown/Independent Newspapers poll, with 61 per cent of Fine Gael voters and 55 per cent of Fianna Fáil voters supporting it, despite differences between the two parties on the issue (see Chapter 11). Most voters in two other Millward Brown/Independent Newspapers polls (31 January and 17 February) thought the Taoiseach's nominees to the Seanad should include non-party figures, with Fine Gael and Labour voters most supportive of this, but few very significant differences between the parties.

18. Cramer's V, a simple measure of association which varies between 0 and 1, is 0.51 for the deficit, 0.41 for health, 0.47 for unemployment and 0.46 for the banks.

19. An earlier Millward Brown/Independent Newspapers poll carried out on January 31 asked the same question. Those with no experience of cuts were much more likely to vote Fianna Fáil (and Independent) and less likely to support Labour and Sinn Féin, but showed no difference in support for Fine Gael.

20. Voters 'also rely on their internal emotional states to signal when to abandon their predispositions and begin conscious political choice.' George E. Marcus

and Michael B. MacKuen, 'Anxiety, enthusiasm, and the vote: the emotional underpinnings of learning and involvement during presidential campaigns', *The American Political Science Review*, 87:3 (1993), pp. 672-85.

21. Cramer's V, a simple measure of association which ranges from 0 to 1, shows the strength of the link between each emotion and vote is 0.12 for angry, 0.07 afraid, 0.09 confident, 0.08 hopeful, 0.07 worried and 0.13 outraged.

22. A Millward Brown/Independent Newspapers poll on 20 February found only 25 per cent of electors, and a bare 50 per cent of Labour voters, agreed this was a 'credible strategy' by the Labour Party. See also p. 72 above.

23. The Lansdowne/RTÉ exit poll also found that only 59 per cent of Labour voters thought that Gilmore would make the best Taoiseach, compared with 74 per cent and 73 per cent for Kenny and Martin among own party supporters. Gilmore was far from the electoral asset that Labour had assumed he would be.

24. Analysis of previous exit polls suggests that coalition preferences are not a good predictor of second preferences: Michael Marsh, 'Voting for government coalitions in Ireland under single transferable vote', *Electoral Studies* 29:3 (2010), pp. 329–38.

25. See Marsh et al., *The Irish Voter*, Table 2.5.

26. Millward Brown/Independent Newspapers poll of 17 February.

27. Millward Brown/Independent Newspapers poll of 31 January.

28. Millward Brown/Independent Newspapers poll of 17 February.

29. See Pat Leahy, 'Labour rescued general election at the death', *Sunday Business Post*, 20 March 2011.

9
Preference Voting under PR-STV 1948–2011

Richard Sinnott and James McBride

Given the seismic shifts that transformed the Irish electoral landscape in February 2011, it is tempting to focus solely on the massive changes in the distribution of first preference votes recorded in that election. However, such an approach would grossly underrate the role of second and subsequent preferences in allocating seats and in uncovering fundamental aspects of Irish voting behaviour.[1] In using these preferences to proceed count by count and elimination by elimination towards the final outcome, proportional representation by the single transferable vote (PR-STV) generates unparalleled additional evidence on how voters relate to the candidates and to the parties. In analysing this evidence, it is important to note several features of the Irish electoral system. In the first place, and contrary to a not uncommon view, in PR-STV each voter has only one vote. Secondly, that vote is transferable, according to the preference order indicated by the voter. Thirdly, although from the point of view of the act of voting, PR-STV is simple and transparent, the mechanics of transferring votes are quite complex. Because the complexities can affect the interpretation of the transfer evidence, the mechanics of PR-STV are addressed in some detail below.

The evidence generated by the transfer of votes can be thought of in terms of three behavioural variables. The first is party loyalty. This manifests itself when votes are being transferred from a candidate of a given party in a situation in which there is a continuing candidate from the same party in contention. In these circumstances a loyal vote or a loyal transfer is one that goes directly from the eliminated or elected candidate to his or her party running mate. The second variable is party plumping. This arises when there is no running mate available to receive the transferable votes. In this situation a party plumper opts to make his or her vote non-transferable rather than transferring the vote to a candidate of another party. The third variable measures inter-party transfers.[2] These arise when a candidate of a given party is being eliminated and there is no running mate available to receive transfers but there is a continuing candidate of another party that is or has been in actual or potential, explicit or implicit alliance with the party of the candidate whose surplus or elimination votes are being distributed.

Before proceeding to the analysis of these variables, we must examine the transfer process, not for its own sake but because the evidence it produces, although voluminous, is incomplete and open to misinterpretation. There are four procedures involved in the transfer of votes and each gives rise to varying degrees of loss of information regarding the size and/or the direction of the transfer taking place. The simplest transfer arises from the elimination of a candidate with the lowest number of votes on the count in question. On the face of it, this aspect of the count should produce comprehensive information about transfer patterns, in that all of the votes of the eliminated candidate are examined and distributed to the continuing candidates or to the category of non-transferable votes. However, the now widespread procedure of multiple eliminations compromises the analysis in so far as it deprives us of vital information regarding the origin of the transfer in question.[3] Given this indeterminacy, all cases of multiple eliminations are excluded from the analysis that follows.

The process is more complex when the votes to be distributed are the surplus votes of a candidate elected on the first count. In this case all the papers of the elected candidate are examined for continuing preferences, papers that do not indicate any preference among the continuing candidates having been first put to one side. This latter step means that the calculation of the proportions in which the surplus is to be distributed to the continuing candidates automatically produces a zero rate of non-transferability. In fact this zero rate is an artefact that is due to the omission of non-transferable votes at the outset.

The process becomes more complicated still when the task is to distribute the surplus votes of an elected candidate that have accrued on a count subsequent to the first count. In this case only the votes in the last parcel received are examined (that is, the votes received by the elected candidate on the count on which he or she was elected). If the number of transferable papers in the last parcel exceeds or equals the surplus, the Returning Officer proceeds along lines similar to those just described for the case of surpluses that accrue on a first count. Obviously, this process will also yield a zero non-transferable vote that is, however, an artefact due to the counting process.

If, on the other hand, the surplus is greater than the number of transferable papers in the last parcel received, a number of votes equal to the difference between the surplus and the number of transferable votes is taken and placed in the non-transferable category so that the votes in the column when added together are equal to the surplus. This of course means that the reported non-transferable vote understates the actual non-transferable vote and that this distortion should be corrected when it occurs. A further distortion can arise if the last parcel received has come from a candidate of a party that is different from the party of the candidate whose votes are being distributed.

With a view to coping with these data problems, the methodology of this analysis is as follows. The first step is to set aside all surplus transfers that report a zero non-transferable vote, as their inclusion distorts the calculation of non-transferability, overestimating loyalty and underestimating plumping. The second step is to recalculate the real rate of non-transferability in the case of transfers of surpluses that do report a non-transferable vote. The rate of non-transferability in such cases is obtained by subtracting the number of transferable votes from the last parcel received. The third step is to note all cases of surplus transfers corrected in this way in which the last parcel received is from a party other than the party of the elected candidate. Because of their potentially distorting effect, these are also omitted from the analysis. Fourthly, support for inter-party alliances is calculated only for those counts in which the allied party is still in contention with any other party or independent candidate and so is available to receive transferred votes. Fifthly and finally, counts involving multiple eliminations are set aside as it is not possible to identify the source of the transfer in question.

Party loyalty 1948–2011

Over the long term, the loyalty profiles of Fianna Fáil and Fine Gael have tended to be quite similar. This is evident firstly in the period from the mid-1950s up to the late 1980s when Fianna Fáil was mostly ahead of Fine Gael, but usually by not much more than a couple of percentage points (see Figure 9.1). The second similarity between the two parties is that party loyalty, as manifested in intra-party transfers, began to decline in both parties at about the same time; that is, between the 1987 and

1992 general elections. Trends after that were somewhat inconsequential until the 2011 election. This saw a small increase in party loyalty among Fine Gael supporters. However, party loyalty in the Fianna Fáil ranks fell significantly, leaving Fine Gael 8 percentage points ahead of Fianna Fáil in party loyalty as expressed in vote transfer preferences.

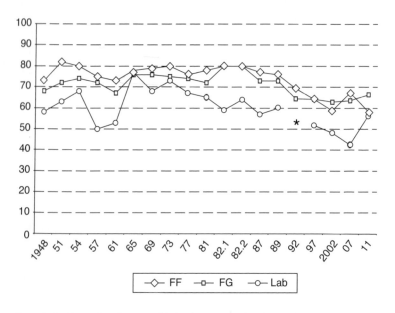

Figure 9.1   Party loyalty in published vote transfer data, 1948–2011

* Labour loyalty could not be calculated for 1992.
Sources: 1948–2007, published election results; 2011, RTÉ results system.

The story of loyalty among Labour Party supporters is quite different. First of all, Labour loyalty is substantially lower than that of Fianna Fáil or Fine Gael in most elections in the period under consideration. Secondly, it is quite volatile, plunging to below 50 per cent in 1957 and 2007 while rising to the heights of the other two parties in 1965 and 1973.[4] Then, in the 2011 election, the downward trajectory in Labour internal loyalty that had been manifest since the mid-1970s was more than halted when Labour loyalty went from 42 per cent in 2007 to 58 per cent in 2011.

The concept of 'party loyalty' underlying the preceding discussion is part of a broader syndrome of attitudes usually referred to as party identification or party attachment and measured by a variety of questionnaire items in opinion surveys. Reliable data on party attachment (operationalised as feeling close to a party) are available for Ireland since the late 1970s.[5] This makes it possible to compare trends in party loyalty expressed in vote transfers with trends in party attachment expressed in survey responses. There is no suggestion here that these different measures should be on identical trajectories. Nonetheless, their relative positions and slopes may suggest the direction that both or either (or neither) may take. As Figure 9.2 shows, in the late 1970s attachment among the electorate was trailing loyalty among party voters by approximately 15 percentage points. In the early 1980s, however, the gap between these two indicators gradually widened until, in the context of the 2011 election, only 20 per cent of the electorate said that they felt close to a party, while rates of loyal behaviour in transferring votes were in the high 50s for Fianna Fáil and in the high 60s for Fine Gael. While, as already suggested, comparisons of this sort are broad-brush rather than exact science, they

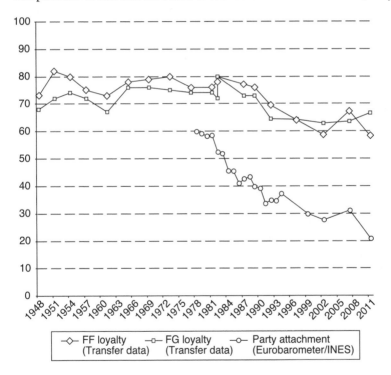

Figure 9.2 Average party loyalty in vote transfers, Fianna Fáil and Fine Gael (1948–2011), and proportion of electorate attached to a party (1977–2011)

Sources: Transfer data from published election results; attachment data from Eurobarometer (1978–94), European Election Study (1999), and INES (2002–11).

do suggest that a very substantial weakening of party attachment in the electorate as a whole is under way, but that this is only having a limited effect on the willingness of a majority of party supporters to behave in a loyal party fashion by transferring their votes to running mates when possible. For now, however, we note this as a preliminary observation to which we shall return when we have considered all of the data on party loyalty, especially that contained in the ballot papers from the e-voting constituencies in the 2002 election.

Party plumping

The story of party plumping (that is, transferring to all the candidates of the party of first preference and only to those candidates, leaving the remainder of the ballot paper blank) is more easily told. In the case of Fianna Fáil it is mainly a story of a contrast between a very high and largely stable level of plumping (mostly in the high 70s) between 1954 and 1977 followed by a period of fluctuation and an overall downward movement resulting in a rate of plumping of about 40 per cent in the 2011 election. At the beginning of our period, Fine Gael had a very low rate of plumping. But then, concomitant with a rising first preference vote, Fine Gael's plumping rate increased steadily, culminating in a rate of 65 per cent in 1981. From then on, however, Fine Gael plumping tended to decline, reaching the mid-40s in 2011. With the single exception of the 1969 election, plumping by Labour Party supporters is exceptionally low, at times dipping below 20 per cent. The very substantial increase in plumping that occurred in 1969 no doubt reflects Labour's go-it-alone approach to that election. The decline in plumping of approximately 30 percentage points in 1973 in turn reflects the abandonment of the 1969 strategy in favour of a pre-election endorsement of coalition with Fine Gael. Even though its rate of plumping increased somewhat in 2007 and increased substantially in 2011, Labour remains a party with a minimal tendency to plump.

But what do these variations in party plumping imply? Perhaps the first point to make is that the rational, party-oriented voter should not plump. This is because, providing the voter has voted for all of the candidates of his or her preferred party, registering a preference for another party or candidate does not in any way diminish or detract from the first preference vote. Accordingly, unless a voter is entirely indifferent as between all of the remaining candidates and parties, the 'rational' thing to do is to keep on expressing those preferences. The second point, however, is that politics is not just about rationality and it is not surprising that a voter may wish to express his or her negative feelings about a particular party or candidate by refusing to transfer their precious single vote to the disliked object.

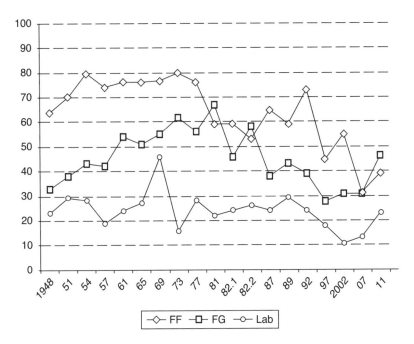

Figure 9.3 Party plumping in published vote transfer data, 1948–2011

Sources: 1948–2007, published election results; 2011, RTÉ results system.

Inter-party transfers: Fine Gael and Labour

While the impact of vote transfers on the outcome of elections can sometimes be exaggerated, transfer arrangements or pacts between parties can have decisive effects. Given the history and structure of the Irish party system, the main focus of interest in this regard is inevitably on the relationship between Fine Gael and Labour. Accordingly, Figure 9.4 charts the responsiveness of Fine Gael and Labour supporters to the varying approaches to coalition strategy and vote transfer arrangements over time. With just a few qualifications, the graph points to three distinct periods in the Fine Gael/Labour relationship. The periods are (a) 1948–69, (b) 1973–82 and (c) 1987–2011.

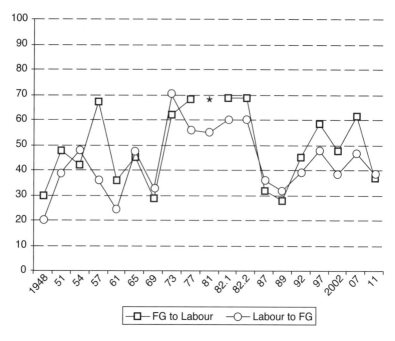

Figure 9.4 Fine Gael to Labour and Labour to Fine Gael inter-party transfers in published vote transfer data, 1948–2011

* FG to Labour cannot be calculated for 1981.

Sources: 1948–2007, published election results; 2011, RTÉ results system.

The first period began with very low rates of transfer of votes both from Fine Gael to Labour and from Labour to Fine Gael, very low in this case being less than 30 per cent. The period ended in 1969 with equally low rates of transfer following an election campaign in which Labour proclaimed that the 'seventies will be socialist'. In between these two time points, the reciprocal transfer of votes was in the low to moderate range. The moderate rate of transfer was associated with the two elections in which the Fine Gael-led Inter-Party government contested the election as an alliance (that is, the elections of 1951 and 1954) and with the election in which Fine Gael's left-of-centre *Just Society* document came to be the party's election manifesto (1965).[6]

The second and the most distinctive period in the Fine Gael–Labour relationship runs from 1973 to 1982. This is clearly the high point of the appeal of coalition electoral strategy. Fine Gael's endorsement of the coalition option was particularly strong and stable and in all five elections was in excess of 60 per cent. However, in January 1987 the Fine Gael–Labour coalition government that had assumed office in November 1982 collapsed in disagreement over the preparation of the budget. In the ensuing general election both government parties suffered serious losses in first preference votes and inter-party transfers plummeted – by 37 percentage points in the case of Fine Gael to Labour and by 24 percentage points in the case of Labour to Fine Gael. Inter-party transfers fell again in 1989, though the falls then were quite slight. Then, in spite of some recovery in the relationship over the next five elections and notwithstanding the fact that it was obvious during and even prior to the 2011 election that the two parties would be forming a coalition government, reciprocal transfers between the parties in 2011, at around 40 per cent, were just about as low as at any time in the previous 60 years.

The e-voting evidence

In presenting the evidence up to this point, we have made repeated references to the 'published vote transfer data'. It has been necessary to draw particular attention to the limitations of the data in this way because the data in question are incomplete and potentially misleading. We have seen that, in analysing the data, some steps can be taken to minimise the potential for distortion. As these corrective measures do not entirely solve the problem, we are fortunate in having a remarkable body of data, namely the full set of ballot papers from the three e-voting constituencies in the 2002 election, that reveals all there is to be revealed about voter preferences and the transfer patterns they imply, albeit in just three constituencies in one single election.[7] The measurement of two variables benefits in particular from the availability of the e-voting data. The two variables in question are the rate of utilisation of preferences, which is impossible to determine accurately without access to the ballot paper data, and party loyalty, which we have already estimated but which requires further qualification in the light of the ballot paper data.

As an alternative to the published vote transfer data, the e-voting dataset has its own limitations (that is, mainly that it covers only three constituencies in one election) but the availability of full information on how each voter filled in his or her ballot paper more than compensates for the fact that the data come from only three constituencies. One should also bear in mind that the e-voting dataset involves a very large number of votes (138,011). In short, viewed as three case studies with a large N of observations, the e-voting data provide invaluable evidence not just on party loyalty, but also on the prior question of the extent of the utilisation of preferences in PR-STV as it operates in the Republic of Ireland.

Preference utilisation: the e-voting evidence

Figure 9.5 shows the rate at which preference utilisation decreases as one moves down the scale of preferences (from left to right along the horizontal axis). In the case of second preferences, the rate of utilisation is extremely high with 95 per cent of voters expressing a second preference. Take-up of the opportunity to express a third preference is only a little behind (88 per cent). At that point, however, a substantial fall in preference utilisation occurs – from almost 90 per cent of voters expressing a third preference to only 57 per cent expressing a fourth. On the other hand, it might be regarded as remarkable that a clear majority of voters go as far as expressing a fourth preference. In any event, the rate of utilisation falls steeply again as we move from four to five preferences: only 39 per cent of voters express at least a fifth preference and the rate drops to 26 per cent when we look at the expression of sixth preferences. Thereafter the downward curve begins to flatten out, reflecting the fact that if a voter reaches a seventh or eighth preference or thereabouts, he or she may go all the way, ranking all the candidates in order of preference. In order to ascertain the proportion of voters who use their ballot to the maximum in this way, one must take into account not just those who are at the end of the line in Figure 9.5 (that is, at the 14th preference in the Meath constituency) but also those who exercised nine preferences in Dublin West and 12 preferences in Dublin North because these were the total numbers of candidates in those two constituencies. This yields 9,952 voters, or 7 per cent of voters, who voted the full array of candidates.[8]

The relationship captured in the curve in Figure 9.5 appears to be a general one, seeming to hold for all three e-voting constituencies, despite each being different in size (in terms of number of seats) and each having a distinctive party composition. Further evidence of the generality of the relationship is contained in Figure 9.6, which shows the proportion of people expressing each preference from first to Nth in four additional surveys (the MRBI/*Irish Times* 1989 European Parliament Election Survey, and the INES Irish National Election Surveys for 2002 and 2007). Finally, Figure 9.7 shows the breakdown of preference utilisation by party. This shows that the curvilinear shape of the data does indeed hold across the political parties. However, Figure 9.7 also shows up significant variations between the parties. Thus, from the outset, Sinn Féin preference utilisation

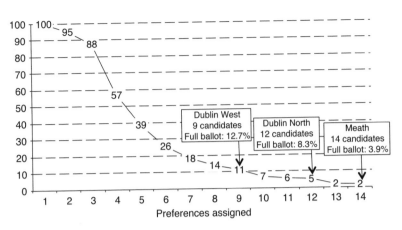

Figure 9.5   Preference utilisation in e-voting constituencies, 2002 general election

Source: E-voting ballot papers published by constituency Returning Officers following 2002 general election.

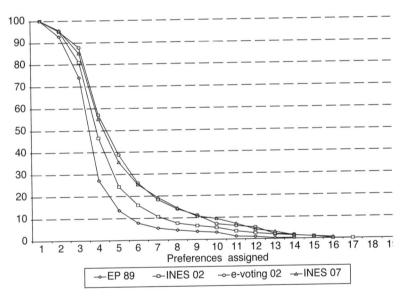

Figure 9.6   Preference utilisation in selected mock ballot surveys and in e-voting constituencies, 2002 general election

Sources: Shaun Bowler and David Farrell, 'Voter behavior under STV-PR: solving the puzzle of the Irish party system', *Political Behavior* 13 (1991), p. 310; INES 2002 and INES 2007 Irish National Election Studies; e-voting 2002 ballot papers published by constituency Returning Officers following the 2002 general election.

is quite distinctive, with only 87 per cent expressing a second preference (compared to 95 per cent for the other parties). As the left-hand line in the graph shows, this distinctiveness continues throughout the range of preferences; see, for example, the 43 per cent of Sinn Féin voters expressing a fourth preference compared to the 64 per cent of Fine Gael/ Labour and the Greens who do so. Note also the distinctive behaviour of Fianna Fáil, who fall precipitously from 88 per cent expressing a third preference to only 53 per cent expressing a fourth preference, moving towards the Sinn Féin side of the graph as it does so.

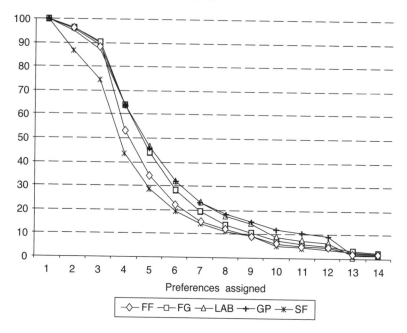

Figure 9.7   Preference utilisation by party in e-voting constituencies, 2002 general election

Source: E-voting ballot papers published by constituency Returning Officers following 2002 general election.

Party loyalty: the e-voting evidence

The concept of party loyalty used so far in this chapter is defined in terms of a one-stage transfer of votes within a party; that is, from one candidate of the party in question to one other candidate of the same party. It is obvious, however, that, given more than two candidates from any particular party, intra-party transfers can be a multi-stage process.[9] In short, we have a second and more rigorous concept of party loyalty, but one that cannot be employed if the analysis is confined to the official record of the results of the election.[10] In order to deal with this difficulty we turn again to the e-voting dataset, which does in fact include three instances in which two-stage party loyalty arises. Accordingly, this dataset will enable us to compare the estimate of party loyalty based on the published results of the election with that based on the e-voting data.

The constituency of Dublin North presents one of the three instances of two-stage loyalty in the e-voting data. The data necessary to estimate Fianna Fáil party loyalty are contained in the eighth count, when the third-ranked Fianna Fáil candidate (Michael Kennedy) was eliminated and his votes distributed. In the event his vote went strongly to Fianna Fáil, dividing fairly evenly between the two Fianna Fáil candidates. As Figure 9.8 shows, these data, which are based on the published, official results, give an estimate of 76 per cent as the rate of intra-party loyalty among Fianna Fáil voters in Dublin North in the 2002 general election. However, this estimate of the extent of party loyalty is based on partial information. With only the published data to hand, we know where Kennedy's transfers went on his elimination, but we know nothing about the next preferences contained in the votes of the other two Fianna Fáil candidates, both of whom were elected without reaching the quota. When we resort to the e-voting data, however, we can accurately and comprehensively estimate the destination of all the second preferences of all three Fianna Fáil candidates. These calculations result in an estimate of Fianna Fáil two-stage loyalty of 46 per cent. In short, compared with using the published results, using the e-voting ballot papers leads to a substantial downward revision of the estimate of party loyalty among Fianna Fáil voters in Dublin North – substantial here meaning a difference of 30 percentage points. The explanation for the difference is that the official results of the election only allow for the estimation of one-stage party loyalty, whereas the e-voting data make it possible to estimate two-stage loyalty for the same constituency and the same count. Both measures have their own validity and their own application. The chief use of the two-stage measure is to remind us that there are two measures and that, as a measure of party loyalty as such, the one-stage measure is likely to err on the generous side. On the other hand, we need the one-stage measure because it is the only basis on which we can undertake the kind of analysis illustrated in Figure 9.1 above.

Very substantial differences also arise in the other two cases in which we have data from the e-voting constituencies. The counts in question are both from the Meath constituency and arise on the second count transfer of Noel Dempsey's (Fianna Fáil) surplus and on the eighth count elimination and redistribution of the votes of John Farrelly of Fine Gael. In the Fianna Fáil case, analysis of the published results indicate a loyalty rate of 67 per cent. However, when the e-voting data are examined, the estimate for full or two-stage loyalty is only 47 per cent. Finally, in the Fine Gael case in the Meath constituency, Figure 9.8 shows a difference of 33 percentage points between the loyalty estimate based on the published data (72 per cent) and the loyalty estimate based on the e-voting data (39 per cent).

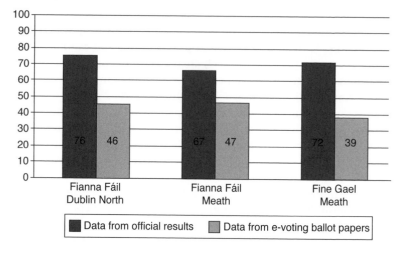

Figure 9.8   Loyalty in published vote transfer data and (two-stage) loyalty in e-voting constituency data, at 2002 general election

Sources: Published election results; E-voting ballot papers published by constituency returning officers following 2002 general election.

Conclusion

PR-STV has the capacity to elicit and process prodigious quantities of information about the preferences of the voters. This gives rise to several questions. Is the capacity of the system fully utilised? What do the transfer preferences tell us about party loyalty, about party plumping and about inter-party relationships? How do these phenomena vary over time and across parties? And, finally, how do the 2011 results fit in with the long-term trends?

Before summarising our findings, we should recall some important caveats. The fundamental problem is that there is a lot of missing data in the published results. This arises from multiple eliminations and particularly from the fact that the preferences of the supporters of the last elected and runner-up contestants are rarely revealed by the counting process. Then there is the problem that all those zero non-transferable votes that arise on the distribution of surpluses cannot be taken at face value. Nor can the origin of the 'last parcels received' be taken for granted. All that said, there is a wealth of information out there about transfers that repays careful attention. It is also worth noting that overcoming the conceptual and measurement issues involved has been made easier by the availability of the full ballot papers from the three e-voting constituencies in the 2002 election.

Evaluating any given rate of utilisation of preferences is a glass half-full/half-empty story that begs the question of what is a satisfactory standard of utilisation of preferences in PR-STV. The instinctive response may be 'the more, the better', with a fully completed ballot being the goal to be aimed at. By this standard, Irish voters fail. On the other hand, the registration of at least a second preference by 95 per cent of voters and at least a third preference by 88 per cent seems impressive. While this 88 per cent expressing a third preference is immediately followed by a substantial decline in registering preferences, the fact remains that a clear majority of voters (57 per cent) express at least four preferences, and four preferences will take the vast majority of voters beyond their first party preference.

Party loyalty as expressed in PR-STV is of two kinds. The minimum measure only captures single stage transfers; that is, from an elected or eliminated candidate to a continuing candidate of the same party. The complete measure (that is, full party loyalty) captures two stages of transfer – from candidate A of party X to candidate B of party X, and from candidate B to candidate C (also of party X). One-stage loyalty has the advantage of being usable over all general elections; two-stage loyalty provides a vital reminder that the one-stage estimates overstate the extent of party loyalty.

Party plumping can be seen either as an extreme form of party loyalty or as total indifference as between the remaining parties and candidates. While it was an integral part of Fianna Fáil electoral strategy in the past, it has been less in evidence in recent elections. It may be, however, that the significant increase in plumping that is evident in the transfer patterns in 2011 reflects some of the inter-party antipathies stemming from the economic crisis.

In the case of Fine Gael-to-Labour and Labour-to-Fine Gael transfers, the evidence suggests three distinct periods of varying voter commitment to that particular alliance. What might be described as the classic electoral coalition period was in fact quite short-lived, spanning merely a decade from 1973 to 1982. It should also be noted that the 2011 election gave little encouragement to advocates of coalition electoral strategy, as both Fine Gael-to-Labour and Labour-to-Fine Gael transfers were significantly down in 2011 compared with 2007. While it is true to say that such transfers weren't needed in 2011, it is also true that they weren't on offer.

Preference utilisation, party loyalty, party plumping, and support for coalition alliances are features of the PR-STV system that are revealed (more or less clearly) by the constituency-by-constituency, count-by-count workings of the electoral system. They illustrate the power and the responsiveness of the PR-STV system and the range of behaviour it can accommodate. As such they should be essential ingredients in any debate about the electoral system that may arise from the country's current economic and political upheavals.

Notes

1. Readers seeking further material on this topic should see: John Curtice and Michael Marsh, 'How did they vote: voters' use of the STV ballot paper in the 2007 Scottish local election', *Representation* 44:4 (2008), pp. 285–300; Shaun Bowler and David Farrell, 'Voter behavior under STV-PR: solving the puzzle of the Irish party system', *Political Behavior* 13 (1991), pp. 303–20; Michael Gallagher, 'Party solidarity, exclusivity and inter-party relationships in Ireland, 1922–1977: the evidence of transfers', *Economic and Social Review* 10:1 (1978), pp. 1–22; Fiachra Kennedy, 'Elite level co-ordination of party supporters: an analysis of Irish aggregate data, 1987–1997', *Representation* 38:4 (2002), pp. 284–93; Michael Laver, 'Analysing structures of party preference in electronic voting data', *Party Politics* 10:5 (2004), pp. 521–41; Michael Marsh, Richard Sinnott, John Garry and Fiachra Kennedy, *The Irish Voter: The nature of electoral competition in the Republic of Ireland* (Manchester: Manchester University Press, 2008); Michael Marsh, 'Voting for government coalitions in Ireland under single transferable vote', *Electoral Studies* 29 (2010), pp. 329–38; Richard Sinnott, *Irish Voters Decide: Voting behaviour in elections and referendums since 1918*, (Manchester: Manchester University Press, 1995), pp. 199–216; Richard Sinnott, 'Party attachment in Europe: methodological critique and substantive implications', *British Journal of Political Science* 28:4 (1998), pp. 627–50.
2. Michael Laver suggests an alternative list of four indicators comprising 'perfect', 'split', 'broken' and 'bust' ballots. See Laver, 'Analysing structures of party preference', pp. 527–8.

3. Changes to the criteria governing multiple eliminations that came into effect in the 1997 election were followed by a dramatic increase in the number of multiple eliminations, from six in 1992 to 27 in 1997. The number has continued to rise since 1997, reaching 37 in 2011.

4. Some of the volatility in Labour loyalty is no doubt due to the small number of cases on which the calculation must at times be based.

5. Sinnott, 'Party attachment in Europe', pp. 627–50.

6. The very high Fine Gael-to-Labour transfer in 1957 (when 66 per cent of Fine Gael terminal transfers went to Labour) is clearly an outlier. The anomaly arises because there is only one case that meets the criteria for inclusion in the calculation of Fine Gael-to-Labour transfers. In short, we cannot rely on this particular instance to draw any inferences about inter-party transfers as such.

7. In February 2000 the Irish government decided to introduce electronic voting and counting at elections. At the 2002 general election e-voting was employed in three constituencies, and it was used in these and an additional four constituencies in a referendum later in 2002, with a view to using it nationwide at subsequent elections. In the event a range of objections, complications and difficulties arose, and e-voting was never used again, the plans being formally abandoned in 2009. See Gary Murphy, 'The background to the election', pp. 1–18 in Michael Gallagher and Michael Marsh, *How Ireland Voted 2007: The full story of Ireland's general election* (Basingstoke: Palgrave Macmillan, 2008), at pp. 14–15.

8. These break down as follows:
   - Dublin North (12 candidates): 3,662 out of 43,942 votes cast (8.3 per cent);
   - Dublin West (9 candidates): 3,800 out of 29,988 votes cast (12.7 per cent);
   - Meath (14 candidates): 2,490 out of 64,081 votes cast (3.9 per cent).

9. As discussed in some detail in Sinnott, *Irish Voters Decide*, p. 209, n3.

10. Out of all 15 elections between 1948 and 1992 Sinnott has identified only seven cases in which two-stage party loyalty can be even approximately measured using the published election results – see Sinnott, *Irish Voters Decide*, p. 209, n4.

10
Women and the Election

Fiona Buckley and Claire McGing

As the results of the 2011 general election flooded in on count day, it quickly transpired that significant changes to the Irish political landscape were afoot. Excited commentators could not resist using words such as 'historic', 'transformative' and 'revolution' to describe the unfolding drama. The Irish electorate had unleashed vengeance on its political masters and in the process had ensured that the composition of the 31st Dáil would be very different from that of its predecessors. However, one constant remained – the low number of women elected to Dáil Éireann.

On 25 February 2011, 25 women were elected to Dáil Éireann. This represents a new record in terms of the number of women elected at a general election. Despite this positive development, the persistent issue of women's under-representation remains. Only 91 women have been elected to Dáil Éireann since 1918. Of the total 4,744 Dáil seats filled since 1918, only 260 have been occupied by women. With just over 15 per cent women's representation in its lower house of parliament, Ireland falls behind both the world average of 20 per cent and the European Union average of 24 per cent.

International research has demonstrated that certain socio-cultural, economic and political variables contribute to women's increased political representation. Given Ireland's dramatic socioeconomic and cultural changes over the past 30 years, coupled with the increasing numbers of women participating in the labour force, women's higher educational attainment, and the use of a proportional representation electoral system, one would have expected an acceleration in women's political representation in Ireland. This has not been the case.

The chapter begins with a brief overview of women's political participation in Ireland since the foundation of the state. This is followed by an examination of women's electoral performance in the 2011 general election. The election campaign is reviewed to identify the presence, if any, of a gendered dimension to the campaign issues. The chapter assesses the current status of women in political decision-making in Ireland and concludes by reviewing the debate surrounding the proposal to introduce a candidate selection quota at the next general election.

Women's political representation in Ireland: a brief history

Despite being active in the nationalist struggle and the suffrage movement of the early twentieth century, Irish women gradually faded from the political stage after the foundation of the state. Diarmaid Ferriter argues that as early as 1917, political parties were sidelining women members.[1] He recounts how a league of women delegates was formed demanding fair representation of women on the Sinn Féin party executive. This league requested the appointment of six women to the 24-person executive. Sinn Féin conceded, but stated that only four 'ladies' could be appointed to the council. Ferriter also highlights the case of Kathleen Clarke, one of the first members of Fianna Fáil and widow of 1916 patriot Tom Clarke. In 1926, Clarke refused to withdraw from the Senate election in favour of Margaret Pearse, after party leader Éamon De Valera informed her that 'the party would not support two women'. Yvonne Galligan argues that 'the supremacy of the nationalist discourse over that of feminism is important in understanding the low representation of women subsequent to independence'.[2] Following the foundation of the state, Frances Gardiner advises 'women's domestic role was singled out as their most important contribution to the building of the new state and eventually became, via social custom and legislation, constitutionally guaranteed in the 1937 constitution'.[3] Article 41.2 of the constitution stated (as it still does today):

> 1° In particular, the State recognises that by her life within the home, woman gives to the State a support without which the common good cannot be achieved.
> 2° The State shall, therefore, endeavour to ensure that mothers shall not be obliged by economic necessity to engage in labour to the neglect of their duties in the home.

This constitutional declaration, coupled with the prominence of the Catholic Church in Irish society, which viewed the role of women as being childbearers, carers and nurturers, meant that Irish women were met with strong cultural, societal and legal barriers in their attempts to enter public life. Accordingly, in 1973 there were fewer women in Dáil Éireann than there had been 50 years earlier (five women were elected to the Dáil in 1923 compared with just four in 1973). Those that did enter politics were often from well-established political families, and several succeeded their husbands in politics. Indeed, the 'widows' inheritance' was the primary route to political office for many women during this period. The second-wave feminism of the 1970s resulted in a remobilisation of women's political activity. This period witnessed the establishment of the Council for the Status of Women (later the National Women's Council of Ireland, NWCI) and the Women's Political Association. These groups engendered a political fervour amongst women, and a new 'feminist' woman politician begun to emerge independent of kinship ties. There was a gradual increase in the number of women seeking political office from the late 1970s onwards, growing steadily from 25 in 1977 to 65 in 1987, and reaching a then high of 89 in 1992. The 1992 general election witnessed the first major breakthrough in terms of women's political representation in Ireland, with a record 20 women elected. However, the number of women TDs has remained relatively static ever since (see Table 10.1).

Table 10.1   Women candidates and TDs at elections, 1973–2011

Election	Candidates			Deputies			Success rate for women %	Success rate for men %
	Total	Women	%	Total	Women	%		
1973	334	16	4.8	144	4	2.7	25.0	44.0
1977	376	25	6.6	148	6	4.1	24.0	40.5
1981	404	41	10.1	166	11	6.6	26.8	42.7
1982 (Feb.)	366	35	9.6	166	8	4.8	22.9	47.7
1982 (Nov.)	365	31	8.5	166	14	8.4	45.2	45.5
1987	466	65	13.9	166	14	8.4	21.5	37.9
1989	371	52	14.0	166	13	7.8	25.0	48.0
1992	482	89	18.5	166	20	12.0	22.5	37.2
1997	484	96	19.8	166	20	12.0	20.8	37.6
2002	463	84	18.1	166	22	13.3	26.2	38.0
2007	470	82	17.4	166	22	13.3	26.8	37.6
2011	566	86	15.2	166	25	15.1	29.1	29.2

Women's political representation in Ireland today

Representation is a key concept in the study and practice of politics. It is about *who* represents, *what* is represented, and *how* it is represented. The normative view is that women's presence in political decision-making is 'essential to the quality of the democratic process'.[4] The main arguments for increasing women's political representation can be categorised into three distinct themes: *justice, difference* and *symbolism*.

Justice arguments for increasing women's political presence are the most powerful, contending that it is simply unfair for men to disproportionately populate politics. This perspective argues that gendered barriers (such as cultural biases) must be dismantled in the name of equal opportunity.

Difference arguments for increasing women's political representation are more contentious and see gender as relevant to the ways in which elected representatives perform their role. In this line of reasoning, gender is a structure that imposes a particular position on women. It is argued that women bring a distinct perspective to policy discussions because of their different life experiences. Others argue that there are particular women's issues or interests that merit political representation and that the inclusion of women representatives is often required to bring these into the discourses of parliament.

Some scholars argue that the presence of women representatives is important for symbolic reasons because they act as role models. Female candidates and elected representatives can help to mobilise women and stimulate their political interest, as well as increase women's confidence in making the decision to run for political office.

Much of the scholarly literature on women's political representation emphasises cultural bias as the principal obstacle to women achieving elected office.[5] In Ireland, feminist scholars have argued that Irish society was historically patriarchal, so women's participation in all aspects of public life, including politics, was minimised and marginalised.[6] The cultural variable clearly plays a major role in explaining women's under-representation in Ireland but, despite this, women do not face discrimination from voters.[7] As the number of women candidates has increased, there has been a concurrent increase in the number of women TDs elected.

Recent academic literature proposes the 'five Cs' model of *care* (childcare or otherwise), *culture, cash, confidence* and *candidate selection* to summarise the main barriers facing Irish women when entering politics. A report by the NWCI in 2009 revealed that over the course of a week, women in Ireland spend on average a fifth of their day engaged in care and household work, three times as much as men do.[8] A Central Statistics Office (CSO) report showed that half a million women were looking after home/family compared with only 7,500 men.[9] These facts indicate that there is a persistent bias towards traditional gender roles in Ireland. The expectation placed on women to maintain the customary role of main home-maker prevents or delays many women from entering politics. The CSO report also indicates that women's annual income is around 70 per cent of that of men. Over 20 per cent of women occupy lowly-paid clerical jobs as compared to just 6 per cent of men. Women continue to be under-represented in senior professional posts; just 34 per cent of medical and dental consultants are women. With not as much cash at their disposal and/ or with different earning potential from that of men, many women find it difficult to enter politics and fund electoral campaigns. The masculine image of politics expressed by comments such as 'macho' and the 'old boys' network' is one that many women feel unable to break through. Politics is a gendered institution. Gendered institutions are those where gender is present in the processes, practices and distribution of power.[10] Political institutions are male-created bodies whereby the structures, rules and procedures were developed by men at a time when women were still fighting for equal voting and political rights. Status characteristics theory suggests that men benefit compared to women on the basis of their gender, as politics has traditionally been seen as a male domain.

Some women politicians question whether it is necessary to emulate masculine behaviour.[11] Shouting, sneering and name-calling have become standard procedure in parliaments in Anglo-American countries. However, feminist studies suggest that women who adopt this combative style are often ridiculed and criticised for being 'unladylike'. Conversely, women who adopt a more collaborative, 'soft' and demure style are labelled weak.[12] The candidate selection procedures of political parties act as a 'gatekeeper' to the ambitions of many an aspiring politician. Party activists will tend to favour the 'tried and tested' incumbent candidate at selection conventions.[13] As most incumbents are men, the opportunities for new women candidates to get onto the party ticket are limited.

The 'five Cs' barriers are not exclusive to Ireland. However, in many other countries, efforts have been made to address women's political under-representation through the introduction of affirmative action measures such as gender quotas. Gender quotas have been identified as an important contributor to changes in women's political representation.[14] They act as a facilitator of women's inclusion into the political arena and give women access to the agenda-setting process. Voluntary party quotas have been used in countries such as Germany, Sweden and Norway since the 1970s to redress the gender imbalance on candidate lists. The first country in the world to introduce a legislative quota was Argentina in 1991. Since then, a number of countries in the European Union, notably Belgium (1994), France (2000) and Spain (2007) have introduced candidate selection laws. The experience of these countries indicates that quotas are successful in increasing the number of women elected. In Belgium, women's representation rose from 13 per cent in 1994 to 35 per cent in 2007; in Spain, it rose from 27 per cent in 1996 to 36 per cent in 2008, and in France the figure rose from 11 per cent in 1997 to 19 per cent in 2007.[15]

The 2011 general election: women candidates

Of the 566 candidates to contest the 2011 general election, 86 (15 per cent) were women. While numerically this was an increase of four on the 2007 figure, it represented a percentage decrease of 2 per cent in the proportion of women candidates. The percentage of women candidates in 2011 was the lowest since 1989 (see Table 10.1).

Women contested the election in 39 of the 43 constituencies, the exceptions being Cork South-West, Kildare South, Limerick and Roscommon–South Leitrim. When one removes independent and smaller party women candidates from the constituency overview, a more negative picture emerges. There were nine constituencies, just over a fifth of the total, in which no woman was selected to run for Fianna Fáil, Fine Gael, Labour, Sinn Féin or the Green Party. Overall, 12 constituencies had only one woman candidate; 16 constituencies had two women candidates, five had three women candidates, three had four women candidates and three had five women candidates.

Political parties varied in their percentage of women candidates, with only two parties increasing their number of women candidates since 2007. Fine Gael increased its number of woman candidates by one. While this numerical increase is welcome, a larger number of women candidates may have been expected, considering the party ran many more candidates than in 2007. Labour took advantage of its rising tide of popularity by running multiple candidate tickets in some constituencies. Labour women benefited from this candidate strategy, the number of women candidates rising from 11 in 2007 to 18 in 2011. Eleven women contested the election on behalf of Fianna Fáil, a decrease of three in numerical terms but a marginal increase in percentage terms. The Greens and Sinn Féin each ran eight women candidates, which represented a decrease of three for the Greens and a decrease of two for Sinn Féin when compared to 2007 (see Table 10.2).

Table 10.2   Women candidates in the 2011 election

Party	Total number of candidates	Women candidates	Total number of TDs	Women TDs
Fianna Fáil	75	11 (14.7%)	20	0
Fine Gael	104	16 (15.4%)	76	11 (14.5%)
Labour	68	18 (26.5%)	37	8 (21.6%)
Sinn Féin	41	8 (19.5%)	14	2 (14.3%)
Greens	43	8 (18.6%)	0	0
United Left Alliance	20	5 (25.0%)	5	2 (50.0%)
Independents/Others	215	20 (9.3%)	14	2 (14.3%)
Total	566	86 (15.2%)	166	25 (15.1%)

Party candidates are selected primarily at constituency level by selection conventions, but party headquarters (HQ) maintains the right to add candidates to the locally-selected tickets (see Chapter 3). In 2011, the larger political parties added a total of 27 candidates to party tickets following the completion of local selection conventions. This was rarely done to achieve a better gender balance of candidates, with geographical considerations being the main reason for additional selections. Of the 27 candidates added after selection conventions, only five (19 per cent) were women.[16] The sole candidate added by Fianna Fáil HQ was a woman. Lisa Chambers, a 24-year-old first-time candidate and chairperson of her local cumann, was selected as running mate to incumbent TD Dara Calleary in Mayo. Fine Gael HQ made 18 late additions. Two were women – councillors Cáit Keane in Dublin South-West and Hildegarde Naughton in Galway West. Two of the eight candidates later added by Labour HQ were women – Mary Moran in Louth and Lorraine Higgins in Galway East. Both women were added as running mates to male councillors.

A gender-related controversy arose in the Fine Gael selection process in Dun Laoghaire. The incumbent deputy, Seán Barrett, contested the nomination along with councillors John Bailey, Marie Baker, Mary Mitchell O'Connor and Barry Ward. Barrett topped the poll, with Ward and Mitchell O'Connor coming second and third respectively. Following the convention vote, a directive by party HQ was read out requiring members to select just one male and one female candidate. Hence Mitchell O'Connor was placed on the ticket ahead of Ward. A number of Monkstown Fine Gael branch members who supported Ward felt 'disenfranchised' and believed that the selection process was undemocratic. However, the Dublin director of elections for Fine Gael, Terry Murphy, denied this, stating that the decision had been reached as part of a party commitment to increasing the number of women candidates.[17]

In Clare, three women – Ann Cronin, Sarah Ferrigan and Madeline McAleer – decided to put their names forward for election at a late stage when it looked as if the constituency would be an all-male contest. Running under the umbrella *Balance the Ballot*, the group announced their desire to create a more inclusive form of politics. 'We are delighted to be able to balance the ballot and give the people of Clare choice', they declared at their press conference launch.

The raft of political retirements in advance of the election posed a concern for those advocating an increased presence of women in the Dáil. Of the 36 TDs who announced their retirement from politics (see Appendix 5), six were women. The number meant that over a quarter of the 23 women deputies in the outgoing 30th Dáil would not be seeking re-election. The decision by Fine Gael's Olwyn Enright (Laois–Offaly) to retire from politics highlighted the difficulties women face when attempting to balance family life with a political career. Enright announced in August 2010 her intention not to seek re-election. With a ten-month-old son and expecting her second child at the time, her decision was prompted by a desire to spend more time with her young family. Olwyn Enright is married to Joe McHugh, a Fine Gael TD representing Donegal North-East. As both deputies spent much time in their respective constituencies, family life became difficult. Given Enright's higher profile, some questioned why it was she and not McHugh who was retiring from politics. In response Enright advised 'I just feel it's a role I want to play as a mother and that Joe can't play.'[18] She said that the political lifestyle posed significant challenges for women as the long hours were not compatible with raising a family. Also, the lack of maternity leave[19] posed particular problems for women. Enright's decision led to calls for a change in the structure of politics to accommodate family life.

Profiling the women candidates

Over half (47) of the women candidates were first-time Dáil challengers, while 22 were contesting the election for the second or subsequent time and 17 were incumbent TDs. In the case of Labour, Fine Gael and Sinn Féin many of their first-time women candidates had successfully contested the 2009 local elections, thus ensuring that these candidates had both name recognition and (some) political experience, important attributes when one is seeking political office. Conversely, in the case of Fianna Fáil and the Green Party, few of their newcomers had previous political experience, something that their parties may have thought advantageous considering the expected backlash that the government was likely to receive. Ultimately, neither incumbency nor inexperience would save the women candidates of these parties, a fate also endured by many of their male party colleagues.

An examination of the demographic profile of women candidates reveals a wide spectrum in age profile. The youngest candidate was Darcy Lonergan (21) of the Green Party in Cavan–Monaghan. The oldest was Loretta Clarke (75), an Independent in Mayo, running on a platform of increasing national awareness of issues relevant to older people. Thirteen women candidates (15 per cent) were aged 35 years or under. The majority of women candidates were clustered in the middle-aged categories. Twenty-five per cent worked in education (teaching at either pre-school, primary, secondary or third level), 17 per cent in business (with some owning their own companies), 14 per cent in advocacy, community or trade union groups, 9 per cent in medicine and social work, 8 per cent in the law profession, with the remainder working in a variety of professions ranging from accountancy to journalism, and engineering to homemaker. The majority of women candidates were married or in long-term relationships. Over 70 per cent of women candidates had children.

Political experience and kinship have traditionally provided a distinct advantage to aspiring women candidates. The 2011 election provides some interesting findings to confirm and contest this assumption. Becoming a local representative (county, city, town councillor) has always been the most common first step or springboard on the road to Dáil Éireann.[20] This was proven again to be the case for women candidates in the 2011 election. Fifty-seven per cent of candidates had prior experience at the local level. All of those elected, with the exception of Áine Collins (Fine Gael) and Mary Lou McDonald (Sinn Féin), served in local government at some point in their political careers.[21] Nine candidates were former senators, with six sitting senators contesting the election. Two of these were elected. Incumbency proved an advantage for Labour and Fine Gael women candidates. All were re-elected with the exception of Deirdre Clune, who lost out to her party colleague, Jerry Buttimer, in Cork South-Central. However, the opposite was the case for Fianna Fáil and Green Party candidates, as all their incumbent women TDs, along with most of their male counterparts, lost their seats. A third of all women candidates had kinship ties to previous or current public representatives. However, unlike in previous elections, family connections did not prove to be electorally advantageous to women candidates. Only three of those elected had a family relationship with a former elected official. Interestingly, none of these relatives were former TDs, meaning that the so-called 'widows' and daughters' inheritance' disappeared in 2011. The 31st Dáil is the first in which none of the women TDs is related to former TDs.

Women's issues: party manifestos and election campaign

While all of the parties referred to specific 'women's issues' in their election manifestos, gender-specific topics garnered minimal interest in the course of the election campaign.

The Fine Gael manifesto referred to a number of policies of specific interest to women. References were made to encouraging female recruitment in the Defence Forces, extending Breast Check to more women, introducing a cervical cancer vaccination catch-programme for all girls up to the age of 18 years, and compensating women who were excluded on age grounds from the Lourdes Hospital Redress Scheme.[22] On a more gender-neutral platform, Fine Gael proposed to re-examine maternity leave entitlements to meet the changing needs of families, stating that it would review current policy in order to permit both parents to share leave entitlements. Fine Gael recognised the need to increase the number of women in decision-making but put no firm solutions forward as to how the current situation could be improved.

Alongside more generalised aims for gender equality in apprenticeship programmes, jobs and sport, the Labour Party manifesto pledged to update the constitution 'to reflect the role of women in 21st century Ireland'. The party also outlined its plans for dealing with the problem of domestic violence. Labour too made reference to the lack of women in decision-making, proposing a legal requirement that would ensure that state boards and committees have at least 40 per cent women and 40 per cent men. It also promised to tie public funding of parties to 'the level of participation by women as public representatives those parties achieve', setting out targets in legislation. Three months after the election, the Fine Gael–Labour government declared an intention to introduce a legislative requirement that at least 30 per cent of each party's candidates be women. This would link state party funding to the number of women candidates on party tickets. If parties fail to meet the 30 per cent quota, they will lose 50 per cent of their state funding.

Only the Fine Gael and Labour manifestos mentioned abortion. The parties diverged considerably in their approach to the issue. In line with longstanding party policy, Labour favoured legislating in accordance with the 1992 'X' case judgment.[23] In contrast, Fine Gael sought to establish an all-party committee that would have access to legal and medical expertise to consider the conclusions of the European Court of Human Rights (ECHR) judgment.[24] Following the election, the agreed Fine Gael–Labour Programme for Government contained a commitment to establish an 'expert group' to make recommendations on the matter.

The Fianna Fáil manifesto made only a few direct references to issues specific to women. Under proposals for targeted constitutional reform, and in a similar vein to Labour, the party pledged 'an amendment to replace the reference to women and mothers in Article 41.2 with a gender neutral version recognising parents in the home'. Within priorities for electoral reform, the party called for the replacement of proportional representation by the single transferable vote (PR-STV) with a mixed-member proportional system along the lines of the German system. A proposal was made as part of this, although somewhat ambiguously, to address the gender imbalance in Irish politics. Fianna Fáil has subsequently given its support to the proposed gender quota legislation announced by the government in May 2011.

Sinn Féin's manifesto contained a number of policies directed at women. The right of women to feel safe in their communities was emphasised. Similar to Fine Gael policy, the party vowed to establish a supplementary Lourdes Redress Scheme, which would compensate the remaining 35 victims of Michael Neary. The party also committed itself to setting up a Commission of Inquiry into the practice of symphysiotomy on women in the past.[25] Under a section dedicated to the pursuit of equality for all citizens, it wished to set up an All-Ireland 'Strategy for Women's Equality' and to 'bind gender targets of at least 40 per cent for either gender on the boards of State and semi-State bodies, the judiciary and the cabinet', while considering the extension of these targets to 'private sector bodies in receipt of government funding'.

The Green Party manifesto made frequent appeals to women. The Greens committed themselves to encouraging women in enterprise, seeking to establish a National Women in Enterprise group to bring together the support currently offered by County Enterprise Boards. In a section dedicated to 'Women and Men', the Greens put forward a number of gendered policy proposals. These included issues related to fathers' rights, domestic and sexual violence, and taking measures to address the gender 'wage gap' in Ireland. They proposed changes to better facilitate the participation of women in political life. The party advocated changes to the Dáil term to make it more compatible with the school term, and suggested that TDs be allowed to take full maternity or parental leave with a pairing arrangement to be put in place to cover any absences. They pledged their support for candidate selection measures that would increase the number of women in politics.

As expected, the campaign was dominated by concerns about the economy, unemployment and the public finances. While women's groups such as the NWCI highlighted the gendered impact of the economic crisis, showing that women suffered disproportionately from reductions in the minimum wage and social welfare payments, as well as from cuts to public services and public sector employment,[26] the differential impact of the economic crisis received very little attention from the media or the political parties.

Abortion failed to emerge as a key election issue.[27] Pro-choice groups called upon the government to legislate for the 1992 Supreme Court judgment on the 'X' case. Conversely, those on the pro-life side sought a referendum to reverse that decision. An alliance, 'Ireland United for Life', led by former MEPs 'Dana' Rosemary Scallon and Kathy Sinnott, called on party leaders and candidates to give an election pledge not to legislate for abortion in the wake of the ECHR ruling. While Labour Party canvassers reported some targeted protest from anti-abortion campaigners, abortion as an election issue did not gather momentum.

The low numbers of women contesting the election spurred a debate about women's political representation in Ireland. Groups such as the *50:50 Group* and *Claiming our Future* advocated the introduction of affirmative action measures such as candidate selection quotas to reduce the gender imbalance in Irish politics.[28] While political parties were reluctant to clearly state their support for such calls in the course of the election campaign, the Programme for Government announced that state funding of political parties would be linked to the number of women candidates a party selects at election time and, as mentioned above, in May 2011 it announced more details of this.

The outcome

Turnover amongst women members of Dáil Éireann was high in 2011 with only nine incumbent women being returned. Six did not seek re-election, eight were not re-elected, 14 women were elected to the Dáil for the first time and two former TDs were re-elected. The average success rate for both men and women candidates was the same at 29 per cent. Yet among candidates of the five main parties, 47 per cent of male party candidates won seats, as opposed to just 34 per cent of female party candidates.

The election was disastrous for incumbent women candidates of the outgoing government. Given their small number, Fianna Fáil women were disproportionately hit by the large scale collapse in their party's support. All incumbent women candidates lost their seats (for full list of defeated TDs, see Appendix 5). Indeed, no woman TD was returned on behalf of the Fianna Fáil party. The Green Party returned no deputies to the Dáil, with Minister of State Mary White losing her seat along with her five male colleagues.

Eleven women were elected for Fine Gael, thus increasing the party's number of women TDs by six. Six of the women elected for Fine Gael have never before been members of the Oireachtas. Eight women were elected for the Labour Party, which represents an increase of one in comparison to the 30th Dáil. All incumbent Labour women retained their seats, and two were elected on the first count. Róisín Shortall (Dublin North-West) received the sixth highest percentage of first preference votes in the country (29 per cent), the highest of all women candidates. Joan Burton (Dublin West) had the honour of being the first TD elected on count day, receiving 9,627 first preference votes. Three new women TDs join the Labour Party ranks. Five of Labour's eight women TDs are based in urban constituencies, in Dublin, Cork and Limerick. Sinn Féin now has two women TDs. Both, Mary Lou McDonald (Dublin Central) and Sandra McLellan (Cork East), are first-time TDs. Two of those that won seats as part of the ULA umbrella group are women. Clare Daly (Dublin North) of the Socialist Party and Joan Collins (Dublin South-Central) of People Before Profit are first-time TDs.

An interesting geography of female representation emerged, with urban and commuter-belt constituencies more gender-balanced than rural areas, a pattern that has been seen in previous elections. Eighteen of the 25 women TDs represent a constituency in either Dublin or the rest of Leinster. In addition, all three constituencies with more than one woman deputy are in Dublin: Dublin Central, Dublin Mid-West and Dublin South-Central. Overall, 21 constituencies of the 43 have no woman TD. In contrast, all constituencies have *at least* two male representatives. Strikingly, despite the Fine Gael and Labour parties winning 113 seats between them, 25 constituencies (58 per cent of the total) have no 'government' woman TD.

Table 10.3 shows first preference votes cast by sex and party in 2011. Overall, female candidates received slightly more first preference votes on average than male candidates. However, looking at the five main political parties only, men received more first preference votes per head than women candidates, though the difference varied considerably between parties. The largest gap emerged for Sinn Féin, with male candidates winning nearly 2,000 more votes on average than their female colleagues. On the other hand, women that ran for the United Left Alliance won just over 700 more votes per head than male candidates, while Independent women received marginally more than male independents.

Table 10.3 First preference vote by sex and party, 2011 election

Party	First preferences (total)	First preferences (men)	First preferences (women)	First prefs per male candidate	First prefs per female candidate
Fianna Fáil	387,358	333,940 (86%)	53,418 (14%)	5,218	4,856
Fine Gael	801,628	688,552 (86%)	113,076 (14%)	7,914	6,652
Labour	431,796	328,054 (76%)	103,742 (24%)	6,561	5,763
Sinn Féin	220,661	190,372 (86%)	30,289 (14%)	5,769	3,786
Green Party	41,039	35,848 (87%)	5,191 (13%)	1,024	649
United Left Alliance	59,423	41,878 (70%)	17,545 (30%)	2,792	3,509
Independents	246,954	221,871 (90%)	25,083 (10%)	1,378	1,568
Others	31,500	29,800 (95%)	1,700 (5%)	851	567
Total	2,220,359	1,870,315 (84%)	350,044 (16%)	3,896	4,070

Women TDs and ministers

While women TDs have traditionally come from the teaching professions, there is greater diversity in the backgrounds of women deputies in the 31st Dáil. Teaching remains near the top of the list but the occupational backgrounds of women TDs are varied (see Table 10.4). Over 80 per cent of women TDs are graduates of third-level institutions. The average age of women TDs is 49.4 years and women deputies have on average two children each.[29]

Table 10.4 Occupational backgrounds of women TDs, 2011

Occupation	Number
Administration (secretarial, clerical)	5
Teaching	5
Activist (advocacy, community, trade union)	3
Law	3
Accountancy	2
Research and development	2
Business	1
Credit union manager	1
Homemaker	1
Industry	1
Social worker	1
Total	25

Of the 181 people who have served in cabinet since 1922, only 12 have been women. The formation of the new cabinet on 9 March led to a debate about women's inclusion in the upper echelons of political decision-making in Ireland. It was expected that the number of women ministers would be maintained at three, as was the precedent set by previous Fianna Fáil-led governments, with some hoping for an increased female presence. However, only two women, Joan Burton and Frances Fitzgerald, were appointed to the cabinet.[30] The appointment of Joan Burton to the Social Protection portfolio caused much debate, and had many people questioning the manner in which cabinet appointments are made. Burton, a qualified accountant with several years of experience as finance spokesperson for the Labour Party, was widely expected to be appointed to one of the finance portfolios, but was not. Some felt that the decision was gender-driven. Writing in the *Irish Times*, Susan McKay, Chief Executive of the NWCI, commented that 'the country is once again to be run by Irish men with brass necks and brass balls'.[31] This perception was rejected by Tánaiste Éamon Gilmore. He denied that Burton had been overlooked in favour of a male colleague, arguing that she was being appointed to one of the biggest-spending government departments (see also Chapter 12, pp. 277–8 below). Frances Fitzgerald's appointment to the Department of Children was viewed by some as stereotypical. When asked if this was so, the new Minister for Education, Ruairí Quinn, advised that 'women know more about children than men because they spend more time with them'.[32] To dilute the gender controversy, the Taoiseach maintained the number of junior ministers at 15, despite election promises to reduce this, and four women were appointed to these ministerial ranks.

Conclusion

Contrary to what many believe, women *are* involved in politics. Taking women's membership of political parties as a barometer of women's political interest and activity, a positive picture emerges. Women make up 34 per cent of Fianna Fáil party members, 42 per cent of Fine Gael, 37 per cent of Labour and 24 per cent of Sinn Féin.[33] The results of the 2011 election show that when women are placed on the ballot, they are as successful as their male colleagues in attaining political office. Getting on the political ticket, however, still proves problematic. In May 2011, Phil Hogan, Minister for the Environment, Community and Local Government, announced his intention to introduce legislation whereby political parties must ensure that 30 per cent of their candidates are women. If parties fail to comply, they will lose 50 per cent of their state funding. The proposed legislation is due to come into effect at the next general election.

This proposal has been welcomed by groups and individuals advocating greater equality in political decision-making. It has received support from parties across the political spectrum. Conversely many have questioned the democratic nature and fairness of such measures arguing that politicians should be selected solely on merit.

Gender quota provisions are used in more than one hundred countries worldwide. They are considered a legitimate equal opportunity measure. The UN Committee on the Elimination of Discrimination Against Women (CEDAW)[34] has continually criticised Ireland for the low representation of women in elected office and has recommended that Ireland introduce measures, such as gender quotas, to increase the number of women in public life.

Merit-based arguments assume naively that all election candidates make it into politics 'on their own'. Many candidates experience forms of advantage, whether it is family connections, large personal resources, favour by the party leadership, or, as is specific to Ireland, strong local profile due to GAA (Gaelic Athletic Association) connections. These forms of advantage are considered normal and are rarely questioned. A gender quota is conceived on the premise that it compensates for the many gendered barriers to politics that women experience (see earlier discussion on the 'five Cs'). A woman who comes through a candidate selection process via a quota will still have to prove she is a vote-getter. If she wins a seat, she does so based on her capacity to attract votes, just like other candidates.

Women's political representation in Ireland remains low. If the current situation continues, former TD Liz O'Donnell advises, 'it will come to a point where decisions taken, from which women are absent in large numbers, will lack credibility in a democracy'.[35] The proposed quota legislation will contribute to redressing the gender imbalance in Irish politics. However, gender quotas will not resolve all of the issues that women face when making a decision to enter politics. To be successful, they must be used in conjunction with other measures to benefit a larger number of women, such as civic education programmes, training, mentoring, financial support and improved childcare facilities.

Notes

1. 'The ultimate old boys' network', *Sunday Business Post*, 13 March 2011, www. sbpost.ie/commentandanalysis/the-ultimate-old-boys-network-55043.html, accessed 13 April 2011.

2. Yvonne Galligan, 'Women in politics', pp. 263–91 in John Coakley and Michael Gallagher (eds), *Politics in the Republic of Ireland*, 5th edn (Abingdon: Routledge and PSAI Press, 2010), p. 263.

3. Frances Gardiner, 'Women in the election', pp. 79–92 in Michael Gallagher and Michael Laver (eds), *How Ireland Voted 1992* (Dublin: Folens and PSAI Press, 1993), p. 79.

4. Miki Caul Kittilson, *Challenging Parties, Changing Parliaments: Women and elected office in contemporary Western Europe* (Columbus: Ohio State University Press, 2006), p. 13.

5. Ronald Inglehart and Pippa Norris, *Rising Tide: Gender equality and cultural change around the world* (Cambridge: Cambridge University Press, 2003), pp. 127–46.

6. Pat O'Connor, 'The Irish patriarchal state: continuity and change', pp. 143–64 in Maura Adshead, Peadar Kirby and Michelle Millar (eds), *Contesting the State: Lessons from the Irish case* (Manchester: Manchester University Press, 2008).

7. Gail McElroy and Michael Marsh, 'Candidate gender and voter choice: analysis from a multimember preferential voting system', *Political Research Quarterly* 63:4 (2010), pp. 822–33.

8. National Women's Council of Ireland (2009) *Who Cares?*, www.nwci.ie/download/pdf/who_cares_october_2009.pdf, accessed 14 April 2011.

9. Central Statistics Office (2011) *Women and Men in Ireland 2010*, www.cso.ie/releasespublications/documents/other_releases/2010/womenandmen2010.pdf, accessed 14 April 2011.

10. Joan Acker, 'Gendered institutions: from sex roles to gendered institutions', *Contemporary Society* 21 (1992), pp. 565–9.

11. Louise Chappell, *Gendering Government* (Vancouver: University of British Columbia Press, 2002).

12. Mary Hawkesworth, 'Engendering political science: an immodest proposal', *Politics and Gender* 1:1 (2005), pp. 150–1.

13. Pádraic McCormack (FG) in Galway West was the only incumbent not selected to contest the 2011 general election – see p. 57 above.

14. Julie Ballington and Francesca Binda, *The Implementation of Quotas: European experiences* (Stockholm: International Institute for Democracy and Electoral Assistance, 2005).

15. Oireachtas Sub-Committee on Women's Participation in Politics (2009) *Women's Participation in Politics*, www.oireachtas.ie/documents/committees30thdail/j-justiceedwr/reports_2008/20091105.pdf, accessed 13 April 2011.

16. Adrian Kavanagh, 'Gender and candidate selection', Irish General Election 2011 Facts and Figures, http://geographyspecialinterestgroup.wordpress.com/2010/12/10/gendercandsge2011/, accessed 16 April 2011.

17. 'Controversy surrounds Fine Gael selection convention', *Dublin People*, 30 December 2010, www.dublinpeople.com/content/view/4112/57/, accessed 7 May 2011.

18. Kathy Sheridan, 'Does politics suit anyone? It suits men. It does really', *Irish Times*, 4 September 2010, www.irishtimes.com/newspaper/weekend/2010/0904/1224278172522.html, accessed 10 May 2011.

19. Statutory maternity leave is not available to women TDs or senators because they are not employees.

20. Liam Weeks and Aodh Quinlivan, *All Politics is Local: A guide to local elections in Ireland* (Cork: Collins Press, 2009), pp. 157–60; see also p. 166 above.

21. Mary Lou McDonald did have previous experience of elected office as she was MEP for the Dublin constituency between 2004 and 2009.

22. A government redress scheme established to compensate women who suffered unnecessary hysterectomies and oopherectomies (removal of ovaries) as a result of the wrongful practices of Dr Michael Neary.

23. In the 'X' case, the Supreme Court declared that Article 40.3.3 of the constitution guarantees a right to an abortion when the life of the mother is at risk.

24. In December 2010 the ECHR made a ruling on the *ABC* v. *Ireland* case, finding that the Irish State had defied a woman's rights, and that it must make life-saving abortion services available.

25. Surgical symphysiotomy is a procedure carried out in childbirth resulting in a permanent widening of the pelvis.

26. National Women's Council of Ireland (2010) *Submission to Budget 2011*, www.nwci.ie/download/pdf/pre_budget_submission_2011.pdf, accessed 17 April 2011.

27. See note 15, p. 203 above.

28. http://5050-group.com/blog/, and www.claimingourfuture.ie/, accessed 31 May 2011.

29. There is some missing data for these background characteristics. Average age is calculated on the basis of 23 women TDs (two missing cases) and number of children on the basis of 22 women TDs (three missing cases). Interestingly, one woman TD refused to reveal her date of birth, stating that such a revelation may have a negative impact on a woman's career in politics.

30. Máire Whelan was appointed to the position of Attorney General, the first woman to hold this position in the history of the state. The Attorney General attends all cabinet meetings but does not have voting rights.

31. 'Normal cabinet service resumes with jobs for the boys ... again', *Irish Times*, 11 March 2011, www.irishtimes.com/newspaper/opinion/2011/0311/1224291883279.html, accessed 13 May 2011.

32. 'Labour women concern over lack of cabinet roles', *Irish Examiner*, 11 March 2011, www.irishexaminer.com/election/analysis/labour-women-concern-over-lack-of-cabinet-roles-147859.html, accessed 12 May 2011.

33. Female membership figures were sourced from political parties in the course of interviews and e-mail correspondence with the authors.

34. UN Committee on the Elimination of Discrimination Against Women, www.un.org/womenwatch/daw/cedaw/committee.htm, accessed 18 April 2011.

35. Oireachtas Sub-Committee on Women in Politics (2009) *Women's Participation in Politics*, www.oireachtas.ie/documents/committees30thdail/j-justiceedwr/reports_2008/20091105.pdf, accessed 13 April 2011.

11
The Final Seanad Election?

John Coakley[1]

The run-up to the election of the 24th Seanad saw a spiral of attacks on the second chamber, and promises that the 2011 election to that body would be the last. The volume of criticism had grown as parties questioned the need to retain the Seanad, even in reformed shape. In October 2009 Fine Gael leader Enda Kenny proposed outright abolition of the house, and this commitment was incorporated in his party's election manifesto. At the beginning of January 2011, as the general election loomed, Fianna Fáil sources indicated that they would trump this, proposing to hold a referendum on the same day as the general election with a view to abolishing the second chamber.[2] The party manifesto duly included a commitment to abolition as part of a broader reform package. The manifesto of the Labour Party was unambiguous, announcing that 'Labour will abolish the Seanad'. Not surprisingly, the formal programme for government of the new Fine Gael–Labour coalition incorporated a promise to abolish this body.

This seeming unanimity between the largest three parties in the Dáil might appear to have sealed the fate of Ireland's apparently unloved second chamber. If political commitments are taken at face value, this chapter in the 2011 version of *How Ireland Voted* will be the last on a Seanad election. But the history of the debate on Seanad reform shows that, as in many other areas, enthusiasm for reform can wilt quickly in the wake of an election; it is precisely this debate that we consider in the section that follows. The remaining sections of this chapter consider three aspects of the election of the largest component of the Seanad, the 43 'panel' members (the nomination process, the electoral process and the political outcome), before looking at the election of the six university senators and the appointment of the Taoiseach's 11 nominees.

The Seanad and its critics

The Irish Seanad continues to be something of an anomaly among its peers. By 2011, most parliaments of sovereign states (111 out of 188) were unicameral; the Irish Oireachtas was one of 77 bicameral parliaments (41 per cent of the total). But its composition made it particularly unusual. In most second chambers the predominant principle of representation is territorial: members are intended to represent populations or territories, whether they are elected directly (as in the USA) or indirectly (as in France, where local councillors have the major say). A further considerable group of second chambers is made up mainly of members nominated by the head of state; and some others are mixed in composition.[3] In only two cases is a second chamber designed to represent functional or vocational interests: Ireland and Slovenia (a third case, the Bavarian Senate, was abolished in 1999, but this was, in any case, a subnational body). The Slovene National Council seeks to give expression to corporate groups: its 40 members comprise 22 representatives of local interests, four of employers, four of employees, four of farmers, crafts, trades and independent professions, and six of non-commercial fields (universities, other education, research, culture and sport, health care, and social welfare). It has also been relatively successful in achieving this form of representation, by ensuring that electoral interests registered in these categories have a decisive voice in determining who is elected.[4]

At first sight, provisions for the election of the Irish senate appear similar (and similarly unusual, in reflecting corporatist thinking of the early twentieth century). As provided for in Article 18.7 of the 1937 constitution, the Seanad has three components. The largest group consists of 43 senators elected from five panels that represent sets of 'interests and services' into which, by implication, Irish society is divided:

1. National language and culture, literature, art, education and such professional interests as may be defined by law for the purpose of this panel;
2. Agriculture and allied interests, and fisheries;
3. Labour, whether organised or unorganised;
4. Industry and commerce, including banking, finance, accountancy, engineering and architecture;

5. Public administration and social services, including voluntary social activities.

A further six senators are elected by graduates of the country's oldest two universities, the National University of Ireland and the University of Dublin (Trinity College). The remaining 11 senators are appointed by the Taoiseach.[5]

One of the strongest criticisms levelled at the Seanad is that it has altogether failed to fulfil the representative function set out for it in 1937 – that it has never really reflected the kinds of interests outlined in the constitution. This chapter will provide yet more evidence – not that it is needed – of the validity of this allegation. Of course, more fundamental criticisms have also been made: that vocational representation is not desirable in any case, and that a second chamber is an unnecessary luxury – if not an entirely inappropriate constitutional device – in the modern democratic state (or, at least, in a unitary state).

Aside from the calls for outright abolition that have been referred to above, one of the commonly cited complaints about the Seanad in the run-up to the 2011 election was that it had been the subject of a long series of reports on which no action had been taken. Specifically, 12 reports (the most recent in 2004) were mentioned, implying an extraordinary tendency to talk about rather than to implement reform. Whatever the faults of the Seanad, though, this criticism is unfair. This number (12 reports whose conclusions had apparently been ignored) seems to have arisen from a misinterpretation of the 2004 report, which simply listed 11 reports that had been compiled earlier. However, one third of these reports dealt with very general topics, such as the composition and powers of the original senate of the Irish Free State (1928), options for a new senate (1936), vocational organisation as a general principle of social organisation (1943), and the overall content of the constitution (1967).[6] Another third was made up of reports into aspects of the election of the 43 panel members, including technical or mechanical issues (in 1937, 1947, 1952 and 1959).[7]

This leaves four more recent reports. The Constitution Review Group (1996) concluded that 'the Seanad does not appear to satisfy the criteria for a relevant, effective and representative second house', but took the view that there was insufficient time to consider so complex an issue in detail.[8] But the three remaining reports addressed the position of the Seanad in some detail and called for far-reaching reform. The Oireachtas committee that considered the review group's report turned on two occasions to the Seanad. In its second report (1997), it made radical proposals for an overhaul of its make-up, and, following a change in the composition of the committee, it returned to the issue in its seventh report (2002) with a rather different blueprint. The Seanad's own Committee on Procedure and Privileges appointed a sub-committee to consider the issue of reform following the 2002 election, and proposed yet another schema (2004).[9]

These three reports acknowledged the impossibility of giving effect to any meaningful form of vocational representation, and each proposed a complex, hybrid alternative:

- A 60-member body with 15 senators elected from European constituencies in the same manner as MEPs, 14 elected by Dáil deputies, 14 by local councillors, six by university graduates, and 11 Taoiseach's nominees (1997 report).[10]
- A 60-member body with 48 members elected from a single state-wide constituency by means of a list system, and 12 Taoiseach's nominees (2002 report).[11]
- A 64-member body with 26 members elected from a single state-wide constituency by means of a list system on the same day as the European and local elections, six elected by university graduates on the same day, 20 elected by an electoral college made up of newly-elected Dáil deputies, outgoing senators and county and city councillors, and 12 Taoiseach's nominees (2004 report).[12]

There is little evidence that implementation of any of these recommendations was given serious consideration; most recently, an All-Party Group on Seanad Reform in 2008–10 sought to find common ground between parties, but little followed from its deliberations.[13] The transition from proposals for reform to calls for abolition was abrupt, and did not appear to be based on any of the research or deliberation that had informed the reports on reform just discussed. The abolitionist position had been foreshadowed in the 1980s by the Progressive Democrats, who initially called for dropping the Seanad from the constitution but changed their stance following their own experience of the operation of the second chamber.[14] This hostile view of the Seanad received new life in the wake of the economic crisis that began in 2008, for which the Seanad, as such, did not have any specific responsibility, and in respect of which its abolition is likely to have virtually no impact. Commitments to do away with the Seanad, however, did little to impede the enthusiasm with which political parties prepared to contest the April 2011 election to that body, the issue to which we now turn.

The schedule for the election was determined by the date of the dissolution of the Dáil, 1 February 2011 (the Seanad election must take place within 90 days of this). Nominations of university candidates closed on 3 March, those from nominating bodies on 11 March, and those from Oireachtas members on 21 March. The panels of candidates were completed on 25 March and published on 29 March, and ballot papers for these and for the two university constituencies were distributed by registered post, with the requirement in each case that they be sent back to the returning officers by the voting deadline of 26 April for the panel elections and the following day for the university elections. The counting of votes began immediately and concluded four days later. The composition of the Seanad was completed when the Taoiseach announced his 11 nominees on 20 May, exactly three weeks after the completion of the other senate counts.

The panel nominations

Nomination of candidates in Seanad elections is more restrictively controlled than in Dáil elections, where any citizen nominated by a registered political party, by 30 people from the Dáil constituency in question, or who pays a deposit of €500, may stand as a candidate. There are two routes. First, a Seanad candidate may be nominated to one or other of the five panels by a nominating body (typically, a public organisation) associated with that panel and registered as entitled to do this. The register is maintained by the Clerk of the Seanad and is updated annually.[15] Second, any four Dáil deputies or senators (or combination of the two) may also nominate a candidate (but each may make only one nomination). Candidates in each panel are grouped into two sub-panels depending on the way in which they have been nominated, and the electoral law requires the election of a minimum number of senators from each sub-panel.

The manner in which this process was conducted in 2011 is summarised in Table 11.1. In three panels with large numbers of nominating bodies each body was entitled to a single nomination, though not all exercised this right. On the Cultural and Educational panel, for instance, 19 bodies made no nomination at all, and another 13 nominated 12 candidates between them (this is because one candidate was nominated by two bodies – an improbable combination of the Pharmaceutical Society of Ireland and the Drama League of Ireland). The nomination of the remaining body evaporated when the candidate later opted for a different panel to which she had also been nominated. On the Industrial and

Commercial panel, 11 bodies made no nomination, and the remaining 32 nominated 26 candidates between them (some candidates secured several nominations). On the Administrative panel, three bodies made no nomination, and the remaining 12 nominated ten candidates in all.

Table 11.1 Seanad candidate nominations by panel and sub-panel, 2011

Panel	Nominating bodies sub-panel		Oireachtas sub-panel	Total candidates	Total senators to be elected	
	No. of bodies	No. of candidates	No. of candidates		Min. per sub-panel	Total
Culture and Education	33	12	5	17	2	5
Agriculture	11	18	10	28	4	11
Labour	2	12	9	21	4	11
Industry and Commerce	43	26	9	35	3	9
Administration	15	10	9	19	3	7
Total	104	78	42	120	–	43

Sources: Calculated from *Iris Oifigiúil* 23, 22 March 2011, and *Iris Oifigiúil Supplement* 25B, 29 March 2011.

On the two remaining panels, where the number of nominating bodies was smaller in relation to the number of senators to be elected, the bodies were entitled to put forward more candidates. On the Agricultural Panel, the 11 bodies were each entitled to two nominations. It is interesting to note that eight of these maintained a form of political balance by nominating one Fianna Fáil and one Fine Gael candidate each (the ninth nominated two Independent candidates, and two bodies made no nominations). On the Labour Panel, with 11 senators to be elected but only two nominating bodies, each was entitled to seven nominations, and each body availed of this. The Irish Congress of Trade Unions nominated two candidates from each of the largest three parties, and an Independent; the Irish Conference of Professional and Service Associations deferred less to political balance, with five Fianna Fáil and two Fine Gael nominees (because of overlapping nominations, this resulted in 12 candidates in all).

The ease with which candidates could appeal to different types of organisation – and even to organisations on different panels – illustrates the weak connection between candidacies in the Seanad election and the vocational principle. One prominent outgoing Fianna Fáil senator, leaving nothing to chance and mopping up potential sources of nomination of rival candidates, secured nominations from four bodies on the Industrial and Commercial panel (Wholesale Produce Ireland, the Chambers of Commerce of Ireland, the Insurance Institute of Ireland, and the Institute of Bankers in Ireland). A Fine Gael county councillor secured a nomination on two panels, Culture and Education (from the Library Association of Ireland) and Administration (from the National Association for Deaf People), but she later opted for the latter. Overall, the overwhelmingly party political character of the nomination process was clear: of the 78 nominating body candidates, 66 were associated with the largest three parties, and five of the remaining 12 candidates were politically active (either in local councils or as candidates in the earlier Dáil election).

The partisan character of the nomination process was even more obvious in the case of the Oireachtas nominees where, as well as candidates from the largest three parties, three Sinn Féin candidates, two Independents and a solitary Green Party candidate were nominated. Of particular interest here was the effort by Fianna Fáil leader Micheál Martin to reinvigorate his party by appealing for priority support for a list of 10 candidates (though four of these were put forward on the nominating bodies sub-panels). This was of particular importance in circumstances where no fewer than 35 Fianna Fáil TDs had been defeated in the general election, and might well have considered careers as senators (though it did not really represent an innovation: there had been a similar 'inner list' in 2002 and 2007, but this was not publicised at the time). Many of this group, however, like those outgoing Fianna Fáil deputies who retired from public life at the Dáil election, seem to have regarded the political trauma associated with the economic collapse as spelling the end of their political careers (only 13 of them contested the Seanad election). Nevertheless, in addition to the party leader's list there were four further nominations of Fianna Fáil candidates by Oireachtas members, as well as 17 from nominating bodies. Alongside the ten Fianna Fáil Oireachtas nominees, Fine Gael parliamentarians nominated 20 candidates and Labour a further six.

By contrast with the proactive approach of the leader of Fianna Fáil, a consequence, no doubt, of the shock the party suffered in the Dáil election, the process of candidate selection in the other parties appeared more open – at least at the level of the initial proposing of candidates. However, the party leadership played a critical role in filtering candidacies. Fine Gael had a five-member selection committee and Sinn Féin used its Ard Chomhairle (executive) to select candidates likely not just to win seats but also to advance the party's longer term strategic interests (such as providing representation in areas where it currently has no

Dáil representation, and offering parliamentary experience to potential future Dáil candidates). The selection process in the Labour Party was more open, and therefore harder for the party leadership to manage, with the decisive vote being made at a large selection meeting including the parliamentary party as well as executive representatives.

The political nature of the contest is reflected in the electoral profile of the 120 candidates. All but 19 had well-established political careers: nine had been Dáil deputies (two of them, indeed, junior ministers) until suffering defeat in the general election, 24 were members of the outgoing Seanad and 68 were, or had recently been, local councillors (of whom 63 were members of the Seanad electorate). No fewer than 47 had stood unsuccessfully in the Dáil election. Truly 'vocational' candidates were hard to find. Most of those who did not have an established political profile were aspirant party politicians; a clear exception was the President of the Royal Institute of Architects of Ireland, nominated by his own organisation – a rare example of the kind of candidate that the vocational panels were originally intended to attract.

The panel electorate

The partisan character of the panel elections is further underscored by the nature of the electorate. This consists of all county and city councillors, newly-elected Dáil deputies and outgoing senators – overwhelmingly associated with political parties, and in any case politically involved. The distribution of the electorate in 2011 is presented in Table 11.2. This shows a considerable change from earlier Seanad elections, with a decline in the position of Fianna Fáil as its most pronounced feature. The 2009 local elections had not been kind to the party: as economic conditions plummeted, it lost the position of dominance it had maintained since the local elections of 1934, trailing far behind Fine Gael for the first time ever. The gap between the two parties widened further in the 2011 general election (see Chapter 7), with Fine Gael now returning almost four times the number of TDs of its historical rival. Only among senators – the smallest component of the electorate – was Fianna Fáil able to hold its own. The previous Seanad panel election in 2007, together with the Taoiseach's nominees, had given that party a relatively strong position in the second chamber, but this was insufficient to compensate for setbacks elsewhere.

The dramatic character of the change in the Seanad electorate is illustrated in figure 11.1, which presents its composition in selected years since 1977. This suggests that the decline in Fianna Fáil's fortunes predates 2011. If we consider 2002 as representing the traditional voting relationship between the three main parties, the big changes that are clear since then are a drop in Fianna Fáil support from 45 per cent to 24 per cent, and corresponding increases in support for Fine Gael (30 per cent to 39 per cent), Labour (9 per cent to 16 per cent) and others (16 per cent to 21 per cent). One important point of qualification about this pattern needs to be noted. As popular hostility towards Fianna Fáil began to manifest itself in the last years of the decade, many long-standing party figures at local level began to distance themselves from the party, and even to contest the local elections of 2009 as Independents. The 'Other' category in Table 11.2 and in Figure 11.1 thus probably includes a number of local councillors who, though formally 'non-party', are in reality close to Fianna Fáil and potentially open to mobilisation by that party at Seanad elections.

Table 11.2   Composition of Seanad electorate, 2011

Component	Fianna Fáil	Fine Gael	Labour Party	Sinn Féin	Others	Independent/ non-party	Total
Local councillors	213	340	131	51	17	129	881
Dáil deputies	20	76	37	14	5	14	166
Senators	27	6	2	0	3	7	45
Total	260	422	170	65	25	150	1,092

Note: 'Others' include People Before Profit, Socialist Party, Green Party, Workers' Party, Republican Sinn Féin, South Kerry Independent Alliance, and former Progressive Democrat.

Sources: Calculated from *Iris Oifigiúil Supplement* 25A, 29 March 2011, *Members of County Councils, City Councils and Borough Councils 2010/2011* (Dublin: Department of the Environment, 2010), information supplied by the political parties, and other sources.

Yet another factor that needs to be borne in mind is a degree of horse-trading between parties, and special deals brokered by individual candidates. Reference has already been made to Fianna Fáil's strategy, and this was matched in different ways on the part of the other parties. Since the political composition of the electorate is known, it was easy for each party to compute the number of electoral quotas available to it on each panel, and to determine where unaffiliated votes might, if available, be most efficiently used. As in 2007, Sinn Féin was able to arrive at understandings with candidates of other parties in the two panels where it was not standing, with Fianna Fáil's Labhrás Ó Murchú (Culture and Education) and Mark Daly (Administration) as potential beneficiaries, but with the Labour Party also appearing to benefit on the latter panel.

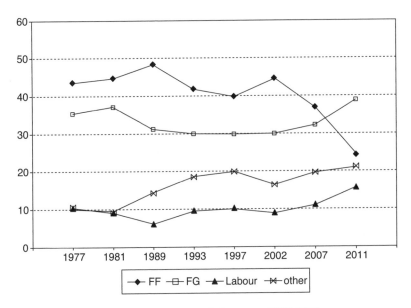

Figure 11.1 Distribution of Seanad panel electorate, 1977–2011

Note: data points refer to share of electorate.

Sources: Derived from Table 11.2, and from John Coakley, 'The Irish Senate election of 1977: voting in a small electorate', *Parliamentary Affairs* 33:3 (1980), pp. 322–31; John Coakley, 'The Senate elections', pp. 195–205 in Howard R. Penniman and Brian Farrell (eds), *Ireland at the Polls 1981, 1982, and 1987: A study of four general elections* (Durham, NC: Duke University Press, for the American Enterprise Institute, 1987); John Coakley, 'The Senate election', pp. 148–61 in Michael Gallagher and Richard Sinnott (eds), *How Ireland Voted 1989* (Galway: Centre for the Study of Irish Elections, 1990); John Coakley, 'The Senate elections', pp. 135–45 in Michael Gallagher and Michael Laver (eds), *How Ireland Voted 1992* (Dublin: Folens; Limerick: PSAI Press, 1993); John Coakley and Maurice Manning, 'The Senate elections', pp. 195–214 in Michael Marsh and Paul Mitchell (eds), *How Ireland Voted 1997* (Boulder, CO: Westview Press, 1999); Michael Gallagher and Liam Weeks, 'The subterranean election of the Seanad', pp. 197–213 in Michael Gallagher, Michael Marsh and Paul Mitchell (eds), *How Ireland Voted 2002* (Basingstoke: Palgrave Macmillan, 2003); Theresa Reidy, 'The Seanad election', pp. 187–204 in Michael Gallagher and Michael Marsh (eds), *How Ireland Voted 2007: The Full Story of Ireland's General Election* (Basingstoke: Palgrave Macmillan, 2008).

While deals between parties mattered, and the support of party headquarters was important for individual candidates, one of the most notorious features of Seanad elections is the hard slog that each candidate must undertake to engage with the electorate. The election campaign is largely invisible: candidates criss-cross the country, trying to make personal contact with individual councillors to secure their support, but are never sure how successful their efforts have been (see the contribution by one Seanad candidate, Averil Power, in Chapter 6, where she describes the campaign as 'the "Discover Ireland" route to the Seanad'). New social and other electronic media may help to bridge some communication gaps, but cannot replace long-standing comradeship and local and partisan loyalties. The role played by the party leadership no doubt helps some candidates more than others, but is calculated primarily to maximise the party vote. Each party circulates a list of its candidates (usually in the form of a mock ballot paper) to party voters; in 2011, Fine Gael prepared an elaborate and detailed booklet for the guidance of its supporters. Party organisations also make every effort to ensure that everyone turns out to vote – whether by bringing voters together in Dublin, as in the case of Sinn Féin, or doing so at county level, as in the case of Fine Gael and Fianna Fáil.

The panel results

As already indicated, the fact that the composition of the electorate is well known is often seen as making the results of the panel elections a foregone conclusion. The electoral system resembles that in the Dáil elections, the single transferable vote.[16] The electoral quota in 2011 ranged from 17 per cent (about 177 votes) on the five-member panel to 8 per cent (about 89 votes) on the 11-member ones. On the basis of their known share of electoral quotas, Fine Gael seemed certain of 17 seats, Fianna Fáil of 11 and Labour of seven. But it was overwhelmingly probable that Sinn Féin would win a seat on each of the two 11-member panels, and quite likely that it would win a further seat on the nine-seat panel and have a good chance on the seven-member panel. Of the remaining four seats, Fine Gael seemed poised to win two, with one each to Fianna Fáil and Labour. If we altogether ignore voters not affiliated to these four parties, then, and make no assumptions about transfers or deals between parties, straightforward arithmetic would suggest that Fine Gael would win 19 seats, Fianna Fáil 12, Labour eight and Sinn Féin four. In the event, as Table 11.3 shows, Fine Gael won one seat fewer than this (18) as did Sinn Féin (not surprisingly, since it ran only three candidates), but Fianna Fáil performed remarkably well in the circumstances, with 14 seats.

Some of the factors behind this outcome have already been referred to. On the smallest two panels, Sinn Féin did not have a candidate of its own, but its members appear to have concentrated their support on a particular Fianna Fáil candidate in each case – and these two candidates were indeed elected, no doubt incurring a certain moral debt to Sinn Féin. The Labour Party also seems to have profited on the Administrative panel. In addition, the large number of unaffiliated electors included a sizeable group of former Fianna Fáil members who had left the party in disillusion with its economic policies or in a tactical response to its growing unpopularity, but who might be reluctant to support candidates of other parties against their former colleagues. Observers also suggested that competition within Fianna Fáil was enhanced by the endorsement of only ten of the party's 31 candidates by the party leader, and that this gave an added vigour to the Fianna Fáil campaign.

Table 11.3   Results of Seanad panel elections by party, 2011

Panel	Fianna Fáil	Fine Gael	Labour Party	Sinn Féin	Others	Total
Culture and Education	385	479	157	0	44	1,065
(candidates–seats)	(4–2)	(11–2)	(1–1)	(0–0)	(1–0)	(17–5)
Agriculture	329	445	166	82	44	1,066
(candidates–seats)	(10–4)	(13–4)	(2–2)	(1–1)	(2–0)	(28–11)
Labour	320	445	166	84	51	1,066
(candidates–seats)	(7–3)	(8–5)	(3–2)	(1–1)	(2–0)	(21–11)
Industry and Commerce	305	459	186	73	44	1,067
(candidates–seats)	(6–3)	(18–4)	(5–1)	(1–1)	(5–0)	(35–9)
Administration	348	434	233	0	49	1,064
(candidates–seats)	(4–2)	(9–3)	(4–2)	(0–0)	(2–0)	(19–7)
Electorate	260	422	170	65	175	1,092
(total candidates–seats)	(31–14)	(59–18)	(15–8)	(3–3)	(12–0)	(120–43)

Note: 'Others' include one Green Party candidate (Industrial and Commercial panel, 19 votes).

Sources: Computed from data made available by the Office of the Clerk, Seanad Éireann, www.seanadcount.ie, and information provided by the political parties.

Analysis of the outcome shows a remarkable uniformity across panels on the part of Fine Gael, though it also suggests that the party had limited success in winning support from the 175 electors not affiliated to the four main parties: assuming support from all of its own electors, it seems to have won the support of between 12 and 57 of the unaffiliated electors. Fianna Fáil, by contrast, seems to have won the support of about 45 of these 'others' on the Industrial and Commercial panel, increasing well above this on all other panels, and exceeding its 'core' vote by 125 on the Cultural and Educational panel (more than half of these additional votes were likely to have been Sinn Féin ones). Labour support, however, fell below its 'core' vote on three panels, but exceeded it on the other two – by a large margin of 63 votes on the Administrative panel (perhaps with the addition of Sinn Féin support). Sinn Féin focused its attention on the largest three panels, where the quota was lowest, winning a handful of first preference votes above its 'core' support and gaining sufficient lower preferences to secure the election of all three of its candidates – though the transferred votes came mainly from Independent and Labour candidates.

The tension between the two categories of Fianna Fáil candidates was particularly interesting. Most votes were cast for candidates not on the party leader's list, but that is not surprising, since there were 21 of these in all (in fact, this group won on average 52 votes each, compared to an average of 60 for the ten on the leader's list). The outcome was that nine of the 14 Fianna Fáil senators elected had not been endorsed by the leader, an outcome that suggested that this strategy had had limited success, and was used by many long-standing but 'excluded' senators to gain sympathy and mobilise support.

As it happens, Fianna Fáil was in the running for an additional seat, but lost this as a consequence of a peculiarity of the electoral rules. As we have seen, there is a requirement that a minimum number of seats be allocated to each sub-panel within each of the five panels. For many years, there was a tendency for candidates on the Oireachtas sub-panels to perform better than those on Nominating Body ones (this perspective is symbolised in the description of the former as 'inside' and the latter as 'outside' candidates). It is true that, other things being equal, candidates nominated by Oireachtas members tend to perform better than candidates of nominating bodies. Furthermore, in the past this often caused special rules to be invoked to ensure minimum representation of nominating body candidates. More recently, the same rules have had to be used to ensure minimum representation of Oireachtas nominees, but 2011 was different. By the 15th count on the Administrative panel, three Fine Gael, two Fianna Fáil and one Labour candidate had been elected. Since four of these were on the Oireachtas sub-panel and two on the Nominating Bodies one, no further Oireachtas nominee could be elected. There were at this stage two continuing candidates who had not reached the quota; and the seat had to be allocated to Labour's Denis Landy (nominated by the Association of Municipal Authorities of Ireland), even though he was nine votes behind Mary Fitzpatrick of Fianna Fáil (one of Micheál Martin's Oireachtas nominees), who was thus a casualty of this little-known but important counting rule.

Once again, then, the results of the panel elections illustrated the highly partisan nature of the process. It is true that there were some high-profile political casualties, including the two Fianna Fáil former ministers of state (Seán Connick, who was supported by party leader Micheál Martin, and Martin Mansergh) and the outgoing Leader of the Seanad, Senator Donie Cassidy. But Independent candidates fared very poorly. The most authentic representative of the vocational sector, the President of the Royal Institute of Architects of Ireland, received only one vote, and was placed between two other Independents who won respectively two votes and none.

At first sight, there appeared to be evidence that 'inside' candidates (nominated by Oireachtas members) had an advantage over 'outside' ones: they won on average 56 votes, as opposed to an average of 38 for 'outside' candidates. But crude comparison of this kind is hazardous, not least because of different levels of competitiveness across panels. It indeed seems likely that the profile of the candidates matters independently of this: those with little political profile are less likely to win 'inside' nominations, and, quite apart from this, they are less likely to win votes. If we exclude them and consider only the 64 candidates with the most established political profiles, the gap between the two nomination pathways diminishes: 'inside' candidates won on average 62 votes, 'outside' candidates 52.[17]

If we look at the question of regional support patterns, it is striking that the distribution of candidates tended to follow closely the distribution of the electorate. But if we compare the final outcome with the distribution of the population, the under-representation of the east becomes obvious. The province of Leinster, including Dublin, accounted for 54 per cent of the population, for 46 per cent of the Seanad electorate, and for 44 per cent of the candidates. But, surprisingly, these candidates won only 35 per cent of the first preference votes, and accounted for only 26 per cent of panel senators elected.

The university seats

In many respects, the provision for the election of six senators by university graduates has drawn even more fire than the character of the panel elections. Giving votes uniquely to university graduates has been criticised as elitist; but giving them to graduates of only two of the state's universities has been faulted as unjustifiably selective. In an era when university representation in parliament was common, the University of Dublin (Trinity College) had returned representatives to the old Irish House of Commons, and after the Act of Union of 1800 these instead attended the UK House of Commons at Westminster. In 1918 the National University of Ireland (NUI) was given similar rights, and both university constituencies continued to be represented in the Dáil after 1922. Although university representation in the Dáil came to an end following a constitutional amendment in 1936, the constitution of the following year allocated three members in the new Seanad to each of the two universities (together with five other members elected in the panel election, these were seen as part of the Cultural and Educational component).

With the expansion of third-level education, it became increasingly difficult to justify the exclusive nature of this representation. By 2009, for example, the NUI accounted for only 32 per cent of all those graduating from undergraduate courses, Trinity College for just 6 per cent, other university-level institutions for 14 per cent and the institutes of technology for 48 per cent.[18] Already in 1979, the constitution was amended by referendum (with a huge majority of 92 per cent voting in favour) to allow this anomaly to be rectified. The amendment allowed university representation to be regulated by ordinary legislation; but no such legislation was ever introduced.

As a result, then, only graduates of the oldest two universities are entitled to vote, with each university returning three senators. The electorate in each case was extremely large in 2011: just under 98,000 in the NUI, and almost 54,000 in the University of Dublin constituency. Given the debate on the allegedly unrepresentative nature of university representation, it is worth looking in greater detail at its composition; this is reported in Table 11.4. Quite significant differences will be noticed between the two universities, and these were much greater in the past. The NUI electorate broadly reflects the distribution of the Irish population, though with a stronger Dublin bias (this accounts for 31 per cent of the electorate, as compared to 28 per cent of the overall population). In the earlier years, the Dublin share was rather higher. The proportion resident outside the state, 3 per cent, has been shrinking over time. The University of Dublin, perhaps not surprisingly, lives up to its name in having a much stronger Dublin orientation (47 per cent of the electorate). A much higher proportion are resident outside Ireland than in the case of the NUI (16 per cent) and in the past this would have been higher still. Of those receiving their degrees before 1960, for example, 66 per cent are now resident outside the Republic, though they are required to be Irish citizens if they wish to be part of the Seanad electorate. This no doubt reflects Trinity College's long but now less marked tradition of recruiting students from Northern Ireland and Britain.

It is likely that getting qualified graduates to register for Seanad elections poses a considerable challenge, especially in the NUI, where the electorate has not kept pace with the growing pool of graduates. This no doubt reflects the university's own diverse structure, with large campuses located around the country, but also its uncertain future (given proposals to abolish it) and the debate about the appropriateness of such representation at all. Even among registered graduates, turnout in the election tends to be low – 36 per cent in the NUI and 29 per cent in the University of Dublin in 2011. Yet, the election was intensely contested, with 27 candidates in the NUI constituency and 19 in the University of Dublin one (though, in fact, 20 names appeared on the ballot paper – after the close of nominations it emerged that one candidate was ineligible as she was not an Irish citizen).[19] Strangely, candidates are not themselves required to be graduates, though they must be nominated by ten graduates of the university whose representation they are contesting.

Table 11.4   Distribution of Seanad university electorate by period of first qualification and region, 2011

Period of first qualification	Dublin (%)	Rest of Rep. of Ireland (%)	Northern Ireland (%)	Great Britain (%)	Rest of world (%)	Total (number)
National University of Ireland						
Before 1960	41.0	52.6	2.3	2.5	1.7	6,261
1960–69	36.9	57.7	1.5	1.6	2.2	9,944
1970–79	32.4	64.2	0.9	1.1	1.4	19,813
1980–89	28.6	68.1	0.7	1.3	1.4	24,552
1990–99	28.5	69.1	0.5	1.0	0.9	22,146
2000–09	29.3	69.4	0.4	0.4	0.5	14,535
Total	31.1	65.7	0.8	1.2	1.3	97,251
University of Dublin						
Before 1960	21.7	12.6	23.0	27.8	14.9	1,983
1960–69	31.0	21.0	16.4	19.2	12.4	1,664
1970–79	44.2	24.2	8.8	11.4	11.4	3,839
1980–89	48.0	30.9	2.7	9.3	9.1	11,024
1990–99	49.4	39.6	2.0	4.3	4.7	17,447
2000–09	49.3	44.3	2.8	1.7	1.9	17,633
Total	47.1	36.7	4.1	6.3	5.8	53,590

Note: The data exclude two electors in the NUI constituency whose qualifications were awarded after 2009 and 481 whose deaths were recorded only after publication of the register, and 75 electors in the University of Dublin constituency where information in respect of region or year of qualification was missing. The full electorates in the respective constituencies were 97,734 and 53,665.

Sources: Computed from anonymised registers supplied by the Registrar, National University of Ireland, and the Vice Provost, Trinity College Dublin (University of Dublin).

On the NUI side, two of the outgoing Independent senators, Rónán Mullen and Feargal Quinn, stood for election again and were comfortably returned. They were joined by another Independent, John Crown, a well-known medical consultant and critic of the health system, who fought off a challenge from several other strong candidates. Those with a distinctive party political background fared poorly, as former Progressive Democrat, Green and Sinn Féin candidates failed to gain momentum – perhaps because, unlike the established candidates, whose campaigns began well before the election was called, their decision to stand was typically a last-minute one. In the University of Dublin constituency, two well-known incumbents were re-elected (David Norris, Independent, who was also looking for support for what proved in the end to be an unsuccessful bid to contest the presidential election, and Ivana Bacik, who had stood as a Labour candidate in the general election). The third seat was won by TCD economist Seán Barrett against a strong challenge from a former Progressive Democrat, Tony Williams, who was backed by the third outgoing senator, Shane Ross, who had himself been elected to the Dáil (see p. 152 above). Canvassing for votes in the university constituencies was particularly challenging, with candidates resorting to mail-shots to all potential voters and circulating publicity leaflets.[20] Some candidates organised public meetings or even engaged in door-to-door canvassing in areas where there was a reasonably high concentration of electors.

The Taoiseach's nominees

The composition of the Seanad was rounded off by the announcement of the Taoiseach's 11 nominees, which contained some surprises. As part of the arrangement that put the Fine Gael–Labour coalition in office, the filling of these positions had been divided between the two party leaders. Taoiseach Enda Kenny (who formally nominated all 11) put forward seven nominees. Only one of these was a full-time politician (a Louth county councillor); two more were known to be associated with Fine Gael, though they had built their reputations outside the area of politics, and did not take the Fine Gael whip; and four were Independent, having come to public prominence by other routes. By contrast, three of the four nominees put forward by Tánaiste Éamon Gilmore were active politically – they had contested the Seanad panel elections as Labour candidates, and two of them had also stood in the earlier Dáil election. In an unusual development, eight of the Taoiseach's nominees agreed to form a separate Independent group in the Seanad, leaving just one taking the Fine Gael whip and two taking the Labour whip.

If the emphasis on party affiliation was weaker in 2011 than in earlier Taoiseach's appointments, that on gender was stronger. A majority of those nominated were women – three from the Taoiseach's own list and all four of the Tánaiste's. This was in part a response to long-standing criticisms of male dominance in the Seanad (and in the Oireachtas more generally). But it was no doubt further encouraged by the negative reaction to the appointment of a strongly male-dominated government just a few weeks earlier. The inclusion among the Tánaiste's nominees of a prominent campaigner for equal rights, Katherine Zappone, offered a further at least symbolic marker of the extent of this change.

A further noteworthy feature of the 11 nominees was the absence of any representative of Northern Ireland's political interests. Such representation had been a feature of Taoiseach's nominations over the period from 1982 to 2002, and the three major parliamentary documents that had considered the composition of the Seanad had all recommended that this practice be formalised.[21] Bertie Ahern had not, however, included any Northern Ireland resident among his nominees in 2007, and Enda Kenny followed suit in 2011. The appointment of the President's husband, Martin McAleese, was no doubt intended as a gesture in this direction, though it was politically sensitive in circumstances where his term as a senator would overlap with the last six months of his wife's term of office as President. Originally from Belfast, Dr McAleese's working life was divided between the Republic and Northern Ireland before he moved to Dublin in 1997 when the President took up office. Though best known publicly as the President's consort, he had been playing a particularly active role behind the scenes, notably in liaising with loyalist groups in Belfast.

A summary of the composition of the new Seanad is given in Table 11.5. While Fine Gael emerged as the largest party with 19 seats, it is noteworthy that its leader, like previous Taoisigh, did not 'go for broke' in seeking to maximise the representation of his own party through his right of nomination. Together with Labour's 11 seats, the government formally controls half of the second chamber. This is likely to provide stability for as long as the coalition lasts – especially since several of the Independent senators are politically close to the government, and any vacancies occurring among the 'panel' senators will be filled by vote of current Dáil and Seanad members, not by the original electorate. Fianna Fáil, with only 14 seats, is at its lowest point ever in this chamber as in the lower house, and here, too, its role in opposition is likely to be challenged by Sinn Féin, even though that party has only three seats. The strength of the unaffiliated component (13 senators) is worth noting. In an adjustment to the tradition of overwhelming male dominance, the proportion of women senators has risen to an historic peak of 30 per cent – still lower than in many other parliaments, but well above the current level in the Dáil (15 per cent).

Table 11.5   Overall result of Seanad election, 2011

Group	Fianna Fáil	Fine Gael	Labour Party	Sinn Féin	Indepen- dents	Total	(women)
Panels							
Culture and Education	2	2	1	0	0	5	(1)
Agriculture	4	4	2	1	0	11	(1)
Labour	3	5	2	1	0	11	(3)
Industry and Commerce	3	4	1	1	0	9	(5)
Administration	2	3	2	0	0	7	(0)
Universities							
National University of Ireland	0	0	0	0	3	3	(0)
University of Dublin	0	0	1	0	2	3	(1)
Taoiseach's nominees	0	1	2	0	8	11	(7)
Total	14	19	11	3	13	60	(18)

Note: Party affiliations for university senators and Taoiseach's nominees are based on the party whip, if any, accepted by the senators in question following the initial meeting of the Seanad. Of the Taoiseach's nominees here placed in the 'Independent' category, two were prominently associated with Fine Gael and one with Labour.

Conclusion

As the discussion above has shown, the idea of the Seanad as a body that reflects party political divisions is much more strongly entrenched than the notion of the Seanad as a chamber that represents vocational interests. This has been the subject of agreement between observers from the beginning: the late doyen of Irish political science, Professor Basil Chubb, described the Seanad four decades ago as 'merely another selection of party politicians chosen in an unnecessarily complicated manner'.[22] The 2011 election inevitably failed to do anything to dispel this perception.

One of the other recurring allegations about the Seanad has been that it is seen all too often as 'a place for grooming new Dáil candidates and as a political resting place for defeated deputies'.[23] This, too, was confirmed by the 2011 experience. As we have seen, in selecting Seanad candidates parties had an eye to providing a platform for potential candidates for the next Dáil election. Indeed, almost half (25) of the outgoing senators had contested the Dáil election. Some senators had used their position to particularly good effect. For example, one of the country's leading poll-toppers in the general election (Shane Ross, who, with 17,075 first preference votes, was second only to Fine Gael leader Enda Kenny in electoral popularity) earned his reputation not just from his financial journalism but also from his robust performance as a senator. Nevertheless, it seems strange that, as it has been remarked, 'candidates receive votes to be elected to one house of parliament based on their potential to successfully challenge for election to another house of parliament'.[24] The other traditional role of the Seanad has been as a safety net for politicians defeated in Dáil elections. Here, too, the 2011 election was no exception: as mentioned above, no fewer than 47 of the candidates in the Seanad election had stood in the immediately preceding Dáil election, and 22 of these unsuccessful Dáil candidates were elected to the Seanad (a further two Labour candidates who had lost out in the Dáil and Seanad panel elections were appointed to the Seanad as part of the 'Taoiseach's eleven').

This role as an apparent antechamber to the Dáil has left critics of the Seanad with plenty of ammunition, even though many argue that its role as a forum in which talented Dáil deputies who happen to have lost their seats can continue to make a political contribution should not be dismissed out of hand. But this criticism reinforces principled objections to the existence of a second chamber in a small, unitary state. Nevertheless, no sustained, broadly supported case for the abolition of the Seanad has been made. The argument that this would save several million euros is no substitute for a careful cost-benefit analysis.[25] Implicitly blaming the Seanad for not helping to prevent the banking and public finance crises diverts attention from the responsibility of the government, the very body which for long has done little to enhance the role of the Seanad.

Abolishing the Seanad would entail a wide range of constitutional changes. The expression 'Seanad Éireann' occurs 65 times in the text of the constitution, and substantive references extend over 16 articles. These of course include articles 18 and 19 which describe the structure and role of the Seanad itself, and a further ten articles that deal with aspects of the legislative or other control functions shared with the Dáil. Abolishing the Seanad and allocating exclusive responsibility to the Dáil in these areas might pose few formal problems. But there are areas where implications for other institutions of state need to be considered. The Chairman of the Seanad is *ex officio* a member of the Council of State, and alternative arrangements would need to be made here. The Seanad also has a role to play in triggering a legislative referendum, but the fact that this has never happened suggests that dropping this provision from the constitution might attract little dissent. However, the Seanad Chairman is one of only three members of the Presidential Commission, which functions when the President is unavailable, and an alternative formula for its composition would need to be devised. The right of the Taoiseach to appoint ministers from the Seanad (sparingly used, but potentially important at a time of crisis) would also disappear.

It seems strange, then, that no considered case for abolishing the Seanad has been made, nor have the implications of abolition been assessed in any degree of detail. The programme for government of the Fine Gael–Labour coalition prioritises abolition of the Seanad as one of three 'urgent parliamentary reform issues', and abolition is conditionally supported by the main opposition party, in the context of wider constitutional reform. This bold commitment implicitly ignores the painstaking deliberations (extending over the past 16 years) of earlier parliamentary evaluations of the composition and role of the second chamber, and prejudges the conclusions of the wide-ranging constitutional convention also promised in the programme for government. Hastily-reached cross-party consensus on this radical departure may ultimately be reinforced by convincing arguments, and may indeed lead to the disappearance of Ireland's unusual second chamber. But it is too early to conclude that the whole set of practical and political difficulties, and issues of principle and procedure, will be overcome in time to allow this change to take place during the lifetime of the government. It would, therefore, be unwise to take it for granted that the 2011 election to Seanad Éireann will be the last.

Notes

1. I am grateful to Paul Sammon (Fianna Fáil), Terry Murphy (Fine Gael), Joe Costello, TD (Labour Party) and Brian Keane (Sinn Féin) for their assistance in the preparation of this article, and to Deirdre Lane (Clerk, Seanad Éireann), Attracta Halpin (Registrar, National University of Ireland) and Michael Marsh (Vice Provost, Trinity College, University of Dublin) for technical advice.
2. Harry McGee, 'Government to consider referendum on abolition of Seanad', *Irish Times*, 3 January 2011.
3. Computed from the Inter-Parliamentary Union's Parline database, available at www.ipu.org, accessed 23 April 2011. This shows 29 second chambers as being based exclusively or mainly on direct election, 22 on indirect election and 18 on appointment, with a further eight based on a mixture of principles. For further discussion, see John Coakley and Michael Laver, 'Options for Seanad Éireann', pp. 32–107 in *Second Report of the All-Party Committee on the Constitution* (Dublin: Government Publications, 1996).
4. See the Council's website at www.ds-rs.si/en/. The role of the National Council is defined in the constitution as largely consultative, but it is generally seen as a second chamber and is so classified by the Inter-Parliamentary Union.
5. For a general description of Seanad Éireann and its work, see the two standard texts: Thomas Garvin, *The Irish Senate* (Dublin: Institute of Public

Administration, 1969), and John MacG. Smyth, *The Theory and Practice of the Irish Senate* (Dublin: Institute of Public Administration, 1972).

6. *Report: Committee on the Constitution and Powers of, and Methods of Election to, Seanad Éireann* (Dublin: Stationery Office, 1928) dealt with a new system to replace direct, popular election of senators. The *Report of the Second House of the Oireachtas Commission* (Dublin: Stationery Office, 1936) suggested that if a new senate were to be established it should comprise a mixture of appointed and indirectly elected members, but its minority report offered a more detailed blueprint close to the model written into the new constitution: it would comprise 50 members, ten nominated by the President of the Executive Council (the prime minister) and 40 elected from four panels (farming and fisheries, labour, industry and commerce, and education and the learned professions), with nominations made by relevant organisations and other interests, and election by Dáil deputies (pp. 26–34). The *Report of the Commission on Vocational Organisation* (Dublin: Stationery Office, 1943) concluded that the existing system of candidate nomination and election to the Seanad was 'only partially' determined by vocational principles, but was instead essentially party political (p. 310); it proposed the creation of a consultative, non-partisan 'national vocational assembly' alongside the existing Seanad. Finally, the *Report of the Committee on the Constitution* (Dublin: Stationery Office, 1967) endorsed retention of a second chamber 'on vocational or functional lines' but recommended little by way of reform to bring about this objective (pp. 29–31).

7. The *Special Report of the Special Committee on the Seanad Electoral (Panel Members) Bill, 1937* (Dublin: Stationery Office, 1937), chaired by de Valera, failed to agree on any blueprint as an alternative to the scheme proposed in the original bill (p. v). The scheme provided for in the resulting act differed from the current scheme in important respects, including use of a single (in practice, extremely large) ballot paper for all candidates on all panels, and a smaller electorate with only seven representatives from each county or county borough. In combination, this produced a much lower electoral quota (of about eight votes). The *Report of the Joint Committee on Seanad Panel Elections 1947* (Dublin: Stationery Office, 1947) recommended a broader range of nominating bodies, separate election to each panel, expansion of the electorate to include all county councillors, and other reforms. The *Report of the Select Committee on the Seanad Electoral (Panel Members) Bill, 1952* (Dublin: Stationery Office, 1952) recommended inter alia reversing one of these reforms, by introducing a formula to restrict the number of candidates any nominating body could propose, thereby removing the need for a special nominating committee to filter candidates (pp. v–vii). The *Seanad Electoral Law Commission 1959: Report* (Dublin: Stationery Office, 1959) suggested a mechanism for ensuring that senators nominated by nominating bodies would also be elected by electoral colleges comprising members nominated by the nominating bodies themselves (pp. 16–20). The recommendations of the 1947 and 1952 reports were reflected in the Seanad Electoral (Panel Member) Acts, 1947 and 1954, but those of the 1959 report were not followed up.

8. *Report of the Constitution Review Group* (Dublin: Stationery Office, 1996), pp. 65–71.

9. There was little overlap in the membership of the three committees. Only three members of the 1997 committee (chaired by Jim O'Keeffe) were on the 2002 committee (chaired by Brian Lenihan), and only one member of the latter committee served on the Seanad committee (chaired by Mary O'Rourke).

10. All-Party Oireachtas Committee on the Constitution, *Second Progress Report: Seanad Éireann* (Dublin: Stationery Office, 1997), pp. 10–12.

11. All-Party Oireachtas Committee on the Constitution, *Seventh Progress Report: Parliament* (Dublin: Stationery Office, 2002), pp. 38–9.

12. Seanad Éireann Committee on Procedure and Privileges: Sub-Committee on Seanad Reform, *Report on Seanad Reform* (Dublin: Stationery Office, 2004), pp. 9–13.

13. Minutes of the meetings of the group are available at www.environ.ie/en/ Publications/LocalGovernment/Voting/. A further report appears to have been overlooked in the various listings of the 12 reports: *Representation of Emigrants in Seanad Éireann: A Consultation Paper Issued by the Minister for the Environment* (Dublin: Department of the Environment, 1996), which proposed that three of the Taoiseach's nominees be replaced by three senators elected by the Irish diaspora.

14. Maurice Manning, 'The Senate', pp. 153–66 in Muiris MacCarthaigh and Maurice Manning (eds), *The Houses of the Oireachtas: Parliament in Ireland* (Dublin: Institute of Public Administration, 2011), p. 165.

15. The current version of the register was published in *Iris Oifigiúil* 23, 22 March 2011, pp. 400–1.

16. One difference between the two elections is that voting is exclusively carried out by mail. Furthermore, because of the small size of the panel electorate (which would exaggerate a certain random element that is sometimes present in surplus distributions), each ballot paper is treated as if it had the value 1,000, allowing for weighting of transferred papers through the use of the Gregory method when transferring surpluses. Extra rules have also been introduced to ensure that a balance is maintained between the two sub-panels in the case of each panel. These rules prevent the elimination of candidates from a sub-panel when this would result in that sub-panel failing to attain its minimum share of seats, and provide for the elimination of candidates of a sub-panel that has already won its maximum number of seats. It is thus possible for a candidate to be eliminated even though he or she has more votes than other continuing candidates on the same panel.

17. This refers to a group of 64 panel candidates who had also been candidates in the 2011 Dáil election, or who were outgoing senators. It should be noted that crude comparison of first preference votes fails to take account of two factors that have a major influence on this: the number of seats on a particular panel, and the number of candidates contesting these.

18. Computed from HEA statistical data for 2009, available at www.hea.ie/en/ statistics, accessed 9 May 2011.

19. One other candidate, Francis Donnelly, an Independent, asked voters *not* to support him as he had belatedly switched his focus to the Labour panel, where he had also secured a nomination.

20. Each candidate was entitled to one free mailing. A collection of Seanad canvassing leaflets is reproduced at http://irishelectionliterature.wordpress. com/index-of-electionsparty-literature/2011-seanad-index.

21. The All-Party Oireachtas Committee on the Constitution had recommended in its *Second Progress Report* (1997, p. 12) that three of the Taoiseach's nominees be 'representative of the various traditions in the North'; its *Seventh Progress Report* (2002, p. 38) had recommended that four of these 'represent citizens resident in Northern Ireland'; and the Seanad Sub-Committee in its *Report on Seanad Reform* (2004, p. 49) had recommended that two of these 11 be from Northern Ireland, 'one from the unionist and one from the nationalist tradition'.

22. Basil Chubb, *The Government and Politics of Ireland* (London: Oxford University Press, 1970), p. 205.

23. Maurice Manning, 'The Senate election', pp. 165–73 in Howard R. Penniman (ed.), *Ireland at the Polls: The Dáil Elections of 1977* (Washington, DC: American Enterprise Institute for Public Policy Research, 1978), p. 167.

24. Theresa Reidy, 'The Seanad election', pp. 187–204 in Michael Gallagher and Michael Marsh (eds), *How Ireland Voted 2007: The Full Story of Ireland's General Election* (Basingstoke: Palgrave Macmillan, 2008), p. 196.

25. The McCarthy Report estimated the annual cost of the Seanad at €25m and took the view that its abolition could make a saving at this level, but noted that 'any such proposition would require careful and extended consideration'; *Report of the Special Group on Public Service Numbers and Expenditure Programmes*, vol. 2 (Dublin: Stationery Office, 2010), pp. 149–50.

12

Government Formation in 2011

Eoin O'Malley

Background

Once again a central aspect of an Irish election campaign related to the likely government to be formed in its aftermath. It was the first election since 1927 where Fianna Fáil was going into an election without a reasonable prospect of forming part of the government. As the campaign progressed, the strong expectation that a Fine Gael-led government would emerge at times gave that party the impression of incumbency.

Unlike in 2007, Fine Gael and Labour campaigned as separate parties and judging from the speeches on the day of the dissolution of the 30th Dáil Labour's strategy of emphasising differences with Fine Gael was in evidence. Éamon Gilmore claimed 'it is clear that Fianna Fáil and Fine Gael are comfortable with each other's policies. They both voted for the blanket bank guarantee. They are happy to embrace austerity.' Gilmore suggested that for 'the first time ever in the 90-year history of this State, we can elect a Government led by neither Fianna Fáil nor Fine Gael. For the first time people have a choice to elect a Government led by Labour.'[1]

Labour designed its campaign around this possibility. Opinion poll results in the autumn showed that it was close to or exceeding Fine Gael in its support and that its leader Éamon Gilmore was a more popular choice for Taoiseach than Fine Gael leader Enda Kenny. On the back of this Labour strategists designed a campaign in which the phrase 'Gilmore for Taoiseach' predominated (see pp. 72–3 above). Although Fine Gael's campaign was less obviously about the nature of the post-election government formation than about its policies, it too ran a campaign that emphasised the possible government on offer, in this case the team of people around Enda Kenny rather than him as an individual.

Quite early in the campaign it was obvious that Gilmore would not be Taoiseach. According to a Millward Brown Lansdowne exit poll for RTÉ, voters had a clear preference for a Fine Gael-led government.[2] Sixty-six per cent preferred some form of government led by Fine Gael compared to only 23 per cent preferring a government led by Labour. Even Labour voters, perhaps being realistic, preferred the Fine Gael–Labour option to Labour–Fine Gael by 43 per cent to 32 per cent. It is also a measure of the extent to which coalition is regarded as a desirable norm in Ireland that Fine Gael voters were evenly split on whether they favoured a single-party Fine Gael government or a coalition with Labour. Fine Gael had, seemingly successfully, labelled Labour a 'high-tax party' and nearing polling day there was some speculation that Fine Gael might achieve an overall majority or be close enough to govern alone. It was just in the final few days that Labour changed its message to one calling for 'balanced government', that is, not single-party government, and it warned against Fine Gael having a 'monopoly of power' (see Chapter 4).

Despite a campaign dominated by criticisms by each party of the other, Fine Gael and Labour had effectively ruled out governing with anyone else. Labour had emphatically ruled out entering government either with Sinn Féin[3] or with Fianna Fáil. There were suggestions, which were not denied at the time, that senior members of each party, Phil Hogan and Pat Rabbitte, had set up 'back channels' to negotiate during the election campaign. The suggestions that there had been formal or informal negotiations prior to the election have since been denied by senior figures in both parties.[4] But it was clear that only one outcome was really envisaged. During the final televised debate Gilmore had suggested to Kenny that the two leaders would be sitting down to talk about the issues in the week after the election. Kenny did not demur.

Labour and Fine Gael had a history of governing together, though not always happily. However the experience in the 'rainbow' government together between 1994 and 1997 was a good one, particularly the relationship between Fine Gael and Democratic Left (DL).[5] Indeed, it is striking that many of the same people who were in that cabinet were still at the forefront of politics in their respective parties in 2011. DL was a small left-wing party that had evolved from the split in Sinn Féin in the 1970s into an anti-irredentist socialist party. The party had struggled to maintain itself and following government with Labour, it merged into Labour in 1999. This merger is better characterised as a reverse takeover given that the small number of Democratic Left TDs went on to take high-profile leadership positions within the Labour Party, two of them (Rabbitte and Gilmore) subsequently becoming Labour leader. Fine Gael and Labour had worked together in the lead-up to the 2007 election, so there were some good personal relationships. Moreover, both parties' impatience to get into power following almost 14 years in opposition might have assuaged any reluctance to work together. The mutual criticisms that had characterised much of the election campaign might have been accepted as simply the stuff of campaigning, but nonetheless they had the potential to give hostages to fortune and to affect the type of agreement the parties eventually struck.

Post-election options

Though other coalition combinations were theoretically possible, the results from the election set out in Table 12.1 pointed to one outcome, that Fine Gael would lead the government. Sinn Féin and Fianna Fáil being 'uncoalitionable', the question was then whether it would be Labour or some independents that supported a Fine Gael-led government. In seat terms it was the party's best ever result (see Chapter 7). On the night of the count some senior Fine Gael figures spoke of having other options – in particular, that they could look to the Independents to form a majority. This was probably best considered as a bargaining ploy. For Labour the results were more a relief than a disappointment. At the start of the campaign a return of 50 seats still looked achievable, but by the end there was a fear that the party's support was slipping. That it was much bigger than Fianna Fáil in terms of seats, and that it too had its best result ever, came as a relief. Labour Party TDs seemed less adept at hiding their eagerness to enter coalition talks.

Table 12.1   Seat distributions in 31st Dáil

Fine Gael	76	
Labour	37	
Fianna Fáil	20	
Sinn Féin	14	
United Left Alliance	5	
Right Independents	2	(Donnelly, Ross)
Left Independents	5	(Halligan, F. McGrath, Murphy, O'Sullivan, Pringle)
Local Independents	5	(Fleming, Grealish, Healy-Rae, Lowry, M. McGrath)
Other Independents	2	(Flanagan, Wallace)
Total	166	

Note: These categorisations of Independent are not definitive or exclusive. For a discussion see Liam Weeks, 'We don't like (to) party: a typology of Independents in Irish political life, 1922–2007', *Irish Political Studies* 24:1 (2009), pp. 1–28.

Who would have more power in those negotiations was not really up for debate either. A number of power indices, such as Shapley–Shubik and Banzhaf, confirm what most people already felt, that Fine Gael appeared in a very strong position.[6] The strength of a party's bargaining position depends on a number of factors; patience, the risk of a breakdown in negotiations and the 'outside options' of the negotiators.[7] As noted above, both sides were impatient to get into office after being in opposition since 1997. The relatively tight schedule for the meeting of the new Dáil – this was set for 9 March, less than two weeks after polling day – and the parlous state of the economy meant that a new government was needed in time for a European Union (EU) summit meeting, and the wish to be in office for St Patrick's Day (17 March) meant that it was unlikely that either party could afford to be 'patient'.

What really mattered were the 'outside options' of the two parties, i.e. what each party would do if the other party was not prepared to offer an acceptable deal. Fine Gael possibly had a viable alternative. It could form a government alone and expect to pick up support from at least some of the Independents. Fianna Fáil had already indicated that it would support the new government if it adhered to the National Recovery Plan agreed with the EU and the International Monetary Fund (IMF) in late 2010 (see Chapter 1, p. 25). A number of the Independents elected had broadly the same policy outlook as Fine Gael, and some others could have been satisfied with the provision of some local services or merely the assurance that these would not be cut. This would have meant that Fine Gael could have kept all 15 cabinet places for itself and it would have avoided inevitable cabinet conflict and the need to negotiate constantly on each new issue. Some of the lower ranks of the party leadership may have been attracted out of self-interest (their chances of securing a cabinet seat would be higher), but within Fine Gael it was the party leader and a small group around him that made the decisions.[8]

In any case this may not have been as attractive as it appeared. The need in Ireland for a Taoiseach and new government to win an investiture vote meant that a minority government really had to be organised in advance. It was unclear whether Fianna Fáil was willing to abstain on such a vote and unlikely that Fianna Fáil would have continued to support the government. Certainly Fine Gael was not willing to rely on it. With 76 seats, Fine Gael was eight short of a majority on which it could govern. Fine Gael could have found itself in a position where it had laborious negotiations with independents, some of who were making demands greater than Fine Gael might have been willing to concede. For instance, Shane Ross, a newly-elected Independent TD who had run for Fine Gael in 1992, was demanding a referendum on the EU/IMF deal. Many more of the independents were either on opposite sides of the policy spectrum or unknown quantities. The subsequent publication of the Moriarty Tribunal report less than a month after the government was formed confirmed in some Fine Gael minds the dangers of relying on Independents. The report was highly critical of Michael Lowry, an Independent TD, for activities undertaken when he had been a Fine Gael minister in the mid-1990s.

So the party leadership claims that given the results of the election it never seriously considered governing except with Labour. This might be seen as somewhat surprising. Coalition theory is one of the most active areas of political science.[9] After any election there are usually a large number of governments that are theoretically possible, but only one emerges. Coalition theories initially assumed that the desire for office was the most important prize that determined which of these would be chosen. The idea of the minimal winning coalition (MWC) predicted that each party would attempt to maximise the spoils of office. Therefore we would not expect oversized coalitions, i.e. ones that included any party that was not strictly necessary to form a majority. We might also expect that the larger party would if possible choose the smallest among those parties that could produce an overall majority. This would predict that Fine Gael would approach Sinn Féin, since such a coalition would command 90 seats and Fine Gael would have to concede fewer government posts to its coalition partner than if it linked up with Fianna Fáil in a 96-seat coalition or with Labour in a 113-seat coalition.

The importance of policy was later incorporated into models so, basing our predictions on these, we might then expect that the government to emerge would be one that was both minimal winning and close in policy terms. Parties whose policies are similar can be expected to be more likely to coalesce because they will have to concede less in policy terms. Recently, theories have incorporated bargaining theory, and some argue that this means that coalitions are less likely when one party is seen as dominant.[10] The smaller party will want to avoid being dominated because it can be smothered – losing its identity and being punished electorally.[11] So these theories would predict a Fine Gael–Fianna Fáil coalition, given the similarity between the policies of these two parties. One area that coalition theory has devoted less attention to is the effect of coalition on a party's vote-gathering capabilities. Though historical enmities would be put forward as explanations for the absence of a Fianna Fáil–Fine Gael coalition, both parties were probably aware that a coalition might have been enough to wipe the weaker party out.

Given the difficult decisions that were to be taken, and having seen Fianna Fáil's experience of having its once iron-clad majority slip away between 2007 and 2011, it is not surprising that Fine Gael preferred the stability and certainty of a formal coalition with a sizeable majority. It also felt that in the circumstances, where the country was in such a difficult situation, the new government should be broadly based. According to a Fine Gael spokesperson, Enda Kenny wanted a stable and secure government to deal with the fiscal crisis facing the country.[12] Having Labour in government might make the government's decisions more acceptable, particularly to the trade union movement. By governing with Labour, Fine Gael was able to frame the new government as one of national unity, which was in office to help Ireland out of the financial crisis, rather than a regular government. It could claim not to be obsessed with power for its own sake. As such Fine Gael's 'outside options' were not all that strong. Despite this, senior Fine Gael figures approached a number of 'local' Independents; it offered them speaking rights and inquired as to which other issues the Independents might want to be addressed. For instance, Fine Gael TDs have shared their speaking time in the Dáil chamber with Michael Healy-Rae.[13]

Labour too had 'outside options'. Government parties tend to lose votes at elections,[14] and this is particularly the case for small parties in Ireland.[15] Labour would have been aware of the losses it suffered in 1997, the election after its previous best performance (in 1992). Labour could have remained in opposition, where it would have been by some way the largest party. From here it might have based its position around opposition to what it had portrayed during the election campaign as deflationary austerity measures. In opposition, Labour would have made Fianna Fáil's job of rebuilding even more difficult and it could thus have cemented itself in its new position as a large, or at least medium-sized, party. In opposition it would have been able to protect its left flank and stunt the growth of Sinn Féin and the ULA. Labour could have reasonably expected to emerge from the election to the 32nd Dáil as the largest party in the state, though this was not a foregone conclusion. Labour was not willing to take this long view, feeling that having run a campaign on the basis of offering balanced government, it could not walk away from a responsibility to govern. Senior party figures interviewed conceded that they never really considered remaining in opposition as an option and one thought it could have been the 'kiss of death' for the party.

Labour's impatience to get into government again might also have been because its leaders were at an age where this was probably their last chance to achieve office.[16] Though parties are sometimes thought of as the salient actors, with the working assumption that they are unitary actors with no internal disagreements or different interests, in reality parties are a collective of the members that make them up. Their positions are chosen by the collective members or leaders of the party, and not all of these have identical preferences or interests. The broad leadership of Labour, many having come from Democratic Left, were people who had held office between 1994 and 1997, and did not have the poor experiences with Fine Gael in their memories.

The government formation process and the Programme for Government

Recounts in Galway West, Wicklow and Laois–Offaly meant the final seat totals were not confirmed on the Monday after the election. Despite this, Enda Kenny and Éamon Gilmore met that evening for 80 minutes 'to discuss potential policies and portfolios'.[17] According to sources they discussed the breakdown of portfolios between the parties, with Labour pitching for a 9–6 split and for the Department of Finance on the basis that if Fine Gael had the office of Taoiseach Labour should be given the next most powerful office. Kenny resisted these, arguing that unlike in 1994, Fine Gael was just seven seats shy of an overall majority and was twice Labour's size and so could reasonably expect to have twice as many seats at cabinet, including Finance. No agreement was reached on this issue, but it was agreed to proceed with talks. Later that night Gilmore briefed the Central Council of the Labour Party, which authorised the leadership to start talks with Fine Gael. Each party leader appointed three senior TDs to his negotiating team. Labour used Joan Burton, Brendan Howlin and Pat Rabbitte, supported by the party leader's economic advisor Colm O'Reardon, the brother of a newly-elected Labour TD. Fine Gael's team comprised Phil Hogan, Michael Noonan and Alan Shatter, supported by economic advisor Andrew McDowell. The two party leaders had agreed that neither they nor the negotiators would speak or leak to the media, a commitment that was adhered to. As a result there was little of the excitement that has surrounded other coalition negotiations, which may also have given the impression that the negotiations were not as fraught as observers were used to.

Coalition negotiations are usually conducted with the parties' election manifestos forming the basis of the discussion. Then the bargaining strength of the parties comes into play. For instance, in 1992 Labour, though the third largest party and significantly smaller than Fianna Fáil, succeeded in getting its agenda followed. In 1992 Labour had significant bargaining strength because it could effectively choose which other party it would deal with. This was the position Fianna Fáil had found itself in between 1997 and 2007. Party size is also important, because even if two parties have equal bargaining strength, the larger party will expect to do better in any negotiations. A fairness principle comes into play.

Negotiations

The outgoing Taoiseach, Brian Cowen, offered the two parties the use of Government Buildings and perhaps more importantly senior civil servants and other officials were made available to brief the two parties. Often one or other party in the negotiations is incumbent and may be thought to have an advantage over the non-incumbent. This is because incumbents will have more developed policy proposals and greater technical support in the process. In this case both sides may have been at a disadvantage, as government secrecy could have meant that each was negotiating from a position of ignorance.

Much of the first two days of the negotiations, Tuesday and Wednesday, was given over to presentations by the Governor of the Central Bank, Patrick Honohan, officials from the National Treasury Management Agency and the Department of Finance, as well as Colm McCarthy, an economist and author of a report on sources of savings in Irish government expenditure. These were regarded as important in setting the context for the subsequent negotiations and were described as sobering, with Fine Gael sources of the opinion that they helped move Labour towards its own position on the fiscal adjustments necessary. These presentations were also important as a bonding experience. Rather than starting the process negotiating across a table from one another, the presentations had the effect of pushing the two parties together. For one participant the briefings were important not so much for what was said, as most already knew the magnitude of the fiscal situation, but because 'it set a tone of constructive engagement' between the two parties and a feeling that they were there to solve a common problem. In any conflict between groups, much of the difference is based on disagreement about basic facts. Having these 'facts' set out for both parties meant that there was a shared basis for any analysis of the situation. Both sides agreed that the EU/IMF Programme of Financial Support had failed, and that this reflected 'uncertainty over the affordability of the rescue package'.[18] There was not, however, full agreement on what measures were needed to tackle the problems the country faced. The 'austerity versus stimulus' debate that economists and political leaders throughout the world had considered was being negotiated by the two parties, with Fine Gael broadly of the view that deficit reduction was imperative, whereas Labour felt that some sort of stimulus was crucial.

Labour early on identified some 'red-line' issues, on which it claimed it would not compromise. These were cuts in child benefit and the reintroduction of third-level fees. It also differed from Fine Gael in wanting to extend the target for reducing the deficit to 3 per cent of national income until 2016, whereas Fine Gael aimed to do this by 2014. The parties differed on the form and extent of tax changes, especially the ratio of cuts to tax increases, where Labour wanted an equal division and Fine Gael suggested that only 27 per cent of the money needed to close the deficit should be made up through tax increases. The number of employees in the public sector was also seen as an area where the two parties had serious differences, though even Labour was willing to accept the need for large-scale redundancies if these were voluntary. So where there were what were characterised as major differences, these were along a continuum rather than polar opposite positions, which had the potential to make striking a compromise easier.

It may have been the case that Labour chose 'red line' issues that were easily deliverable. In many ways Fine Gael did not mind conceding on specific issues such as child benefit as long as the underlying fiscal targets were in place and there was an agreed formula for the make-up of the fiscal correction. If the money was not going to be saved in child benefits then it would have to be found somewhere else.

Another factor that the negotiators had to deal with was the opinion of external actors. It is normal that negotiators of a programme for government need to consider the needs and expectations of their parliamentary party, their wider party membership and their voters. In this case the EU and IMF had what was essentially a veto over any agreement, in that this was being negotiated within parameters set by the EU/IMF deal (see also Chapter 13). Furthermore, both parties were acutely aware that the programme for government would be scrutinised by the financial markets for any signals.

The two negotiating teams agreed the headings for the negotiations that can be seen in the Programme for Government. Both sides agreed that Ireland's fiscal position and jobs should be the main focus and so they agreed that there would be a 'Jobs Budget' early in the new government's term, and set about agreeing what it should contain. The group also interpreted the election as having been one in which voters were looking for reform, and so they put some emphasis on political reform. This area also had the advantage of offering change without any real cost to the exchequer.

Because the Tuesday and Wednesday after the election were largely taken up with presentations the negotiations proper did not start until the evening of Wednesday 2 March. The two sides discussed the need for fiscal correction and how this should be constituted between taxation and cuts. This issue was never fully resolved, but the sides went on to agree certain positions regarding the EU/IMF deal and some policies designed to facilitate economic growth. The procedure for the negotiations had been that all eight participants would agree on issues and then the six politicians would break while the two advisors would draft the document. This turned out not to be an efficient use of time and from Friday 4 March a new model was introduced where the parties' advisors in various areas were brought into discussions on their areas of expertise. Then, when agreements were made the advisors from Labour and Fine Gael would leave to work together to draft a section on that area, while the negotiators could move on to a new area, with new special advisors coming in for those discussions.

So drafting the programme for government only got under way on the Friday, and working over Friday and Saturday the two sides had the draft of an agreement, which went to the leaders on the evening of Saturday 5 March. Some issues took more time than others. The sale of state assets generated a good deal of negotiation. The final wording on the formula for fiscal adjustments – the ratio of tax increases to expenditure cuts – was not agreed and had to go to the leaders for resolution. Participants felt that while there were serious and hard-nosed negotiations, there were never really moments where one side or the other was going to walk out. Both sides felt that they had to come to an agreement and where there were disagreements carefully worded language was found to 'gloss over' the differences between the parties. The fiscal formula was one such example as was the absence of a specific figure for the level of savings – €9 billion had been extensively thought to be the likely necessary figure for savings in annual current spending, a figure that Labour had wanted to reduce to €6 billion. Because mentioning any figure might have left one of the parties open to accusations of having lost, none was mentioned. On Saturday night the leaders agreed a programme for what they styled a Government for National Recovery.

The Programme for Government and its ratification

The negotiations were unusual in the way both parties felt they had little option but to agree a deal and because there was less horse-trading of manifesto commitments than usual. The programme for government reflects the unusual nature of the negotiations and the speed with which the document was produced. At 23,000 words long it is shorter than its 2007 counterpart, which ran to 33,000 words, but still longer than those of 1997 or 2002. Unlike in 2007, where Fianna Fáil obviously dominated the negotiations and three-quarters of the programme was taken directly from its manifesto, in 2011 there was much more drafting of the document from scratch, especially the section on the economy.

Half of the programme for government was taken directly from the two parties' manifestos with each party supplying about 25 per cent. Though no agreement was reached on the formula for the fiscal correction, we can read a formula into the document in which most forms of tax increase were ruled out (apart from water charges and a property tax). This meant that unless the new government could agree very high property taxes it was likely that deficit reduction measures had to come primarily from cuts in expenditure. The parties split the difference on the target date for the deficit reduction to 3 per cent of gross domestic product (GDP), agreeing on 2015; Fine Gael wanted 2014 and Labour 2016. A similar compromise was achieved on the reduction of the size of the public sector, with the parties agreeing that 25,000 jobs would go by 2015 – Fine Gael had wanted 30,000, whereas Labour said 18,000 was sufficient. There was agreement about the sale of non-strategic state assets up to the value of €2 billion, with the implied condition that this would happen only if the money were reinvested in the economy. That the parties could only agree an amount rather than specify which non-strategic state assets would be likely targets perhaps points to this being a problem. Another problem is that this seems to conflict with the conditions in the Memorandum of Understanding (MoU) of the EU/IMF programme, which states that such monies would have to be used to reduce Ireland's debt. Other measures, such as the decision to restore the minimum wage and reduce a value added tax (VAT) rate needed the agreement of the EU and IMF, which was subsequently received. When it came to identifying areas where the spending cuts might fall there was a commitment to a 'Comprehensive Spending Review', and again, since the parties failed to agree on social welfare cuts, they agreed to establish a 'Tax and Social Welfare Commission to examine ... the elimination of disincentives to employment.'[19]

In other policy areas one party could be said to have won out over the other. Fine Gael retained its NewEra proposals (to invest in new telecom, water and electricity networks) and Labour won a commitment to set up a Strategic Investment Bank. In health both parties had sought to introduce a system based on universal health insurance. Fine Gael had a place for private insurance, and health provision by private hospitals, in its proposals and this is what was agreed in the programme. In education much of what was agreed came from the Labour manifesto, and the absence of provision for a graduate tax or the reintroduction of fees was sold as a victory for the party.

The Labour Party had scheduled a special delegate conference in University College Dublin (UCD) for the Sunday afternoon, as the party's constitution specifies that such a conference has the final say on whether Labour enters a coalition government. Although the question of coalition had animated the party's 'passions probably more than any other single subject' in the past, there was little evidence of soul searching.[20] The conference, which was streamed live on the party's website, saw one TD and a leader of a small Labour-affiliated union warn against going into government. But even some of those scheduled to speak against the motion voted in favour. Just two TDs, Tommy Broughan and Joanna Tuffy, voted against. Some of the younger members spoke against, arguing that Labour could expect to grow by remaining in opposition. But the show of hands of the estimated 1,000 delegates was overwhelmingly in favour of accepting the programme for government and entering government. At the same time the Fine Gael parliamentary party met at the Shelbourne Hotel where Kenny made a brief speech and Michael Noonan fielded questions on the contents of the programme. It received the unanimous backing of the meeting. That evening the two party leaders met to discuss cabinet composition.

Cabinet selection

The Taoiseach must be elected by the Dáil before being formally appointed by the President. Then the new Taoiseach can construct his cabinet, which also must receive Dáil approval. Ireland is unusual in the constitutional restrictions that are placed on a Taoiseach's choice of ministers. All but two cabinet ministers must be elected TDs. It is possible for a Taoiseach to appoint up to two non-elected members of the Oireachtas to the cabinet but there are practical restrictions on appointing senators as ministers, a mechanism that has rarely been used.[21] As most political power is located in the cabinet or with ministers, there is a high demand for ministerial office among TDs, who generally see it as the pinnacle of a political career.[22] The cabinet has an upper limit of 15 members,[23] but the demands of coalition politics meant that a means of creating a sixteenth position at the cabinet table was found in 1994 through what is known as a 'super-junior' minister. This refers to a junior minister who is not in charge of a department but who has responsibilities that often run across a number of departments and who has the right to sit at and, depending on the relationship with the Taoiseach, to speak at, cabinet, and this device has been employed since then. The two party leaders agreed on the Saturday night that Fine Gael would get ten cabinet places and Labour five ministers. The 10–5 split was almost exactly proportional, which is unusual in that smaller parties usually get a disproportionate share of cabinet places. Perhaps for this reason the super-junior position was given to Labour, and the appointment to the position of Attorney General, who also sits at cabinet, was of a Labour supporter.

As the negotiations on cabinet appointments were left until the programme for government had been agreed, it became almost impossible for Labour to make a coalition conditional on the cabinet make-up. Gilmore was forced to concede Finance and the 10–5 cabinet split to Fine Gael. Those who had remained loyal to Kenny during the challenge to his leadership of Fine Gael in June 2010 were also seen to have got their desired portfolios, so Phil Hogan got Environment, Alan Shatter got Justice and James Reilly got Health. Fine Gael also got the other main economic portfolio of Jobs, Enterprise and Innovation. Labour's cabinet selection seemed more chaotic (see below) but four of the five places were already allocated given that the party leader and three negotiators knew in advance that they would be in cabinet. Having lost its two main battles, on Finance and the 10–5 split in portfolio allocation, Labour was keen to maximise its impact on economic policy. It saw the break-up of the Department of Finance's responsibilities with a new Department of Public Expenditure and Reform (PER), something that had been planned in advance of the negotiations. Finance retained control over the overall fiscal policy (taxation and budgetary policy) as well as banking. The new department is to negotiate annual estimates with the ministers, and so will determine the detail of where spending goes within the broad framework set out by Finance. PER will look for reforms in public sector pay, work practices and the form of the public sector generally. This split was criticised by opposition parties but the split makes some sense as it will mean the PER minister will be able to concentrate on the spending side and he is more likely to be able to enforce agreements with departments and public sector bodies as he controls the purse strings. An 'economic council', which comprises the Taoiseach, Tánaiste, the Minister for Finance and the Minister for Public Expenditure and Reform, was set up. It is essentially a committee of the cabinet and will effectively be able to set economic policy.

When the new Dáil met on 9 March, Enda Kenny was elected Taoiseach by a record margin of 117 votes to 27. As well as the 112 TDs of the two government parties (this excludes the Ceann Comhairle, or Speaker of the Dáil, who does not vote except in the event of a tie) he was supported by a number of Independents, while Fianna Fáil TDs and one other Independent abstained. He presented his new cabinet some hours later for ratification by the Dáil, announcing as he did so some other changes to the structure of government. The Department of Defence was grouped with Justice and Equality under a single minister and a new stand-alone Department of Children was set up. There were a number of notable features of the new cabinet, one being its age. The average age is 56 and only two ministers were under 50. (The average age of Brian Cowen's government when it was formed in 2008 was 48.) Despite the high average age, just five of the new cabinet had previous cabinet experience, though another four had been junior ministers. The cabinet included three former party leaders, which is rather unusual in Ireland. One of these, Ruairí Quinn, had been offered the super-junior post but refused it. The paucity of cabinet-level experience on the front benches of the two parties may explain why Quinn was then offered a senior post. Willie Penrose, who eventually took the super-junior post, also caused some problems, delaying the vote on the new government for a number of hours. He was said to have been concerned that the super-junior was not a real job, but having been reassured by Pat Rabbitte, who had held it himself once, Penrose agreed to take the position. One Labour minister reported having been given about five minutes' notice of the portfolio they were to be given before the formal announcement in the Dáil, possibly highlighting the unplanned nature of cabinet formation in Ireland.

Another notable feature was the relative absence of women. Only two were appointed to cabinet and this was seen at the time as a snub for women (see also Chapter 10, p. 236). The low number was hardly a surprise given that so few of the outgoing Fine Gael parliamentary party were women; indeed, the only female Fine Gael TD appointed to cabinet had not been a member of the outgoing Dáil. In Labour most of those available with cabinet experience were men and it might have been seen as necessary to favour experience over gender. Another surprise for many was that Joan Burton, who had been seen to shadow Finance successfully, did not receive an important economic policy-making portfolio. This caused some disquiet in Labour, but it was said that Gilmore made the decision on the basis that Burton's expertise had been in banking policy and when the Department of Finance, which controlled this, was not available he thought that Brendan Howlin's experience of having run a government department would be important. Burton was reported to have been annoyed at having been given a portfolio without a major policy input.

Taoisigh rarely admit to being guided by factors such as gender and geography when selecting a cabinet. But Taoisigh rarely construct cabinets that lack geographical balance. Certain areas such as Cork expect to be represented at cabinet. This cabinet was more Dublin-centric than any since the state was founded. Nine of the 15 ministers are Dublin-based, though many of these are not originally from Dublin. Though ministers are not meant to be representatives of their regions, many ministers assume that role. In this first Kenny cabinet it was noted by some that there was no representative from the midlands or north-west (other than Kenny himself). This geographical imbalance is in some part due to the concentration of senior Labour politicians in Dublin, so Kenny may not be to blame as he had no input into choosing the Labour ministers or into which department they were put.

Loyalty to the leadership is also denied as a factor affecting cabinet selection, but is unquestionably an important reason behind the appointment of ministers. However, most Taoisigh recognise that they need to retain support within the party and so senior party figures, even ones who have not been loyal, might have to be accommodated. The leadership challenge to Enda Kenny in the summer of 2010 saw a majority of his then front bench come out against him. Kenny promised during that challenge not to punish the rebels, but many of the young Turks who would have aspired to senior cabinet posts were demoted. Kenny rewarded loyalists where he could. Richard Bruton, the main challenger, had been demoted by Kenny after the failed heave, but was regarded as too senior to leave out of cabinet. Simon Coveney, another challenger, was probably appointed because there was a perceived need to have a minister from Cork. Leo Varadkar had performed well in opposition and in the media, and despite some suggestions that he might not be promoted, he made the cabinet. The others, Phil Hogan, Jimmy Deenihan, Frances Fitzgerald, James Reilly and Alan Shatter had been loyal and close to the leadership, and Michael Noonan had remained neutral. So although it was suggested that Kenny had left ego at the door and treated his enemies the same as his friends,[24] this is probably not true as just three of the 'rebels' made it to cabinet. Some of the enemies he brought in were ones who might have turned out to cause more trouble had they been left out. Kenny was still in a weak position even after he won his leadership battle in summer 2010 and so needed to reunite the party. It is clear that being close to Kenny was an important factor in promotion.

If the distribution of cabinet seats is an important mechanism to strengthen one's hold on the party, the upper limit of 15 is one that Taoisigh would prefer not to have. While it is not possible to change the size of the cabinet pie that was to be divided between the two parties, junior ministers are available for this. Their number had been steadily expanded up to 2007 when 20 were appointed. The need to be seen to cut back at the political level meant that this was reduced to 15 in 2009. Though Fine Gael said at that time it would have reduced the number to 12,[25] the new government maintained that number and used the 15 appointments to alleviate some of the criticisms of age, gender and geographic imbalance.

In some countries junior ministers are thought to have a watchdog role between parties in coalition, the idea being that a junior minister from Fine Gael, say, can keep an eye on the senior minister from Labour in the department. Of the 15 junior ministers nine might possibly be shadowing; that is, a department's junior and senior minister are from different parties. In fact junior ministers cannot really act as a watchdog because they have no right to observe what their senior minister is doing. Junior ministers in Ireland have quite specific roles within a department and cannot go beyond that brief unless the senior minister wishes them to. Even in the junior minister's specific brief, the cabinet minister can constrain even the slightest degree of autonomy if s/he is so minded.

The new cabinet was approved by a large majority, 115 votes to 26. The ministers were warned by Kenny that if they were not seen to perform they would be sacked, and he hinted that there would be a major reshuffle in the summer of 2013. This might give the government an opportunity to bring in younger ministers, more women and a more balanced geographical spread, which might enable both parties to prepare for the next election.

Conclusion: how long will it last?

Though formed from highly unusual circumstances, the actual government that emerged was hardly revolutionary. When Fianna Fáil is not in office Labour and Fine Gael had always formed the basis of the alternative government. This was the case again in 2011. There were a number of reasons for this. One is that most of the other parties were uncoalitionable. However, this is unlikely to remain the case. Fianna Fáil will probably be a legitimate coalition partner after the next election and Sinn Féin could continue to move to the mainstream of Irish politics, making the government formation process after the next election much more open. Another reason why government formation was so familiar was that no new party emerged in the election to shake up the party system.

The government was unusual in some ways. It is the government with the largest support base in the Dáil (113 seats, or 68 per cent of all TDs) if not the largest electoral base (its 55 per cent vote is less than that achieved by Fianna Fáil and Labour between them in 1992). It is also a first in that this was a government of the largest two parties in the state, and so could legitimately claim to be a national unity government.

The government took office with some goodwill behind it and in the first months a majority of those expressing an opinion were impressed with the government's performance.[26] Enda Kenny, whose ability was questioned by so many before the election, received generally positive press and his cabinet colleagues were impressed with his efficient management of cabinet meetings. He was said to approach issues without a predetermined outcome in mind, and facilitated good debate in cabinet. It was also said that cabinet meetings were notable for not being divided on party lines. Whether this can be maintained over the desired five-year lifetime of the government is questionable.

One problem is that the Programme for Government is quite vague on issues on which the two parties found hard to agree. The quote that the two parties claimed guided the programme – 'Learn from yesterday, live for today, hope for tomorrow' – seemed to reflect the hope that certain problems will not have to be faced. Many of those problems were, in the words of one participant in the negotiations, 'glossed over'. If decisions need to be taken about further cuts the two parties may find themselves in disagreement over where those cuts should come. Within the first 100 days of the new administration one Labour minister had compromised on what had previously been a red-line issue for the party: the reintroduction of fees for third-level students. By the summer of 2011 tensions over unpopular decisions regarding hospital closures were publicly aired, and Fine Gael removed the whip from one TD for voting against the government.

This relates to a difficulty in having such a large majority and broad ideological base. The large number of backbench government TDs may become restless, particularly if there is no good news on the economy. Five constituencies have only government party TDs and many more are dominated by the government parties. It is unlikely that both parties will maintain their current number of seats at the next election, and as that approaches TDs will attempt to distinguish themselves from their colleagues. The large majority will not protect it from the possible tensions the government could face in the coming years.

Notes

1. Éamon Gilmore, *Dáil Éireann Debates*, vol. 727 no. 6 (unrevised), 1 February 2011.
2. www.rte.ie/news/election2011/election2011-exit-poll.pdf, accessed 10 May 2011.
3. Deaglán de Bréadún and Harry McGee, 'Coalition pact with Sinn Féin "impossible"', *Irish Times*, 6 January 2011.
4. This chapter relies heavily on off-the-record interviews with senior figures in Fine Gael and Labour who were close to the negotiations.
5. Kevin Rafter, *Democratic Left: The life and death of an Irish political party* (Dublin: Irish Academic Press, 2011), pp. 174–6.
6. These indices estimate the power that each group has when it comes to forming majority coalitions; 1 indicates complete power and 0 no power. The Banzhaf index indicated that power was distributed thus: .669 for Fine Gael, .063 for Labour, .063 for Fianna Fáil, .063 for Sinn Féin and the rest to various independent blocks. The Shapley–Shubik index indicated power was distributed .599, .087, .087, .087 respectively to the main parties.
7. See Abhinay Muthoo, 'A non-technical introduction to bargaining theory', *World Economics* 1:2 (2000), pp. 145–66.
8. See Stephen Collins, 'FG–Labour pact must be defined by national interest', *Irish Times*, 5 March 2011.
9. See Kaare Strøm and Benjamin Nyblade, 'Coalition theory and government formation', pp. 782–802 in Carles Boix and Susan C. Stokes (eds), *The Oxford Handbook of Comparative Politics* (Oxford: Oxford University Press, 2007), for a discussion of these theories.
10. Strøm and Nyblade, 'Coalition theory and government formation', p. 790.
11. Eoin O'Malley, 'Punch bags for heavyweights? Minor parties in Irish government', *Irish Political Studies* 25:1 (2010), pp. 539–61.
12. 'Fine Gael and Labour start coalition talks in Dublin', *Irish Times*, 28 February 2011.
13. For example, Fine Gael TD Jerry Buttimer gave ten minutes to Michael Healy-Rae in *Dáil Éireann Debates*, vol. 729 no. 5 (unrevised), 12 April 2011.
14. Belén Barriero, 'Explaining the electoral performance of incumbents in democracies', pp. 17–44 in José María Maravall and Ignacio Sánchez-Cuenca (eds), *Controlling Governments: Voters, Institutions, and Accountability* (New York: Cambridge University Press), p. 24.
15. O'Malley, 'Punch bags for heavyweights?', at pp. 547–48. Labour suffered a nine-point loss in 1997, losing almost half its 1992 support.
16. Eoin O'Malley, 'Labour's dilemma', *Sunday Business Post*, 6 March 2011.
17. 'Fine Gael and Labour start coalition talks in Dublin', *Irish Times*, 28 February 2011.
18. *Towards Recovery: Programme for a Government of National Recovery*, p. 4, available at www.taoiseach.gov.ie/eng/Publications/Publications_2011/Programme_for_Government_2011.html.

19. *Towards Recovery*, p. 15.
20. Michael Gallagher, *Political Parties in the Republic of Ireland* (Dublin: Gill and Macmillan, 1985), p. 86.
21. See Eoin O'Malley, 'Building and maintaining Irish governments', pp. 179–93 in Patrick Dumont and Keith Dowding (eds), *Ministerial Selection in Europe* (Abingdon: Routledge, 2009).
22. See Eoin O'Malley and Shane Martin, 'The government and the Taoiseach', pp. 295–326 in John Coakley and Michael Gallagher (eds), *Politics in the Republic of Ireland*, 5th edn (Abingdon: Routledge and PSAI Press, 2010).
23. There is also a minimum size of seven, which had not been regarded as relevant until the botched reshuffle by Brian Cowen (see Chapters 1 and 4) meant that the minimum size was reached in January 2011.
24. Noel Whelan, 'Kenny will stay upbeat despite the short honeymoon', *Irish Times*, 19 March 2011.
25. Fine Gael published a bill to reduce the numbers to 12 on 21 April 2009. See also O'Malley and Martin, 'The government and the Taoiseach', p. 301.
26. Red C Research, 'Voting intention tracking poll' for *Sunday Business Post* (11 April and 29 May, 2011), http://redcresearch.ie/wp-content/uploads/2011/04/SBP-10th-Apr-Poll-2011-Report.pdf, and http://redcresearch.ie/wp-content/uploads/2011/05/SBP-29th-May-Poll-2011-Report.pdf.

13
The Election in Context

Peter Mair

Three years ago, in his assessment of the implications of the 2007 election, Ken Carty noted that one of the most basic questions asked by analysts about an election outcome is whether it was marked by continuity or change.[1] The answer for the 2007 election was clearly continuity, although, as Carty also noted, it was a continuity that was achieved on a very insecure and shifting foundation. The answer for 2011 is clearly change – an enormous change by any standard, as we shall see below, but, perhaps paradoxically, a change that might eventually be reversed, and that might not have done very much to disturb the fundamentals. In 2007, analysts expected change and got continuity, even though the continuity was fragile. In 2011, they expected change and got change, even though in some crucial respects the outcome was not that different from what had been experienced in earlier momentous contests. This chapter will first look at the evidence and implications of this electoral change, and will show that the scale of the shift in Ireland in 2011 was exceptional even by comparative standards. The chapter then goes on to discuss the problems now faced by many party systems, including that of Ireland, in seeking to reconcile the preferences of the voters with the constraints imposed by external actors and institutions. These problems, which were brought into sharp relief in the 2011 election, have major implications for the legitimacy of the electoral process.

Ireland's earthquake election

In retrospect, it is probably easier to explain the major shift in 2011 than it was to explain the non-shift in 2007. The earlier election, as

Michael Gallagher put it, was the earthquake that never was, and a story of 'dramatic changes that, in the event, simply did not happen'.[2] Why this was the case has never been very clear, however. To be sure, this was the last good year before the Celtic Tiger collapsed, and the sense of well-being was still pronounced. As Michael Marsh concluded, the economy clearly worked to Fianna Fáil's advantage.[3] Nonetheless, as the Rainbow coalition had learned to its cost in 1997, a good economic record was not always enough to ensure re-election, and in 2007 voters had seemingly tired of a decade of Fianna Fáil rule. Elsewhere in Europe, moreover, established mainstream parties were losing a lot of ground to new populist challengers from the right and from the left. It was therefore somewhat of a surprise that Fianna Fáil was re-elected to government and that no other major shifts in the party balance were recorded. The 2011 election, by contrast, turned out much as predicted. Coming as it did in the midst of the most severe economic crisis ever experienced by the state, and offering the first proper electoral test of what was commonly viewed as the most incompetent and damaging government ever to hold office in Ireland, it resulted in a record high shift in votes, leaving Fianna Fáil with its lowest vote ever and its Green coalition partner with a total Dáil wipe-out. This was, as had been expected, a major transformation.

The explanations for the outcome in 2011 are explored at length by the various chapters elsewhere in this volume, and will not be revisited here. The sheer scale of the change is worth emphasising, however. In the first place, the loss of votes suffered by Fianna Fáil is itself almost unprecedented in a long-established democracy. This was a party which had twice in its history polled more than 50 per cent of the vote, and which, with two narrow exceptions, always polled more than 40 per cent. In terms of the strength of its support and the longevity of its success, its record is unrivalled across the democratic world. In 2011, however, the party fell to just over 17 per cent of the vote, a figure which is roughly the same as that which the British Liberals were receiving at the end of the 1990s, and which is only slightly more than the new right-wing populist parties now poll in Denmark and the Netherlands. Indeed, the dramatic loss of votes suffered by Fianna Fáil seems comparable only to that experienced by the Union of the Democratic Centre in Spain (then a fledgling democracy) in 1982, the Christian Democrats in Italy in 1994, and the Progressive Conservatives in Canada in 1993. Few other parties have ever been battered so badly in a single election.

In this sense, it is interesting to compare Fianna Fáil's electoral trajectory with that of the Ulster Unionist Party (UUP) north of the border. Both Fianna Fáil and the UUP had long dominated their respective polities, although party politics in the Republic was obviously always more competitive than that in Northern Ireland. The UUP was also bigger than Fianna Fáil, and commanded a substantially greater share of votes and seats, and was still polling some 60 per cent of the vote in the 1960s. Thereafter, however, challenged by more hardline unionists, on the one side, and by more liberal elements, on the other, and also losing ground to the nationalist parties as a result of the slow demographic shifts in the electorate, the party went into a steady decline, falling to 30 per cent in the 1970s and early 1980s, to just over 20 per cent in the 1990s, to 15 per cent in the Assembly elections of 2007, and then to a record low of 13 per cent in the Assembly elections in May 2011. Both Fianna Fáil and the UUP have now become, at least for now, minor parties, but the collapse that Fianna Fáil experienced virtually overnight was spread over 30 years in the case of the UUP.

Since Fianna Fáil was not the only loser in 2011, the overall shift in votes was also remarkably high. The Greens, though very small by comparison to their senior coalition partner, also lost a substantial share of their support, while the Progressive Democrats (PDs), which had entered the 2007 election as an independent party, and which had dissolved themselves mid-term, can also be counted as a loser. When we add these to the Fianna Fáil figure, we get a total loss of votes of 29.6 per cent experienced by three parties in 2011, a figure that is unprecedented in Irish political history and almost unprecedented on a European scale. The best summary measure of this sort of aggregate electoral change is provided by the index of *total electoral volatility*, which is a simple measure recording the sum of the aggregate losses of all losing parties (or, which is more or less the same, the aggregate gains of all winning parties) from one election to the next. This index is easily calculated for any election, and hence it is also easy to compare levels of total electoral volatility over time. As can be seen from Table 13.1, the index of volatility for the 2011 election has a value of 29.6 per cent, which is equivalent to the total losses of the losing parties (Fianna Fáil, Greens, PDs) or the total gains of the winners (all the others).

Prior to 2011, the highest level of volatility recorded in post-independence Ireland was in the election of September 1927, when the index reached 20.8 per cent. This was the election which followed Fianna Fáil's decision to take its seats in Dáil Éireann, and which helped give shape to the party system as it subsequently developed over the following decades. The next most volatile election was that of 1943, with an index of 20.6, when Clann na Talmhan made a major breakthrough and Labour made substantial gains. Thereafter, as can be seen from

Figure 13.1, volatility tended to decline, with occasional peaks in 1987, when the PDs broke through, and 1992, when Labour suddenly doubled its vote. In historical terms, the 2011 election was therefore exceptional, even though it is possible that it may yet signal a return to the sort of extended *sequence* of highly unstable electoral outcomes that marked the late 1920s and 1930s.

Table 13.1   Aggregate electoral change in Ireland, 2007–11

Party	% Votes 2007	% Votes 2011	Difference
Fianna Fáil	41.6	17.4	–24.1
Fine Gael	27.3	36.1	+8.8
Labour	10.2	19.4	+9.3
Sinn Féin	6.9	9.9	+3.0
Green	4.7	1.8	–2.8
Progressive Democrats	2.7	–	–2.7
Socialist Party	0.7	1.2	+0.5
People Before Profit	0.5	1.0	+0.5
United Left Alliance	0	0.5	+0.5
Inds/Others	5.4	12.4	+7.0
Total	100.0	100.0	29.6

Source: www.tcd.ie/Political_Science/staff/michael_gallagher/Election2011.php.

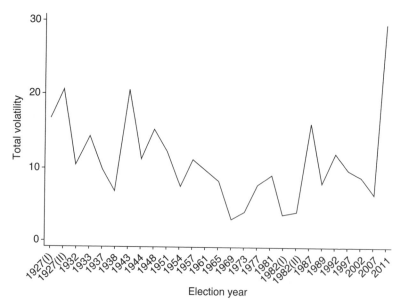

Figure 13.1   Volatility in Irish elections 1927–2011

By comparative standards, levels of electoral volatility in Ireland have usually ranked close to or below the average level recorded in Europe's other long-established democracies. The relevant data are shown in Table 13.2, which reports the mean level of electoral volatility in western Europe during each of the postwar decades, and which also reports the equivalent Irish figure. In each of these decades, barring the 1950s, the average level in Ireland was below that in Western Europe as a whole, although elsewhere, as in Ireland, we see a sharp upsurge after the 1980s. The Irish electoral earthquake in 2011 might therefore be seen as part of the more widespread drift towards electoral instability in Europe, being all the more pronounced because of the lack of build up in 2002 and 2007, when higher levels of electoral change might have been expected.

Table 13.2 Mean levels of volatility in Western Europe and Ireland, 1950s–2000s

Decade	1950s	1960s	1970s	1980s	1990s	2000–09
Western Europe	8.0	7.4	8.6	8.4	12.0	11.0
Ireland	10.3	7.0	5.7	8.1	11.7	7.5

Source: Based on figures in Michael Gallagher, Michael Laver and Peter Mair, *Representative Government in Modern Europe*, 5th edn (London: McGraw Hill, 2011), p. 310.

That said, the scale of the change in 2011 was dramatic even by recent European standards. This can be seen from the data in Table 13.3, which ranks the most volatile postwar elections among the long-standing European democracies, and which includes only those with levels of volatility greater than 20 per cent. As might be expected, these are relatively unusual elections: of the 290 elections held in these 16 countries since 1945, only 11 (3.8 per cent) have recorded a level of volatility of 20 per cent or more. Moreover, the distribution of these elections is quite skewed, both geographically and through time. Three of these elections have occurred in Italy, in 1948, 1994 and 2001; three in the Netherlands, in 1994, 2002 and 2010; and one each in Austria (2002), Denmark (1973), France (1958), Germany (1953), and now Ireland (2011). Although three occurred before 1960, the large majority come after 1990, when European elections began their present upward spiral of instability. What is perhaps most striking, however, is that the recent Irish election emerges as the third most volatile on the list, being surpassed only by Italy in 1994, when the Christian Democrats and Socialists collapsed and Berlusconi's Forza Italia first came to power, and by the Netherlands in 2002, when Pim Fortuyn led the first Dutch populist revolt. In other words, despite

Table 13.3   Europe's most volatile elections since 1945

Country	Year	Level of volatility (%)
Italy	1994	36.7
Netherlands	2002	30.7
Ireland	2011	29.6
France	1958	26.7
Italy	1948	23.0
Netherlands	2010	22.5
Italy	2001	22.0
Netherlands	1994	21.5
Denmark	1973	21.2
Germany	1953	21.2
Austria	2002	21.1

Note: All elections with a level of volatility greater than 20.0 per cent. These data refer only to the long-established European democracies. High-volatility elections have tended to occur with greater frequency in the newer post-communist democracies.

little change in the turnout levels, the 2011 election in Ireland was the third most unstable election in postwar Western Europe.

What is also striking to note is that the Irish election is one of only two elections on this list in which a high level of volatility occurred in the absence of a major new party suddenly storming the polls, or in the absence of a major constitutional upheaval – the other exception is Austria in 2002, where the instability was due to the sudden collapse in support for Jörg Haider's Freedom Party. The rapid mobilisation and electoral success of new parties constituted the major source of change in Italy in 1994, in Denmark in 1973, and in the Netherlands in both 2002 and 2010. In France in 1958, Italy in 1948, and in Germany in 1953 the high level of volatility accompanied a major constitutional upheaval and restructuring. And although the instability in Italy in 2001 was similar to that in Ireland in that it involved a shake-up of existing parties rather than the mobilization of new alternatives, most of the parties involved in the election had already been heavily transformed in the turbulent years that followed the scandals of 1992. Needless to add, there is no other election on this list in which the revolt of the electorate acted to the benefit of a party that had last enjoyed the status of the single biggest party almost 80 years before.

Two other features of this election reveal somewhat contradictory signals – the one, at the level of government formation, suggesting underlying continuity; the other, at the level of partisan alignments, suggesting potentially long-term change. In the first place, while the electoral upheaval was itself unprecedented, the eventual outcome seems remarkably familiar. Since Fianna Fáil established its dominant position in the 1930s, competition in the Irish party system has tended to revolve around the opposition between Fianna Fáil and a coalition of more or less all the other relevant parties – the familiar divide of Fianna Fáil versus the Rest. Over time, this opposition has been adapted, on the one hand, by Fianna Fáil's engagement in a coalition strategy of its own, which, since the late 1980s, has led it to form coalitions with the PDs, Labour, and, most recently, the Greens; and, on the other hand, by the simplification of the non-Fianna Fáil coalition, which steadily became more predictable and familiar, and which was usually built around the relatively enduring alliance between Fine Gael and Labour. In other words, party competition has come to revolve around the opposition between two blocs: a Fianna Fáil *plus* bloc, and a Fine Gael–Labour bloc. The only occasion on which this pattern was seriously disturbed was when the second Reynolds coalition took office in January 1993 and crossed the traditional political divide by bringing Fianna Fáil and Labour together in government. The collapse of this novel government less than two years later was also unprecedented, in that it led to the formation of a new government (composed of Labour, Fine Gael and Democratic Left (DL)) that was the first such coalition to be formed without a prior election.

In the case of the 2011 election, therefore, the outcome seems to signal a reversion to the more traditional pattern of government formation: a Fine Gael–Labour coalition under the leadership of a Fine Gael Taoiseach (Fine Gael and Fianna Fáil remain the only parties to have occupied the office of Taoiseach since the birth of the modern party system) and a Labour Tánaiste, and with Labour holding about one-third of the cabinet seats. The same formula had been adopted in 1973, 1981, 1982 and – with the addition of DL, now merged with Labour, with many former DL leaders now holding leadership positions in Labour[4] – at the end of 1994. And while the formation of such a government might have been unavoidable in 2011, it nevertheless serves to emphasise that despite the economic crisis, despite the collapse of Fianna Fáil, and despite one of the most dramatic elections in modern European political history, political opposition in Ireland continues to be organised along familiar lines. Indeed, Ireland's traditional political opposition retains the sort of visibility that brings to mind Churchill's 'dreary steeples',[5] and in the longer run, it is the integrity of this particular parliamentary divide that may yet hasten the restoration of Fianna Fáil to centre stage. Now that Fine Gael and Labour are yet again in government together, it is likely that opposition to their alliance will come to focus largely on Fianna Fáil – after all, this is how political opposition in Ireland has always worked. Moreover, unless the more radical left is courted into office, Fianna Fáil will surely be seen as the basis for any alternative government. In other words, while the cabinet has changed, the fundamentals of the party system might still have been preserved by the decision of Fine Gael and Labour to join forces in government once again. Indeed this may well provide the necessary life support system for Fianna Fáil, allowing it to regroup its once formidable organisational and affective resources and – sometime in the future – challenge for power once again. Given the familiarity of the alternatives, it would therefore be a mistake to write Fianna Fáil off – at least in the medium term.

Second, despite the familiar outcome at the level of government formation, the electoral upheaval seems to have signalled a partial electoral realignment that is not only of relevance to the future development of the Irish political debate, but that may also have lessons for other European polities. This was the shift of votes to the left of the political spectrum, and hence to the side of politics that has always been marked in Ireland by its comparative debility. One of the principal features to have long distinguished Ireland from its political neighbours has been the relative weakness of the traditional socialist or social democratic left, and the relative strength of the centre right. Even through to the early 2000s, at a time when the left throughout Europe was beginning to decline, the Irish case continued to be exceptional. During the 1990s, for example, the left in Europe was polling an average of 40 per cent of the vote in the long established democracies (roughly 30 per cent for the Social Democrats, 4 per cent for the present and former Communists, and 7 per cent for the New Left and Green parties). In the early 2000s, this had fallen slightly to just over 39 per cent. In Ireland, by contrast, the respective figures were 20 per cent and 16 per cent – an underestimate, to be sure, since it fails to count the support offered to many Independent candidates of the left, but one which still falls substantially below the average Western European polity.[6] Even if we add Sinn Féin to this total, the contrast remains very marked.

In 2011, however, the balance changed (see Table 13.1 above). Labour almost doubled its support, and Sinn Féin, promoting a strong anti-austerity programme, gained 3 per cent. When we add the gains of the small Socialist Party and the People Before Profit Alliance, the total gain is almost 14 per cent, taking the overall left (including Sinn Féin, but excluding the Greens on this occasion) to some 32 per cent of the vote, a level unrivalled in the postwar period and one that is now quite comparable to that in a number of other European countries. Given that this was the first austerity election in the increasingly troubled euro zone, the move to the left may not have been very surprising and might yet be echoed elsewhere. Having long been the exception to trends common to mass politics in most European polities, it may be that Ireland has finally become a trend-setter, or at least a forerunner.

Government by the people and government for the people

In terms of the policies and issues at stake, the 2011 election was distinctive in a number of ways. First, as Jane Suiter has pointed out in a contribution to the valuable *Political Reform* blog,[7] it was one of the few elections in which national policy played an important role, also at the local constituency level. Policy differences between the parties have often been quite marked, even though this has tended to be underestimated by the conventional focus on personalities and constituency politics. In practice, however, even when marked, these differences rarely impact at the local level, with party competition being more akin to a two-level game in which the sphere of national politics rarely connects with that of the constituency. At local level, the candidate seeking election responds to and seeks to represent the demands of her constituents, most of which are framed within local terms of reference. At national level, the TD in the Dáil responds to and seeks to represent the programme advanced by her party leadership, most of which is framed within the terms of reference of national policy. Since these spheres rarely intersect, however – except when, as in the case of health policy, for example, national policies have significant local implications – they are easily reconciled.[8] This also means, of course, that national issues and policy differences usually play little role in local electioneering or in determining the distribution of voter preferences, but are rather held at one remove. In most Irish elections, to paraphrase US Congressman Tip O'Neill, politics has been local. In 2011, by contrast, as Jane Suiter suggests, much of the politics was also national. As the exit poll reported in Chapter 8 (p. 185 above) indicates, while choosing a candidate to look after the needs of the constituency remained a priority for many voters (37 per cent in 2011 compared to 39 per cent in 2007), choosing between the set of policies set out by the parties was the option that was now preferred by a plurality (41 per cent in 2011 compared to 24 per cent in 2007).

A second distinctive feature of the debates in the 2011 election was the tension that they revealed between the policies proposed by the winning parties, and hence what we can assume to have been the preferences of the voters, on the one hand, and the policies that were effectively imposed by external authorities, most notably the European Union (EU) and the International Monetary Fund (IMF), on the other.[9] Although the broad outlines of the EU/IMF loan package to Ireland had already been agreed prior to the election by all mainstream parties, including Fine Gael and Labour, the opposition parties began the campaign by pledging that they would seek to renegotiate the agreement, including the interest rate on the loan itself.[10] Indeed, in a special RTÉ *Prime Time* programme on the issue, broadcast on 27 January 2011, spokespersons from both parties suggested that they might try to lower the latter figure to closer to 3 or 3.5 per cent. This was clearly an attractive election pledge, since it promised the possibility of being able to pull back from the most severe elements of the austerity programme. However, it also seemed unrealistic. Interviewed for the same RTÉ programme, Lorenzo Bini Smaghi, a member of the European Central Bank (ECB) Executive Board, and the official in charge of European and international relations, flatly denied the possibility that the loan might be renegotiated, as, in a separate interview, did Ajai Chopra, who had headed the IMF mission to Ireland. All of this clearly had the potential to lead to a conflict between a set of parties that sought to win government with a representative mandate to renegotiate a loan, and a set of external actors who insisted on sticking to the terms of an agreement that has already been signed on behalf of the state rather than on behalf of any particular party or government.

Every modern democracy is faced by the need to balance what the parties or their voters might like to happen and the real room for manoeuvre that is available to government to meet these demands. This balance is all the more difficult to achieve when the government in question is subject to external constraints, particularly when, as is currently the case in most of the EU, these constraints are becoming increasingly weighty and increasingly limiting. Indeed, with time, most of the EU polities have ceded a substantial degree of their autonomy in a process that has steadily weakened the capacity and legitimacy of their party governments.[11] For Ireland, which is a relatively small and highly open economy, and which is fully embedded within both the 27-member EU and the 17-member euro zone, these external constraints are especially severe. In other words, in Ireland most obviously – but also in other economically troubled polities – it is becoming more and more difficult to reconcile the preferences of the citizens with the strictures of external actors, particularly when the range of policy choices that are in practice available to government grows ever narrower.

At one level, we might see this problem as being equivalent to what Fritz Scharpf has spoken of as the more conventional trade-off between 'input legitimacy' and 'output legitimacy', or, as he also puts it, adopting Abraham Lincoln's famous terms, the trade-off between government 'by' the people and government 'for' the people.[12] In the Irish case, however, the conflict is of a different order – at least on one side of the equation. That is, while it is easy in the Irish case to see what input legitimacy would entail, and to see how government by the people might be expressed, it is less clear what form of output legitimacy is involved, or how policies that are expressive of government for the people might be shaped, and it is this which risks damaging the legitimacy of the electoral process.

In the Irish case, it seems clear that the push for a renegotiation of the EU/IMF agreement would be something that could be considered expressive of government *by* the people. The parties that favoured renegotiation – even if without precise detailed plans – were those preferred by the electorate and were those that won a commanding Dáil majority. Indeed, precisely because of its associated austerity costs, the EU/IMF agreement had quickly proved extremely unpopular with voters, with more than 80 per cent of respondents to a pre-election poll by Millward Brown in the *Sunday Independent* (30 January 2011) indicating a preference for renegotiation. Should the people have been allowed to decide, the decision would therefore have been likely to favour new terms, if only because this would have eased the pressure on the government to adopt an austerity programme.[13]

On the other side of the equation, however, it is difficult to view acceptance of the status quo, and hence acceptance of the EU/IMF strictures, which was the position advocated by the outgoing Fianna Fáil–Green coalition, as being expressive of government *for* the people. According to many interpretations, for example, including those of renowned economists Ken Rogoff and Paul Krugman, as well as financier George Soros, this agreement is actually damaging to the interests of the Irish people and to the long term prosperity of the Irish state. 'How long can Ireland take the pain that's necessary?', asked Rogoff. 'A year, two years? Maybe. But three or four? Countries outside of Romania maybe, under Ceausescu, really haven't done this and so it's possible but it's very demanding.'[14] According to Krugman, 'you have to wonder what it will take for serious people to realize that punishing the populace for the bankers' sins is worse than a crime; it's a mistake'.[15] For Soros, finally, it is a case of 'the bondholders of insolvent banks ... being protected at the expense of taxpayers. This is politically unacceptable. A new Irish government to be elected next spring is bound to repudiate the current arrangements.'[16] In other words, a policy that advocates staying with the present commitments does not seem expressive of government for the people. Indeed, for some commentators, it is more akin to government *against* the people, and hence is a policy that not only lacks input legitimacy, but also lacks all sense of output legitimacy.

So, if not for the people, for whom was government acting? And in whose interests was the decision to go for a bailout and to accept the terms of the EU/IMF agreement? In the first place, and most obviously, it was in the interests of the banks that were bailed out, and in the interests of the senior management of these banks who had busily lobbied the government leaders on the night of 29–30 September 2008 when the original guarantee was given. This also means that it was in the interests of the bondholders of the failing banks, who are mainly European banks, and who were together owed an estimated €360 billion, including €100 billion owed to German banks, and €110 billion to UK banks. Since any default would have major knock-on effects on their balance sheets, it was also clearly in the interests of these other European banks and their national governments that the debts are covered. Finally, the decision was also taken in the interests of the ECB and the leadership of the Eurozone more generally, as well as of the EU authorities, since an Irish default would seriously undermine the euro, and hence risk irreparable damage to the EU itself.

Perhaps, then, it was a decision expressive of government for the *European* people(s). Indeed, it was argued by some commentators and politicians that the ECB and the EU had forced the rescue package on Ireland in an effort to protect the European banks and the currency.[17] In a heated exchange in the European Parliament, for example, the Irish Socialist MEP, Joe Higgins, condemned the transferring of the costs of the bailout to the Irish taxpayers, who, he claimed, were not responsible. The bailout mechanism, he argued, 'is in practice nothing more than another tool to cushion major European banks from the consequences of their reckless speculation on the financial markets'. To which the president of the European Commission, José Manuel Barroso, responded angrily:

> the problems of Ireland were created by the irresponsible financial behaviour of some Irish institutions and by the lack of supervision in the Irish market ... Europe is now part of the solution; it is trying to support Ireland. But it was not Europe that created this fiscally irresponsible situation and this financially irresponsible behaviour.

Europe is trying to support Ireland. It is important to know where the responsibility lies.[18]

Lorenzo Bini Smaghi was also explicit on this issue, emphasising that the whole problem was the responsibility of the Irish, and that it was 'totally wrong' to suggest that the ECB had pressured the government:

Democracies have to be accountable and consistent with their own choices. I don't think anybody outside Ireland should tell Ireland what to do, but you should not complain if now you have to increase taxes as a result of the choice of economic model the Irish people made … The driving force was the collapse of investor confidence and the decision was entirely the Government's own.[19]

Brian Cowen, the soon to be outgoing Taoiseach, pushed the same line, emphasising that the request for European help had not been forced on his government: 'It was an Irish decision made by Irish people', he insisted.[20] What is less clear, however, is whether it was also an Irish decision made *for* Irish people.

Although the particular economic difficulties currently faced by the Irish state make it a relatively exceptional and extreme case, the issues that it raises are symptomatic of a more general problem facing modern party systems. On the one hand, there are the voter preferences to which the parties are expected to respond, and which they must also seek to represent. On the other hand, there are various international and supranational actors that expect and demand that certain policies are pursued by domestic authorities. In between these two sets of pressures move the national governments, constituted by the parties, but also obliged to follow the conditions and procedures specified by the external institutions of which they form part.

Governments in this sense are agents with two distinct principals. In some cases, the principals concur, and the demands and opportunities stemming from the international environment prove perfectly compatible with those emanating from the citizens. In other cases, there is a moderate clash, and governments seek to square the circle through negotiation and fudge, gaining concessions from the external actors, on the one hand, while pursuing blame avoidance with their domestic audience, on the other. In yet other and probably exceptional cases, however, including that of contemporary Ireland, the two principals are completely at odds, and the government ends up by being squeezed between two sets of largely incompatible pressures. It is then that the decision-making process becomes most difficult and most easily subject to challenge.

Conclusion: a democracy without choices

In the end, of course, at least in these circumstances, it is the external principals who are likely to hold sway. Although some changes may be negotiated at the margins, and although wider Eurozone developments might permit the lowering of interest rates, as proved to be the case in July 2011, the Irish government will still have to come to terms with the conditions laid down by the EU, the ECB and the IMF, and will therefore be left to manage a politics of austerity for the foreseeable future. But this also means that the election outcome, however dramatic, will have mattered little in the sense of any real mandate for action. Regardless of the vote, in other words, the path that will be followed in the coming years will be much the same.

Some years ago, in an evaluation of developments in the newly democratised Balkan states, Ivan Krastev emphasised how policy outcomes in these polities had been 'ensured largely by outside pressure and constraints in the form of EU or IMF conditionalities, currency pegs and the like'.[21] The current situation in Ireland, which is one of the longest enduring of the European democracies, but which is now in thrall to the ECB and IMF, is little different. In such circumstances, as Krastev went on to argue, relations between politicians and public worsen, since in such circumstances we see regimes 'in which the voters can change governments far more easily than they can change policies'. In the Balkans, he argued, this signalled the failure of representation, and the onset of a democracy without choices which risked undermining and eventually damaging the legitimacy of the electoral process.

In Ireland, where democracy is much more solidly established, this also signals a failure of representation, and this might also, in time, serve to undermine the legitimacy of the electoral process. The Irish failure does not so much derive from any unwillingness of political leaders to listen to their citizens, although that may well be the case, but rather from the growing incapacity of these leaders to act in a way that responds to the demands of their voters or that meets their interests. In present circumstances, in short, democracy in Ireland is also becoming a democracy without choices, one in which elections might continue to be full of drama, sound and fury, but in which the outcomes might signify little.

Notes

1. R. Kenneth Carty, 'Fianna Fáil and Irish party competition', pp. 218–31 in Michael Gallagher and Michael Marsh (eds), *How Ireland Voted 2007: The full story of Ireland's general election* (Basingstoke: Palgrave Macmillan, 2008), p. 218.

I am grateful to the editors for their comments, and to Dorothee Bohle, Conor Little and Thomas Bourke for ongoing discussions of the themes developed here.

2. Michael Gallagher, 'The earthquake that never happened: analysis of the results', pp. 78–104 in Gallagher and Marsh, *How Ireland Voted 2007*, p. 78.

3. Michael Marsh, 'Explanations for party choice', pp. 105–31 in Gallagher and Marsh, *How Ireland Voted 2007*.

4. See the account of the Democratic Left fusion with Labour in Kevin Rafter, *Democratic Left: The life and death of an Irish political party* (Dublin: Irish Academic Press, 2011).

5. Speaking of the changes wrought in the aftermath of the First World War, Churchill famously recalled in the House of Commons debate on the Irish Free State Bill of 1922: 'The modes of thought of men, the whole outlook on affairs, the grouping of parties, all have encountered violent and tremendous changes in the deluge of the world. But as the deluge subsides and the waters fall short, we see the dreary steeples of Fermanagh and Tyrone emerging once again. The integrity of their quarrel is one of the few institutions that has been unaltered in the cataclysm which has swept the world.' Cited by Richard Rose, *Governing without Consensus: An Irish perspective* (London: Faber and Faber, 1971), p. 359.

6. Michael Gallagher, Michael Laver and Peter Mair, *Representative Government in Modern Europe*, 5th edn (London: McGraw Hill, 2011), pp. 240–52.

7. See Jane Suiter, 'Policy and the election campaign', 25 February 2011, http://politicalreform.ie/2011/02/25/policy-and-the-election-campaign/#more-2360.

8. These questions are discussed at greater length in David Farrell, Peter Mair, Séin Ó Muineacháin and Matthew Wall, 'Courting, but not always serving: Perverted Burkeanism and the puzzle of the Irish TD under PR-STV'. Paper presented to the Workshop on Parties as Organizations and Parties as Systems, University of British Columbia, May 2011.

9. It is easy to predict the make-up of the next government, noted Gene Kerrigan in his *Sunday Independent* column of 5 March: it will be an EU/IMF/FG coalition.

10. See Dan O'Brien, 'The Opposition parties want to renegotiate the bailout. Is it possible?', *Irish Times*, 1 February 2011. The following section of the chapter is drawn from the lengthier analysis in Peter Mair, 'Bini Smaghi vs. the Parties', EUI Working Papers, RSCAS 2011/22, http://cadmus.eui.eu/handle/1814/16354.

11. Fritz W. Scharpf, 'Legitimacy in the multilevel European polity', *European Political Science Review* 1:2 (2009), pp. 173–204.

12. See Fritz W. Scharpf, *Governing in Europe* (Oxford: Oxford University Press, 1999).

13. This was also how Icelandic voters responded in a referendum on proposed solutions to their economic problems in April 2011. In the Irish case, where voters were also pessimistic about the possibilities for renegotiation, it might be argued that their preferences were a sign of the triumph of hope over expectation.

14. *Irish Times*, 27 January 2011.

15. *New York Times*, 25 November 2010.

16. *Financial Times*, 14 December 2010.

17. See also the arguments in Morgan Kelly, 'Ireland's future depends on breaking free from bailout', *Irish Times*, 7 May 2011.

18. *European Parliament Debates*, 19 January 2011.

19. *Irish Times*, 15 January 2011.

20. Interview with Brian Cowen, *Prime Time*, 8 December 2010.

21. Ivan Krastev, 'The Balkans: democracy without choices', *Journal of Democracy* 13:3 (2002), pp. 39–53, at p. 51.

Appendices

Michael Courtney

Appendix 1: results of the general election, 25 February 2011

Table A1.1 Electorate, valid votes and votes for each party

Constituency	Electorate	Valid votes	Fine Gael	Labour	Fianna Fáil	Sinn Féin	ULA	Green Party	Others
Carlow–Kilkenny	105,449	73,743	28,924	11,980	20,721	7,033	1,135	2,072	1,878
Cavan–Monaghan	99,178	71,275	28,199	4,011	14,360	18,452	0	530	5,723
Clare	82,745	57,916	24,524	8,572	12,804	0	0	1,154	10,862
Cork East	83,651	56,933	20,847	17,563	9,642	6,292	0	635	1,954
Cork North-Central	75,302	52,137	13,669	13,801	7,896	7,923	4,803	524	3,521
Cork North-West	62,870	45,740	22,321	6,421	11,390	3,405	1,552	651	0
Cork South-Central	91,619	64,040	22,225	11,869	17,936	5,250	0	1,640	5,120
Cork South-West	62,967	45,658	22,162	6,533	10,787	3,346	0	765	2,065
Donegal North-East	59,084	37,918	11,987	4,090	6,613	9,278	0	206	5,744
Donegal South-West	64,568	43,263	8,589	2,209	9,745	14,262	0	527	7,931
Dublin Central	56,892	34,612	6,903	9,787	5,141	4,526	0	683	7,572
Dublin Mid-West	64,880	42,722	13,214	13,138	5,043	5,060	3,093	1,484	1,690
Dublin North	70,413	49,347	15,488	13,014	7,634	0	7,513	4,186	1,512
Dublin North-Central	52,992	38,774	14,644	8,731	5,017	2,140	1,424	501	6,317
Dublin North-East	58,542	41,839	12,332	14,371	4,794	5,032	869	792	3,649
Dublin North-West	49,629	32,811	5,496	14,158	3,869	7,115	677	328	1,168
Dublin South	102,387	72,646	26,404	13,059	6,844	1,915	1,277	4,929	18,218
Dublin South-Central	80,268	50,927	11,956	18,032	4,837	6,804	6,574	1,015	1,709
Dublin South-East	58,217	34,919	12,402	8,857	3,922	1,272	629	2,370	5,467
Dublin South-West	70,613	46,964	13,044	17,032	5,059	8,064	2,462	480	823
Dublin West	62,348	42,472	11,549	12,313	7,044	2,597	8,084	605	280

Dun Laoghaire	80,115	56,676	19,591	17,217	8,632	0	6,206	2,156	2,874
Galway East	83,651	59,276	25,409	7,831	10,694	3,635	0	402	11,305
Galway West	88,840	60,625	18,627	7,489	12,703	3,808	0	1,120	16,878
Kerry North–Limerick West	63,614	45,614	18,599	9,159	5,230	9,282	0	239	3,105
Kerry South	59,629	44,380	14,482	4,926	5,917	0	0	401	18,654
Kildare North	77,959	51,222	17,050	14,979	7,436	2,896	0	905	7,956
Kildare South	58,867	38,270	12,755	10,645	8,307	2,308	0	523	3,732
Laois–Offaly	108,142	74,158	25,032	5,802	19,860	8,032	561	306	14,565
Limerick	65,083	45,041	21,925	7,910	9,361	0	0	354	5,491
Limerick City	64,909	43,188	18,696	8,764	9,259	3,711	721	490	1,547
Longford–Westmeath	85,918	57,525	21,887	15,366	11,197	4,339	0	309	4427
Louth	99,530	69,319	21,825	13,264	10,858	15,072	0	3,244	5056
Mayo	101,160	74,154	48,170	3,644	11,920	4,802	0	266	5,352
Meath East	64,873	42,752	17,471	8,994	8,384	3,795	0	461	3,647
Meath West	62,776	40,178	18,450	5,432	7,285	6,989	0	479	1,543
Roscommon–South Leitrim	60,998	47,504	18,303	4,455	7,103	4,637	0	220	12,786
Sligo–North Leitrim	63,432	44,428	16,378	4,553	9,708	5,911	2,284	432	5,162
Tipperary North	63,235	48,273	11,425	9,559	7,978	3,034	0	409	15,868
Tipperary South	57,420	41,361	14,298	4,525	5,419	1,860	8,818	367	6,074
Waterford	78,435	53,720	20,416	10,192	7,515	5,342	0	462	9,793
Wexford	111,063	75,539	26,034	15,462	14,027	4,353	741	391	14,531
Wicklow	95,341	70,500	27,926	12,087	7,467	7,089	0	1,026	14,905
Dublin	807,296	544,709	163,023	159,709	67,836	44,525	38,808	19,529	51,279
Rest of Leinster	869,918	593,206	217,354	114,011	115,542	61,906	2,437	9,716	72,240
Munster	911,479	644,001	245,589	119,794	121,134	49,445	15,894	8,091	84,054
Connacht–Ulster	620,911	438,443	175,662	38,282	82,846	64,785	2,284	3,703	70,881
Ireland	3,209,604	2,220,359	801,628	431,796	387,358	220,661	59,423	41,039	278,454

Notes: The number of votes obtained refers to first preference figures. A further 22,817 were deemed invalid.

The United Left Alliance (ULA) is an alliance of the Socialist Party (26,770), People Before Profit Alliance (21,551), the Workers and Unemployed Action Group (South Tipperary) (8,818) and an Independent (2,284).

In this and all subsequent tables 'Others (Non-ULA)' includes New Vision (which was an informal association of Independents) (25,422), The Peoples Convention (1,512), The Christian Solidarity Party (2,102), the Workers' Party (3,056), Fis Nua (938), South Kerry Independent Alliance (4,939), along with Independents (240,485).

Table A1.2 Turnout, and percentage votes for each party

Constituency	Turnout	Fine Gael	Labour	Fianna Fáil	Sinn Féin	ULA	Green Party	Other
Carlow–Kilkenny	69.9	39.2	16.2	28.1	9.5	1.5	2.8	2.5
Cavan–Monaghan	71.9	39.6	5.6	20.1	25.9	0.0	0.7	8.0
Clare	70.0	42.3	14.8	22.1	0.0	0.0	2.0	18.8
Cork East	68.1	36.6	30.8	16.9	11.1	0.0	1.1	3.4
Cork North-Central	69.2	26.2	26.5	15.1	15.2	9.2	1.0	6.8
Cork North-West	72.8	48.8	14.0	24.9	7.4	3.4	1.4	0.0
Cork South-Central	69.9	34.7	18.5	28.0	8.2	0.0	2.6	8.0
Cork South-West	72.5	48.5	14.3	23.6	7.3	0.0	1.7	4.5
Donegal North-East	64.2	31.6	10.8	17.4	24.5	0.0	0.5	15.1
Donegal South-West	67.0	19.9	5.1	22.5	33.0	0.0	1.2	18.3
Dublin Central	60.8	19.9	28.3	14.9	13.1	0.0	2.0	21.9
Dublin Mid-West	65.8	30.9	30.8	11.8	11.8	7.2	3.5	4.0
Dublin North	70.1	31.4	26.4	15.5	0.0	15.2	8.5	3.1
Dublin North-Central	73.2	37.8	22.5	12.9	5.5	3.7	1.3	16.3
Dublin North-East	71.5	29.5	34.3	11.5	12.0	2.1	1.9	8.7
Dublin North-West	66.1	16.8	43.2	11.8	21.7	2.1	1.0	3.6
Dublin South	71.0	36.3	18.0	9.4	2.6	1.8	6.8	25.1
Dublin South-Central	63.4	23.5	35.4	9.5	13.4	12.9	2.0	3.4
Dublin South-East	60.0	35.5	25.4	11.2	3.6	1.8	6.8	15.7
Dublin South-West	66.5	27.8	36.3	10.8	17.2	5.2	1.0	1.8
Dublin West	68.1	27.2	29.0	16.6	6.1	19.0	1.4	0.7
Dun Laoghaire	70.7	34.6	30.4	15.2	0.0	10.9	3.8	5.1
Galway East	70.9	42.9	13.2	18.0	6.1	0.0	0.7	19.1
Galway West	68.2	30.7	12.4	21.0	6.3	0.0	1.8	27.8
Kerry North–Limerick West	71.7	40.8	20.1	11.5	20.3	0.0	0.5	6.8
Kerry South	74.4	32.6	11.1	13.3	0.0	0.0	0.9	42.0

Kildare North	65.7	33.3	29.2	14.5	5.7	0.0	1.8	15.5
Kildare South	65.0	33.3	27.8	21.7	6.0	0.0	1.4	9.8
Laois–Offaly	68.6	33.8	7.8	26.8	10.8	0.8	0.4	19.6
Limerick	69.2	48.7	17.6	20.8	0.0	0.0	0.8	12.2
Limerick City	66.5	43.3	20.3	21.4	8.6	1.7	1.1	3.6
Longford–Westmeath	67.0	38.0	26.7	19.5	7.5	0.0	0.5	7.7
Louth	69.6	31.5	19.1	15.7	21.7	0.0	4.7	7.3
Mayo	73.3	65.0	4.9	16.1	6.5	0.0	0.4	7.2
Meath East	65.9	40.9	21.0	19.6	8.9	0.0	1.1	8.5
Meath West	64.0	45.9	13.5	18.1	17.4	0.0	1.2	3.8
Roscommon–South Leitrim	77.9	38.5	9.4	15.0	9.8	0.0	0.5	26.9
Sligo–North Leitrim	70.0	36.9	10.2	21.9	13.3	5.1	1.0	11.6
Tipperary North	76.3	23.7	19.8	16.5	6.3	0.0	0.8	32.9
Tipperary South	72.0	34.6	10.9	13.1	4.5	21.3	0.9	14.7
Waterford	68.5	38.0	19.0	14.0	9.9	0.0	0.9	18.2
Wexford	68.0	34.5	20.5	18.6	5.8	1.0	0.5	19.2
Wicklow	73.9	39.6	17.1	10.6	10.1	0.0	1.5	21.1
Dublin	67.5	29.9	29.3	12.5	8.2	7.1	3.6	9.4
Rest of Leinster	68.2	36.6	19.2	19.5	10.4	0.4	1.6	12.2
Munster	70.7	38.1	18.6	18.8	7.7	2.5	1.3	13.1
Connacht–Ulster	70.6	40.1	8.7	18.9	14.8	0.5	0.8	16.2
Ireland	69.2	36.1	19.4	17.4	9.9	2.7	1.8	12.5

Notes: Turnout is defined as the valid votes expressed as a percentage of the electorate; of the votes cast, 0.9 per cent were invalid.
Main constituent groups of the ULA: Socialist Party (1.2), People Before Profit Alliance (1.0).
Others (Non-ULA): New Vision 1.1 per cent, Peoples Convention 0.1 per cent, Christian Solidarity 0.1 per cent, Workers' Party 0.1 per cent, Fís Nua 0.04 per cent, South Kerry Independent Alliance 0.2 per cent, Independents 10.8 per cent.

Table A1.3 Seats and candidates by party

Constituency	Total	Fine Gael	Labour	Fianna Fáil	Sinn Féin	ULA	Green Party	Others
Carlow–Kilkenny	5–19	3–3	1–2	1–3	0–2	0–1	0–1	0–7
Cavan–Monaghan	5–14	3–4	0–1	1–2	1–2		0–1	0–4
Clare	4–16	2–3	1–1	1–2			0–1	0–9
Cork East	4–13	2–3	1–2	0–2			0–1	0–4
Cork North-Central	4–15	1–2	1–2	1–1	1–1	0–1	0–1	0–7
Cork North-West	3–9	2–3	0–1	1–2	1–1	0–1	0–1	
Cork South-Central	5–17	2–3	1–2	2–2	0–1		0–1	0–8
Cork South-West	3–13	2–3	1–1	0–2	0–1		0–1	0–5
Donegal North-East	3–11	1–2	0–1	1–1	1–1		0–1	0–5
Donegal South-West	3–9	1–1	0–1	0–2	1–1		0–1	1–3
Dublin Central	4–16	1–1	1–2	0–2	1–1		0–1	1–9
Dublin Mid-West	4–14	2–2	2–2	0–1	0–1	0–2	0–1	0–5
Dublin North	4–9	2–2	1–2	0–2		1–1	0–1	0–1
Dublin North-Central	3–9	1–2	1–1	0–1		0–1	0–1	1–2
Dublin North-East	3–11	1–1	2–2	0–1	0–1	0–1	0–1	0–4
Dublin North-West	3–12	0–2	2–2	0–1	1–1	0–1	0–1	0–4
Dublin South	5–16	3–3	1–2	0–1	0–1	0–1	0–1	1–7
Dublin South-Central	5–18	1–3	2–3	0–1	1–1	1–1	0–1	0–8
Dublin South-East	4–16	2–2	2–2	0–1	0–1	0–1	0–1	0–8
Dublin South-West	4–10	1–2	2–2	0–2	1–1	0–1	0–1	0–1
Dublin West	4–10	1–2	1–2	1–2	0–1	1–1	0–1	0–1
Dun Laoghaire	4–13	2–2	1–2	0–2		1–1	0–1	0–6
Galway East	4–13	2–4	1–2	1–2	0–1		0–1	0–3
Galway West	5–17	2–4	1–1	1–3	0–1		0–1	1–7
Kerry North–Limerick West	3–11	1–2	1–1	0–1	1–1		0–1	0–5
Kerry South	3–10	1–2	0–1	0–1			0–1	2–5

Kildare North	4-12	2-2	1-2	0-2	0-1		0-1	1-4
Kildare South	3-8	1-1	1-1	1-2	0-1		0-1	0-2
Laois-Offaly	5-21	2-4	0-1	2-3	1-1	0-1	0-1	0-10
Limerick	3-10	2-3	0-1	1-1			0-1	0-4
Limerick City	4-13	2-2	1-2	1-2	0-1	0-1	0-1	0-4
Longford-Westmeath	4-15	2-3	1-2	1-3	0-1		0-1	0-5
Louth	5-17	2-2	1-2	1-3[a]	1-1		0-1	0-8
Mayo	5-15	4-4	0-1	1-2	0-2		0-1	0-5
Meath East	3-9	2-2	1-1	0-2	0-1		0-1	0-2
Meath West	3-13	2-3	0-1	0-2	1-1		0-1	0-5
Roscommon–South Leitrim	3-10	2-2	0-1	0-2	0-1		0-1	1-3
Sligo–North Leitrim	3-13	2-2	0-1	0-2	1-1	0-1	0-1	0-5
Tipperary North	3-8	1-1	1-1	0-1	0-1		0-1	1-3
Tipperary South	3-8	1-2	0-1	0-1	0-1	1-1	0-1	1-1
Waterford	4-15	2-2	1-2	0-1	0-1		0-1	1-8
Wexford	5-14	2-3	1-2	1-2	0-1	0-1	0-1	1-4
Wicklow	5-24	3-3	1-3	0-2	0-1		0-1	1-14
Dublin (12)	47-155	17-24	18-24	1-17	4-10	4-12	0-12	3-56
Rest of Leinster (10)	42-152	21-26	8-17	7-24	3-11	0-3	0-10	3-61
Munster (13)	46-158	21-31	9-18	7-19	3-10	1-4	0-13	5-63
Connacht–Ulster (8)	31-102	17-23	2-9	5-16	4-10	0-1	0-8	3-35
Ireland (43)	166-567[a]	76-104	37-68	20-76	14-41	5-20	0-43	14-215[b]

[a] Figures include outgoing Ceann Comhairle Séamus Kirk (FF), who was automatically returned for Louth.

[b] This figure includes two independents who ran in two constituencies each.

Notes: ULA candidates: Socialist Party nine candidates (two elected), People Before Profit nine candidates (two elected) and Others two candidates (one elected).

Others (Non-ULA): New Vision 20 candidates (one elected), Peoples Convention four candidates (none elected), Christian Solidarity eight candidates (none elected), Workers' Party six candidates (none elected), Fís Nua five candidates (none elected), South Kerry Independent Alliance one candidate (not elected), Independents 171 (13 elected).

Appendix 2: members of the 31st Dáil

Table A2.1 Members of the 31st Dáil

TD (constituency)	Party	Occupation	Date of birth	First elected	Times elected	First pref. votes in 2011
Gerry Adams (Louth)	SF	Barman	Oct 1948	2011	1	15,072
James Bannon (Longford–Westmeath)	FG	Farmer, auctioneer	Mar 1958	2007	2	9,129
Seán Barrett (Dun Laoghaire)	FG	Insurance broker	Aug 1944	1981	9	10,504
Tom Barry (Cork E)	FG	Agri-business entrepreneur	Oct 1968	2011	1	5,798
Richard Boyd Barrett (Dun Laoghaire)	ULA	Teacher	Nov 1967	2011	1	6,206
Pat Breen (Clare)	FG	Farmer, architect	Mar 1957	2002	3	9,855
Tommy Broughan (Dublin NE)	Lab	Teacher	Aug 1947	1992	5	10,006
John Browne (Wexford)	FF	Salesman	Aug 1948	N1982	8	7,352
Richard Bruton (Dublin NC)	FG	Economist	Mar 1953	F1982	9	9,685
Joan Burton (Dublin W)	Lab	Accountant	Feb 1949	1992	4	9,627
Ray Butler (Meath W)	FG	Small trader	Dec 1965	2011	1	5,262
Jerry Buttimer (Cork SC)	FG	Director of adult education	Mar 1967	2011	1	7,128
Catherine Byrne (Dublin SC)	FG	Homemaker	Feb 1956	2007	2	5,604
Eric Byrne (Dublin SC)	Lab	Carpenter	Apr 1947	1989	3	8,357
Dara Calleary (Mayo)	FF	Employee of Chambers Ireland	May 1973	2007	2	8,577
Ciarán Cannon (Galway E)	FG	Publican	Sep 1965	2011	1	6,927
Joe Carey (Clare)	FG	Accountant	Jun 1975	2007	2	7,840
Paudie Coffey (Waterford)	FG	ESB official	May 1969	2011	1	9,698
Áine Collins (Cork NW)	FG	Accountant	Sep 1969	2011	1	7,884
Joan Collins (Dublin SC)	ULA	An Post Clerk	Jun 1961	2011	1	6,574
Niall Collins (Limerick)	FF	Lecturer, accountant	Mar 1973	2007	2	9,361
Michael Colreavy (Sligo–N Leitrim)	SF	IT project manager	Sep 1948	2011	1	5,911
Michael Conaghan (Dublin SC)	Lab	College principal	Sep 1944	2011	1	5,492
Seán Conlan (Cavan–Monaghan)	FG	Solicitor	Jan 1975	2011	1	7,864

Name (Constituency)	Party	Occupation				
Paul Connaughton (Galway E)	FG	Foróige youth worker	Jan 1982	2011	1	7,255
Ciara Conway (Waterford)	Lab	Service design and development facilitator	Aug 1980	2011	1	5,554
Noel Coonan (Tipperary N)	FG	Auctioneer	Jan 1951	2007	2	11,425
Marcella Corcoran-Kennedy (Laois–Offaly)	FG	Company director	Jan 1963	2011	1	5,817
Joe Costello (Dublin C)	Lab	Teacher	Jul 1945	1992	4	6,273
Simon Coveney (Cork SC)	FG	Manager of family business	Jun 1972	B-1998	4	9,447
Barry Cowen (Laois–Offaly)	FF	Auctioneer	Aug 1967	2011	1	8,257
Michael Creed (Cork NW)	FG	Farmer	Jun 1963	1989	5	10,112
Lucinda Creighton (Dublin SE)	FG	Barrister	Jan 1980	1980	2	6,619
Seán Crowe (Dublin SW)	SF	Printing operative	Mar 1957	2002	2	8,064
Clare Daly (Dublin N)	ULA	Trade unionist	Apr 1968	2011	1	7,513
Jim Daly (Cork SW)	FG	Teacher	Dec 1972	2011	1	8,878
John Deasy (Waterford)	FG	US Congressional aide	Oct 1967	2002	3	10,718
Jimmy Deenihan (Kerry N–Limerick W)	FG	Teacher	Sep 1952	1987	7	12,304
Pat Deering (Carlow–Kilkenny)	FG	Farmer	Feb 1967	2011	1	7,470
Pearse Doherty (Donegal SW)	SF	Civil engineer	Jul 1977	B-2010	2	14,262
Regina Doherty (Meath E)	FG	Sales director	Jan 1971	2011	1	8,677
Stephen Donnelly (Wicklow)	Ind	Management consultant	Feb 1975	2011	1	6,530
Paschal Donohue (Dublin C)	FG	Sales & marketing director	Sep 1974	2011	1	6,903
Timmy Dooley (Clare)	FF	IT and publishing salesman	Feb 1969	2007	2	6,789
Robert Dowds (Dublin MW)	Lab	Teacher	May 1953	2011	1	5,643
Andrew Doyle (Wicklow)	FG	Farmer	Jul 1960	2007	2	10,035
Bernard Durkan (Kildare N)	FG	Agricultural contractor	Mar 1945	1981	9	10,168
Dessie Ellis (Dublin NW)	SF	Television repairman	Oct 1952	2011	1	7,115
Damien English (Meath W)	FG	Accountant	Feb 1978	2002	3	9,290
Alan Farrell (Dublin N)	FG	Estate agent	Dec 1977	2011	1	5,310
Frank Feighan (Roscommon–S Leitrim)	FG	Newsagent, businessman	Jul 1962	2007	2	8,983
Anne Ferris (Wicklow)	Lab	Political aide	Sep 1954	2011	1	5,436
Martin Ferris (Kerry N–Limerick W)	SF	Fisherman	Mar 1952	2002	3	9,282
Frances Fitzgerald (Dublin MW)	FG	Social worker	Aug 1950	1992	3	7,281

Table A2.1 continued

TD (constituency)	Party	Occupation	Date of birth	First elected	Times elected	First pref. votes in 2011
Peter Fitzpatrick (Louth)	FG	Regional business manager	May 1962	2011	1	7,845
Charlie Flanagan (Laois–Offaly)	FG	Solicitor	Nov 1956	1987	6	10,427
Luke 'Ming' Flanagan (Roscommon–S Leitrim)	Ind	Merchandiser	Jan 1972	2011	1	8,925
Terence Flanagan (Dublin NE)	FG	Accountant	Jan 1976	2007	2	12,332
Seán Fleming (Laois–Offaly)	FF	Accountant	Feb 1958	1997	4	6,024
Tom Fleming (Kerry S)	Ind	Publican	Feb 1951	2011	1	6,416
Éamon Gilmore (Dun Laoghaire)	Lab	Trade union official	Apr 1955	1989	6	11,468
Noel Grealish (Galway W)	Ind	Company director	Dec 1965	2002	3	6,229
Brendan Griffin (Kerry S)	FG	Publican	Mar 1982	2011	1	8,808
John Halligan (Waterford)	Ind	Radio operator	Jan 1955	2011	1	5,546
Dominic Hannigan (Meath E)	Lab	Civil engineer	Jul 1965	2011	1	8,994
Noel Harrington (Cork SW)	FG	Postmaster	Dec 1970	2011	1	6,898
Simon Harris (Wicklow)	FG	Political aide	Oct 1986	2011	1	8,726
Brian Hayes (Dublin SW)	FG	Teacher	Aug 1969	1997	3	9,366
Tom Hayes (Tipperary S)	FG	Farmer	Feb 1952	B-2001	4	8,896
Séamus Healy (Tipperary S)	ULA	Hospital administrator	Aug 1950	1997	3	8,818
Michael Healy-Rae (Kerry S)	Ind	Shop and plant hire owner	Jan 1967	2011	1	6,670
Martin Heydon (Kildare S)	FG	Farmer	Aug 1978	2011	1	12,755
Joe Higgins (Dublin W)	ULA	Teacher	May 1949	1997	3	8,084
Phil Hogan (Carlow–Kilkenny)	FG	Insurance broker, auctioneer	Jul 1960	1989	6	10,525
Brendan Howlin (Wexford)	Lab	Teacher	May 1956	1987	7	11,005
Heather Humphreys (Cavan–Monaghan)	FG	Credit union manager	n/a	2011	1	8,144
Kevin Humphreys (Dublin SE)	Lab	Pharmaceutical technician	Feb 1958	2011	1	3,450
Derek Keating (Dublin MW)	FG	Charity director	May 1955	2011	1	5,933
Colm Keaveney (Galway E)	Lab	Trade unionist	Jan 1971	2011	1	4,254
Paul Kehoe (Wexford)	FG	Sales representative	Jan 1973	2002	3	8,386

Name (Constituency)	Party	Occupation				
Billy Kelleher (Cork NC)	FF	Farmer	Jan 1968	1997	4	7,896
Alan Kelly (Tipperary N)	Lab	Semi-state eBusiness manager	Jul 1975	2011	1	9,559
Enda Kenny (Mayo)	FG	Teacher	Apr 1951	B-1975	12	17,472
Seán Kenny (Dublin NE)	Lab	CIÉ official	Oct 1942	1992	2	4,365
Séamus Kirk (Louth)	FF	Farmer	Apr 1945	1982	8	—
Michael Kitt (Galway E)	FF	Teacher	May 1950	B-1975	10	6,585
Seán Kyne (Galway W)	FG	Agri-environment consultant	May 1975	2011	1	4,550
Anthony Lawlor (Kildare N)	FG	Teacher/farmer	Jun 1959	2011	1	6,882
Brian Lenihan (Dublin W)	FF	Barrister	May 1959	B-1996	5	6,421
Michael Lowry (Tipperary N)	Ind	Company director	Mar 1954	1987	7	14,104
Ciarán Lynch (Cork SC)	Lab	Adult literacy organiser	Jun 1964	2007	2	8,481
Kathleen Lynch (Cork NC)	Lab	Homemaker	Jun 1953	B-1994	4	7,676
John Lyons (Dublin NW)	Lab	Teacher	Jun 1977	2011	1	4,799
Éamon Maloney (Dublin SW)	Lab	Recycling plant owner	May 1952	2011	1	4,165
Micheál Martin (Cork SC)	FF	Teacher	Aug 1960	1989	6	10,715
Peter Mathews (Dublin S)	FG	Banking consultant	Aug 1951	2011	1	9,053
Michael McCarthy (Cork SW)	Lab	Pharmaceutical company employee	Nov 1976	2011	1	6,533
Charlie McConalogue (Donegal NE)	FF	Farmer	Oct 1977	2011	1	6,613
Mary Lou McDonald (Dublin C)	SF	Productivity consultant	May 1969	2011	1	4,526
Shane McEntee (Meath E)	FG	Publican, farmer	Dec 1956	B-2005	3	8,794
Nicky McFadden (Longford–Westmeath)	FG	Building society employee	Dec 1962	2011	1	6,129
Dinny McGinley (Donegal SW)	FG	Teacher	Apr 1945	F1982	9	8,589
Finian McGrath (Dublin NC)	Ind	School principal	Apr 1953	2002	3	5,986
Mattie McGrath (Tipperary S)	Ind	Plant hire contractor	Sep 1958	2007	2	6,074
Michael McGrath (Cork SC)	FF	Chartered accountant	Aug 1976	2007	2	7,221
John McGuinness (Carlow–Kilkenny)	FF	Transport company director	Mar 1955	1997	4	9,531
Joe McHugh (Donegal NE)	FG	Teacher	Jul 1971	2007	2	7,330
Sandra McLellan (Cork E)	SF	Trade union official	May 1961	2011	1	6,292
Pádraig MacLochlainn (Donegal NE)	SF	Community worker	Jun 1973	2011	1	9,278
Tony McLoughlin (Sligo–N Leitrim)	FG	Sales representative	Jan 1949	2011	1	7,715
Michael McNamara (Clare)	Lab	Barrister, farmer	Mar 1974	2011	1	8,572
Olivia Mitchell (Dublin S)	FG	Teacher	Jul 1947	1997	4	9,635

Table A2.1 continued

TD (constituency)	Party	Occupation	Date of birth	First elected	Times elected	First pref. votes in 2011
Mary Mitchell O'Connor (Dun Laoghaire)	FG	School principal	n/a	2011	1	9,087
Michael Moynihan (Cork NW)	FF	Farmer	Jan 1968	1997	4	8,845
Michelle Mulherin (Mayo)	FG	Solicitor	Jan 1972	2011	1	8,851
Catherine Murphy (Kildare N)	Ind	Clerical worker	Sep 1953	B-2005	2	6,911
Dara Murphy (Cork NC)	FG	Catering entrepreneur	Dec 1969	2011	1	6,597
Eoghan Murphy (Dublin SE)	FG	Speechwriter	Apr 1982	2011	1	5,783
Ged Nash (Louth)	Lab	Public relations	Dec 1975	2011	1	8,718
Denis Naughten (Roscommon–S Leitrim)	FG	Research scientist	Jun 1973	1997	4	9,320
Dan Neville (Limerick)	FG	Personnel manager	Dec 1946	1997	4	9,176
Derek Nolan (Galway W)	Lab	Trainee solicitor	Oct 1982	2011	1	7,489
Michael Noonan (Limerick City)	FG	Teacher	May 1943	1981	10	13,291
Jonathan O'Brien (Cork NC)	SF	Community worker	Dec 1971	2011	1	7,923
Caoimhghín Ó Caoláin (Cavan–Monaghan)	SF	Bank official	Sep 1953	1997	4	11,913
Éamon Ó Cuív (Galway W)	FF	Cooperative manager	Jun 1950	1992	5	7,441
Willie O'Dea (Limerick City)	FF	Accountant, barrister	Nov 1952	F1982	9	6,956
Kieran O'Donnell (Limerick City)	FG	Chartered accountant	May 1963	2007	2	5,405
Patrick O'Donovan (Limerick)	FG	Teacher	Mar 1977	2011	1	8,597
Fergus O'Dowd (Louth)	FG	Teacher	Sep 1948	2002	3	13,980
Seán O'Fearghaíl (Kildare S)	FF	Farmer	Apr 1960	2002	3	4,514
John O'Mahony (Mayo)	FG	Teacher	Jun 1953	2007	2	8,667
Joe O'Reilly (Cavan–Monaghan)	FG	Teacher, publican	Apr 1955	2011	1	8,333
Aodhán Ó Riordáin (Dublin NC)	Lab	School principal	Jul 1976	2011	1	8,731
Aengus Ó Snodaigh (Dublin SC)	SF	Teacher	Aug 1964	2002	3	6,804
Jan O'Sullivan (Limerick City)	Lab	Teacher	Dec 1950	B-1998	4	6,353
Maureen O'Sullivan (Dublin C)	Ind	Teacher	Mar 1951	B-2009	2	4,139
Willie Penrose (Longford–Westmeath)	Lab	Barrister	Aug 1956	1992	5	11,406

Name	Party	Occupation	Date of birth	First elected	Elections	Vote
John Perry (Sligo–N Leitrim)	FG	Businessman	Aug 1956	1997	4	8,663
Ann Phelan (Carlow–Kilkenny)	Lab	Secretary	Sep 1961	2011	1	8,072
John Paul Phelan (Carlow–Kilkenny)	FG	Law student	Sep 1978	2011	1	10,929
Thomas Pringle (Donegal SW)	Ind	Water treatment plant manager	Aug 1967	2011	1	5,845
Ruairí Quinn (Dublin SE)	Lab	Architect	Apr 1946	1977	10	5,407
Pat Rabbitte (Dublin SW)	Lab	Trade union official	May 1949	1989	6	12,867
James Reilly (Dublin N)	FG	Medical doctor	Aug 1955	2007	2	10,178
Michael Ring (Mayo)	FG	Auctioneer	Dec 1953	B-1994	5	13,180
Shane Ross (Dublin S)	Ind	Stockbroker, journalist	Jul 1949	2011	1	17,075
Brendan Ryan (Dublin N)	Lab	Food chemist	Feb 1953	2011	1	9,809
Alan Shatter (Dublin S)	FG	Solicitor	Feb 1951	1981	9	7,716
Seán Sherlock (Cork E)	Lab	Parliamentary assistant	Dec 1972	2007	2	11,862
Róisín Shortall (Dublin NW)	Lab	Teacher of the deaf	Apr 1954	1992	5	9,359
Brendan Smith (Cavan–Monaghan)	FF	Ministerial adviser	Jun 1956	1992	5	9,702
Arthur Spring (Kerry N–Limerick W)	Lab	Juice bar owner	n/a	2011	1	9,159
Emmet Stagg (Kildare N)	Lab	Laboratory technician	Oct 1944	1987	7	9,718
Brian Stanley (Laois–Offaly)	SF	Truck driver, builder	Jan 1961	2011	1	8,032
David Stanton (Cork E)	FG	Teacher	Feb 1957	1997	4	10,019
Billy Timmins (Wicklow)	FG	Army officer	Oct 1959	1997	4	9,165
Peadar Tóibín (Meath W)	SF	Management consultant	Jun 1974	2011	1	6,989
Robert Troy (Longford–Westmeath)	FF	Postmaster	Jan 1982	2011	1	4,275
Joanna Tuffy (Dublin MW)	Lab	Solicitor	Mar 1965	2007	2	7,495
Liam Twomey (Wexford)	FG	Medical doctor	Apr 1967	2002	2	9,230
Leo Varadkar (Dublin W)	FG	Medical doctor	Jan 1979	2007	2	8,359
Jack Wall (Kildare S)	Lab	Electrician	Jul 1945	1997	4	10,645
Mick Wallace (Wexford)	Ind	Builder and property developer	Nov 1955	2011	1	13,329
Brian Walsh (Galway W)	FG	Financial entrepreneur	Sep 1972	2011	1	5,425
Alex White (Dublin S)	Lab	Barrister	Dec 1958	2011	1	8,524

Notes: Most TDs are full-time public representatives. For such TDs, the occupations given here are those previously followed. Séamus Kirk was automatically returned as outgoing Ceann Comhairle. There were two general elections in 1982, in February (F) and November (N). B- indicates that deputy was first elected at a by-election.

Appendix 3: the government and ministers of state

The government

The Fine Gael–Labour government was approved by the Dáil on 9 March 2011. Enda Kenny was elected as Taoiseach by 117 votes (comprising 75 Fine Gael, 37 Labour and five Independent TDs) to 27. The Independents who supported the nomination were Stephen Donnelly, Noel Grealish, Michael Healy-Rae, Michael Lowry and Mattie McGrath. The Fianna Fáil TDs abstained. The government subsequently appointed was:

Enda Kenny (FG)	Taoiseach
Éamon Gilmore (Lab)	Tánaiste and Minister for Foreign Affairs and Trade
Richard Bruton (FG)	Minister for Jobs, Enterprise, and Innovation
Joan Burton (Lab)	Minister for Social Protection
Simon Coveney (FG)	Minister for Agriculture, Fisheries and Food
Jimmy Deenihan (FG)	Minister for Arts, Heritage and Gaeltacht
Frances Fitzgerald (FG)	Minister for Children and Youth Affairs
Phil Hogan (FG)	Minister for the Environment, Community and Local Government
Brendan Howlin (Lab)	Minister for Public Expenditure and Reform
Michael Noonan (FG)	Minister for Finance
Ruairí Quinn (Lab)	Minister for Education and Skills
Pat Rabbitte (Lab)	Minister for Communications, Energy and Natural Resources
James Reilly (FG)	Minister for Health
Alan Shatter (FG)	Minister for Justice and Equality, and for Defence
Leo Varadkar (FG)	Minister for Transport, Tourism and Sport
(Máire Whelan SC	Attorney General)

Ministers of state, their departments and special areas of responsibility

Paul Kehoe (FG)	Taoiseach; Defence (Government Chief Whip)
Willie Penrose (Lab)	Environment, Community and Local Government (Housing and Planning)
Ciarán Cannon (FG)	Education and Skills (Training and Skills)
Lucinda Creighton (FG)	Taoiseach; Foreign Affairs and Trade (European Affairs)
Brian Hayes (FG)	Finance (Public Service Reform and the OPW)
Alan Kelly (Lab)	Transport, Tourism and Sport (Public and Commuter Transport)
Kathleen Lynch (Lab)	Health; Children and Youth Affairs (Disability, Equality and Mental Health)
Shane McEntee (FG)	Agriculture, Fisheries and Food (Food, Horticulture and Food Safety)
Dinny McGinley (FG)	Arts, Heritage and Gaeltacht (Gaeltacht Affairs)
Fergus O'Dowd (FG)	Communications, Energy and Natural Resources; Environment, Community and Local Government (NewEra Project)

Jan O'Sullivan (Lab)	Foreign Affairs and Trade (Trade and Development)
John Perry (FG)	Jobs, Enterprise and Innovation (Small Business)
Michael Ring (FG)	Transport, Tourism and Sport (Tourism and Sport)
Seán Sherlock (Lab)	Jobs, Enterprise and Innovation; Education & Skills (Research and Innovation)
Róisín Shortall (Lab)	Health (Primary Care)

Note: Both Paul Kehoe, as chief whip, and Willie Penrose as the 'super-junior' minister (see Chapter 12, pp. 275–7), attend cabinet meetings.

Appendix 4: the Irish electoral system

The Irish electoral system for Dáil, Seanad and local elections is proportional representation by the single transferable vote (PR-STV). PR-STV is a relatively rare system compared to the family of PR-list systems. In 2011, 165 TDs were elected (and a 166th, the outgoing Ceann Comhairle, was returned automatically) from one of the 43 geographical constituencies. District magnitude varies in size between three and five seats. There are 17 three-seat constituencies, 15 four-seat constituencies and 11 five-seat constituencies. The minimum number of seats returned from each constituency is fixed by the constitution at three; no upper limit is stated, but in practice no constituency has returned more than five TDs since 1948. The ratio of population to TDs must, under the constitution, fall within the range between 20,000 and 30,000. All citizens of the Republic of Ireland and resident British citizens are eligible to vote.

Candidates appear on the ballot paper in alphabetical order of their surnames with a photograph, their affiliated party and usually their occupation and contact address. Independent candidates are listed without a label or as 'non-party' (they are not permitted to describe themselves as 'Independent'). To cast a valid vote, a voter simply ranks the candidates numerically in order of preference. Each voter is free to rank one, some, or all of the candidates, and may do this on any basis they choose, not being constrained by party lines. Polling stations are usually open between 7 a.m. and 10 p.m. Some early voting is permitted to accommodate island voters and those who qualify for a postal vote, the sick, the disabled and those whose occupations base them away from their constituency. Those who are voluntarily absent from the state are not entitled to a postal vote.

A candidate is deemed elected once they reach a specified quota of votes either on the first round of counting or after a transfer process has been completed. The number of votes that candidates need to reach is determined by the Droop quota. This is the number of valid votes cast in the constituency divided by the number of seats plus one. So if there are 60,000 valid votes in a constituency with four seats, the quota is 12,001 (60,000 / (4 + 1) + 1). Only four candidates can possibly reach this number.

After the polls close the boxes are taken to a designated count centre and stored until they are opened, usually at 9 a.m. the following morning. Following the first count the returning officer for the constituency announces the result. Candidates whose first preferences exceed the quota on the first count are deemed elected. Assuming that some seats remain to be filled, the transfer of votes takes place; this is the distinctive feature of PR-STV, which, as well as enabling voters to convey rich information on their preferences, provides the opportunity for analysts to draw inferences about voters' perceptions of the relationships between parties and about the relative importance they attach to party and to candidate when deciding how to vote (see Chapters 7 and 9). The 'surplus' votes of elected candidates – that is, the number of votes an elected candidate has over and above the quota, which they did not need to secure election – are distributed to the other candidates in proportion to the second preferences marked on each ballot paper. In addition, the candidates with the lowest votes who could not possibly reach the quota on further preferences are eliminated, each vote being transferred to the next candidate in the voter's ranking. This process continues until all of the seats are filled (for full explanations of how PR-STV works, see the sources listed below under 'Further reading'). The shortest count was in Tipperary North (three) and the longest was Wicklow (19).

Candidates can be deemed elected without reaching the quota if the number of seats to be filled is equal to the number of candidates not yet elected or eliminated. More than one candidate may be eliminated simultaneously in situations where this could not possibly affect the final result, at a saving in time but a cost in transparency (see Chapter 9). Successful candidates and eliminated candidates whose votes at any stage of the count amount to a quarter of a quota may claim their declared election expenses back from the exchequer up to a maximum of €8,700.

Further reading

Department of the Environment, Heritage and Local Government, *Guide to Ireland's PR-STV Electoral System*, www.environ.ie/en/LocalGovernment/Voting.

Michael Gallagher, 'Ireland: the discreet charm of PR-STV', pp. 511–32 in Michael Gallagher and Paul Mitchell (eds), *The Politics of Electoral Systems* (Oxford: Oxford University Press, 2008).

Richard Sinnott, 'The electoral system', pp. 111–36 in John Coakley and Michael Gallagher (eds), *Politics in the Republic of Ireland*, 5th edn (Abingdon: Routledge and PSAI Press, 2010).

Appendix 5: retirements and defeated incumbents from the 30th Dáil

Members of the 30th Dáil who did not contest the election to the 31st Dáil

Bertie Ahern	(Dublin C)	FF
Dermot Ahern	(Louth)	FF
Noel Ahern	(Dublin NW)	FF
Bernard Allen	(Cork NC)	FG
Seán Ardagh	(Dublin SC)	FF
Niall Blaney	(Donegal NE)	FF
Ulick Burke	(Galway E)	FG
Paul Connaughton	(Galway E)	FG
Brian Cowen	(Laois–Offaly)	FF
Seymour Crawford	(Cavan–Monaghan)	FG
John Cregan	(Limerick W)	FF
Martin Cullen[a]	(Waterford)	FF
Noel Dempsey	(Meath W)	FF
Jimmy Devins	(Sligo–Leitrim N)	FF
Olwyn Enright	(Laois–Offaly)	FG
Michael Finneran	(Roscommon–Leitrim S)	FF
Beverley Flynn	(Mayo)	FF
Mary Harney	(Dublin MW)	Ind
Jackie Healy-Rae	(Kerry S)	Ind
Michael D. Higgins	(Galway W)	Lab
Tony Killeen	(Clare)	FF
Tom Kitt	(Dublin S)	FF
George Lee[a]	(Dublin S)	FG
Pádraic McCormack	(Galway W)	FG
James McDaid[a]	(Donegal NE)	FF
Liz McManus	(Wicklow)	Lab
Arthur Morgan	(Louth)	SF
M.J. Nolan	(Carlow–Kilkenny)	FF
Noel O'Flynn	(Cork NC)	FF
Rory O'Hanlon	(Cavan–Monaghan)	FF
Batt O'Keeffe	(Cork NW)	FF
Jim O'Keeffe	(Cork SW)	FG
Ned O'Keeffe	(Cork E)	FF
Brian O'Shea	(Waterford)	Lab
P.J. Sheehan	(Cork SW)	FG
Noel Treacy	(Galway E)	FF
Mary Upton	(Dublin SC)	Lab
Mary Wallace	(Meath E)	FF
Michael Woods	(Dublin NE)	FF

[a] These three TDs had resigned their seats in 2010, and the seats were vacant at the time of the 2011 general election.

Members of the 30th Dáil who were defeated at the 2011 election

Michael Ahern	(Cork E)	FF
Barry Andrews	(Dun Laoghaire)	FF
Chris Andrews	(Dublin SE)	FF
Bobby Aylward	(Carlow–Kilkenny)	FF
Joe Behan	(Wicklow)	Ind
Áine Brady	(Kildare N)	FF
Cyprian Brady	(Dublin C)	FF
Johnny Brady	(Meath W)	FF
Thomas Byrne	(Meath E)	FF
Pat Carey	(Dublin NW)	FF
Deirdre Clune	(Cork SC)	FG
Margaret Conlon	(Cavan–Monaghan)	FF
Seán Connick	(Wexford)	FF
Mary Coughlan	(Donegal SW)	FF
Ciarán Cuffe	(Dun Laoghaire)	Green
John Curran	(Dublin MW)	FF
Michael D'Arcy	(Wexford)	FG
Frank Fahey	(Galway W)	FF
Michael Fitzpatrick	(Kildare N)	FF
Paul Gogarty	(Dublin MW)	Green
John Gormley	(Dublin SE)	Green
Mary Hanafin	(Dun Laoghaire)	FF
Seán Haughey	(Dublin NC)	FF
Máire Hoctor	(Tipperary N)	FF
Peter Kelly	(Longford–Westmeath)	FF
Brendan Kenneally	(Waterford)	FF
Michael Kennedy	(Dublin N)	FF
Conor Lenihan	(Dublin SW)	FF
Martin Mansergh	(Tipperary S)	FF
Tom McEllistrim	(Kerry N)	FF
John Moloney	(Laois–Offaly)	FF
Michael Mulcahy	(Dublin SC)	FF
Darragh O'Brien	(Dublin N)	FF
Charlie O'Connor	(Dublin SW)	FF
John O'Donoghue	(Kerry S)	FF
Mary O'Rourke	(Longford–Westmeath)	FF
Christy O'Sullivan	(Cork SW)	FF
Peter Power	(Limerick E)	FF
Seán Power	(Kildare S)	FF
Dick Roche	(Wicklow)	FF
Éamon Ryan	(Dublin S)	Green
Trevor Sargent	(Dublin N)	Green
Éamon Scanlon	(Sligo–Leitrim N)	FF
Tom Sheahan	(Kerry S)	FG
Mary White	(Carlow–Kilkenny)	Green

Index